LEARNING TEXT

CONSUMER LAW

LEARNING TEXT

CONSUMER LAW

Ewan MacIntyre LLB, Cert Ed
Distance Learning Tutor, Nottingham Law School

First published in Great Britain 1999 by Blackstone Press Limited,
Aldine Place, London W12 8AA.   Telephone (020) 8740 2277
www.blackstonepress.com

© Nottingham Law School, Nottingham Trent University, 1999

ISBN: 1 85431 988 4

British Library Cataloguing in Publication Data
A CIP catalogue record for this book is available from the British Library.

Typeset by Style Photosetting Limited, Mayfield, East Sussex
Printed by Livesey Limited, Shrewsbury, Shropshire

All rights reserved. No part of this book may be reproduced or transmitted in any form or by any means, electronic or mechanical, including photocopying, recording, or an information storage or retrieval system without prior permission from the publisher.

FOREWORD

The books in the LLB series have been written for students studying law at undergraduate level. There are two books for each subject. The first is the *Learning Text* which is designed to teach you about the particular subject in question. However, it does much more than that. By means of Activities, Self Assessment, and End of Chapter Questions, the *Learning Text* allows you to test your knowledge and understanding as you work. Each chapter starts with 'Objectives' which indicate what you should be able to do by the end of it. You should use these Objectives in your learning — check them frequently and ask yourself whether you have attained them.

The second book is a volume of *Cases and Materials*. This is cross-referenced from the *Learning Text*. It contains the primary sources of law such as statutes and cases plus subsidiary sources such as extracts from journals, law reform papers and textbooks. This is your portable library. Although each volume can stand alone, they are designed to be complementary.

The two-volume combination aims to support your learning by challenging you to demonstrate your mastery of the principles and application of the law. They are appropriate whatever your mode of study — full-time or part-time.

CONTENTS

Foreword   v

Preface   xi

Table of Cases   xiii

Table of Statutes   xix

Introduction   1

Objectives — The development of consumer law — The definition of a consumer — The way this book is organised

1 The Law of Contract as a Means of Consumer Protection   6

1.1 Objectives — 1.2 Introduction — 1.3 Formation of contracts (general principles) — 1.4 Privity of contract — 1.5 Pre-contractual statements (general principles) — 1.6 Exclusion clauses — 1.7 Discharge of contractual liability (general principles) — 1.8 Remedies for breach of contract and misrepresentation (general principles) — 1.9 Losing the right to rescind or to treat the contract as repudiated — 1.10 Damages for breach of contract and for actionable misrepresentations — 1.11 Summary — 1.12 End of chapter assessment questions

2 Defective Goods and Services: the Classification of Transactions   47

2.1 Objectives — 2.2 Introduction — 2.3 Contracts to which the Sale of Goods Act 1979 applies — 2.4 Contracts of hire-purchase — 2.5 Contracts to transfer the property in goods, contracts of hire and contracts for the supply of a service — 2.6 End of chapter assessment question

3 Contract Based Remedies: Statutory Implied Terms as to Quality and Fitness   63

3.1 Objectives — 3.2 Introduction — 3.3 Quality in business sales — 3.4 Satisfactory quality — 3.5 Fitness for the buyer's purpose — 3.6 The status of the implied terms — 3.7 Flexibility of satisfactory quality and fitness for purpose — 3.8 The terms implied into contracts for the supply of a service — 3.9 Summary

4 Contract Based Remedies: Statutory Implied Terms as to Correspondence with Description and as to Title   89

4.1 Objectives — 4.2 Introduction — 4.3 Correspondence with description — 4.4 The right to sell — 4.5 Sale by sample — 4.6 No implied term in a sale by model — 4.7 The status of the implied terms — 4.8 The supply of a service — 4.9 Summary — 4.10 End of chapter assessment questions

5 Miscellaneous Aspects of the Sale of Goods Act 1979 — 111

5.1 Objectives — 5.2 Introduction — 5.3 Sales of goods: the passing of the property and the risk — 5.4 The seller's duty to deliver — 5.5 The duty to pay the price — 5.6 Sale by a seller in possession after a sale — 5.7 Sale of a motor vehicle obtained on hire purchase — 5.8 Unsolicited Goods and Services Act 1971 — 5.9 Summary — 5.10 End of chapter assessment question

6 Exclusion and Limitation Clauses — 152

6.1 Objectives — 6.2 Introduction — 6.3 Freedom of contract — 6.4 The common law approach to exclusion clauses — 6.5 The Unfair Contract Terms Act 1977 — 6.6 The Unfair Terms in Consumer Contracts Regulations 1994 — 6.7 Summary — 6.8 End of chapter assessment question

7 Product Liability (Safety) — 177

7.1 Objectives — 7.2 Introduction — 7.3 Product liability in contract and tort — 7.4 The law of tort — 7.5 The Consumer Protection Act 1987, Part I — 7.6 Criminal liability for unsafe products — 7.7 Summary — 7.8 End of chapter assessment question

8 The Consumer Credit Act 1974: History, Structure and Definitions — 203

8.1 Objectives — 8.2 Introduction — 8.3 The History and Structure of the 1974 Act — 8.4 The definitions contained in the 1974 Act

9 Consumer Credit: Advertising, Canvassing and Entry into an Agreement — 220

9.1 Objectives — 9.2 Introduction — 9.3 Advertising — 9.4 Canvassing — 9.5 Entry into credit or hire agreements — 9.6 Summary — 9.7 End of chapter assessment question

10 Matters Arising during Currency of Credit or Hire Agreements — 237

10.1 Objectives — 10.2 Introduction — 10.3 Liability of creditor for breaches by supplier — 10.4 Duty to give notice before taking certain action — 10.5 Duty to give notice of termination in non-default cases — 10.6 The duty to give information — 10.7 Appropriation of payments — 10.8 Variation of agreements — 10.9 Liability for misuse of credit facilities — 10.10 Duty on issue of new credit-tokens — 10.11 Death of debtor or hirer — 10.12 Summary — 10.13 End of chapter assessment question

11 Consumer Credit: Termination and Remedies — 248

11.1 Objectives — 11.2 Introduction — 11.3 Need for default notices — 11.4 Early payment by debtor — 11.5 Termination by the debtor of hire-purchase and conditional sale agreements — 11.6 Right to terminate regulated consumer hire agreement — 11.7 Remedies of the creditor — 11.8 Provisions protecting hirers of goods — 11.9 The court's powers in hire-purchase and conditional sale agreements — 11.10 Protection orders — 11.11 Extortionate credit bargains — 11.12 Summary

12 The Trade Descriptions Act 1968: Goods — 262

12.1 Objectives — 12.2 Introduction — 12.3 False trade descriptions of goods — 12.4 False trade descriptions — 12.5 False descriptions — 12.6 Disclaimers — 12.7 Summary — 12.8 End of chapter assessment question

13 The Trade Descriptions Act 1968: Services and Defences — 289

13.1 Objectives — 13.2 Introduction — 13.3 Misdescription of services, accommodation or facilities — 13.4 Defences — 13.5 Summary — 13.6 End of chapter assessment question

CONTENTS

14 Misleading Price Indications   313

14.1 Objectives — 14.2 Introduction — 14.3 The offence of giving a misleading indication as to the price — 14.4 Goods, services, accommodation or facilities — 14.5 Misleading indications — 14.6 Defences — 14.7 Time limits — 14.8 The Code of Practice — 14.9 Summary

Index   325

PREFACE

This book is intended for LLB students. As the law of contract and the law of tort are studied by LLB students as subjects in their own right, this caused some difficulty in deciding what matters to include. The law of contract is in many ways the basis of consumer law. I have therefore reiterated the basic principles of contract law very briefly and concentrated only on those areas which are of particular importance to consumers.

The Consumer Credit Act 1974 is dealt with in four chapters. This is a notoriously difficult Act for students to understand, but I hope that I have made the more important aspects of the Act comprehensible.

The terms implied by the Sale of Goods Act 1979 and related statutes are dealt with in two fairly lengthy chapters. Other relevant aspects of the 1979 Act are dealt with in one chapter. There is little doubt that the 1979 Act lays down many of the rules of consumer law. The difficulty with the Act is that it was written to regulate the affairs of nineteenth century merchants and consequently some of the Act's provisions do not fit in with the expectation of modern consumers.

Product safety requirements, both civil and criminal, are explored. The book also examines the law on false trade descriptions and misleading price indications.

Although the Civil Procedure Rules 1998 has substituted the word 'plaintiff' for 'claimant' the old terminology has been retained when discussing cases decided before 1999.

The emphasis throughout the book is on self-discovery and on appreciation of why the law is as it is. I hope that students using the book will find it entertaining as well as instructive.

Ewan MacIntyre

TABLE OF CASES

Adler v Dickson and Another [1955] 1 QB 158	157
AG Stanley Ltd (T/A Fads) v Surrey County Council (1994) 159 JP 691	323
Airtours plc v Shipley (1994) 158 JP 835	301
Aldridge v Johnson (1857) 7 E & B 885	50, 57
Anderson v Ryan [1964] IR 34	121
Andrews Bros Ltd v Singer & Co. Ltd [1934] 1 KB 17	158
Arcos Ltd v E. A. Ronaasen & Son [1933] AC 470	93, 94, 113, 114
Asfar & Co Ltd v Blundell [1896] 1 QB 123	133, 134
Ashington Piggeries Ltd v Christopher Hill Ltd [1971] 1 All ER 847, [1972] AC 441	80, 93, 183
Ashley v Sutton London Borough Council (1994) 156 JP 631	296, 297
Aswan Engineering Establishment Co. v Lupdine Ltd [1987] 1 All ER 135	73, 74
Attwood v Small (1838) 6 Cl & Fin 232	14
Avery v Bowden (1855) 5 E & B 714	22
BAB v Taylor [1976] 1 All ER 65	297
Bannerman v White (1861) 10 CB NS 844	16
Barber v NWS Bank plc [1996] 1 All ER 906	98, 101
Barrow, Lane and Ballard Ltd v Phillip Phillips & Co Ltd [1929] 1 KB 574	134
Bartlett v Sydney Marcus Ltd [1965] 1 WLR 1013	67, 113, 114
Beale v Taylor [1967] 3 All ER 253	20
Becket v Cohen [1972] 1 WLR 1593	275, 302
Beckett v Kingston Brothers (Butchers) Ltd [1970] 1 QB 606	278
Bernstein v Pamson Motors Ltd [1987] 2 All ER 220	29
Beswick v Beswick [1968] AC 58	185, 187
Birkenhead Co-operative Society v Roberts [1970] 1 WLR 1497	304, 305
Bisset v Wilkinson [1927] AC 177	14, 21
Bolam v Friern Hospital Management Committee [1957] 2 All ER 118	83
Bowerman v ABTA Ltd (1995) 145 NLJ 1815	12, 13
Brace v Calder [1895] 2 QB 253	23
Breed v Cluett [1970] 2 QB 459	293, 297, 298
British Airways Board v Taylor (1976) 140 JP 96	303
British Crane Hire Corporation Ltd v Ipswich Plant Hire Ltd [1975] QB 303	14
Brown (BS) & Sons Ltd v Craiks Ltd [1970] 1 All ER 823	71, 72, 77, 114
Byrne v Van Tienhoven (1880) 5 CPD 344	7
Cadbury Ltd v Halliday [1975] 1 WLR 653	281
Cahalne v Croydon LBC (1985) 149 JP 561	274
Car and Universal Finance Co. Ltd v Caldwell [1965] 1 QB 525	38
Carlill v Carbolic Smoke Ball Co. [1893] 1 QB 256	1, 7, 11, 12
Carlos Federspiel & Co. SA v Charles Twigg & Co. Ltd [1957] 1 Lloyd's Rep 240	126
Cavendish Woodhouse Ltd v Wright (1985) 149 JP 497	269, 270, 271
Cehave NV v Bremer Handelsgesellschaft mbH, The Hansa Nord [1975] 3 All ER 739	22

Cellulose Acetate Silk Ltd v Widnes Foundry (1925) Ltd [1933] AC 20	23
Central London Property Trust Ltd v High Trees House Ltd [1947] 1 KB 130	8
Chapelton v Barry UDC [1940] 1 KB 532	155, 156, 160, 161
Chappell & Co. Ltd v Nestlé Co. Ltd [1960] 2 All ER 701	8
Charles Rickards Ltd v Oppenheim [1950] 1 All ER 420	141
Clarke v Dickson (1858) El Bl & El 148	15, 37
Clay v Yates (1856) 1 H & N 73	58
Cottee v D. Seaton Ltd [1972] 1 WLR 1408	273, 279, 280, 283
Coupe v Guyett [1973] 1 WLR 669	309
Cowburn v Focus Television Rentals Ltd [1983] Crim LR 563	295
Curtis v Chemical Cleaning and Dyeing Co. [1951] 1 All ER 631	155, 156
Cutter v Powell (1795) Term Rep 320	22
Dakin & Co. Ltd v Lee [1916] 1 KB 566	22
Daniels v White and Tarbard [1938] 4 All ER 258	179, 188
Daulia Ltd v Four Millbank Nominees [1978] 2 All ER 557	13
Davies v Leighton [1979] Crim LR 575	118, 122
Davies v Sumner [1984] 3 All ER 831, [1984] 1 WLR 1301	65, 163, 265, 267, 272
Dawson, G.J., (Clapham) Ltd v H & G Dutfield [1936] 2 All ER 232	58
Demby Hamilton & Co Ltd v Barden [1949] 1 All ER 435	132
Denard v Smith and Dixons Ltd (1990) 155 JP 253	275
Dennant v Skinner and Collom [1948] 2 All ER 29	114, 139
Derry v Peek (1889) 14 App Cas 337	14, 294, 295
Devlin v Hall [1990] RTR 320	266, 267
Dick Bentley Productions Ltd v Harold Smith Motors Ltd [1965] 1 WLR 623	15
Dickinson v Dodds (1876) 2 ChD 463	8
Dodd v Wilson [1946] 2 All ER 691	58
Donnelly v Rowlands [1971] 1 WLR 1600	271, 282
Donoghue v Stevenson [1932] AC 562	2, 188
Doyle v Olby Ltd [1969] 2 QB 158	38
Drummond v Van Ingen (1887) 12 App Cas 284	102
Dunlop Pneumatic Tyre Co. v New Garage and Motor Co. Ltd [1915] AC 79	23
Dunlop Pneumatic Tyre Company Limited v Selfridge and Company Limited [1915] AC 847	180
Durham Trading Standards v Kingsley Clothing (1990) 154 JP 124	278, 279
E & S Ruben Ltd v Faire Bros & Co. Ltd [1949] 1 All ER 215	102
Ealing London Borough Council v Taylor (1996) 159 JP 460	307
East v Maurer [1991] 2 All ER 733	40
Ecay v Godfrey (1974) 80 Lloyd's Rep 286	17
Edwards v Dinn [1976] 1 WLR 943	127
Elton Cop Dyeing Co. v Broadbent and Son Ltd (1919) 89 LJKB 186	22
Entores v Miles Far East Corporation [1955] 2 QB 327	7
Erlanger v New Sombrero Phosphate Co. (1878) 3 App Cas 1218	37
Errington v Errington & Woods [1952] 1 KB 290	7, 13
Esso Petroleum Co. Ltd v Mardon [1976] QB 801	16, 21
Esso Petroleum Ltd v Commissioners of Customs and Excise [1976] 1 All ER 117, [1976] 1 WLR 1	8, 49, 50, 58
Falcke v Gray (1859) 4 Drew 651	24
Farnworth Finance Facilities v Attryde [1970] 1 WLR 1053	35
Felthouse v Bindley (1862) 11 CBNS 869	7
Financings Ltd v Baldock [1963] 2 QB 104	256, 257
Fisher v Bell [1961] 1 QB 394	8, 9, 10, 274, 275
Fletcher v Budgen [1974] 1 WLR 1056	267, 268, 317
Fletcher v Sledmore [1973] RTR 371	268, 290
Foakes v Beer (1884) 9 App Cas 605	8
Formula One Autocentres Ltd v Birmingham City Council, The Times, 29 December 1998	274

TABLE OF CASES

Forthright Finance Ltd v Carlyle Finance Ltd [1997] 4 All ER 90	55, 56
Geddling v Marsh [1920] 1 KB 668	69
George Mitchell Ltd v Finney Lock Seeds Ltd [1983] 2 AC 803; [1983] 1 QB 296	153, 157
Godley v Perry [1960] 1 All ER 36	103, 183
Grainger & Son v Gough [1896] AC 325	11
Grant v Australian Knitting Mills Ltd [1936] AC 85	20, 78, 114, 183
Greaves & Co. Contractors Ltd v Baynham, Meickle & Partners [1975] 3 All ER 99, [1975] 1 WLR 1095	83, 84
Griffiths v Peter Conway Ltd [1939] 1 All ER 685	79, 80
Hadley v Baxendale (1854) 9 Exch 341	23, 183, 256
Hall v Wickens Motors Ltd [1972] 1 WLR 1418	293
Haringey London Borough Council v Piro Shoes Ltd [1976] Crim LR 462	307
Harlingdon & Leinster Enterprises Ltd v Christopher Hull Fine Art Ltd [1991] 1 QB 564	19, 21, 91, 114
Havering London Borough v Stevenson [1970] 3 All ER 609	65, 265, 267
Head v Tattersall (1871) LR 7 Ex 7	33
Healy v Howlett and Sons [1917] 1 KB 337	126
Hedley Byrne v Heller & Co. Ltd [1963] 2 All ER 575	82
Heilbut, Symons & Co. v Buckleton [1913] AC 30	18
Helby v Mathews [1895] AC 471	55, 56
Henderson v Merrett Syndicates Ltd [1994] 3 All ER 506	82
Hochster v De La Tour (1853) 2 E & B 678	22
Hollier v Rambler Motors (AMC) Ltd [1972] 2 QB 71	155, 156
Holloway v Cross [1981] 1 All ER 1012	281, 283
Holwell Securities Ltd v Hughes [1974] 1 All ER 161	7
Hong Kong Fir Shipping Co. Ltd v Kawasaki Kisen Kaisha Ltd [1962] 1 All ER 474	23
Hopkins v Tanqueray (1854) 15 CB 130	17, 18
Houghton v Trafalgar Insurance [1954] 1 QB 247	158
Hyde v Wrench (1840) 3 Beav 334	8
Ingram v Little [1960] 1 QB 31	118, 119
Jackson v Horizon Holidays Ltd [1975] 1 WLR 1468	184, 185
John v Mathews [1970] 2 QB 443	274
Jones v Padavatton [1969] 1 WLR 328	8
Karflex Ltd v Poole [1933] 2 KB 251	97, 101
Kendall (Henry) & Sons v William Lillico & Sons Ltd [1969] 2 AC 31	71, 72, 76, 78, 113, 114
Kensington and Chelsea (Royal) London Borough Council v Riley [1973] RTR 122	276
Kent County Council v Price (1993) 157 JP 1161	279
Ketley, A., Ltd v Scott and Another [1981] ICR 241	260
Kirkham v Attenborough [1895–9] All ER Rep 450	123
Krell v Henry [1903] 2 KB 740	22
L'Estrange v F. Graucob Ltd [1934] 2 KB 394	155, 157
Lacis v Cashmarts [1969] 2 QB 400	117, 119, 139
Lampleigh v Brathwaite (1615) Hob 105	8
Laurelgates Ltd v Lombard North Central Ltd (1983) 133 NLJ 720	34
Leaf v International Galleries [1950] 2 KB 86	15, 36
Lee v Griffin (1861) 1 B & S 272	51, 52, 58
Lewis v Averay [1972] 1 QB 198	37
Lewis v Maloney [1977] Crim LR 436	306
Lill, K., Holdings Ltd v White [1979] RTR 120	309

TABLE OF CASES

Case	Page
Lockett v Charles Ltd [1938] 4 All ER 170	58
Lombard North Central v Butterworth [1987] 1 All ER 267	257
London Wine Co. (Shippers) Ltd, Re 1986 PCC 121	128, 130
Long v Lloyd [1958] 1 WLR 753	35, 36
Luxmoore-May and another v Messenger May Baverstock [1990] 1 All ER 1067	84
Luxor (Eastbourne) Ltd v Cooper [1941] AC 108	13, 14
Manchester Diocesan Council for Education v Commercial and General Investments Ltd [1970] 1 WLR 241	8
May and Butcher v R [1934] 2 KB 17	7
McArdle, Re [1951] Ch 669	8
McCutcheon v David MacBrayne Ltd [1964] 1 All ER 430	155, 157
McDougall v Aeromarine of Emsworth Ltd [1958] 3 All ER 431	140
MFI Warehouses Ltd v Nattrass [1973] 1 WLR 307	295
Microbeads AC and another v Vinhurst Road Markings Ltd [1975] 1 All ER 529	100
Midland Bank plc v Cox McQueen, The Times, 2 February 1999	84
Millars of Falkirk Ltd v Turpie 1976 SLT 66	74, 75, 106
Miller v FA Sadd & Son Ltd [1981] 3 All ER 285	319
Moore and Co. Ltd and Landauer and Co. Ltd, Re [1921] 2 KB 519	93, 94
Morgan v Russell & Sons [1909] 1 KB 357	51
Mountford v Scott [1975] 2 WLR 114	14
Nettleship v Weston [1971] 2 QB 691	85
New Zealand Shipping Co. Ltd v A.M. Satterthwaite & Co. Ltd [1975] AC 154	8
Newell and Another v Hicks [1984] RTR 135	296, 297, 299, 300
Newman v Hackney London Borough Council [1982] RTR 296	284
Niblett Ltd v Confectioners Materials Co. Ltd [1921] 3 KB 387	96
Nichol v Godts (1854) 10 Ex 191	104
Nicolene Ltd v Simmonds [1953] 1 All ER 822	7
Norman v Bennett [1974] 1 WLR 1229	285
Olgiersson v Kitching [1986] 1 All ER 764	309
Olley v Marlborough Court Hotel Ltd [1949] 1 KB 532	156, 157, 160
Oscar Chess Ltd v Williams [1957] 1 WLR 370	15
Parker v Clark [1960] 1 WLR 286	8
Partridge v Crittenden [1968] 1 WLR 1204	7, 11, 12, 274, 275
Peyman v Lanjani [1985] 1 Ch 457	36
Pharmaceutical Society of Great Britain v Boots Cash Chemists (Southern) Ltd [1953] 1 QB 401	9, 10
Philip Head & Sons Ltd v Showfronts Ltd [1970] 1 Lloyd's Rep 140	58, 121
Phillips Products Ltd v Hyland [1987] 2 All ER 620	169
Poole v Smith's Car Sales (Balham) Ltd [1962] 2 All ER 482	123
Printing and Numerical Registering Co. v Samson (1875) LR 19 Eq 462	153
Queensway Discount Warehouses Ltd v Burke (1985) JP 150	276
R & B Customs Brokers Co. Ltd v United Dominions Trust Ltd [1988] 1 All ER 847, [1988] 1 WLR 321	65, 66, 162, 171
R.V. Ward Ltd v Bignall [1967] 1 QB 534	117, 119, 120
R v Anderson (1987) 152 JP 373	276, 277, 282
R v Avro plc (1993) 157 JP 759	302
R v Bevelectric Ltd (1992) 157 JP 323	293
R v Bow Street Magistrates Court, ex parte Joseph (1986) 150 JP 650	291
R v Breeze [1973] 1 WLR 994	290, 301
R v Bull (1996) 160 JP 240	284, 285
R v Clarksons Holidays (1972) 57 Cr App R 38	300
R v Ford Motor Co. Ltd [1974] 1 WLR 1220	272, 277
R v Hammerton Cars Ltd [1976] 1 WLR 1243	280, 284, 285, 286

TABLE OF CASES xvii

R v Inner London Justices, ex parte Wandsworth London Borough Council
  [1983] RTR 425   282
R v Piper 1995 JP 116   300, 301
R v Shrewsbury Crown Court, ex parte Venables [1994] Crim LR 61   268
R v Southwood [1987] 3 All ER 556   273, 284, 285, 304, 307
R v Sunair Holidays Ltd [1973] 1 WLR 1105   302
R v Thomson Holidays Ltd [1974] 2 WLR 371   291
R v Veys (1992) 157 JP 567   278
Reardon Smith Line Ltd v Hansen-Tangen [1976] 3 All ER 570   93
Ritchie v Atkinson (1808) 10 East 295   22
Roberts v Leonard (1995) 94 LGR 284   267, 291
Robertson v Dicicco [1972] RTR 431   276, 282
Robinson v Graves [1935] 1 KB 579   51, 58
Rogers v Parish (Scarborough) Ltd [1987] QB 933   74, 75
Routledge v Ansa Motors (Chester-Le-Steet) Ltd [1980] RTR 1   272, 282
Rowland v Divall [1923] 2 KB 500   97, 99, 113, 114
Royscot Trust Ltd v Rogerson [1991] 3 All ER 294   41
Rylands v Fletcher (1866) LR 1 Ex 265   160

Schawel v Reade [1913] 2 IR 81   17, 18
Shine v General Guarantee Corporation Ltd [1988] 1 All ER 911   71, 72, 77, 113, 114
Sky Petroleum Ltd v VIP Petroleum Ltd [1974] 1 WLR 576   24
Smith New Court Securities Ltd v Scrimgeour Vickers (Asset Management) Ltd
  [1996] 4 All ER 769   23, 39, 41
Smith v Land and House Property Corporation (1884) 28 ChD 7   21
South Australia Asset Management Corp v York Montague Ltd
  [1996] 3 All ER 365   42
St Albans City and District Council v International Computers Ltd
  [1996] 4 All ER 481   52
Stevenson v McLean (1880) 5 QBD 346   8
Stevenson v Rogers [1999] 1 All ER 613   65
Sumner Permain & Co. v Webb & Co. [1922] 1 KB 55   71, 72, 77
Sumpter v Hedges [1898] 1 QB 673   22

Tarling v Baxter (1827) 6 B & C 360   115, 131, 132
Taylor v Caldwell (1863) 3 B & S 826   22
Tesco Supermarkets Ltd v Nattrass [1972] AC 153   305, 306, 308
Thake and another v Maurice [1986] 1 All ER 497   83
Thomas Witter Ltd v TBF Industries Ltd [1996] 2 All ER 573   43
Thompson v London, Midland and Scottish Railway Co [1930] 1 KB 41   156, 157
Thompson, W.L., v Robinson (Gunmakers) Ltd [1955] Ch 177   23
Thornton v Shoe Lane Parking Ltd [1971] 1 All ER 686   156, 157
Toys 'R' Us v Gloucestershire County Council (1994) 158 JP 338   314, 317
Tweddle v Atkinson (1861) 1 B & S 393   8, 180

Underwood Ltd v Burgh Castle Brick and Cement Syndicate [1922] 1 KB 343
      116, 117, 119, 121

Wait, Re [1927] 1 Ch 606   129
Waltham Forest London Borough Council v TG Wheatley (Central Garage) Ltd
  [1978] RTR 157   283, 286
Warner Bros Pictures Ltd v Nelson [1937] 1 KB 209   24
Warwickshire County Council v Johnson [1993] 1 All ER 299   316, 317
Webster v Higgin [1948] 2 All ER 127   18, 19, 157
Westminster City Council v Ray Allan Manshops Ltd [1982] 1 WLR 383   298
White and Carter (Councils) Ltd v McGregor [1962] AC 413   24
William Sindell plc v Cambridgeshire CC [1994] 3 All ER 932   23, 42, 43
Wings Ltd v Ellis [1985] 1 AC 272   292, 294, 295, 303
Wolkind and Another v Pura Foods Ltd (1987) 85 LGR 782   282

Wood v Letric Ltd, The Times, 13 January 1932	12, 19
Woodar Investment Developments Ltd v Wimpey Construction UK Ltd [1980] 1 WLR 277	184, 201
Wren v Holt [1903] 1 KB 610	77, 80
Wycombe Marsh Garages Ltd v Fowler [1972] 1 WLR 1152	264, 269
Yoeman Credit Ltd v Apps [1962] 2 QB 508	34
Yoeman Credit Ltd v Waragowski [1961] 1 WLR 1124	256

TABLE OF STATUTES

Cheques Act 1957, s.4   244
Civil Liability (Contribution) Act 1978, s.3   240
Consumer Credit Act 1974   3, 55–6, 203–19
  Part I-Part III   204
  Part IV   204, 220, 221–2, 223
  Part V   204, 221, 225, 227
  Part VI-Part XI   204
  s.8   205
  s.8(1)   205, 206
  s.8(2)   205
  s.8(3)   207
  s.9(1)   205
  s.10   212
  s.10(1)(a)-(b)   216
  s.10(3)   212
  s.10(3)(a)   212
  s.11(1)-(2)   216
  s.11(3)   213, 216
  s.12   214
  s.12(1)   216
  s.12(a)   214, 215, 216, 226, 238, 246
  s.12(b)   214, 215, 216, 226, 234, 238, 239, 240, 241, 242, 246
  s.12(c)   214, 216, 226, 238, 239, 240, 241, 242, 246
  s.13(a)   216
  s.13(c)   216
  s.14(1)-(2)   217
  s.14(4)   218
  s.15   205
  s.15(1)   208
  s.16   205, 209
  s.17(1)   217
  s.19   218
  s.19(3)   219
  s.23(3)   224
  s.43(1)-(4)   221
  s.44   222, 223
  s.45-s.47   223
  s.48   223–4
  s.49   224
  s.50   224

Consumer Credit Act 1974 – *continued*
  s.50(1)-(3)   224
  s.51   224, 225
  s.51(2)-(3)   224
  s.52-s.53   225
  s.55   225
  s.56   220, 225, 227, 241
  s.56(1)   225, 238
  s.56(1)(a)   225–6, 227, 238
  s.56(1)(b)   225, 226, 227, 238
  s.56(1)(c)   225, 226, 227, 238, 239, 241
  s.56(2)   226, 237, 238, 239, 241, 242
  s.56(3)   239
  s.56(4)   226
  s.57   227
  s.57(1)-(4)   227
  s.58   227–8
  s.58(1)-(2)   228
  s.59   228
  s.60   228, 245
  s.61   245
  s.61(1)-(2)   228
  s.62   229, 231, 245
  s.62(1)-(2)   229, 230, 233
  s.62(3)   229, 230, 231
  s.63   229, 231, 245
  s.63(1)   229, 230
  s.63(2)   229, 230, 232, 233
  s.63(2)(a)   229, 230
  s.63(2)(b)   230
  s.63(5)   229, 230
  s.64   245
  s.64(1)   231, 232
  s.64(1)(a)   231
  s.64(1)(b)   231, 232
  s.64(4)   232
  s.65   245
  s.65(1)   231
  s.66   245
  s.67   231–2
  s.68   232
  s.69(1)   232, 234
  s.69(2)   234
  s.69(4)   232

Consumer Credit Act 1974 – *continued*
  s.69(7) 232, 233
  s.70(1) 234
  s.70(1)(a)-(c) 233
  s.70(2)-(3) 234
  s.70(6) 234
  s.71(1)-(3) 234
  s.72 234
  s.72(4) 234
  s.72(8)-(9) 234
  s.73(2)-(3) 234
  s.73(5) 234
  s.74 227
  s.74(1)(a)-(b) 227
  s.74(2) 227
  s.74(4) 227
  s.75 239, 240, 241, 246
  s.75(1) 237, 239, 241, 242
  s.75(2) 240, 241
  s.75(3) 239
  s.75(4) 240
  s.76 243, 253, 257
  s.76(1) 242, 243, 254
  s.76(2)(a) 242
  s.76(4) 243
  s.77-s.79 243
  s.80(1)-(2) 243
  s.81(1)-(2) 243
  s.82(1) 243
  s.82(2)-(3) 244
  s.83 244, 245
  s.83(1)-(2) 244
  s.84 244, 245
  s.84(1) 244
  s.84(2)-(3) 245
  s.84(5) 245
  s.85 245
  s.85(1)-(3) 245
  s.86(1) 245
  s.87 249, 253, 255, 257
  s.87(1) 250, 254
  s.87(2) 249
  s.88 255, 257
  s.88(2) 249
  s.88(3) 250
  s.89 249, 255, 257
  s.90 258
  s.90(1) 257, 258
  s.90(2) 257
  s.90(5) 257, 258
  s.91 258
  s.92(1)-(3) 258
  s.93 250, 254
  s.94 251
  s.94(1) 250
  s.95 256
  s.95(1) 250
  s.96(1) 250
  s.98 243, 255, 257

Consumer Credit Act 1974 – *continued*
  s.98(1) 243, 254
  s.99 250, 251, 253, 256
  s.99(1) 250-1
  s.99(2)-(3) 251
  s.100 250, 251, 252, 256
  s.100(1) 251, 252, 256, 258
  s.100(2) 252
  s.100(3) 252, 258
  s.100(4) 251
  s.101 253, 254
  s.101(1)-(7) 253
  s.127(1) 231
  s.127(3) 231
  s.127(4)(a)-(b) 231
  s.129 254
  s.129(1)(b)(ii) 243
  s.130(5) 255
  s.131-s.132 258
  s.133 258
  s.133(6) 258
  s.135-s.136 258
  s.137(1) 258
  s.138(1)-(4) 258
  s.139 260
  s.145(2) 226
  s.168 223
  s.170(1) 223, 224, 225
  s.173 254, 258
  s.173(1) 234, 240, 244, 250, 252, 258
  s.173(3) 258
  s.173(b) 217
  s.187(3) 215
  s.187(3A) 215
  s.189 217
  s.189(1) 204, 205, 206, 221, 222, 226, 229, 232, 250
  s.189(2) 221, 222
  sch.1 204
  sch.2 204, 218, 227, 232
Consumer Protection Act 1987 2, 3, 10, 11, 199
  Part I 177, 179, 181, 183, 188, 189–94, 201
  Part II 177, 195–7, 199, 201
  Part III 296, 313
  s.1(1) 189
  s.1(2)(a) 189, 191
  s.1(2)(b) 191
  s.1(2)(c) 190, 191
  s.2 189
  s.2(2) 190
  s.2(2)(a) 189
  s.2(2)(b)-(c) 190
  s.2(3) 190
  s.2(4) 189, 190, 191
  s.2(5)-(6) 190
  s.3(1) 191-2
  s.3(2) 192

TABLE OF STATUTES

Consumer Protection Act 1987 – *continued*
   s.5(1)-(2)   193
   s.5(3)   194
   s.5(5)   190
   s.6(4)   193
   s.7   194
   s.10   197, 198
   s.10(1)-(2)   195
   s.10(4)   196
   s.10(4)(a)   196
   s.10(4)(b)   196, 198
   s.10(4)(c)   196
   s.10(7)   196
   s.11   196
   s.13   197
   s.13(1)(a)-(b)   197
   s.14-s.16   197
   s.18   197
   s.19(1)   195
   s.20   313, 315, 318, 319, 321, 322
   s.20(1)   313–14, 315, 316, 317, 318, 319, 324
   s.20(2)   314, 315, 316, 324
   s.20(2)(a)   316
   s.20(3)   316
   s.20(5)   322
   s.20(6)   317–18
   s.20(6)(a)   317
   s.21(1)   319–20
   s.21(2)   320
   s.22(1)   319
   s.23   319
   s.24   321
   s.24(1)   321
   s.24(2)-(4)   321, 322
   s.25(2)   322
   s.26   321
   s.39   321
   s.40   196
   s.40(2)   316
   s.45   191, 319
   s.46   192, 196

Factors Act 1889, s.8   146

Hire-Purchase Act 1964   148
   Part III   148
   s.27   41
   s.27(2)   148
   s.29(1)   148

Larceny Act 1916   118
Law Reform (Frustrated Contracts) Act 1943   135, 136
Limitation Act 1980
   s.11A   194
   s.11A(3)   194
   s.11A(4)   194
   s.32   37

Merchandising Marks Acts 1887–1953   3, 262, 271
Misrepresentation Act 1967   16, 21, 40
   s.1   21–2, 23, 36
   s.2(1)   14, 16, 23, 40, 41, 43
   s.2(2)   15, 19, 23, 25, 35, 42, 43, 46
   s.2(3)   43
   s.3   159, 168
   s.6(4)   159

Occupier's Liability Act 1957   160

Pharmacy and Poisons Act 1933   9
Protection of Birds Act 1964, s.6(1)   11, 274

Restriction of Offensive Weapons Act 1959
   s.1   8
   s.1(1)   274–5

Sale of Goods Act 1893   1, 2, 19, 47, 48, 65, 66, 70
   s.4   58
   s.13   20, 158
   s.14(2)   65, 66
Sale of Goods Act 1979   1, 2, 7, 10–11, 20, 24, 25, 34, 47, 48–54, 55, 56, 57, 60, 63, 64, 65, 66, 70, 89, 111, 112, 113, 122, 178, 181, 182, 183, 191, 200
   s.2(1)   49, 51
   s.2(4)-(5)   52
   s.5(1)-(2)   52
   s.5(3)   53
   s.6   133, 134, 135, 150
   s.7   119, 120, 134, 150
   s.8   143
   s.8(1)-(3)   143
   s.10   141
   s.10(1)   143
   s.10(2)   140
   s.11(4)   23, 25, 30, 31
   s.12   58, 63, 64, 90, 161, 163
   s.12(1)   95, 96, 97, 98, 99, 100, 101
   s.12(2)   100, 101
   s.12(2)(a)-(b)   100
   s.12(3)   99
   s.13   30, 58, 63, 64, 90–5, 159, 161, 163, 166
   s.13(1)   90, 91, 92, 94, 95, 102
   s.13(2)   104
   s.13(3)   91
   s.14   30, 58, 63, 64, 103, 104, 161, 180, 193
   s.14(1)   64
   s.14(2)   25, 45, 64, 65, 66, 67–77, 78–9, 81, 82, 103, 179, 180, 181, 183, 276
   s.14(2A)   68, 69, 104
   s.14(2B)   70, 72, 73, 76, 77, 96, 104

Sale of Goods Act 1979 – *continued*
  s.14(2C) 67, 68, 103
  s.14(3) 64, 65, 66, 77–81, 155, 162, 180
  s.14(5) 66
  s.14(6) 69, 70
  s.15 30, 58, 63, 64, 90, 101–4, 161
  s.15(1) 102
  s.15(2) 101
  s.15(2)(a) 102, 103
  s.15(2)(b) 104
  s.15(2)(c) 103, 104
  s.15A 81, 105, 106
  s.15A(1)-(3) 105
  s.16 111, 124, 126, 130, 149, 150
  s.17 111, 114, 115, 117, 119, 120, 121, 124, 130, 147, 149, 150
  s.17(1)-(2) 114
  s.18 111, 114, 115, 116, 117, 119, 120, 121, 122, 123, 124, 125, 126, 127, 135, 147, 149, 150
  s.19 111
  s.19(1) 127
  s.20 111
  s.20(3) 34, 119
  s.20A 124, 128, 129, 130, 149, 150
  s.20B 128, 129, 149
  s.23 37
  s.24 146, 147
  s.25 56
  s.25(1)-(2) 56
  s.27 136
  s.28 136, 143
  s.29 138
  s.29(1) 138
  s.29(2) 138, 139
  s.29(5) 141
  s.30(1)-(2) 141
  s.30(2A) 141
  s.30(3) 141
  s.31(1) 142
  s.32(1)-(2) 138
  s.34 26, 104
  s.35 26–9
  s.35(1) 26, 27
  s.35(2) 26, 27
  s.35(2)(b) 104
  s.35(3) 26, 27
  s.35(4) 26, 27, 29
  s.35(5) 26, 29
  s.35(6) 26
  s.35(6)(b) 183
  s.35(7) 32, 33
  s.35A 30, 32
  s.35A(1) 30–1
  s.35A(2) 31
  s.35A(3) 31, 32
  s.35A(4) 31
  s.36 33
  s.38 143

Sale of Goods Act 1979 – *continued*
  s.39(1)-(2) 143
  s.39 118
  s.41 143
  s.41(1)-(2) 143
  s.43(1) 143
  s.48(1)-(3) 145
  s.59 29
  s.61 50, 130, 136
  s.61(1) 50, 54, 113, 116
  s.61(5) 116
Sale of Goods (Amendment) Act 1995 128
Sale and Supply of Goods Act 1994 26, 30, 32, 69
  s.1 69
Supply of Goods (Implied Terms) Act 1973 2, 7, 34, 47, 48, 56, 63, 64, 65, 66, 77, 81, 89, 241
  s.8 90, 161
  s.8(1)-(2) 101
  s.9 90, 159, 166
  s.9(1) 95
  s.10(2) 34, 77
  s.10(2C) 77
  s.10(3) 81
  s.11 90, 104
  s.11A 81, 105
  s.15 55
Supply of Goods and Services Act 1982 2, 7, 34, 47, 48, 56, 61, 63, 64, 77, 81, 83, 89
  s.1 56–7, 58
  s.1(1) 56
  s.1(2) 57
  s.2 58, 90, 164
  s.2(1) 101
  s.3 58, 90, 164
  s.3(2) 95
  s.4 58, 60, 164
  s.4(2)-(3) 77
  s.4(4)-(6) 81
  s.5 58, 90, 104, 164
  s.5A 81, 105
  s.6 59
  s.6(1)-(3) 59
  s.7 90, 101, 164
  s.7(1) 101
  s.8 90, 105, 161, 164
  s.8(2) 95
  s.9 59, 161, 164
  s.9(2)-(3) 77
  s.9(4)-(6) 81
  s.10 90, 104, 161, 164
  s.10A 81, 105
  s.11 161
  s.12 59
  s.12(1)-(2) 59
  s.12(3) 59, 60, 106

TABLE OF STATUTES

Supply of Goods and Services Act 1982 – *continued*
  s.13 58, 59, 60, 82, 86, 87, 88, 106, 143, 160, 161, 164, 189
  s.14 59, 86, 88
  s.14(1) 86
  s.14(2) 60, 86
  s.15 59, 86, 88
  s.15(1)-(2) 86
  s.16 59

Theft Act 1968 118

Trade Descriptions Act 1968 3, 65, 66, 196, 262–87, 289–311
  s.1 263, 264, 267, 269, 293, 296, 297, 298, 305, 309
  s.1(1) 265, 266, 274, 304
  s.1(1)(a) 262, 263, 264, 266, 267, 268, 269, 270, 273, 274, 276, 280, 284, 285, 286, 287, 290, 304
  s.1(1)(b) 262, 263, 264, 266, 267, 268, 269, 270, 273, 274, 275, 276, 279, 280, 281, 282, 283, 284, 285, 286, 287, 304, 307, 308, 311
  s.2 262, 275, 277, 278, 279, 280, 281, 282, 287
  s.2(1) 275, 279, 281, 283
  s.2(1)(a) 277
  s.2(1)(b) 277, 281
  s.2(1)(c) 276, 277
  s.2(1)(d) 276, 277, 280, 282
  s.2(1)(e)-(f) 277
  s.2(1)(g) 278
  s.2(1)(i) 278
  s.2(1)(j) 277, 279
  s.3(1) 279, 281
  s.3(2) 281, 282, 283
  s.3(3) 279, 281, 282, 283
  s.4 270, 271, 287
  s.4(1)(a)-(c) 271
  s.4(2) 271
  s.4(3) 272
  s.5 272–3
  s.5(2) 272, 273
  s.5(3) 273
  s.6 275
  s.11 313
  s.11(2) 305, 319
  s.14 198, 274, 289, 290, 291, 293, 296, 297, 298, 299, 301, 304, 305, 310
  s.14(1) 296, 297, 299, 302, 303
  s.14(1)(a) 289, 290, 292, 294, 310
  s.14(1)(b) 289, 291, 292, 293, 294, 296, 297, 300, 301, 302, 309, 310
  s.14(2)(a) 301, 302
  s.14(2)(b) 294
  s.14(4) 301
  s.20 264

Trade Descriptions Act 1968 – *continued*
  s.23 264, 279, 280, 305, 308–10, 311
  s.24 273, 283, 306, 309
  s.24(1) 303, 305, 307, 309, 311
  s.24(1)(a) 303, 304
  s.24(2) 305
  s.24(3) 308, 311
  s.25 273, 310, 311
  s.29(1)(a) 274
  s.39 273
  s.39(1) 269

Trading Stamps Act 1964, s.4 61

Unfair Contract Terms Act 1977 2, 3, 65, 66, 152, 153, 157, 158, 159–70, 171, 211
  s.1 159
  s.1(1) 159–60
  s.1(1)(a) 164
  s.1(3) 159, 164, 166
  s.1(4) 160
  s.1(a) 86
  s.2 159, 160, 161, 164
  s.2(1) 86, 160, 161, 164, 166
  s.2(2) 86, 160, 164, 166, 169
  s.2(3) 160
  s.3 161, 164–5, 169
  s.3(2) 166
  s.4 167
  s.4(1)-(2) 167
  s.5 161, 167–8, 182
  s.5(2)(b) 168
  s.5(3) 167
  s.6 30, 163, 164, 165, 166, 169, 170, 182
  s.6(1) 161
  s.6(2) 85, 161
  s.6(3) 86, 163
  s.6(4) 163
  s.7 161, 164, 166, 169, 182
  s.7(2) 85
  s.8 159, 168
  s.10 170
  s.11 168
  s.11(1)-(5) 169
  s.12 3, 161, 163
  s.12(1) 163
  s.12(1)(c) 162
  s.12(2)-(3) 162
  s.13(1) 161, 170
  s.13(1)(a) 170
  s.13(1)(b) 169, 170
  s.13(1)(c) 170
  s.13(2) 170
  s.14 159
  Sch.2 169–70

Unsolicited Goods and Services Act 1971 111, 112, 124, 148–9, 150
  s.1 148–9
  s.2 149

INTRODUCTION

Objectives

By the end of this chapter you should be able to:

■ outline the way in which consumer law has developed;

■ describe the characteristics of a typical consumer transaction;

■ find your way around this book.

The Development of Consumer Law

Consumer law has only recently been recognised as a subject in its own right. As yet there is no statutory code which attempts to encapsulate consumer law, nor is there any prospect of such a code coming into being in the foreseeable future. The law which protects consumers is a mixture of civil and criminal law, of contract and tort, of common law and statute. Some recent legislation is overtly consumer law, in that it is designed to protect consumers and has no other purpose. But often consumer law must be extracted from other well-established areas of law. Here the law was not created with the consumer in mind, but rather the principles of law which have evolved can be adapted to protect the consumer.

In the nineteenth century the concept of a consumer was quite unknown. Those who we would today classify as consumers might be provided with a remedy by the Sale of Goods Act 1893 or by the common law of contract if they bought a defective or dangerous product. However, neither the common law nor the 1893 Act (which codified the common law on contracts of sale of goods) were concerned primarily with consumers. The 1893 Act was intended to be a code which regulated the affairs of merchants. The 1893 Act has evolved into the Sale of Goods Act 1979 but, as we shall see in later chapters, it is still concerned more with business sales than with consumer sales. The consumer has to make do by applying the Act as best he can. There are signs, however, that this might be changing. Recent amendments to the 1979 Act are distinguishing between consumer and commercial buyers with the object of affording consumer buyers better protection.

There has never been a reason why a consumer should not sue a retailer on general common law contract principles. But if you think back to your study of the law of contract, and of the cases which created the law, you are likely to remember that the majority of those cases concerned commercial contracts rather than consumer contracts. (There are of course memorable exceptions, even in the Victorian era, such as *Carlill v Carbolic Smoke Ball Co.* [1893] 1 QB 256.)

In the nineteenth century the principle *caveat emptor* was regarded as fundamental to the law of contract and to a considerable extent it remains fundamental today. We shall see that consumers who buy defective goods are given statutory remedies and that exclusion clauses can no longer deny them these remedies, but there is still no law which protects a consumer against making an unwise or overpriced purchase. In a business context this attitude is perfectly rational; if a business continues to make bad contracts it should not be protected from its own folly. If necessary the business should cease to exist and, it is to be hoped, be replaced by a more efficient business. In a consumer context the argument holds less force. Some consumers habitually buy products they do not really want or pay too high a price for goods or services. There is an argument that they should be afforded some protection in this regard, although it is difficult to see how such protection might be conferred other than by curbing excessive advertising. The free market economy takes it for granted that consumers will make rational choices.

The Sale of Goods Act 1893 codified the law on sales of goods but, like its successor the 1979 Sale of Goods Act, it left untouched contracts which could not be classified as sales of goods. As we shall see, the statutory implied terms which first the 1893 Act, and now the 1979 Act, have implied in the buyer's favour are one of the most significant sources of consumer law. But for most of the twentieth century no statute implied terms into contracts which could not be classed as sales of goods. It was left to the common law to imply terms into such contracts and these common law implied terms were naturally less certain than those set out in the Sale of Goods Acts. However, in the past 30 years other important statutes have implied terms very similar to those implied by the 1979 Act into other types of contracts. The Sale of Goods (Implied Terms) Act 1973 implies the terms into contracts of hire-purchase, the Sale of Goods and Services Act 1982 implies the terms into contracts of hire, and into contracts for the transfer of property in goods. (The 1982 Act also implies rather different terms into contracts to supply a service.) These more recent statutes have provided considerable help to consumers, although none of them is confined to helping consumers. There is no reason why a business should not invoke any of the statutory implied terms.

The Unfair Contract Terms Act 1977 has dealt a heavy blow to the doctrine of *caveat emptor*, at least in the context of exclusion clauses and notices which purport to exclude liability for breach of contract or liability for negligence. Until the 1977 Act came into force the common law was grotesquely inadequate in protecting consumers against terms which denied them a remedy for breach of contract or for the tort of negligence. On the one hand the Sale of Goods Act 1893 gave consumers important rights, and on the other hand exclusion clauses which the consumer had little choice but to sign routinely took these rights away. The 1977 Act is not restricted to the protection of consumers but it does draw a distinction between those who deal as a consumer and those who do not. The purpose of drawing this distinction is to confer greater protection on those who do deal as consumers than on those who do not. The 1973, 1979 and 1982 Acts now all confer extra protection upon consumers. The making of the distinction between those who deal as a consumer and those who do not is a significant milestone in consumer protection legislation.

EC inspired legislation, such as the Unfair Terms in Consumer Contracts Regulations 1994, and the Consumer Protection Act 1987 are overt examples of consumer protection. It seems likely that consumer legislation which was passed to comply with EC Directives will become increasingly important.

The law of tort has always been capable of being used by a consumer who is injured by a service or a product. (*Donoghue* v *Stevenson* [1932] AC 562 is perhaps the most famous consumer case of them all.) However, the law of tort is a blunt instrument in the hands of a consumer. Under the common law it can be very difficult indeed to prove that the business which manufactured the product or the service is liable for the injuries which the product or service caused. The Consumer Protection Act 1987 removes the burden of proving negligence when a consumer is injured by a dangerous product, but the Act gives no help when a consumer is injured by a defective service.

INTRODUCTION

The criminal law has dealt with dishonest traders since the Middle Ages. However, the concern of the criminal law was mainly to prevent a dishonest trader gaining an advantage over his more scrupulous business rivals. This attitude has been carried over into the Trade Descriptions Act 1968. Although not confined to the protection of consumers, this is a major piece of consumer protection legislation. However the 1968 Act replaced the Merchandising Marks Act 1887 to 1953 and these Acts had as their object the prevention of dishonest traders gaining a business advantage by means of their dishonesty. The 1968 Act imposes criminal liability on those who, in the course of a trade or business, misdescribe goods or services. The 1968 Act also created offences relating to misleading price indications, although these have been replaced by provisions in the Consumer Protection Act 1987.

The Definition of a Consumer

One of the consequences of there being no historical sense of consumer law as a subject in its own right is that there is no universally applicable definition of a consumer. As we study the legislation which confers protection upon consumers, we must in each case examine exactly to whom the legislation applies. The Consumer Credit Act 1974, for example, generally confers protection on individuals, but individuals are defined in such a way as to include partnerships, although not in such a way as to include companies. The Unfair Terms in Consumer Contracts Regulations 1994 define a consumer as a natural person who, in making a contract is acting for purposes which are outside his business. The protection conferred by the 1994 Regulations applies when a consumer makes a contract with a seller or supplier. (Sellers and suppliers are defined as making the contracts in relation to their trades or businesses.)

When considering a statute we are at least aware of who is within the ambit of the statute. When considering the protection which the common law confers on consumers it is necessary to have in mind a definition of a consumer. If such a definition is not clearly identified then it is impossible to know which aspects of the common law to include or exclude. Perhaps the most widely accepted definition of when a person is dealing as a consumer is contained in the Unfair Contract Terms Act 1977, s. 12. We examine this definition in detail in **Chapter 6**. Here it is enough to say that s. 12 classifies a person as dealing as a consumer if:

(a) he makes a contract while neither acting in the course of a business nor holding himself out to be doing so; and

(b) the other party does make the contract in the course of a business; and

(c) the goods bought are of a type ordinarily supplied for private use or consumption.

Section 12 also makes it plain that purchases at auction sales are not to be included.

So, when considering who is a consumer as far as the common law is concerned, in this book I have adopted the widely accepted definition contained in s. 12. We are all consumers when we buy books and catch buses. Unless the particular legislation being considered stipulates otherwise, business buyers cannot be consumers. A person who buys otherwise than from a business, or at an auction, or who buys goods or services which would not ordinarily be supplied for private use or consumption, is not a consumer.

The Way This Book is Organised

The first part of this book deals with the ways in which the civil law protects the consumer. The second part examines statutes which impose criminal liability on traders who deal with consumers.

The civil law on consumer protection is to a very large extent based on the law of contract, as supplemented by various statutes which imply terms into contracts. The law of contract will already have been studied as a subject in its own right by LLB students, and so there is no need in this book to re-examine the subject in any detail. However, **Chapter 1** of this book does reiterate the general principles of the law of contract very briefly, and goes on to consider two matters in detail. The first of these matters is the formation of unilateral contracts, the second is the effect of untrue statements made by a party to a contract. Although both of these subjects will have been studied in the law of contract programme, they seem particularly relevant to consumer law and therefore call for an in depth examination as part of this book. (When consumers are urged to buy a product or save labels and promised something in return they may be being offered the chance to make a unilateral contract, and one of the most common causes of consumer dissatisfaction is that goods or services were bought on the strength of promises or assurances which transpire not to have been true.)

Chapters 2–4 examine the statutory terms implied in the consumer's favour. These terms are probably the most important source of consumer law and need to be examined in detail. **Chapter 2** classifies the different types of contracts into which the terms are implied. The Sale of Goods Act 1979 implies the terms into contracts of sale of goods, the Supply of Goods (Implied Terms) Act 1973 implies the terms into contracts of hire-purchase, and the Supply of Goods and Services Act 1982 implies terms into three separate categories of contracts — contracts for the transfer of property in goods, contracts for the hire of goods, and contracts for the supply of a service. We therefore begin by classifying the five different types of contracts into which statutory terms are implied. Having classified the various types of terms, **Chapters 3 and 4** examine in detail the nature of the terms implied. **Chapter 3** examines the implied terms as to quality and fitness for purpose and the terms implied into contracts to supply a service. **Chapter 4** examines the implied terms as to the right to sell, correspondence with description and correspondence with sample.

In **Chapter 5** we examine miscellaneous aspects of the Sale of Goods Act 1979. Although any aspect of the 1979 Act might affect a consumer, we concentrate on those areas which are most likely to be of practical importance, namely, the passing of the risk and the property in goods, the seller's duty to deliver the goods, payment of the price, the rights of an unpaid seller, and sale by a seller in possession after a sale. We also consider two matters dealt with by other statutes: the position where a consumer buys a motor vehicle which is subject to a hire-purchase agreement and the position where a consumer is sent unsolicited goods and services.

Chapter 6 examines the effect of exclusion clauses on consumers. Such clauses attempt to take away a consumer's rights under a contract or attempt to prevent liability in tort from arising. The common law offered little help to consumers in this regard, and the Unfair Contract Terms Act 1977 has proved to be one of the most successful statutes conferring consumer protection. The 1977 Act has been supplemented by the Unfair Terms in Consumer Contracts Regulations 1994, which were passed to comply with an EC Directive. We shall see that these Regulations apply alongside the 1977 Act rather than replacing that Act. Both the 1977 Act and the 1994 Regulations are examined in detail.

In **Chapter 7** we consider product safety. As the law of tort will already have been studied as a subject in its own right we do not consider again the tort of negligence. We begin the chapter by looking at problems which the doctrine of privity of contract creates and then go on to consider the civil and criminal protection conferred by the Consumer Protection Act 1987.

Chapters 8–11 deal with the Consumer Credit Act 1974. This Act has conferred valuable rights on consumers who obtain credit, but the Act is not easy to read or understand. The four chapters attempt to make the more important provisions of the Act comprehensible. **Chapter 8** deals with the history and structure of the Act and examines the

INTRODUCTION

definitions which must be mastered before the Act can be understood. **Chapter 9** deals with the advertising and canvassing of consumer credit agreements and the making of such agreements. **Chapter 10** deals with matters arising under a consumer credit agreement. Some of these matters confer important rights on consumer creditors. **Chapter 11** deals with the termination of consumer credit agreements and the remedies available for wrongful termination.

The Trade Descriptions Act 1968 imposes criminal liability on those who misdescribe goods or services in the course of a trade or business. **Chapter 12** examines the Act as it applies to the misdescription of goods, **Chapter 13** examines the Act as it applies to the misdescription of services. Defences under the Act are also considered in **Chapter 13**. **Chapter 14** examines the criminal law on misleading trade prices.

I have not included a separate chapter on the enforcement of consumer law. LLB students will already have studied civil and criminal procedure and the circumstances in which legal aid and advice can be obtained.

CHAPTER ONE

THE LAW OF CONTRACT AS A MEANS OF CONSUMER PROTECTION

1.1 Objectives

By the end of this chapter you should be able to:

- explain the process by which a contract is formed;

- distinguish an offer from an invitation to treat;

- analyse whether advertisements, or the display of goods in shops, are likely to amount to offers or invitations to treat;

- explain the circumstances in which an offer of a unilateral contract can be revoked;

- explain the tests which the courts have used to distinguish terms and representations, and apply these tests to problem situations;

- give an account of the different remedies available for breach of contract and for an actionable misrepresentation;

- analyse the circumstances in which a consumer will be regarded as having accepted goods which have been bought, and explain the consequences of such an acceptance;

- explain the circumstances in which a consumer with the right to treat a contract of hire-purchase or hire as repudiated will lose the right on account of having affirmed the contract;

- explain the circumstances in which a consumer with the right to rescind a contract on account of an actionable misrepresentation will lose this right;

- assess the measure of damages available for fraudulent and negligent misrepresentations;

- analyse the circumstances in which damages can be awarded in lieu of rescission in cases of innocent misrepresentation, and assess how such damages are quantified.

1.2 Introduction

If a consumer buys goods or services which prove to be defective, then in order to gain a remedy it is to the law of contract which the consumer must look. In the three chapters which follow this one we examine the terms implied by the Sale of Goods Act 1979, the Supply of Goods (Implied Terms) Act 1973 and the Supply of Goods and Services Act 1982. These statutory implied terms are the most significant source of civil consumer protection legislation. However, the statutory terms are only implied if a consumer has made a contract to acquire the goods or services which prove to be defective and they do not deprive the consumer of the right to sue under the common law. In order to understand the statutory implied terms it is therefore necessary to have an understanding of the basic principles of the law of contract.

By the time LLB students study consumer law they will already have studied contract law, one of the LLB foundation subjects. As the law of contract will already have been studied in depth, there is no point in us examining the whole subject again. However, certain aspects of contract law are of particular importance in consumer law, and these aspects need to be studied in detail. So in this chapter the general principles of contract law are outlined very briefly, while the issues which are of particular relevance to consumer law are considered in more detail.

1.3 Formation of Contracts (General Principles)

Contracts are formed when an offer is accepted. One of the parties, the offeror, makes an offer by proposing a set of terms by which he is willing to be bound. If the other party, the offeree, accepts the offer then a contract is formed and both parties will be bound by the terms proposed and accepted. An offer can be made to one person, to a class of people or to the world at large, and only those to whom the offer was made can accept it (*Carlill* v *Carbolic SmokeBall Co.* [1893] 1 QB 256). An invitation to treat is not an offer, but only an invitation to negotiate. Although a person who makes an offer makes a definite promise to be bound if the offer is accepted, a person who makes an invitation to treat makes no such definite promise. Consequently, an invitation to treat cannot be accepted in such a way that this leads to a binding contract (*Partridge* v *Crittenden* [1968] 1 WLR 1204).

Most contracts are bilateral, and in these contracts the parties exchange promises. A person who makes an offer of a unilateral contract agrees to be bound if the offeree performs some act, rather than if the offeree promises to perform some act. The contracts are called unilateral because only one of the parties, the offeror, makes a promise. The offeree cannot accept by promising to do the act requested, but only by actually doing it.

Generally an acceptance creates a binding contract as soon as it is received by the offeror (*Entores* v *Miles Far East Corporation* [1955] 2 QB 327). There are, however, two exceptions to this rule. First, acceptance of a unilateral contract often does not need to be communicated (*Carlill* v *Carbolic Smoke Ball Co.*) Second, in certain circumstances an acceptance of an offer by post or telegram may become effective when the letter or telegram is posted rather than when it is received (*Holwell Securities Ltd* v *Hughes* [1974] 1 All ER 161). It is not possible to accept an offer by doing nothing, even if the offer stipulates that it should be accepted in this way (*Felthouse* v *Bindley* (1862) 11 CBNS 869).

In order for a contract to exist, all of its terms must have been agreed and the reasonable person must be able to ascertain exactly what has been agreed (*May and Butcher* v *R* [1934] 2 KB 17). If meaningless terms have been agreed this will not make the contract uncertain, as meaningless terms can be ignored if this would leave behind a good contract (*Nicolene Ltd* v *Simmonds* [1953] 1 All ER 822.)

An offer can be revoked at any time before acceptance and revocations are always effective when received, even if sent by letter or telegram (*Byrne* v *Van Tienhoven* (1880) 5 CPD 344). Generally, a unilateral offer cannot be revoked once the offeree has embarked on acceptance (*Errington* v *Errington & Woods* [1952] 1 KB 290). Refusal of an offer ends the offer (at least as far as the person who refused is concerned). A counter-offer amounts to a refusal and therefore ends the original offer (*Hyde* v *Wrench* (1840) 3 Beav 334). However, a mere request for more information does not end the offer (*Stevenson* v *McLean* (1880) 5 QBD 346). An offer can cease to be effective through the passage of time. If an offer is expressed to be open for a certain time then it will remain open for that time, unless it is revoked (*Dickinson* v *Dodds* (1876) 2 ChD 463). If no time limit is stipulated by the offeror then an offer will remain open for a reasonable time (*Manchester Diocesan Council for Education* v *Commercial and General Investments Ltd* [1970] 1 WLR 241).

Even if an offer is accepted, there will be no contract unless it can be objectively inferred that the parties intended to create legal relations (*Parker* v *Clark* [1960] 1 WLR 286). In a business or commercial context it is presumed that the parties do intend to create legal relations (*Esso Petroleum* v *Commissioners of Customs and Excise* [1976] 1 WLR 1), in a social or domestic context it is presumed that they do not (*Jones* v *Padavatton* [1969] 1 WLR 328). Either of these presumptions may be rebutted by the evidence.

A contract is a bargain and therefore both sides must give some consideration to the other. The consideration of both parties must be sufficient, that is to say it must amount to something of recognisable value. The consideration given does not need to be adequate, that is to say it does not need to be equal in value to the consideration received (*Chappell & Co Ltd* v *Nestlé Co. Ltd* [1960] 2 All ER 701). An act already performed, or a service already rendered, cannot be promised as consideration — past consideration is no consideration (*Re McArdle* [1951] Ch 669). However, if the act or service performed was requested by the other party, and if an implied promise to pay can be inferred at the time of the request, then the performance of the act or service can amount to good consideration (*Lampleigh* v *Brathwaite* (1615) Hob 105). As a contract is a bargain under which the parties exchange their respective considerations, only a person who is a party to a contract can acquire rights under the contract or be made liable on it (*Tweddle* v *Atkinson* (1861) 1 B & S 393). A lesser sum of money cannot be consideration for a greater sum owed (*Foakes* v *Beer* (1884) 9 App Cas 605), although it is possible that in some circumstances promissory estoppel may act as a defence in favour of a person who agreed to provide a lesser sum in satisfaction of a greater sum owed (*Central London Property Trust Ltd* v *High Trees House Ltd* [1947] 1 KB 130).

1.3.1 OFFERS AND INVITATIONS TO TREAT

The principles of the modern law of contract evolved in the nineteenth century, as the Victorian judges applied the rules of offer and acceptance to commercial disputes. The vast majority of contractual disputes which were brought to the attention of the judiciary involved disputes between two merchants, rather than disputes between a consumer and a retailer. When examining the negotiations of merchants the courts could generally find a proposition which amounted to a definite offer, and then find a definite indication that this offer either had been accepted or had not.

This analysis has never worked so well with consumers, but nevertheless the courts have consistently applied the rules on offer and acceptance to discover when a consumer contract is concluded. (For a criticism of this approach, see Lord Wilberforce in *New Zealand Shipping Co. Ltd* v *A.M. Satterthwaite & Co. Ltd* [1975] AC 154 at 167 in **Cases and Materials** (1.1.1).)

1.3.1.1 Goods displayed in shops

In Victorian times shops were seen to some extent as places to bargain. As far as the law on formation of contracts is concerned, this notion still holds good today.

Fisher v *Bell* [1961] 1 QB 394
The defendant displayed a flick-knife in his shop window. Behind the knife was a ticket saying, 'Ejector knife — 4s'. The defendant was charged with offering for sale a flick-knife, contrary to s. 1 of the Restriction of Offensive Weapons Act 1959.

THE LAW OF CONTRACT AS A MEANS OF CONSUMER PROTECTION

Held: The defendant was not guilty. The display of the knife amounted only to an invitation to treat not to an offer. Lord Parker CJ stated, at 399:

> It is perfectly clear that according to the ordinary law of contract the display of an article with a price on it in a shop window is merely an invitation to treat. It is in no sense an offer for sale the acceptance of which constitutes a contract. That is clearly the general law of the country.

Do you think that most consumers would be surprised to find that goods displayed in shops were not offered for sale? Write down your views.

You might well have written that most consumers would be surprised to find that this is the legal position. In *Fisher* v *Bell*, Lord Parker, at 399, said:

> I confess that I think that most lay people and, indeed, I myself when I first read the papers, would be inclined to the view that to say that if a knife was displayed in a window like that with a price attached to it was not offering it for sale was just nonsense. In ordinary language it is there inviting people to buy it, and it is for sale; but any statute must of course be looked at in the light of the general law of the country.

As the following case shows, goods displayed on supermarket shelves are invitations to treat and not offers.

Pharmaceutical Society of Great Britain v *Boots Cash Chemists (Southern) Ltd* [1953] 1 QB 401
The defendants ran a supermarket in Edgware. The Pharmacy and Poisons Act 1933 required that certain drugs be sold only by or under the supervision of a registered pharmacist. Some such drugs were displayed on the supermarket shelves in packages or containers on which the price was marked. Customers took the packages to the cashier's desk where they paid for them. When the cashiers stated the price which had to be paid for the drugs, and took the money, they were supervised by a pharmacist.
Held: The defendants were not guilty of breaching the 1933 Act. The display of goods in a self-service system did not amount to an offer to sell, but merely to an invitation to buy. The customers made the offer to buy at the cashier's desk. The cashier accepted the offer and so the contract was made at the cashier's desk under the supervision of the pharmacist.

A consumer buys goods displayed inside a non self-service shop. At what stage is the contract concluded?

This is a surprisingly difficult question to answer. In the *Pharmaceutical Society of Great Britain* case Somervell LJ, at 406, explained his view on the matter:

> in the case of an ordinary shop, [one in which there is no self-service,] although goods are displayed and it is intended that customers should go and choose what they want, the contract is not completed until, the customer having indicated the articles which he needs, the shopkeeper, or someone on his behalf, accepts that offer.

This analysis is consistent with the decision in *Fisher* v *Bell* and there seems to be no reason to draw a distinction between goods displayed inside a shop and those displayed in a shop window. Somervell LJ's explanation seems obviously to be correct, but unfortunately he did not indicate exactly how the shopkeeper accepts the offer. Is it by ringing up the price, or taking the money, or saying 'Thank you very much' or whatever?

Why do we need to know precisely when a consumer makes the contract with a shop?

There are two main reasons why it may become necessary to know exactly when the contract between consumer and shop is concluded. The first and more obvious reason is that once the contract has been concluded then it will no longer be possible for either party to change their mind about the contract. The second reason is that if the goods harm the consumer in some way, the consumer will only be able to bring an action in contract if a contract has been concluded at the time the harm is caused. Each of these reasons needs to be considered carefully.

Until such time as the contract is concluded either of the parties can refuse to go ahead with it. In the *Pharmaceutical Society of Great Britain* case Somervell and Romer LJJ seemed guided by the principle that a customer ought to be able to put goods in his basket and then change his mind. Both thought that if the goods constituted an offer this would not be possible (see the extracts in **Cases and Materials** (**1.1.1.1**).) If goods displayed in supermarkets were offers, and if these offers could be accepted by the act of placing goods in a wire basket, this might have two serious consequences for supermarket owners: first, if they accidentally priced goods too low they would be bound to sell to consumers who accepted the price shown in good faith; second, they might also find that a large number of consumers accepted the same offer, so that they would find it impossible to supply all of these customers with the goods they had bought.

A second reason why we need to know exactly when the contract is formed becomes apparent if the goods cause a loss to the consumer in some way. For example, if a liquid leaks from a package and stains the consumer's clothes, then if a contract has been concluded the shop will be strictly liable under the Sale of Goods Act 1979 because the goods, which include their packaging, would not have been of satisfactory quality. If no contract had been concluded, then the 1979 Act would not apply and the consumer would need to sue the shop or the manufacturer in negligence. This would involve the difficult process of proving that the defendant had owed a duty of care to the consumer and had breached it. (Liability would be strict under the Consumer Protection Act 1987 if the consumer was injured or if his clothes or other property were damaged to more than the tune of £275, but not otherwise. The different regimes of liability under the Sale

THE LAW OF CONTRACT AS A MEANS OF CONSUMER PROTECTION

of Goods Act 1979, the Consumer Protection Act 1987 and in negligence are all considered in later chapters.)

The precise moment at which a contract is concluded between customer and supermarket is open to several different analyses, as shown in Bernard S Jackson, 'Offer and acceptance in the supermarket' (1979) 129 NLJ 775 (see *Cases and Materials* (1.1.1.1)). The article also deals with the formation of contracts in non-self-service shops.

1.3.1.2 Advertisements

It is reasonably clear that advertisements which promote goods or services will generally not amount to offers. The vast majority of advertisements are either mere 'puffs' or invitations to treat.

Partridge v *Crittenden* [1968] 1 WLR 1204
The defendant placed the following advertisement in the classified advertisements section of *Cage and Aviary Birds* magazine: 'Quality British A.B.C.R. . . . bramblefinch cocks, bramblefinch hens . . . 25s. each.' In response to the advertisement T wrote asking for a hen and enclosing 25 shillings. The defendant sent a hen to T and was charged with offering for sale a wild bird contrary to s. 6(1) of the Protection of Birds Act 1964.
Held: The defendant was not guilty of the offence as his advertisement was an invitation to treat rather than an offer. Consequently he did not offer for sale the wild bird.

In *Partridge* v *Crittenden* Lord Parker CJ thought that it was necessary to treat advertisements and circulars as invitations to treat because if they were treated as offers an unlimited number of people might accept. As the advertiser's stock would necessarily be limited, it would not be possible for him to fulfil all the contracts which would then be made. Lord Parker quoted with approval the following statement of Lord Herschell in *Grainger & Son* v *Gough* [1896] AC 325 at 334, in which it was decided that sending a list of wine prices to customers did not amount to an offer:

> The transmission of such a wine list does not amount to an offer to supply an unlimited quantity of the wine described at the price named, so that as soon as an order is given there is a binding contract . . . If it were so, the merchant might find himself involved in any number of contractual obligations to supply wine of a particular description which he would be quite unable to carry out, his stock of wine of that description being necessarily limited.

However, some advertisements do amount to a definite offer, as the manufacturers of Hoover vacuum cleaners recently learnt to their cost. The manufacturers advertised that customers buying a new Hoover between certain dates would be given a free flight to America (worth considerably more than the cost of a new vacuum cleaner). Although initially unwilling to honour their promise, the manufacturers were eventually obliged to do so.

The classic case of *Carlill* v *Carbolic Smoke Ball Co.* [1893] 1 QB 256 established that an advertisement aimed at consumers may amount to an offer of a unilateral contract. Such an offer is made when one of the parties makes a definite promise to be bound if the other party performs some action. In bilateral contracts the consideration of both parties is executory because both promise to do something, they exchange one promise for another. In unilateral contracts the consideration of the offeree is executed. The offeree cannot accept by promising to perform the act requested, but only by actually performing the act.

Carlill v *Carbolic Smoke Ball Co.* [1893] 1 QB 256
The defendants manufactured a product known as the Carbolic Smoke Ball. They advertised in various newspapers that they would pay £100 reward to anyone who caught influenza after using the ball properly three times a day for two weeks. The advertisements also said that, '£1,000 is deposited with Alliance Bank, Regent Street,

showing our sincerity in the matter.' The plaintiff bought a smoke ball on the strength of the advertisement. She used it three times a day for eight weeks, but then caught influenza. She claimed that she was entitled to the £100 reward.

Held: The plaintiff was entitled to the reward. The advertisement amounted to the offer of a unilateral contract. By performing the acts requested the plaintiff had accepted the offer.

Partridge v *Crittenden* and *Carlill* are traditionally used to set the parameters of advertisements which do amount to offers and advertisements which do not. However, it can be extremely difficult to know on which side of the line a particular case will fall.

In *Wood* v *Letric Ltd*, *The Times*, 13 January 1932, the manufacturer of an electric comb advertised that the comb would cure grey hair. The advertisement went on to state that there was a £500 guarantee. Having bought a comb the plaintiff found that it did not cure his grey hair, but only served to irritate his scalp. The retailer from whom the plaintiff bought the comb had not made any promise about the comb. Rowlatt J held that the manufacturers were liable on their advertisement, as it was an offer. The word 'guarantee' suggested that a definite promise was being made to customers in a collateral contract. The customers accepted this promise by purchasing one of the combs.

Bowerman v *ABTA Ltd* (1995) 145 NLJ 1815

The plaintiff, a 15-year-old schoolgirl, booked a skiing holiday which was being organised by one of her teachers, the second plaintiff. The tour operator was a member of the Association of British Travel Agents (ABTA). As required by ABTA's rules, the tour operator prominently displayed a notice 'describing ABTA's scheme of protection against the financial failure of ABTA members'. Inter alia, the notice stated that 'ABTA seeks to arrange for you to continue with the booked arrangement as far as possible', and 'ABTA ensures that you will be able to return to the United Kingdom', 'the scheme is for your benefit' and 'ABTA still protects you'. A second written document, which the plaintiff's teacher had read, said, 'Where holidays or other travel arrangements have not yet commenced at the time of failure, ABTA arranges for you to be reimbursed the money you have paid in respect of your holiday arrangements'. The tour was cancelled when the tour operator went out of business. The plaintiff received all of her money back except for a £10 holiday insurance premium. She claimed that this premium should also have been returned.

The Court of Appeal held that the plaintiff should get the return of her £10, as the ordinary member of the public would have regarded the words in the notice and the written document as promising to enter into legal relations with customers who booked holidays with ABTA members on the strength of them. (For the judgments of Waite and Hobhouse LJJ, see *Cases and Materials* (1.1.1.2).

As regards advertisements which do amount to offers of a unilateral contract, we need to analyse the circumstances in which the offer can be withdrawn.

A retailer makes a definite unilateral offer that the first person to arrive at the New Year sale can have a new television for £1. Immediately, Joe Consumer queues up outside the store, camping there at night. At what stage, if any, can the offer be withdrawn? Write down your views.

The answer to this question is not at all certain. In *Errington* v *Errington & Woods* [1952] 1 KB 290, a father who had bought a house for £750, taking out a mortgage of £500, promised his son and daughter-in-law that if they paid the mortgage instalments as they became due they could have the house when all of the instalments were paid. The son and daughter-in-law did pay all of the instalments until the father's death. In his will the father left the house to his widow. The son returned to live with his mother. The daughter-in-law continued to live in the house in question and continued to pay the mortgage instalments. The Court of Appeal held that the daughter-in-law was entitled to continue living in the house. Denning LJ said, at 295:

> The father's promise was a unilateral contract — a promise of the house in return for their act of paying the instalments. It could not be revoked by him once the couple entered on performance of the act, but it would cease to bind him if they left it incomplete and unperformed, which they have not done . . . it is clear that the father expressly promised the couple that the property should belong to them as soon as the mortgage was paid, and impliedly promised that so long as they paid the instalments to the building society they should be allowed to remain in possession.

Support for Denning LJ's view can be found in the following statement of Goff LJ in *Daulia Ltd* v *Four Millbank Nominees* [1978] 2 All ER 557:

> Whilst I think the true view of a unilateral contract must in general be that the offeror is entitled to require full performance of the condition which he has imposed and short of that he is not bound, that must be subject to one important qualification, which stems from the fact that there must be an implied obligation on the part of the offeror not to prevent the condition becoming satisfied, which obligation it seems to me must arise as soon as the offeree starts to perform. Until then the offeror can revoke the whole thing, but once the offeree has embarked on performance it is too late for the offeror to revoke his offer.

However, the House of Lords' decision in the following case weakens this implied term approach.

Luxor (Eastbourne) Ltd v *Cooper* [1941] AC 108
Estate agents were offered £10,000 commission for selling two cinemas, the commission to be paid on completion. The estate agents found buyers for the cinemas, but the cinema owners changed their minds and refused to sell. The estate agents asked for an implied term that the cinema owners would not act in such a way as to prevent them from earning their commission.
Held: No such term could be implied. The commission was so huge that the contract was in the nature of a gamble. If the whole deal went through the estate agents would get their commission. But if anything went wrong, they would not. Lord Russell stated, at 125:

> I can find no safe ground on which to base the introduction of any such implied term. Implied terms, as we all know, can only be justified under the compulsion of some necessity. No such compulsion or necessity exists in the case under consideration. . . . The chances are largely in favour of the deal going through, if a purchaser is introduced. The agent takes the risk in the hope of a substantial remuneration for comparatively small exertion.

So whether or not a term can be implied will depend upon the circumstances of the case. It is still the case that a term will be implied only where it is necessary to do so in order to give the contract business efficacy. That is to say, to make the contract work as the parties as reasonable people must have intended it to work. In answer to **SAQ 1/4** we must therefore ask whether or not it would be necessary, in order to give the contract business efficacy, to imply a term that the retailer's unilateral offer would not be revoked once a consumer had begun to accept it. My own opinion is that it would be necessary to imply such a term. In *Bowerman* v *ABTA Ltd* the majority of the Court of Appeal stressed that the guiding consideration was the impression which would be made on the hypothetical member of the public. No consumer would camp outside the shop if he or she knew that it would be possible for the shop to withdraw the offer at the last moment.

It is certain that an offer cannot be revoked if a person has given some consideration in return for the offer being kept open. In *Mountford v Scott* [1975] 2 WLR 114, the defendant gave the plaintiffs a six-month option to purchase his house for £10,000 in consideration of the plaintiff paying the sum of £1. One month later the defendant tried to withdraw the offer. Two months later still the plaintiff exercised the option. The Court of Appeal had no doubt that the offer could not be revoked within the six-month period and that the plaintiff had purchased the house by exercising the option. This case differs from the previous two in that there was no need to imply a term that the offer would not be revoked. The parties expressly contracted that the offer would be kept open.

1.4 Privity of Contract

The doctrine of privity of contract holds that a contract is a private bargain between the parties who made the contract. Those who did not make the contract cannot therefore become liable under the contract or enforce it. The effect of the privity rule upon consumers is considered in Chapter 7.

1.5 Pre-contractual Statements (General Principles)

The terms of the contract are the undertakings and promises which the parties exchange. Terms may be express, in which case they were expressly proposed in the offer which was accepted, or they may be implied. Terms are implied by various statutes, as we shall see in Chapters 3 and 4, and these terms are of very considerable significance to consumers. Terms may also be implied by the courts, either to give the contract business efficacy (*Luxor (Eastbourne) Ltd v Cooper* [1941] AC 108) or on the ground of custom or usage (*British Crane Hire Corporation Ltd v Ipswich Plant Hire Ltd* [1975] QB 303). If a term of the contract is broken then the injured party will have a right to damages. In addition the injured party will be able to treat the contract as repudiated if the term which was breached was a condition, or if the breach of an innominate term deprived the injured party of substantially the whole benefit of the contract. The right to treat a contract of sale of goods as repudiated will be lost once the goods have been accepted. The right to treat other types of contracts as repudiated will be lost once the contract is affirmed. (The circumstances in which goods are accepted or contracts are affirmed are examined at **1.9.1.1** below.)

Statements made prior to the contract which do not amount to terms may be representations, but the fact of a representation being untrue does not necessarily provide the party to whom it was made with any remedy. However, if the representation is an actionable misrepresentation then the injured party may have a remedy. An actionable misrepresentation might be defined as an untrue statement of fact which induced the other party to make the contract. Statements of mere opinion, and statements which did not induce the other party to make the contract, cannot be actionable misrepresentations and will have no legal effect (*Bisset v Wilkinson* [1927] AC 177, *Attwood v Small* (1838) 6 Cl & Fin 232).

There are three types of actionable misrepresentations: fraudulent, negligent and wholly innocent. A fraudulent misrepresentation is one made either knowing that it was false, or without belief in its truth, or being reckless or careless as to whether it was true or false (*Derry v Peek* (1889) 14 App Cas 337). The remedies available are to rescind the contract and/or to sue for tort damages. A negligent misrepresentation could be defined as a misrepresentation made honestly believing that it was true but without reasonable grounds for such a belief (Misrepresentation Act 1967, s. 2(1)). The remedies are to rescind the contract and/or claim tort damages, although the court has the power to award damages in lieu of rescission if it would be equitable to do so (Misrepresentation Act 1967, s. 2(2)). A wholly innocent misrepresentation is one made honestly believing that it was true and with reasonable grounds for such a belief. The only remedy usually available is to rescind the contract, although the court has the power to award damages in lieu of rescission if it would be equitable to do so (Misrepresentation Act 1967, s. 2(2)).

The right to rescind for an actionable misrepresentation can be lost if the contract has been affirmed (*Leaf* v *International Galleries* [1950] 2 KB 86), if it becomes impossible to return the parties to their pre-contract position (*Clarke* v *Dickson* (1858) El Bl & El 148), or if an innocent third party has acquired rights in the subject matter of the contract. (The loss of the right to rescind is considered at **1.9** below.)

1.5.1 DISTINGUISHING TERMS AND REPRESENTATIONS

Having stated the general contract principles with which you should already be familiar, we can now concentrate on examining the distinction between terms and representations. Statements made to a consumer before a contract is made, whether verbally or in advertisements, may amount either to terms of the contract, or to actionable misrepresentations, or to mere representations. We need to distinguish the three because there is no remedy when a mere representation proves to be untrue, and the remedies for breach of contract differ from those for an actionable misrepresentation. So before considering the remedies available, we need to distinguish terms and representations and examine the circumstances in which a representation becomes an actionable misrepresentation.

The basic premise sounds fairly straightforward — that only those statements which can be taken to amount to definite promises or undertakings will be classified as part of the contract and hence terms. Statements which do not amount to definite undertakings will only amount to representations. In making this distinction the courts try to give effect to the objective intentions of the parties to the contract. If the court thinks that the parties appeared to intend that a statement be a term then it will be a term, if the parties did not appear to intend this then the statement will only be a representation. Over the years several factors have been regarded as important in making the distinction.

1.5.1.1 The relative degrees of the parties' knowledge

Where the parties have less than equal knowledge about the subject matter of the contract, statements by the party with the more knowledge are likely to be classed as terms, statements by the party with the less knowledge are more likely to be classed as representations. As the remedies for breach of contract are more secure than those for an actionable misrepresentation, this is good news for the consumer. Almost always the business from which the consumer buys will have more knowledge about the type of goods or services which are bought. The following two cases are often used to illustrate this first principle.

Oscar Chess Ltd v *Williams* [1957] 1 WLR 370
In 1954 W acquired a second-hand Morris car on hire-purchase. The registration book showed that the car was first registered in 1948. In 1955 W traded the car in to a dealer in exchange for a new Hillman Minx. W described the car as a 1948 model. W believed this to be true and, as the car looked like a 1948 model, so did the dealer. Eight months later the dealer discovered that the Morris was in fact a 1939 model and consequently worth much less than the amount he had allowed against it.
Held: W's statement was not a term. The dealer, having much more expertise about the age and condition of cars, could not regard W as having promised that the car was a 1948 model. (An extract from the judgments of Denning and Hodson LJJ can be read in **Cases and Materials** (1.2.1).)

Dick Bentley Productions Ltd v *Harold Smith Motors Ltd* [1965] 1 WLR 623
The defendants were car dealers and the plaintiff, a private motorist, told them that he wanted to buy a quality, well-vetted British car, whose history could be obtained. S,

acting for the defendants, said he had found such a car, a Park Ward coupé Bentley. The plaintiff looked at the car and S told him that the car had only done 20,000 miles since being fitted with a new engine and gearbox. Later in the day the plaintiff brought his wife to look at the car and the statement about the mileage was repeated. The car soon proved troublesome, and the plaintiff discovered that it had done about 100,000 miles since having a new engine fitted.

Held: The statement about the mileage was a term of the contract. The plaintiff could regard the defendant as having promised that the car's engine had done only 20,000 miles. (The judgments of Lord Denning MR and Salmon LJ can be read in *Cases and Materials* (1.2.1).)

A statement of mere opinion cannot amount to a term or a representation. However, if one of the parties to the contract is in the position of having far more knowledge than the other party could possibly have, it may be the case that even a mere opinion can give rise to a term.

Esso Petroleum Co. Ltd v *Mardon* [1976] QB 801
The defendant entered into a written tenancy agreement of a petrol station from Esso. He did this because an Esso employee with over 40 years' experience of trade told him that the throughput of petrol would be about 200,000 gallons annually within three years. The defendant thought that 100,000 to 150,000 was more likely but allowed himself to be swayed by the greater experience of Esso's employee. Despite being managed well, the petrol station never achieved anything like 200,000 gallons annually. After the issue of a writ, the defendant (in March 1967) counterclaimed for damages for breach of warranty.
Held: There was no warranty that the petrol station would achieve 200,000 gallons a year, because this was only an opinion. There was however an implied term in the form of a collateral warranty that the forecast was sound and reliable and made with reasonable care and skill. This term had been broken.

An extract from the judgment of Lord Denning MR can be read in *Cases and Materials* (1.2.1).)

(Esso would now incur liability under the Misrepresentation Act 1967. However, as the misrepresentation in this case was made before the Act came into force, an effective remedy would not have been available for a non-fraudulent misrepresentation. Even before a contract was made Esso could have been liable for the tort of negligent misstatement. It is not proposed to analyse negligent misstatement in this book, as it is unlikely to be of much importance in a consumer context and will anyway have been studied in the tort programme. Where the representation induces the making of a contract, and thus becomes an actionable misrepresentation, a consumer would prefer to sue for negligent misrepresentation rather than for negligent misstatement because as regards negligent misstatement the consumer must prove negligence. As regards negligent misrepresentation the defendant must prove that he had reasonable grounds for believing that the facts represented were true (Misrepresentation Act 1967, s. 2(1)). Negligent misstatement is nowadays only likely to be useful to a consumer where there was no contract between the consumer and the maker of the statement.

1.5.1.2 The reliance shown to be placed on the statement

If one of the parties to the contract demonstrates that a particular matter is of great importance to him then an assurance about the matter in question is likely to be regarded as a term.

Bannerman v *White* (1861) 10 CB NS 844
The plaintiff was a hop-grower in Kent, the defendants were hop-merchants. The Burton Brewers told hop-merchants that they would no longer buy hops which had been treated with sulphur. The hop-merchants sent a circular to the hop-growers informing them of this. The defendants bought hops from the plaintiff, saying that if the hops had been treated with sulphur they would not buy them at any price. The plaintiff replied that the

hops had not been treated with sulphur. In fact about five acres of the three hundred acres of hops sold had been treated with sulphur. The plaintiff sued for the price of the hops but the defendants claimed to repudiate the contract as a condition had been broken. The jury found that the affirmation that no sulphur had been used was understood and intended by the parties to be a part of the contract.
Held: As a condition of the contract had been broken, the plaintiff could not sue for the price. Erle CJ, giving the judgment of the Court of Common Bench, said:

> This undertaking was a preliminary stipulation; and if it had not been given, the defendants would not have gone on with the treaty which resulted in the sale. In this sense it was the condition upon which the defendants contracted; and it would be contrary to the intention expressed by this stipulation that the contract should remain valid if sulphur had been used.

1.5.1.3 The strength of the statement

If a pre-contract statement is particularly strong, so that it can be taken to be incorporated into the offer which is subsequently made and accepted, then the statement will be a term of the contract. If however a pre-contract statement is very guarded, then it is more likely to be a mere representation.

Schawel v *Reade* [1913] 2 IR 81
The plaintiff inspected a horse belonging to the defendant, a horse dealer, and made plain that he was looking for a horse suitable for stud purposes. The defendant said to the plaintiff, 'You need not look for anything; the horse is perfectly sound. If there was anything the matter with the horse I would tell you.' A few days later a price was agreed, although the sale was not finally completed for about a month. The horse was later found to be suffering from an incurable hereditary disease of the eyes which made it quite unsuitable for stud purposes.
Held: The defendant's words amounted to an express term that the horse was sound. Lord Atkinson stated, at 84:

> I think it is perfectly plain that the jury must have understood that that [the statement about the horse's soundness] was part of the transaction, and meant to be the basis of the sale. If that was the intention of the man who made the statement, and if the person to whom it was addressed acted upon it, then that constitutes a [term].

Ecay v *Godfrey* (1974) 80 Lloyd's Rep 286
The plaintiff, the Spanish Vice-Consul at Newcastle-on-Tyne, bought a boat from the defendant for £750. Although the boat had recently been painted and looked in nice enough condition, it was in fact unsound and becoming barely seaworthy. Before selling the boat the defendant said that he believed that it was sound but he advised the plaintiff to have it surveyed. The plaintiff neglected to have the boat surveyed because he wanted the boat in a hurry.
Held: The defendant's statement that the boat was sound was not a term, but only a representation. The guarded nature of the statement meant that the defendant could not be taken to have promised that the boat was sound.

However, even very strong words will not amount to a term of the contract if it is understood by the parties that the statement is not to be a term.

Hopkins v *Tanqueray* (1854) 15 CB 130
The defendant's horse, California, was sent to Tattersall's to be sold by public auction. The day before the sale the defendant found the plaintiff examining the horse's legs. The defendant said, 'You have nothing to look for; I assure you that he is perfectly sound in every respect.' The plaintiff replied, 'If you say so, I am perfectly satisfied', and bought the horse at the auction the following day. It was well known that horses auctioned at Tattersall were sold without a warranty.
Held: The defendant's statement could not amount to a term. Jervis CJ stated, at 139:

On the day following, Mr Tattersall announces that he is about to sell California without a warranty; and the defendant becomes the purchaser. It seems to me to be perfectly clear, that, in what took place between them on the Sunday, the defendant did not mean to warrant the horse, but was merely making a representation of that which he bona fide believed to be the fact; and that the plaintiff so understood it.

1.5.1.4 The time at which the statement was made

Because the decision as to whether or not a statement is a term of the contract depends upon the intention of the parties, the shorter the delay between the making of the statement and the conclusion of the contract the more likely it is that the parties intended the statement to be a term. However, like the other tests, this is only one factor to be considered. For example, the statement in *Schawel v Reade*, which was held to be a term, was made a month before the contract was concluded, whereas the virtually identical statement in *Hopkins v Tanqueray*, which was held not to be a term, was made the day before the contract was made. In *Schawel v Reade* the strength of the statement proved to be a more important factor and in *Hopkins v Tanqueray* the fact that both parties understood that horses were auctioned without warranty proved to be a more important factor.

Finally, it should be remembered that the matters we have considered cannot in themselves amount to conclusive tests. In all of the cases subsequent to 1913 which we have considered, the following dictum of Lord Moulton in *Heilbut, Symons & Co. v Buckleton* [1913] AC 30 was considered binding:

> It may well be that [various tests used to tell a term from a representation] may be criteria of value in . . . coming to a decision whether or not a warranty was intended; but they cannot be said to furnish decisive tests, because it cannot be said as a matter of law that the presence or absence of these features is conclusive of the intention of the parties. The intention of the parties can only be deduced from the totality of the evidence, and no secondary principles of such a kind can be universally true.

So when considering whether or not a statement made to a consumer was a term or a representation it is an objective view of what the consumer and the retailer intended which will count. The relative degrees of the parties' knowledge, the importance shown to be attached to the statement, the strength of the statement and the length of time which elapsed until the contract was made, are all indications of the parties' intentions. But they are no more than that.

1.5.1.5 Written contracts

If a contract is written then the terms of the contract will be contained in what was written. The parol evidence rule, to which there are several exceptions, prevents extrinsic evidence from being admitted to add to or vary what was written. Therefore oral statements cannot be terms of the written contract and the factors which we have considered above will have no application.

However, even where the contract is written a collateral contract might help the consumer, as the following case shows.

Webster v Higgin [1948] 2 All ER 127
During the negotiations for the hire-purchase of a second-hand car the defendant told the plaintiff that if he signed the contract the defendant would guarantee that the car was in good condition. The plaintiff therefore signed the contract, which contained a clause excluding all liability regarding the condition of the car.
Held: The exclusion clause prevented the defendant from being liable on the written contract. However, the exclusion clause could not prevent liability under a separate collateral contract. Under this collateral contract the defendant's promise that the car was in good condition was exchanged for the plaintiff's signing of the contract.

THE LAW OF CONTRACT AS A MEANS OF CONSUMER PROTECTION

Today this exclusion clause would not be effective against a consumer, as we shall see in **Chapter 6**. However, the principle which *Webster* v *Higgin* demonstrates still holds good. If a consumer is promised something in return for entering into a contract, a court can enforce this promise even if the contract was written and made no mention of the promise. Earlier, we examined *Wood* v *Letric Ltd* and saw that a collateral contract may also be made by the manufacturer rather than by the seller of the product which the consumer buys. (In that case the contract was not written.)

SAQ 1/5

We have examined in a fair amount of detail the difference between terms and representations. Why does it matter to a consumer whether a pre-contract statement made to him is a term or a representation?

If the statement is a term of the contract then the consumer is always going to have a remedy for breach of contract. If the statement made to the consumer is a representation which does not qualify as an actionable misrepresentation then there will be no remedy for breach of contract or for misrepresentation (although there is the possibility of a remedy for negligent misstatement). If the statement made to the consumer is an actionable misrepresentation then the consumer will always have the right to rescind, but this right can easily be lost. If the misrepresentation is fraudulent or negligent then the consumer will also be able to sue for tort damages (which are likely, as regards untrue statements made to consumers, to amount to much the same thing as contract damages). However, if the misrepresentation is innocent, then there is no right to damages. Although the court has a discretion to award damages in lieu of rescission under s. 2(2) of the Misrepresentation Act 1967, this right is rarely exercised. In addition, the damages awarded will only cover the cost of remedying the defect or the reduced market value caused by the defect (*William Sindall plc* v *Cambridgeshire CC* [1994] 3 All ER 932). (At the end of this chapter we examine the ways in which a consumer's right to rescind for an actionable misrepresentation or to repudiate for breach of contract can be lost. The purpose of **SAQ 1/5** is to remind you not to lose sight of the reasons for making the distinction between terms and representations.)

1.5.1.6 Difficulties with pre-1967 cases

In **Chapters 3** and **4** we examine the terms implied into consumer contracts. We shall see that if goods are sold, hired etc. *by description* then various statutes imply a term that the goods must correspond with the description. We shall also see that, if the sale is to be made by description, the description must be an important term of the contract, on which the consumer relied (*Harlingdon & Leinster Enterprises Ltd* v *Christopher Hull Fine Art Ltd* [1991] 1 QB 564).

The older cases on statutory terms all concern the Sale of Goods Act 1893. (The statutory implied terms were not extended to contracts other than sales of goods until the second half of the twentieth century.) Some of the earlier cases can cause difficulty in that the description in question can hardly be said to be a term of the contract but nevertheless the courts held that the sale was made by description.

In *Beale* v *Taylor* [1967] 3 All ER 253 the defendant, a private motorist, advertised a car for sale as a white 1961 Herald convertible. The plaintiff inspected the car and noticed a 1200 badge on the back of the car. After the plaintiff had bought the car he discovered that it was made up of two cars. The rear of a 1200 Triumph Herald had been welded to the front of an older model 948 car. The Court of Appeal held that the badge was part of the description of the car and so the buyer could reject the car under s. 13 of the SGA 1893.

SAQ 1/6

Applying the tests to tell a term from a representation, would the defendant's description of the car in *Beale* v *Taylor* (either the advertisement or the 1200 badge) have been classified as a term or as a representation?

Beale v *Taylor* seems a hard case to explain. The defendant did not know that his car was made up of two cars welded together. He had no special expertise about cars and it is hard to see how either the advertisement or the 1200 badge could amount to a term of the contract. The usual explanation given for the different analysis of some of the older cases is that where specific goods were sold prior to the SGA 1979 the goods were required to be of merchantable (now satisfactory) quality only if they were sold by description. For this reason the courts strove to find that goods were sold by description in order to do justice in cases where a consumer would otherwise be left with no remedy. For example, in *Grant* v *Australian Knitting Mills Ltd* [1936] AC 85, a consumer bought a pair of woollen underpants which gave him severe dermatitis. Obviously, the underpants were not of merchantable quality. However, there would (in those days) have been no implied term as to merchantable quality unless the goods were sold by description. The Privy Council held that the sale was by description, as almost every sale to a consumer in a shop must be. Lord Wright said, at 100:

> It may also be pointed out that there is a sale by description even though the buyer is buying something displayed before him on the counter: a thing is sold by description, though it is specific, so long as it is sold not merely as the specific thing but as a thing corresponding to the description, e.g., woollen under-garments, a hot-water bottle . . .

However, this analysis cannot explain *Beale* v *Taylor*. In that case the seller did not sell the car in the course of a business and so there was no possibility of a statutory implied term that the goods were of merchantable quality.

SAQ 1/7

What would have been the outcome of *Beale* v *Taylor* if the Court of Appeal had held that the defendant's statement was not a term of the contract?

If the defendant's statement had not been a term of the contract then the plaintiff could only have had a remedy if the statement was an actionable misrepresentation. (The statement would have amounted to an actionable misrepresentation if it was an untrue statement of fact which persuaded the plaintiff to enter into the contract.) Even on the assumption that the statement was an actionable misrepresentation, the case pre-dated the Misrepresentation Act 1967 and as it would have been classified as a non-fraudulent misrepresentation the buyer would have had no right to damages.

The reason why the sale in *Harlingdon & Leinster Enterprises Ltd* v *Christopher Hull Fine Art Ltd* was not a sale *by* description was that the buyer did not rely on the description and the seller knew this. The exact status of the old cases is hard to ascertain, but it seems likely that in consumer cases the consumer's reliance on a description will be implied fairly readily.

2.5.1.7 Statements of opinion

A statement which, taken objectively, was merely an opinion and did not assert any fact cannot amount to an actionable misrepresentation or a term of the contract.

Bisset v *Wilkinson* [1927] AC 177
The plaintiff bought a farm because the defendant told him that the farm would support 2,000 sheep. The plaintiff knew that the farm had never before been used for sheep farming. After buying the farm the plaintiff discovered that, no matter how well managed, it could not support anything like 2,000 sheep. He sued the defendant for misrepresentation.
Held: The statement was just an opinion and could not therefore amount to an actionable misrepresentation.

However, some statements of opinion impliedly assert statements of fact, and can therefore amount to an actionable misrepresentation, as the following case shows.

Smith v *Land and House Property Corporation* (1884) 28 ChD 7
The plaintiffs offered their hotel for sale, stating that it was let to 'F. (a most desirable tenant), at a rental of £400 for an unexpired term of 27 years'. Before the sale went through F became bankrupt. The defendants discovered that for some time F had been badly in arrears with his rent. The defendants refused to go ahead with the purchase of the hotel, claiming that the statement that F was a most desirable tenant amounted to an actionable misrepresentation.
Held: The statement was an actionable misrepresentation. It sounded like a mere statement of opinion, but it implied facts (such as the fact that the tenant paid the rent), which justified the opinion. Bowen LJ stated, at 7:

> It is often fallaciously assumed that a statement of opinion cannot involve the statement of fact . . . if the facts are not equally known to both sides, then a statement of opinion by the one who knows the facts best involves very often a statement of a material fact, for he impliedly states that he knows facts which justify his opinion.

The decision in this case was affirmed and applied in *Esso Petroleum Co. Ltd* v *Mardon*. In that case, as we saw earlier in this chapter, a term was implied that Esso's representative had made his opinion about the likely throughput of petrol using reasonable care and skill. We also saw that Esso were liable for the tort of negligent misstatement and that if the case were to arise today Esso would have been liable for making a negligent misrepresentation. So statements of opinion which assert facts can amount to either terms or to actionable misrepresentations.

1.5.1.8 Statements which are both terms and actionable misrepresentations

Section 1 of the Misrepresentation Act 1967 states:

Where a person has entered into a contract after a misrepresentation has been made to him, and—
  (a) the misrepresentation has become a term of the contract; or
  (b) the contract has been performed;
or both, then, if otherwise he would be entitled to rescind the contract without alleging fraud, he shall be so entitled, subject to the provisions of this Act, notwithstanding the matters mentioned in paragraphs (a) and (b) of this section.

We will return to the effect of this section later in this chapter. At the moment we should merely notice that the Act clearly contemplates that what started as a misrepresentation may also become a term of the contract.

1.6 Exclusion Clauses

The effect of exclusion clauses is the subject matter of **Chapter 7**.

1.7 Discharge of Contractual Liability (General Principles)

The liabilities imposed under a contract can be discharged in four ways: by performance, by agreement, by frustration or by breach.

A contract is discharged by performance when both parties perform the contract exactly as agreed (*Cutter v Powell* (1795) Term Rep 320.) A contract can be discharged without exact performance if the contract is severable (*Ritchie v Atkinson* (1808) 10 East 295), or if the contract is substantially performed (*Dakin & Co. Ltd v Lee* [1916] 1 KB 566), or if the other party accepts partial performance (*Sumpter v Hedges* [1898] 1 QB 673).

Contractual liabilities can be discharged by agreement between the parties to the contract. This is known as accord and satisfaction (agreement and consideration). The agreement to discharge the liabilities must itself be a contract (*Elton Cop Dyeing Co. v Broadbent and Son Ltd* (1919) 89 LJKB 186).

A contract is discharged by frustration if, after its creation, it becomes either impossible to perform (*Taylor v Caldwell* (1863) 3 B & S 826), or illegal to perform (*Avery v Bowden* (1855) 5 E & B 714), or if performance would be radically different from what the parties contemplated when they made the contract (*Krell v Henry* [1903] 2 KB 740). If the contract was for the sale of specific goods which perished before the risk passed to the buyer then the contract is avoided (SGA 1979, s. 7). Other frustrated contracts will be governed by the Law Reform (Frustrated Contracts) Act 1943. Under the 1943 Act all money still owed under the contract ceases to be due, money already paid is recoverable, a party who has received a valuable benefit under the contract may have to pay for it on a quantum meruit and the court has a discretion to award expenses up to the amount paid or payable under the contract at the time of the frustrating event.

The injured party will have the right to treat the contract as repudiated in response to breach of a condition or breach of an innominate term which substantially deprived him of the whole benefit of the contract (*Cehave NV v Bremer Handelsgesellschaft mbH, The Hansa Nord* [1975] 3 All ER 739). An anticipatory breach occurs when a party indicates, before performance of the contract is due, that he does not intend to perform the contract. The injured party can terminate the contract immediately and sue for damages (*Hochster v De La Tour* (1853) 2 E & B 678), or alternatively wait until the breach becomes actual and then seek a remedy for breach of contract. However, if the contract becomes frustrated before the injured party elects to sue then the right to sue for breach of contract will be lost (*Avery v Bowden* (1855) 5 E & B 714).

1.8 Remedies for Breach of Contract and Misrepresentation (General Principles)

The remedies available for breach of contract will have been studied in the contract programme. It is not therefore proposed to consider the remedies in detail here, but only to reiterate the basic principles. The amount of damages recoverable for an actionable misrepresentation is considered because this is an area of law which has been the subject of several important recent cases. A consumer's right to get his money back from a retailer can be of considerable importance. We therefore examine in some detail how a consumer with the right to rescind a contract as a consequence of an actionable misrepresentation or to treat a contract as repudiated for breach of contract can lose these rights.

All three types of misrepresentation give rise to rescission of the contract. A fraudulent misrepresentation gives the right to tort damages (*Smith New Court Securities Ltd* v *Scrimgeour Vickers (Asset Management) Ltd* [1996] 4 All ER 769) and so does a negligent misrepresentation (Misrepresentation Act 1967, s. 2(1)). It is possible for the court to award damages in lieu of rescission in cases of negligent or wholly innocent misrepresentation under the Misrepresentation Act 1967, s. 2(2). When this right is exercised the damages are assessed on a breach of contract basis (*William Sindall plc* v *Cambridgeshire CC* [1994] 3 All ER 932). The remedies for actionable misrepresentation are considered in more detail at **1.10** below.

A contract can be treated as repudiated if a condition of the contract is broken but not if a warranty is broken. (However, if the warranty had earlier been an actionable misrepresentation then the right to rescind on account of this survives, as the Misrepresentation Act 1967, s. 1, explains. There will then be a choice of remedies available.) Some terms are classified as innominate terms rather than as conditions or warranties. If this is the case then a party can treat the contract as repudiated if breach of the term deprived him of substantially the whole benefit of the contract, but not otherwise (*Hong Kong Fir Shipping Co. Ltd* v *Kawasaki Kisen Kaisha Ltd* [1962] 1 All ER 474). To treat the contract as repudiated for breach is not the same as to rescind for misrepresentation. In non-severable contracts of sale of goods the right to treat the contract as repudiated will be lost if the buyer accepts the goods (Sale of Goods Act 1979, s. 11(4)). In contracts other than sales of goods the right to treat the contract as repudiated is lost if the contract is affirmed. (The circumstances in which acceptance or affirmation are deemed to have taken place are examined later in this chapter.)

Damages for breach of contract are designed to put the injured party into the position he would have been in if the contract had been performed as agreed (*W.L. Thompson* v *Robinson (Gunmakers) Ltd* [1955] Ch 177). (Tort damages, which are available for fraudulent or negligent misrepresentation, are designed to put the injured party into the position he would have been in if the tort had never been committed.) To be recoverable as contract damages a loss must be within one of the two rules in *Hadley* v *Baxendale* (1854) 9 Exch 341. Rule 1 allows a loss to be recovered if it arose naturally from the breach in the usual course of things. Rule 2 allows other losses to be recovered if it can reasonably be supposed that the parties would have contemplated the losses as a probable result of the breach when the contract was made. A loss which could have been mitigated by taking reasonable steps cannot be recovered (*Brace* v *Calder* [1895] 2 QB 253). If the measure of damages is spelled out in the contract this may be liquidated damages or a penalty. Liquidated damages are a genuine pre-estimate of the loss and will be applied by the courts no matter what the actual loss (*Cellulose Acetate Silk Ltd* v *Widnes Foundry (1925) Ltd* [1933] AC 20). Penalties are not a genuine pre-estimate of the loss. They are ignored by the courts who calculate damages in the usual way as if the penalty clause had never existed (*Dunlop Pneumatic Tyre Co.* v *New Garage and Motor Co. Ltd* [1915] AC 79).

A party who sues for the contract price brings an action for an agreed sum, and has no duty to mitigate loss (*White and Carter (Councils) Ltd* v *McGregor* [1962] AC 413).

Specific performance is a discretionary equitable remedy whereby a party is ordered to actually perform the obligations which he contracted to perform. Specific performance is not ordered where damages are an adequate remedy and is therefore rarely ordered to enforce a sale of goods (*Sky Petroleum Ltd* v *VIP Petroleum Ltd* [1974] 1 WLR 576). Specific performance will not be awarded for a party if it could not be awarded against him, nor in favour of a party who has behaved inequitably (*Falcke* v *Gray* (1859) 4 Drew 651). Nor, as equity does nothing in vain, will specific performance be ordered as regards contracts which would require constant supervision.

An injunction can be obtained to prevent a party from acting in breach of contract. However, this is relatively rare and will not be ordered if to do so would in effect amount to specific performance of a contract in circumstances in which specific performance would not be ordered (*Warner Bros Pictures Ltd* v *Nelson* [1937] 1 KB 209).

1.9 Losing the Right to Rescind or to Treat the Contract as Repudiated

Earlier in this chapter we outlined the circumstances in which a person will be able to treat a contract as repudiated for breach of a term or rescind a contract on account of an actionable misrepresentation having been made. Here we examine how these rights can be lost, a matter which can be of considerable importance to consumers. First, let us briefly remind ourselves of the circumstances in which the rights to rescind or to treat the contract as repudiated arise.

SAQ 1/8

A consumer buys a car from a garage. Has the consumer a right to treat the contract as repudiated or to rescind if:

(a) The car is not of satisfactory quality, thereby breaching one of the statutory implied terms in the Sale of Goods Act 1979?

(b) The radio is not as the salesperson described it, and

   (i) The description was an actionable misrepresentation?

   (ii) The description was a condition of the contract?

   (iii) The description was an innominate term?

   (iv) The description was only an opinion, which did not amount to a term or an actionable misrepresentation?

(a) The statutory implied terms in the Sale of Goods Act 1979 are conditions when the purchaser is a consumer. If any of the terms are broken the consumer will

THE LAW OF CONTRACT AS A MEANS OF CONSUMER PROTECTION

therefore have the right to treat the contract as repudiated. (The statutory terms and their status are examined in **Chapters 2–4**.)

(b)(i) If the description was an actionable misrepresentation then the consumer will have the right to rescind the contract. (However, it is possible if the misrepresentation was negligent or innocent that the court would award damages in lieu of rescission under the Misrepresentation Act 1967, s. 2(2).)

(ii) If the description was a condition of the contract then the consumer would have the right to treat the contract as repudiated.

(iii) If the description was classified as an innominate term then the consumer would have the right to treat the contract as repudiated if breach of the term deprived him or her of substantially the whole benefit of the contract.

(iv) If the description was neither a term nor an actionable misrepresentation then the consumer will have no redress in respect of it.

Now that we have reminded ourselves of the circumstances in which the rights to rescind and to treat the contract as repudiated arise, we can examine the ways in which the two remedies can be lost.

1.9.1 LOSING THE RIGHT TO TREAT THE CONTRACT AS REPUDIATED

In contracts of sale of goods the right to treat the contract as repudiated for breach of a condition, or breach of an innominate term which did deprive the buyer of substantially the whole benefit, is lost if the goods are 'accepted' within the meaning of the Sale of Goods Act 1979. As regards contracts which cannot be classified as sales of goods, the right to treat the contract as repudiated is lost if the contract is affirmed.

1.9.1.1 Acceptance in a contract of sale of goods

Section 11(4) of the Sale of Goods Act 1979 states:

> [Subject to section 35A below] Where a contract of sale is not severable and the buyer has accepted the goods or part of them, the breach of a condition to be fulfilled by the seller can only be treated as a breach of warranty, and not as a ground for rejecting the goods and treating the contract as repudiated, unless there is an express or implied term of the contract to that effect.

SAQ 1/9

Jane buys a new television from a shop. The television breaches the condition as to satisfactory quality required by s. 14(2) of the Sale of Goods Act 1979. Can Jane reject before she has accepted the goods?

What remedies, if any, will be available after Jane has accepted the goods?

> Before acceptance Jane will be able to reject the goods and treat the contract as repudiated, and/or claim damages. After acceptance Jane may be able to claim damages, but will not be able to reject the goods and repudiate the contract.

Methods of accepting
The Sale and Supply of Goods Act 1994 amended the Sale of Goods Act 1979 rules on acceptance. These rules used to be contained in ss. 34 and 35 of the Sale of Goods Act 1979. The new law is complex, and contained in s. 35 of the Sale of Goods Act 1979. To understand the amended s. 35 we need to examine its wording carefully. Section 35 states:

(1) The buyer is deemed to have accepted the goods, subject to subsection (2) below—
   (a) when he intimates to the seller that he has accepted them, or
   (b) when the goods have been delivered to him and he does any act in relation to them which is inconsistent with the ownership of the seller.
(2) Where goods are delivered to the buyer, and he has not previously examined them, he is not deemed to have accepted them under subsection (1) above until he has had a reasonable opportunity of examining them for the purpose—
   (a) of ascertaining whether they are in conformity with the contract, and
   (b) in the case of a contract for sale by sample, of comparing the bulk with the sample.
(3) Where the buyer deals as a consumer . . . the buyer cannot lose his right to rely on subsection (2) above by agreement, waiver or otherwise.
(4) The buyer is also deemed to have accepted the goods when after the lapse of a reasonable time he retains the goods without intimating to the seller that he has rejected them.
(5) The questions that are material in determining for the purposes of subsection (4) above whether a reasonable time has elapsed include whether the buyer has had a reasonable opportunity of examining the goods for the purpose mentioned in subsection (2) above.
(6) The buyer is not by virtue of this section deemed to have accepted the goods merely because—
   (a) he asks for, or agrees to, their repair by or under an arrangement with the seller, or
   (b) the goods are delivered to another under a sub-sale or other disposition.

ACTIVITY 1/1

John buys a new washing machine which is delivered to his house. Section 35 of the 1979 Act mentions three ways in which a seller might accept the goods. Read s. 35 and then write down the three ways in which John could be deemed to have accepted the washing machine.

(a)

(b)

(c)

You should have written that John will be deemed to have accepted the washing machine either (a) when he intimates to the seller that he has accepted it, or (b) when he does an

THE LAW OF CONTRACT AS A MEANS OF CONSUMER PROTECTION

act which is inconsistent with the seller's ownership, or (c) when he keeps the washing machine for more than a reasonable time without rejecting it.

ACTIVITY 1/2

Elaine orders a new washing machine, which is delivered to her house. The same day, before Elaine has had a chance to unpack the washing machine, her job unexpectedly requires her to go to the USA for six months. When Elaine returns home she finds that the washing machine does not work properly. Read s. 35 carefully and decide whether Elaine accepted the machine?

It would seem quite likely that Elaine has accepted the machine. There are three ways in which acceptance can be made. The two of these which are contained in s. 35(1) can be discounted: Elaine has not intimated acceptance, and does not appear to have done any act which is inconsistent with the seller's ownership. However, s. 35(4) might mean that Elaine has accepted the washing machine because she has retained it for more than a reasonable time. Elaine might argue that she has not had a reasonable time to examine the goods, to ascertain whether they were in conformity with the contract. The court must try to balance the interest of both the buyer and the seller and would, I think, taking an objective view, conclude that Elaine had had a reasonable opportunity of examining the goods.

We now need to examine the three methods of acceptance in turn.

Intimation of acceptance

A buyer intimates acceptance by letting the seller know that the goods have been accepted, or by giving the impression that they have. Before the changes made by the Sale and Supply of Goods Act 1994, it was not clear whether or not a buyer could intimate acceptance before having had a chance to examine the goods. This matter is now clarified. Section 35(2) makes it plain that a buyer will not be deemed to have accepted the goods by intimating acceptance until the buyer has had a reasonable opportunity of examining the goods to see that they are in conformity with the contract. Furthermore, s. 35(3) tells us that consumer buyers cannot lose the protection given by s. 35(2).

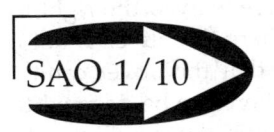

SAQ 1/10

Mary orders a new bed from a shop. The bed is delivered to Mary's house where she signs a delivery note. This note says that the bed has been delivered and that it is in good condition. Has Mary accepted the bed?

Mary will not be deemed to have accepted the bed until she has had a reasonable opportunity to examine it (s. 35(2)). As Mary is a consumer she cannot lose this right to rely on s. 35(2) by agreement, waiver or otherwise (s. 35(3)).

Doing an act which is inconsistent with the seller's continuing ownership

ACTIVITY 1/3

This section of the text is complex and describes the effect of the amended s. 35. The subsection numbers have been left blank. Refer back to s. 35, and fill in the relevant subsection numbers as you read the text. You will find this section, with the relevant subsections inserted, reproduced in *Cases and Materials* **(1.3.1.1).**

Section 35( )( ) tells us that a buyer who does an act which is inconsistent with the seller's continuing ownership of goods which have been delivered will be deemed to have accepted the goods, and will therefore no longer be able to reject the goods. The buyer must, however, have had a reasonable opportunity to examine the goods to see that they are in conformity with the contract (s.35( )).

Section 35( ) tells us that the buyer is not deemed to have accepted the goods merely on account of having done two types of act which are inconsistent with the seller's ownership; asking for them to be repaired or selling them on to another buyer. Unfortunately the 1979 Act does not spell out what acts of the buyer will be deemed to be inconsistent with the seller's continuing ownership. Atiyah, *The Sale of Goods*, Pitman Publishing, 9th ed. at p. 466, states that:

> The truth is that the phrase 'an act inconsistent with the ownership of the seller' is one with no fixed meaning. The court is, in effect, empowered to decide whether it thinks that the buyer ought to be entitled to reject the goods according to the circumstances of the case.

The main reason for wanting to know what constitutes acceptance is that once acceptance has been made the buyer will no longer be able to reject the goods, even if the seller has breached a condition. Here we need to distinguish two situations. Those where the buyer knows of the seller's breach when doing the act inconsistent with the seller's ownership, and those where the buyer does not.

If the buyer knows of the seller's breach, then any act such as reselling the goods, or offering them for sale, or putting them into an auction, will be enough to constitute acceptance under s. 35(1)(b). This might seem to conflict with the proviso in s. 35( ) that the buyer is not deemed to have accepted until he has been given a reasonable opportunity to examine the goods. But if the buyer knew of the right to reject, there would be no point in examining the goods. By doing the act inconsistent with the seller's ownership, while aware of the right to reject, the buyer would have waived the right to examine the goods. This then will be the position in contracts where the buyer is not a consumer. But where the buyer is a consumer s. 35( ) provides that the buyer cannot waive the right to rely on s. 35(2). Consumer buyers will never therefore be deemed to have accepted by doing an act inconsistent with the seller's continuing ownership, until they have had a reasonable opportunity to examine the goods (s. 35( )).

If the buyer did not know of the right to reject the goods, the position will again depend upon whether the buyer was a consumer or not.

A non-consumer buyer who has had a reasonable opportunity to examine the goods, or who has chosen to take the goods as they are without an examination, will accept by doing almost any act which is inconsistent with the seller's ownership. However, a non-consumer buyer who has neither had, nor waived, a reasonable opportunity to examine will not be deemed to have accepted by doing an inconsistent act.

THE LAW OF CONTRACT AS A MEANS OF CONSUMER PROTECTION

The position of a consumer buyer is different. Section 35( ) still protects a consumer buyer, who cannot accept by doing an act inconsistent with the seller's continuing ownership before having had a reasonable opportunity to examine the goods.

Even if it is the buyer's fault that the goods cannot be surrendered in the correct condition, s. 35( ) will protect a buyer to whom goods have been delivered if the buyer had not yet examined the goods or had a reasonable opportunity to do so.

Retaining the goods for more than a reasonable time
Section 35(4) states that a buyer who keeps the goods for more than a reasonable time, without intimating to the seller that they have been rejected, will be deemed to have accepted the goods. It is not necessary that the buyer should have had a reasonable opportunity to examine the goods to see that they are in conformity with the contract. However, whether or not the buyer has had such an opportunity is now expressly mentioned by s. 35(5) as a material question in deciding whether the buyer has retained the goods for a sufficiently long time.

The following consumer case was decided before the provision now contained in s. 35(5) found its way into the Act.

Bernstein v *Pamson Motors Ltd* [1987] 2 All ER 220
On 7 December B bought a car for £8,000. B was then ill for a short time and could not drive the car until after Christmas. On 3 January the car seized up because a lump of sealant in the lubrication system caused the camshaft to become starved of oil. The car had then done 140 miles. The next day B wrote to S, rejecting the car as not being of merchantable quality. S arranged for the car to be repaired under the manufacturer's warranty. When the car was repaired, and as good as new, B refused to take it back. S sued for the price, claiming that B had accepted the goods.
Held: The car was not of merchantable quality. B had had the car for three weeks during which time he was not ill. This was more than a reasonable time to try out and examine the goods, even if not a reasonable time to discover hidden defects. B had therefore accepted the goods.

SAQ 1/11

Clearly the car would not now be of satisfactory quality. Would the case be decided differently in the light of the amended s. 35?

B would initially have had a right to reject the car, but might have lost this right by retaining the car for more than a reasonable time. However, B would probably not have had the car for long enough to examine it for the purpose of ascertaining whether it conformed with the contract description. If this was the case, then s. 35(5) would include this as a material factor to be taken into account in deciding whether a reasonable time had elapsed. In the light of this, it seems likely that B would not have accepted the car. (Before the 1994 amendments the test was whether or not the seller had retained the goods for more than a reasonable time. Section 59, unaltered by the amendments, states that what is a reasonable time is a matter of fact. Now the 1979 Act requires that the buyer must have had a reasonable opportunity to examine the goods. This would seem to mean that factors such as Mr Bernstein's illness have become relevant. The courts must consider the interests of both parties. If goods were seasonal, such as Christmas trees, the right to reject would be lost more easily than it would in the case of goods such as cars.)

If a term of the contract fixes the time within which the goods must be rejected then this term will apply. However, if such a term amounted to an exclusion or restriction of the right implied by ss. 13–15 of the 1979 Act, the Unfair Contracts Terms Act 1977, s. 6 would render the term ineffective against a consumer and only effective against a non-consumer if the term satisfied the test of reasonableness.

ACTIVITY 1/4

Read paras 5.6–5.18 of the Law Commission Report 160, 'Sale and Supply of Goods' (1987) in *Cases and Materials* (1.3.1.1).

Write your answers to the questions which follow:

(a) Why did the Law Commission reject the idea of a long-term right to reject goods?

(b) Why were contracts of hire considered to be different?

(c) Why did the Law Commission reject the idea of a stated fixed period during which the buyer would have the right to reject?

(d) Why did the Law Commission reject the idea of different fixed periods for different types of goods?

1.9.1.2 Acceptance of part of the goods

A new section, s. 35A, was added to the Sale of Goods Act 1979 by the Sale and Supply of Goods Act 1994. The new section deals with the problem of partial acceptance of goods.

First, we need to remember s. 11(4), which stated:

> [Subject to section 35A below] Where a contract of sale is not severable and the buyer has accepted the goods or part of them, the breach of a condition to be fulfilled by the seller can only be treated as a breach of warranty, and not as a ground for rejecting the goods and treating the contract as repudiated, unless there is an express or implied term of the contract to that effect.

This section was examined in **1.9.1.1** above. If you have forgotten this it might be a good idea to have another quick look at it.

Next we need to consider the new s. 35A which states:

> (1) If the buyer—
>   (a) has the right to reject the goods by reason of a breach on the part of the seller that affects some or all of them, but

THE LAW OF CONTRACT AS A MEANS OF CONSUMER PROTECTION

(b) accepts some of the goods, including, where there are any goods unaffected by the breach, all such goods,

he does not by accepting them lose his right to reject the rest.

(2) In the case of a buyer having the right to reject an instalment of goods, subsection (1) above applies as if references to the goods were references to the goods comprised in the instalment.

(3) For the purposes of subsection (1) above, goods are affected by a breach if by reason of the breach they are not in conformity with the contract.

(4) This section applies unless a contrary intention appears in, or is to be implied from, the contract.

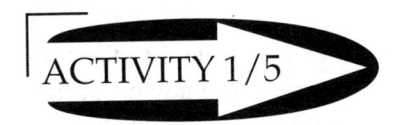

ACTIVITY 1/5

(a) Paraphrase s. 35(1) into one reasonably short sentence.

(b) Do ss. 11(4) and 35A apply to all contracts, whether severable or entire? (For the meaning of severable and entire contracts you might need to refer back to the contract programme. Put simply, an entire contract is one in which a party promises to perform one obligation. A severable contract is one in which a party's obligations under a contract can be regarded as severable into different parts.)

(a) You might have written something like: 'A buyer who has the right to reject a package of goods will not, by accepting some of the goods, lose the right to reject the rest.'

(b) Section 11(4) only applies to entire contracts. It does not apply to severable contracts. Section 35A applies to all contracts, severable and entire.

Let us assume that John, who is building himself a garage, buys 30 bags of cement from a DIY retailer. Ten of the bags are not of satisfactory quality. John has a right to reject all of the goods, but s. 35A gives him the following options:

(a) Accept the 20 bags which are of satisfactory quality and reject the 10 which are not.

(b) Accept the 20 bags which do conform to the contract and some of the bags which do not, rejecting others which do not.

What John cannot do is accept some of the 20 bags which are of satisfactory quality and reject other of these bags which are of satisfactory quality. If none of the goods were of satisfactory quality, John could still reject some of the bags, even though he might have accepted others.

Subsection (4) makes it plain that s. 35A is subject to a contrary intention having been shown by the parties.

SAQ 1/12

What does s. 35A(3) mean?

Subsection (3) means that s. 35A only applies where the buyer is entitled to reject the goods because they do not conform with the contract. It would not apply, for example, where the right to reject was due to late delivery.

In *Cases and Materials* (1.3.1.2), you should read paragraphs 6.6–6.11 of the Law Commission Report 160 'Sale and Supply of Goods' (1987), in which the law on partial rejection is explained. (The Law Commission's proposals were added to the Sale of Goods Act 1979, as s. 35A, by the Sale and Supply of Goods Act 1994.)

1.9.1.3 Acceptance of goods forming one commercial unit

Section 35(7) of the 1979 Act, another amendment brought in by the 1994 Act, reads as follows:

> Where the contract is for the sale of goods making one or more commercial units, a buyer accepting any goods included in a unit is deemed to have accepted all the goods making the unit; and in this subsection commercial unit means a unit division of which would materially impair the value of the goods or the character of the unit.

ACTIVITY 1/6

Write down three examples of goods which make a commercial unit.

Countless examples might be given. The Law Commission, at whose suggestion the subsection was enacted, gave the examples of a pair of shoes, a set of encyclopaedias, or a motor car.

SAQ 1/13

A buyer of a set of encyclopaedias accepts Volume 1. Volume 2 is not of satisfactory quality. Can the buyer reject any of the goods?

Section 35(7) seems to say that the buyer could not. The right of partial rejection given by s. 35A does not apply where, as is the case here, the goods form one commercial unit. (The Law Commission Report 160 used a similar example, and recommended that the buyer should be deemed to have accepted the whole set of encyclopaedias. See paragraphs 6.12–6.13 of the Law Commission Report 160 in *Cases and Materials* (1.3.1.3).)

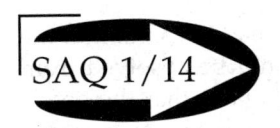

THE LAW OF CONTRACT AS A MEANS OF CONSUMER PROTECTION

SAQ 1/14

Frank buys a set of encyclopaedias and accepts the first 10 volumes. Volume 11 is entirely blank. The remaining 25 volumes are in good order.

(a) What is the simplest solution to this problem?

(b) Is s. 35(7) likely to achieve this solution?

(a) The simplest solution would seem to be that the seller should provide another Volume 11.

(b) Section 35(7) is likely to achieve this solution. Frank would not be able to hand back the volumes accepted, but would have a right to damages. However, Frank would have to mitigate his loss, and this is likely to mean that he would have to accept a Volume 11 which was of satisfactory quality.

At whose risk are the goods before rejection?
A buyer who wishes to reject goods for breach of a condition will have to make the goods available to the seller (the buyer has no duty physically to return the goods: 1979 Act, s. 36). What is the position if the goods cannot be returned because they have become damaged? If the goods have become damaged as a consequence of breach of the condition which gives the right to reject, then it seems clear that the risk remains with the seller. For example, a consumer buys a hair dryer, the motor of which is not of satisfactory quality. As a consequence of this defect the hair dryer catches fire when first used. Obviously the consumer can treat the contract as repudiated, and reject the hair dryer, even though the hair dryer is now damaged.

If the damage to the goods is not caused as a consequence of the breach of condition then there is very little authority on what the position is. In *Head* v *Tattersall* (1871) LR 7 Ex 7, a horse was sold with a description that it had hunted with the Bicester hounds. A term of the contract stated that if the horse did not match the description by which it was sold it had to be returned to the seller by 5 pm Wednesday or the buyer would have to keep it with all its faults. While in the buyer's custody the horse took fright and injured itself. The buyer returned it to the seller before 5 pm Wednesday. The Court of Exchequer held that the buyer was entitled to reject the horse even though it was now damaged.

Head v *Tattersall* was an unusual case because the right to reject was expressly contemplated and had to be exercised before a certain time. As regards the right to reject goods for breach of condition generally, three views seem possible. First, that the property in the goods (ownership of them) remains with the seller because the passing of the property was conditional upon the seller fulfilling all of his contractual obligations. Second, that the property in the goods passes to the buyer defeasibly, although the risk does not pass, and the property will pass back again if the buyer properly rejects the goods. Third, that the property in the goods passes defeasibly to the buyer, and the risk also passes, and that the property will pass back again if the buyer rejects the goods. If this third view is correct then a buyer will not be able to reject goods which have become accidentally damaged before rejection is effected. If the first or second view is correct then the buyer will be able to reject notwithstanding the accidental damage. (In *Cases and Materials* (1.3.1.3) see the extract from '"Risk" in the Law of Sale' by LS Sealy [1972] CLJ 225. It can be seen that the author regards the first view as 'basically incompatible with any sale of specific goods'.) If specific goods 'perish' after the contract has been made but before the risk has passed to the buyer then the contract would be frustrated. In effect this would amount to rejection by the buyer. The seller would be excused for not performing the contract. The buyer could recover the price if it had been paid on the basis that there had been a total failure of consideration and would be absolved from paying the price if he had not already done so. If it is the buyer's fault that the goods are damaged before the risk has passed to him then the buyer will be liable for breaking the duty of a bailee (1979 Act, s. 20(3)). This will mean that the buyer will have to compensate the seller for the diminution in the value of the goods.

1.9.1.4 Affirmation of contracts other than sales of goods

The Sale of Goods Act 1979 rules on acceptance of the goods have no statutory equivalent in either the Supply of Goods (Implied Terms) Act 1973 or the Supply of Goods and Services Act 1982. The right to treat the contract as repudiated in contracts of hire, hire-purchase and for the transfer of property in goods will be lost once the contract has been affirmed.

In sales of goods it is at the time of delivery that the goods must be of satisfactory quality and comply with the other terms of the contract. As we have seen, this causes considerable difficulties for a consumer where the defect does not become apparent until some later time. In contracts of hire-purchase the relevant time is the time at which the defects become apparent.

Laurelgates Ltd v *Lombard North Central Ltd* (1983) 133 NLJ 720
In October 1979 L took a Daimler on hire-purchase from N Ltd. The hire-purchase price was £17,727, payable over three years. By January several defects had been rectified. By February the brakes began to judder. By March there were 12 more defects and the juddering came back. In April an oil leak appeared, by May the oil leak and the judder were still giving problems although the car had been worked on four times. On 2 June L cancelled his standing order payments. On 11 June L's solicitor wrote rejecting the vehicle and claiming all the money L had paid under the contract. By 19 August there were defects with oil leaks, juddering and the exhaust falling off. L's solicitor again wrote rejecting the car, which had spent four weeks with the manufacturer. In September the heating and electrical systems failed. L claimed damages for breach of 1973 Act, s. 10(2). Held: L was entitled to the damages. The car was not of merchantable (now satisfactory) quality and L had rejected the car promptly enough. He had not affirmed the contract.

Yoeman Credit Ltd v *Apps* [1962] 2 QB 508
The plaintiff took a second-hand car on hire-purchase on 21 April 1959. An initial payment of £125 was paid and 30 monthly instalments of £14 19s. 1d were to be paid. When the car was delivered it was unroadworthy and the defects would have cost between £70 and £120 to rectify. The defendant complained about the defects to the hire-purchase company, but nevertheless paid the May, June and July monthly instalments. He failed to pay the August and September payments and in October the hire-purchase company repossessed the car. The Court of Appeal held that the defendant could not have treated the contract as repudiated while he kept up the payments and kept possession of the car. However, in September the hire-purchase company were still in breach of their obligations and so the defendant was then entitled to treat the contract as repudiated.
Held: There was no total failure of consideration by the finance company because the plaintiff had not treated the agreement as repudiated, and he had therefore had possession and some use of the car. However, the finance company was still in breach of its obligations in September 1959 and so the defendant was then entitled to treat the contract as repudiated. The defendant was awarded damages of £100 but had to pay the August instalment as he had not treated the contract as repudiated until after that payment became due.

In *Yoeman* the defendant was somewhat out of pocket. He had paid an initial deposit of £125 and four instalments of about £15 and only been awarded £100 damages. He had therefore paid a net £85 for the very limited use of the car.

THE LAW OF CONTRACT AS A MEANS OF CONSUMER PROTECTION

In the following case the consumer did rather better.

Farnworth Finance Facilities v *Attryde* [1970] 1 WLR 1053
In July 1964 the defendant took a specialist motorbike on hire-purchase from a finance company. The motorbike proved defective from the start. As each defect arose the defendant returned the bike to the finance company to be remedied. After four months the plaintiff had had only seven weeks' use of the motorbike and done only 4,000 miles. Then the rear chain broke shattering the crank case. The defendant therefore told the finance company that he was ceasing all payments and that they should come and repossess the vehicle. The company did this and, after re-selling the motorbike, sued the defendant for £149, the balance of the hire-purchase price. The defendant counterclaimed for the £195 he had already paid.
Held: The defendant was awarded the full £195, without any deduction for the use of the motorbike which he had had. He had not affirmed the contract by using the bike for the 4,000 miles and paying the four instalments, but had shown by his conduct that he would only affirm the contract if the defects were rectified. (See the extract from the judgment of Lord Denning MR in *Cases and Materials* (**1.3.1.4**).)

1.9.2 LOSING THE RIGHT TO RESCIND FOR MISREPRESENTATION

First it should be noticed that there is a right to rescind for fraudulent misrepresentation, but no such right as regards non-fraudulent misrepresentation. In cases of negligent or innocent misrepresentation s. 2(2) of the Misrepresentation Act 1967 gives the court the power to award damages in lieu of rescission where it would be equitable to do so, taking account of the nature of the misrepresentation, the loss which would be caused if the contract were to be upheld and the loss that rescission would cause to the other party. However, it must be said that s. 2(2) is very rarely used.

The right to rescind a contract for misrepresentation can be lost in three ways: if the contract is affirmed, if it is impossible to return the parties to their pre-contractual position, or if a third party has acquired rights under the contract. The first two of these methods commonly affect a consumer's right to rescind a contract.

1.9.2.1 Affirmation and the right to rescind for misrepresentation

The following case shows how easily the right to rescind for misrepresentation can be lost in a commercial contract.

Long v *Lloyd* [1958] 1 WLR 753
The plaintiff, a haulage contractor in Kent, bought a lorry for £750 because of non-fraudulent misrepresentations that it was in 'first-class condition', that it did 11 miles to the gallon, and could be driven at 40 miles an hour. Before buying, the plaintiff went for a trial drive with the defendant. Two days after the sale the plaintiff used the lorry on a short business journey and the dynamo ceased to work. He also found that an oil seal was leaking, that one of the wheels was cracked and the lorry was only doing five miles to the gallon. The plaintiff complained to the defendant about these defects and the defendant agreed to pay half the cost of putting the dynamo right. The next day, with the dynamo fixed, the plaintiff's brother drove the lorry to Middlesbrough. The lorry broke down on the journey. The plaintiff wrote to the defendant complaining that the oil seal leaked, that the lorry was only doing nine miles to the gallon, and that its top speed when loaded was 25 miles an hour.
Held: The short business journey did not amount to affirmation as it was a reasonable trial of the lorry. However, the agreement to accept half the cost of fixing the dynamo and the act of sending the lorry on the journey to Middlesbrough did amount to affirmation. The plaintiff had therefore lost the right to rescind.

SAQ 1/15

If the plaintiff in *Long* v *Lloyd* had been suing for breach of condition, would the right to treat the contract as repudiated have been lost?

It seems most unlikely that the right to treat the contract as repudiated would have been lost. The plaintiff would not have accepted the goods by intimating to the seller that he had accepted. Nor would he have accepted by doing an act inconsistent with the seller's continuing ownership, as he had hardly had the goods for long enough to ascertain whether they were in conformity with the contract. Nor would he have retained the goods for more than a reasonable time.

A consumer with a right to rescind for an actionable misrepresentation will lose the right to rescind if he affirms the contract. Affirmation can also take place through lapse of time, if this shows an intention to affirm or prejudices the position of the seller. So if a consumer buys a product or service as a result of an actionable misrepresentation, then failure to rescind within a reasonable time may well mean that the contract has been affirmed and the right to rescind therefore lost.

Leaf v *International Galleries* [1950] 2 KB 86
The plaintiff bought a painting from International Galleries because of an actionable misrepresentation that the painting was by John Constable. When the plaintiff tried to resell the painting five years later he discovered that it was not by Constable.
Held: The plaintiff was too late to rescind on account of a non-fraudulent misrepresentation because he had affirmed the contract by doing nothing for five years.

Unfortunately this case does not show us exactly what length of time must have passed for the consumer to be taken to have affirmed the contract. Denning LJ thought that the right to rescind an executed contract for a non-fraudulent misrepresentation must necessarily have been lost by the time the right to treat the contract as repudiated for breach of condition would have been lost. His reasoning was that 'an innocent misrepresentation is much less potent than a breach of condition'. However, s. 1 of the Misrepresentation Act 1967 now states that:

> Where a person has entered into a contract after a misrepresentation has been made to him, and—
> (a) the misrepresentation has become a term of the contract . . .
> then, if otherwise he would be entitled to rescind the contract without alleging fraud, he shall be so entitled, notwithstanding [the misrepresentation having become a term of the contract].

This section envisages that the right to rescind for misrepresentation might be a more potent remedy than the remedy for breach of a term.

In *Peyman* v *Lanjani* [1985] 1 Ch 457 the Court of Appeal held that where a person had the choice whether or not to affirm a contract or rescind it for misrepresentation his choice would only be irrevocable if he knew of the facts which gave him the right to rescind and also knew that he had the right to rescind.

If the misrepresentation was fraudulent then, as we have seen, the consumer can sue for the tort of deceit. Deceit is very difficult to prove, as the consumer must show that the defendant actually did not believe the truth of what he said. However, if deceit can be proved then the lapse of a reasonable time will not prevent the consumer from rescinding. Instead s. 32 of the Limitation Act 1980 will prevent the consumer from rescinding only six years after the fraud has been or should have been discovered.

1.9.2.2 Inability to restore pre-contract position

We have already examined the circumstances in which the right to treat a contract as repudiated for breach of a condition will be lost and we considered the position where the goods had become damaged prior to rejection for breach of condition. A consumer who seeks to rescind for misrepresentation must be able to return the subject matter of the contract to the seller. If this is not possible, either because the subject matter has been consumed or has become altered, then rescission will not be possible.

Clarke v *Dickson* (1858) El Bl & El 148
The plaintiff bought shares in what we would today classify as a partnership. The partnership was turned into a limited company and when the company was being wound up the plaintiff discovered that he had bought the shares because of a misrepresentation. The plaintiff claimed to rescind the contract.
Held: The plaintiff had lost the right to rescind. The partnership had ceased to exist. The shares in it had become something else and therefore could not be returned. Crompton J stated, at 155: 'The plaintiff must rescind in toto or not at all. . . . The true doctrine is, that a party can never repudiate [rescind] a contract after, by his own act, it has become out of his power to restore the parties to their original position.' Crompton J gave the example of a butcher buying live cattle, butchering them and selling the meat to customers. If the butcher discovered that the grazier from whom he bought had made a fraudulent misrepresentation damages would be available for the tort of deceit, but rescission of the contract would not be possible.

However, it is not always strictly necessary to return the subject matter in exactly the state it was in when the contract was made. As rescission is an equitable remedy the court can allow for a monetary payment to take account of the fact that what is being returned has diminished in value. For example, in *Erlanger* v *New Sombrero Phosphate Co.* (1878) 3 App Cas 1218 a phosphate mine was sold and by the time the buyer wanted to rescind for misrepresentation he had extracted phosphate from the mine. The House of Lords did allow rescission but the buyer had to account to the seller for profits made since the sale of the mine.

Rescission will remain possible if the inability to restore the subject matter was due to the matter which was misrepresented, or due to the consumer reasonably testing what was bought. When a consumer claims back the purchase price on account of an actionable misrepresentation made by the vendor the price is recoverable even if it had been paid into a bank account by the vendor.

1.9.2.3 Third party has acquired rights

An actionable misrepresentation makes the contract voidable. Section 23 of the Sale of Goods Act 1979 states:

> When the seller of goods has a voidable title to them, but his title has not been avoided at the time of the sale, the buyer acquires a good title to the goods, provided he buys them in good faith and without notice of the seller's defect of title.

The following case shows an example of this.

Lewis v *Averay* [1972] 1 QB 198
Lewis sold his car to a rogue who paid for it with a bad cheque. The rogue made fraudulent misrepresentations that he was Richard Greene the television actor and that

his cheque would be honoured. By the time Lewis sought to rescind the rogue had sold the car to Averay, a student acting in good faith who had paid a reasonable price for it. Held: Lewis was too late to rescind the contract and so Averay was entitled to keep the car.

If, however, the person to whom the misrepresentation was made has done all that he can to show his intention to rescind then rescission can be effective against a third party who subsequently acquires the subject matter of the contract.

Car and Universal Finance Co. Ltd v Caldwell [1965] 1 QB 525
A rogue bought a car from the defendant, paying with a bad cheque. (This of course was a fraudulent misrepresentation.) The defendant found out about the rogue's misrepresentation. He wanted to rescind the contract but could not find the rogue to tell him so. Instead the defendant told the police what had happened and alerted the AA to look out for the car.
Held: Informing the police and the AA of what had happened was enough to rescind the contract. The defendant was therefore entitled to recover the car from a third party acting in good faith who had subsequently purchased the car.

A party who does rescind a contract for misrepresentation has the right to refuse to perform his side of the contract. He cannot be sued for specific performance of the contract or for damages.

1.10 Damages for Breach of Contract and for Actionable Misrepresentations

As stated at the beginning of this chapter, the law of contract will have been studied by LLB students as a foundation subject and there is therefore no point in re-examining general principles of contract law in detail. As regards the quantification of damages for breach of contract it is enough to remind you that the purpose of contract damages is to put the injured party in the position that he would have been in if the contract had been performed properly.

1.10.1 DAMAGES FOR FRAUDULENT MISREPRESENTATION

We have seen already in this chapter that a person suing for a fraudulent misrepresentation is suing for the tort of deceit. Hence the damages are assessed on the fraud basis, that is to say they are designed to put the injured party in the position which he would have been in if the tort had never been committed. Where the damages are for fraud then all expenses and losses subsequently suffered can be recovered. The following case gives an example of such damages.

Doyle v Olby Ltd [1969] 2 QB 158
Mr Doyle bought an ironmongery because of fraudulent misrepresentations that the turnover was achieved without employing a travelling salesman. He paid £4,500 for the lease, the business and the goodwill. He also paid £5,000 for the stock and took out a longer lease, at a greatly increased rent, from the vendor of the business. About half of the turnover was dependent upon the employment of a travelling salesman. Mr Doyle could not afford a travelling salesman so that business was lost. Mr Doyle had little option but to carry on the business as best he could. At the time of the case he owed £4,000 to various creditors, having been sued several times in the County Court.

THE LAW OF CONTRACT AS A MEANS OF CONSUMER PROTECTION 39

SAQ 1/16

(a) How would the damages have been assessed if the statement that there was no need to employ a travelling salesman had been a term of the contract?

(b) How were the damages assessed for the tort of deceit?

(a) The purpose of contract damages would have been to put Mr Doyle in the position he would have been if the statement had been true. The trial judge calculated damages at £1,500 on this basis. This figure was reached either by calculating how much it would have cost to employ a travelling salesman or by calculating how much the goodwill would have been reduced if the business dependent on a travelling salesman was lost. The judge calculated damages as 'the cost of making good the representation' or 'the reduction in value of the goodwill', both coming to the same thing.

(b) The damages for the tort of deceit were greater, being assessed by the Court of Appeal as £5,500. This figure took account not only of the money Mr Doyle put into the business at the start, but also damages for all the expenses and loss which he had subsequently suffered.

Lord Denning MR stated:

In contract, the damages are limited to what may reasonably be supposed to have been in the contemplation of the parties. In fraud, they are not so limited. The defendant is bound to make reparation for all the actual damages flowing directly from the fraudulent inducement.

The judgment of Lord Denning MR is reproduced in *Cases and Materials* (1.4.1).

In the following case the House of Lords recently considered the amount of damages for fraudulent misrepresentation.

Smith New Court Securities Ltd v *Scrimgeour Vickers (Asset Management) Ltd* [1996] 4 All ER 769
In July 1989 the plaintiffs bought 28 million shares in F Ltd which a bank caused to be sold through the defendant, who were stockbrokers owned by the bank. The plaintiffs were told that they were in competition with two other bidders and bid 82.5p per share, making a total price of around £23 million. This was about 4.25p above the current market price. In September F Ltd announced that it had been the victim of a major fraud, and this caused its share price to plummet. Between November and April the plaintiffs sold the shares at between 30 and 40p, making an overall loss of £11 million. When the share prices collapsed the plaintiffs discovered that there had not been two other bidders for the shares. They claimed damages for fraudulent misrepresentation and the House of Lords accepted that there had been deceit as the bank had falsely represented that it had received other bids for the shares.
Held: the primary rule was that in the case of fraud the victim was entitled to compensation for all the actual loss directly flowing from the transaction which was induced by the deceit. This would include consequential loss. The normal measure of damages would therefore be the price paid less the actual value of the subject matter at

the date of sale. However, this rule would not apply where the misrepresentation continued to operate after the contract so as to cause the plaintiff to retain the asset, or where the circumstances of the case meant that the fraud locked the plaintiff into the contract. The plaintiff should be entitled to all the loss directly flowing from the transaction, and not merely loss which was reasonably foreseeable. The plaintiffs were locked into the transaction, because they could not sensibly sell the shares immediately, and so their damages should be the difference between the contract price and the amount for which they resold the shares.

In the cases we have looked at the measure of tort damages for deceit is considerably greater than the measure of contract damages. However, it should be remembered that fraud damages can sometimes be less than contract damages, as tort damages do not include an amount for loss of the bargain. Let us assume that a consumer pays £500 for an antique table because of a statement that the table was Georgian. If this statement had been true then the table would have been worth £1,000. However, the statement is not true and so the table is only worth £250. If the statement that the table was Georgian was an untrue warranty then the consumer's damages would take account of the loss of bargain, and would prima facie be £750. If the statement was a fraudulent misrepresentation then the damages would prima facie be only £250. There would be no damages for loss of bargain, the damages would be designed to put the consumer into the position he would have been in if he had never made the deal. In *East* v *Maurer* [1991] 2 All ER 733 Beldam LJ said:

> Damages for deceit are not awarded on the basis that the plaintiff is to be put in as good a position as if the statement had been true; they are to be assessed on a basis which would compensate the plaintiff for all the loss he has suffered, so far as money can do it.

1.10.2 DAMAGES FOR NEGLIGENT MISREPRESENTATION

Before the Misrepresentation Act 1967 came into force a person who had made a contract in reliance on a non-fraudulent misrepresentation had no right to damages. Section 2(1) of the 1967 Act now provides:

> Where a person has entered into a contract after a misrepresentation has been made to him by another party thereto and as a result thereof he has suffered loss, then, if the person making the misrepresentation would be liable to damages in respect thereof had the misrepresentation been made fraudulently, that person shall be so liable notwithstanding that the misrepresentation was not made fraudulently, unless he proves that he had reasonable ground to believe and did believe up to the time the contract was made that the facts represented were true.

It is perhaps unfortunate that this section takes the form of one lengthy sentence. However, its meaning can be discerned by taking it one step at a time.

The first requirement is that the injured party must have suffered loss because he has entered a contract after an actionable misrepresentation has been made to him. We then ask whether the person making the misrepresentation would have been liable in damages if the misrepresentation had been fraudulent. If the answer to this question is 'yes', then the person making the misrepresentation shall be so liable. Finally, we see that this is not the case if the person making the misrepresentation can show that it was made wholly innocently, that is to say if he can show that he did believe its truth, with reasonable grounds for such a belief, at the time of the contract. You should notice that the burden of proof here is on the defendant.

Section 2(1) of the 1967 Act also spells out the measure of damages. It says that if the negligent misrepresenter would have been liable in damages had the misrepresentation been fraudulent, he shall be 'so liable' for a negligent misrepresentation. What does this mean?

THE LAW OF CONTRACT AS A MEANS OF CONSUMER PROTECTION

Royscot Trust Ltd v *Rogerson* [1991] 3 All ER 294
The first defendant (a consumer) wanted to buy a car from the second defendant (the car dealer) on hire-purchase financed by the plaintiff (the finance company). The price of the car was £7,600 and the deposit paid by the consumer was £1,200. The deposit was therefore only 15.8% of the price. The car dealer knew that the finance company's policy was to demand a deposit of 20% of the price and so he falsified the figures to say that the price was £8,000 and the customer had paid a deposit of £1,600. This left the balance to be paid as £6,400, which was the true balance the consumer agreed to pay. The deal went ahead and the finance company paid the dealer £6,400. After repaying instalments totalling £2,775, the consumer dishonestly sold the car to a private purchaser for £7,200 and made no more payments. The private purchaser gained complete title to the car under s. 27 of the Hire-Purchase Act 1964. The finance company sued the dealer for negligent misrepresentation.

SAQ 1/17

(a) Why did the plaintiffs sue for negligent misrepresentation, when the misrepresentation was almost certainly fraudulent?

(b) Were the damages assessed on the contract basis, the ordinary tort basis or the fraud basis?

(a) The plaintiffs sued for negligent misrepresentation because this shifted the burden of proof on to the defendant to show that he had reasonable grounds to believe and did believe up to the time the contract was made that the facts represented were true (Misrepresentation Act 1967, s. 2(1)). If the defendant could prove this then the misrepresentation would be wholly innocent. If the plaintiff had alleged fraudulent misrepresentation the burden of proof would have been on the plaintiff to establish the tort of deceit, a difficult matter as it would entail proving the defendant's actual dishonest state of mind.

(b) The damages were based on the fraud basis. Balcombe LJ stated 'the wording of the subsection is clear: the person making the innocent [negligent] misrepresentation shall be "so liable", i.e. liable to damages as if the representation had been made fraudulently'. Balcombe LJ held that the plaintiffs were entitled to recover all the losses which flowed from their entering into the contracts with the dealer and the consumer, even unforeseeable losses, as long as these were not too remote. The consumer's breaking the contract and selling the car was not a *novus actus interviens* which broke the chain of causation. The finance company therefore received £3,625, which represented the difference between the amount it had paid to the dealer (£6,400) and the amount it had received from the consumer (£2,775). However, if the finance company did recover any money from the consumer then credit would have to be given for this. At first instance the damages against the dealer had been assessed on the contract basis, as £1,600. (If the dealer had revealed that the true deposit was only £1,200 the finance company would have assumed that the car's price was £6,000 and only have paid the dealer £4,800 instead of the £6,400 which they did pay the dealer. The contract measure of damages was therefore £6,400 − £4,800 = £1,600.) Extracts from the judgments of Balcombe and Ralph Gibson LJJ can be read in *Cases and Materials* (1.4.2).

The decision in *Royscot* was neither approved nor disapproved in *Smith New Court Securities Ltd* v *Scrimgeour Vickers (Asset Management) Ltd*. However, in the light of the

House of Lords' decision in *South Australia Asset Management Corp v York Montague Ltd* [1996] 3 All ER 365 it must now be viewed with some suspicion. In this case the House of Lords considered the liability of valuers who broke a duty of care by negligently valuing property at a higher value than its true value. After the property was purchased its value plummeted due to the fall in the property market. For example, in one of the cases under consideration the plaintiffs advanced £1.75 million on the security of a property which the defendants had valued at £2.5 million. At the time of valuation the correct value was £1.8 million, but at the depths of the slump in property prices the property was sold for £0.95 million. The correct measure of damages was £0.7 million (the difference between the over-valuation and what the property was worth at that date) not all the money lost by the plaintiff. Although this case is concerned with liability for negligent misstatement, rather than liability for negligent misrepresentation, it is hard to see why the same yardstick should not be applied in cases of negligent misrepresentation.

1.10.3 DAMAGES FOR WHOLLY INNOCENT MISREPRESENTATION

Section 2(2) of the Misrepresentation Act 1967 allows a court to award damages even for an innocent misrepresentation:

> Where a person has entered into a contract after a misrepresentation has been made to him otherwise than fraudulently, and he would be entitled, by reason of the misrepresentation, to rescind the contract, then, if it is claimed, in any proceedings arising out of the contract, that the contract ought to be or has been rescinded, the court or arbitrator may declare the contract subsisting and award damages in lieu if rescission, if of opinion that it would be equitable to do so, having regard to the nature of the misrepresentation and the loss that would be caused by it if the contract were upheld, as well as to the loss that rescission would cause to the other party.

Again, this lengthy sentence can be understood by tackling it in stages. First, the misrepresentation must have been non-fraudulent. Second, it must entitle the injured party to rescind the contract. Third, if the injured party claims that the contract has been or ought to be rescinded the court may award damages instead. (Notice that rescission is not a right which the injured party can demand. The court may award damages instead of rescission.) The court will only award damages instead of rescission where it would be equitable to do so. In deciding whether or not it is equitable to award damages instead of rescission the court will consider three things: the nature of the misrepresentation; the loss which would be caused by the misrepresentation if the contract were upheld; and the loss that rescission would cause to the misrepresentor.

In *William Sindell plc v Cambridgeshire CC*, see below, the Court of Appeal considered the measure of damages under s. 2(2), as well as the circumstances in which damages would be available. Unfortunately, all of what was said was obiter, as the Court of Appeal decided that there had been no actionable misrepresentation.

William Sindell plc v Cambridgeshire CC [1994] 3 All ER 932
In 1988 a building company agreed to purchase land from the county council for £5m. In response to pre-contractual enquiries the council stated that they did not know of any easements and that they had no notice of any matters likely to affect the use and enjoyment of the land. The sale was concluded in March 1989. Eighteen months later the builders started building but by that time the property market had collapsed and the land was worth about half the price paid for it. In October 1990 the builders discovered a nine inch foul sewer, which had been built in 1970, under the land. The trial judge allowed the builders to rescind, exercising his discretion (under s. 2(2) of the Act) not to award damages in lieu. The Court of Appeal held that there had been no actionable misrepresentation. (The court reached this conclusion applying the National Conditions of Sale — a point with which we are not concerned.) However, the Court of Appeal did consider the effect of s. (2) of the 1967 Act. In this case the misrepresentation was a matter of minor importance, which would have cost about £18,000 to put right. If rescission were

THE LAW OF CONTRACT AS A MEANS OF CONSUMER PROTECTION

ordered the county council would have to return about £8 million (in purchase price and interest) for land currently worth £2 million. As there was such a disparity between what the builders had lost due to the misrepresentation and what the council would lose if rescission were ordered, the court would have awarded damages in lieu of rescission if there had been an actionable misrepresentation. The correct measure of damages would not have included an amount for the loss caused by the fall in market value of the land. Instead it should have been either the cost of remedying the defect or alternatively the lesser amount the land was worth because of the defect.

SAQ 1/18

Was the measure of damages which the Court of Appeal considered appropriate the same as a damages for breach of warranty would have been?

In effect the measure was the amount which would have been available for breach of warranty. In *William Sindell plc* Hoffman LJ explained the anomalous situation before the 1967 Act came into force, when rescission was available for an innocent misrepresentation but the contract could not be terminated for breach of warranty. He said, at 955:

> I think that s. 2(2) was intended to give the court a power to eliminate this anomaly by upholding the contract and compensating the plaintiff for the loss he has suffered on account of the property not having been what it was represented to be. In other words, damages under s. 2(2) should never exceed the sum which would have been available if the representation had been a warranty.

An extract from the judgment of Hoffman LJ can be read in *Cases and Materials* (1.4.3).

In *Thomas Witter Ltd* v *TBF Industries Ltd* [1996] 2 All ER 573 Jacob J held that the right to award damages in lieu of rescission applied even when the right to rescind had been lost. What was important was that there had once been a right to rescind. The case also established that damages could be available under s. 2(2) even though damages would not have been available under s. 2(1) (because the defendant could prove that he made the statement believing, on reasonable grounds, that it was true). Section 2(3) of the Misrepresentation Act 1967 allows for damages to be claimed under s. 2(2) even though damages can also be claimed under s. 2(1) (i.e. damages also claimed for negligent misrepresentation). But where such damages are awarded under s. 2(2) they should be deducted from the damages payable under s. 2(1).

For a worked example of the damages claimable for actionable misrepresentation and breach of contract, see items (2) and (3) of the End of Chapter Assessment Question.

1.11 Summary

In this chapter we have covered the following:

- goods displayed in shops with a price ticket attached to them will be invitations to treat rather than offers;

- advertisements which state the price at which goods are available are likely to be invitations to treat rather than offers;

- an advertisement which contains a definite promise to be bound if some action is performed can amount to an offer of a unilateral contract;

- it may be the case that an implied term will prevent the revocation of the offer of a unilateral contract once the offeree has embarked on performance;

- whether or not a pre-contractual statement will amount to a term of the contract or not will depend upon the intentions of the parties;

- statements of mere opinion cannot amount to terms or to actionable misrepresentations. However, a term may be implied to the effect that the statement of opinion was made using reasonable care and skill. It may also be the case that the opinion impliedly makes a statement of fact which could amount to an actionable misrepresentation. A pre-contract statement can also give rise to liability for negligent misstatement;

- the right to treat a contract of sale of goods as repudiated for breach of condition will be lost once the buyer has affirmed the contract;

- the right to treat contracts other than sales of goods as repudiated for breach of condition will be lost once the contract has been affirmed;

- the right to rescind for misrepresentation will be lost if the contract is affirmed, if it is impossible to restore the parties to their pre-contract position, or if a third party acting in good faith has acquired rights in the subject matter of the contract;

- damages for fraudulent or negligent misrepresentation will compensate for all actual losses flowing directly from the misrepresentation;

- damages in lieu of rescission may be awarded for non-fraudulent misrepresentation. Such damages will be assessed as if the misrepresentation had been a breach of warranty.

1.12 End of Chapter Assessment Questions

(1) In a series of radio and newspaper advertisements, Dicey Motors Ltd advertises its New Year sale of Yakoxen cars. (Yakoxen are a new car manufacturer, based in Mongolia.) The advertisements are as follows:

Unbeatable price promise! Buy any new Yakoxen car from us in our January sale and you will be guaranteed to be onto a winner. Why? Because if you buy in our New Year sale we know that you cannot buy cheaper locally. We are so sure of this that we will refund ten times the difference in price if you show within 28 days of purchase that you could have bought the same car cheaper locally. That's right! Ten times the difference. Have we gone mad? No! It's our competitors who are getting mad, because they know we cannot be beaten on price or service. Don't forget, ten times the difference will be refunded as regards cars bought during the New Year sale. No arguments. Sale ends January 3rd, so be quick.

Alan visits Dicey Motors' showroom on 2 January. Alan wants to buy a new Yakoxen car and has already had a quote from a garage three miles away. Alan is surprised to find that Dicey Motors' price is £250 more than this quote. While in the showroom Alan signs a contract to buy a new Yakoxen car, reluctantly accepting that it will have to be in a deep shade of Avocado, as this is the only colour Dicey Motors have in stock. The written contract makes no mention of the advertised price promise. Alan pays for the car with a banker's draft.

On 4 January the new car is delivered to Alan. He uses it to visit his parents in Scotland, and then goes on to take a two week touring holiday. On 21 January Alan goes to Dicey Motors' showroom, taking with him the cheaper quote from the other garage, and claims £2,500, representing ten times the amount by which the other garage's car was cheaper. Dicey Motors' managing director tells Alan that the car which the other garage offered to supply is not identical as, although it was exactly the same model, it was not avocado in colour. He says that he knows this to be true as Dicey Motors are the only garage in the region to have been supplied with avocado Yakoxens. On hearing that he would not be receiving the £2,500 Alan tells the managing director that he is not keeping the car if he does not get the £2,500. The managing director replies that a contract has been made and that Alan must stick to it. He points out that as Alan has already travelled 3,000 miles in the car, and that as the paint work is badly scratched and the driver's seat has been modified it would be impossible for Dicey Motors to resell the car as anything like new. (The paint work was scratched by vandals when Alan had parked the car outside his house.) Alan hands over the keys and says that he wants the £2,500 and that he is still not taking the car. Alan also points out that the car has been doing 12 miles to the gallon since the date of purchase, rather than the 40 miles to the gallon which the managing director had claimed that it would. The managing director examines the car and says that this is caused by a twisted fuel pipe. He spends five minutes straightening the pipe and says that this has cured the defect. (You should assume that the excessive fuel consumption was a breach of s. 14(2) of the Sale of Goods Act 1979, and that the managing director's actions cured the problem permanently.)

The following day Alan receives a letter from Dicey Motors Ltd saying that they do not intend to pay the £2,500, that they do not accept that Alan has the right to return the car, but that they have stored it on their premises until Alan picks it up. The letter says that the cost of storage is £40 a week and that Alan will have to pay this.

Advise Alan of his legal position in respect of the above facts.

(2) John pays £1,000 for an antique table because of a statement that the table was made by Chippenmunk, a famous artist. In fact the table is not by Chippenmunk and is therefore worth only £100. If the table had been made by Chippenmunk it would have been worth £1,000.

(a) How would damages be assessed on the basis that the statement was (i) a warranty, (ii) a fraudulent misrepresentation, (iii) a negligent misrepresentation?

(b) How would damages be assessed if the court elected to award damages in lieu of rescission under s. 2(2) of the Misrepresentation Act 1976?

(c) How would the damages be assessed if John had unexpectedly spent a further £800 having the table restored, only to find that as the table was not made by Chippenmunk it was still worth only £100?

(3) John buys an antique vase for £850 because of a statement that it is by Chippenmunk and therefore worth £1,000. In fact the vase is not by Chippenmunk and is therefore worth £500. (If it had been by Chippenmunk it would have been worth £1,850.) How much would John's damages be if the statement was (a) a warranty, (b) a fraudulent misrepresentation?

See *Cases and Materials* (**1.6**) for specimen answers.

CHAPTER TWO

DEFECTIVE GOODS AND SERVICES: THE CLASSIFICATION OF TRANSACTIONS

2.1 Objectives

By the end of this chapter you should be able to:

- define and recognise a contract of sale of goods;

- differentiate between sales and agreements to sell; between existing and future goods; and between specific and unascertained goods;

- define and recognise a contract of hire-purchase;

- define and recognise contracts for the transfer of the property in goods, contracts of hire, and contracts for the supply of a service;

- classify contracts as either contracts of sale of goods, of hire-purchase, of transfer of the property in goods, of hire or of the supply of a service.

2.2 Introduction

Whenever a consumer buys goods or services from a business, a statute will imply terms which favour the consumer into the contract. These terms are implied by different statutes, depending upon how the contract is classified. This situation has arisen because the statutory implied terms have developed in a piecemeal fashion.

The first statutory terms in the consumer's favour were implied: by the Sale of Goods Act 1893. As we shall see, this Act was a codification of the common law and was intended to regulate the affairs of merchants rather than those of consumers. The 1893 Act has been replaced by the (virtually identical) Sale of Goods Act 1979, and the implied terms contained in the 1979 Act are now seen as one of the most important sources of consumer protection. Two other statutes imply very similar terms in the consumer's favour: the Supply of Goods (Implied Terms) Act 1973 implies these similar terms into contracts of hire-purchase; the Supply of Goods and Services Act 1982 implies the terms into contracts of hire and contracts for the transfer of the property in goods. The 1982 Act also implies somewhat different terms in the consumer's favour into contracts for the supply of a service.

48 DEFECTIVE GOODS AND SERVICES: CLASSIFICATION OF TRANSACTIONS

In this chapter we classify the various types of consumer transactions. We also examine the various ways in which sales of goods can themselves be classified. (These classifications are not relevant to the statutory implied terms but are important in other ways, as we shall see in later chapters.) It is important to remember that in this chapter we are not concerned with the substance of the terms implied by the various statutes. The terms themselves are examined in detail in **Chapters 3** and **4**.

To discover which statute governs a particular transaction we consider the three statutes in the order in which they (originally) came into force. As the original Sale of Goods Act was passed in 1893, we first ask whether the contract is a sale of goods. If so, the terms are implied by the Sale of Goods Act 1979. If the transaction cannot be classified as a sale of goods, is it a contract of hire-purchase? If so, the terms are implied by the Supply of Goods (Implied Terms) Act 1973. Finally, if the transaction cannot be classified as either a contract of sale of goods or of hire-purchase, is it a contract for the transfer of the property in goods, a contract of hire or a contract for the supply of a service? If so, the terms are implied by the Supply of Goods and Services Act 1982.

2.3 Contracts to which the Sale of Goods Act 1979 Applies

The Sale of Goods Act 1979 applies only to contracts of sale of goods. We therefore need to examine exactly which contracts fall within this definition.

ACTIVITY 2/1

Using only your intuition to guide you, put a tick or a cross next to the following transactions, to indicate whether or not you think that they amount to contracts of sale of goods:

(a) Alice acquires a car on hire-purchase.

(b) In a shop which sells second-hand goods, Belinda exchanges her bicycle for a video recorder.

(c) Charles buys a new car, paying with a cheque for £12,000.

(d) A supermarket advertises that it will give a 'free' chicken to customers who spend £20 in any one visit. Davina spends £20 and receives a 'free' chicken.

(e) Eric, who has won a National Lottery rollover jackpot, buys a very large yacht.

(f) Frank leases a flat for one year for £3,500.

(g) Gertrude buys 100 shares in a company for £2,000.

(h) Henry pays £2 for a pound of 'pick your own' strawberries.

(i) Ian spends £6 on a haircut.

(j) Joan commissions a sculptor to make a sculpture of her dog for a price of £1,000.

(k) Kevin orders a new set of spectacles. The price is £185, and the optician is to put the appropriate lenses into a frame which Kevin has chosen and to make sure that the spectacles are a good fit.

DEFECTIVE GOODS AND SERVICES: CLASSIFICATION OF TRANSACTIONS 49

(l) Liza agrees to pay £70,000 for a specialist sports car which has yet to be manufactured.

(m) Martin agrees to pay an antique dealer £400 for a particular painting. The sale is made subject to the condition that the dealer can purchase the painting from its current owner.

(n) Naomi agrees to pay £9,000 for a new Ford Fiesta. Neither she, nor the garage from whom she is purchasing, have any particular car in mind.

We will discover the answers to this Activity as we work our way through the rest of this chapter. It will be interesting to see how many of the examples you intuitively got correct. A complete list of the answers can be found in *Cases and Materials* (2.1)

2.3.1 DEFINITION OF A CONTRACT OF SALE OF GOODS

Section 2(1) of the Sale of Goods Act 1979 states:

> A contract of sale of goods is a contract by which the seller transfers or agrees to transfer the property in goods to the buyer for a money consideration, called the price.

SAQ 2/1

Applying s. 2(1), we can see that transactions (a) and (b) in Activity 2/1 are not sales. Why do these transactions not fit within the definition given by s. 2(1)?

Transaction (a) is not a sale because the property in the car was not transferred to Alice. Possession of the goods was transferred, but the property (ownership) was not. (The nature of a hire-purchase contract is considered later at **2.4**.) In transaction (b) Belinda's acquisition of the video recorder was not a sale. Her consideration was not money, it was other goods (her bicycle). She did not therefore give 'a money consideration called the price'. By contrast, in transaction (c) Charles pays money for the property in the new car and so this transaction would be a sale and would be covered by the 1979 Act. There is no requirement that the money consideration should be paid in cash rather than by cheque or credit card.

In the following case the House of Lords had to decide whether or not a 'free gift' was a sale of goods. An entirely free gift, that is to say a gift for which no consideration was demanded in return, would not be a sale of goods. However, such gifts are rare. The old adage that you get nothing for nothing, and very little for a ha'penny, is generally borne out by so called free gifts. Usually, as in the case which follows, the recipient of the 'gift' has to provide some consideration for it. The contract will only amount to a sale of the 'gift' if the consideration given in return is 'a money consideration called the price'.

Esso Petroleum Ltd v *Commissioners of Customs and Excise* [1976] 1 All ER 117
In 1970, in order to promote their petrol, Esso promised to give motorists one World Cup coin for every four gallons of petrol purchased. The coins bore the likeness of one of the

members of England's 1970 World Cup soccer team. The coins were worth very little, but Esso hoped that motorists would attempt to collect all 30 coins and therefore buy Esso's petrol. The coins were advertised with slogans such as: 'Going free, at your Esso Action Station now', and, 'we are giving you a coin with every four gallons of Esso petrol you buy'. For tax reasons, it became necessary to know whether or not the World Cup coins were sold.

ACTIVITY 2/2

In *Esso Petroleum Ltd* v *Commissioners of Customs and Excise* there was little doubt that the customers had to provide some consideration in order to get their World Cup coins. However, the House of Lords held, by a majority of four to one, that the coins were not sold. Read the extract from Lord Simon's speech in *Cases and Materials* (2.1.1) and then write down why he held that the coins were not sold.

You should have written that Lord Simon decided that the coins were not transferred for a money consideration. Rather they were transferred in consideration of the motorist entering into a contract for the sale of petrol. For this reason Lord Simon, and the majority, held that the coins were not sold. Looking back to **Activity 2/1**, transaction (d), we can therefore see that the 'free' chicken which Davina received did not amount to a sale of goods. Davina's consideration for the chicken was not 'a money consideration called the price', but rather the act of spending £20 on other groceries.

When goods are taken in part-exchange for other goods it can be difficult to tell whether or not this amounts to a sale of goods. In *Aldridge* v *Johnson* (1857) 7 E & B 885 the plaintiff took 100 quarters of barley (valued by the parties at £215) in exchange for 32 bullocks (valued at £192). The plaintiff agreed to pay the balance of £23 in cash. This was held to be two contracts of sale, as both the barley and the bullocks were valued in money terms. However, this does not amount to an authority that all part-exchanges will be classified as one or more contracts of sale of goods. Each case must be viewed on its facts. The court will try to find what the parties intended the consideration for the transfer of the property in the goods to be.

2.3.1.1 The definition of 'goods'

Section 61 of the Sale of Goods Act 1979 is the interpretation section. Section 61(1) gives the following definition of goods:

> . . . 'goods' includes all personal chattels other than things in action and money . . . and in particular 'goods' includes emblements, industrial growing crops, and things attached to or forming part of the land which are agreed to be severed before sale or under the contract of sale . . .

To understand this definition we need to know the meaning of 'personal chattels', 'things in action' and 'emblements'.

Personal chattels other than things in action would include all physical objects which can be touched and moved. Looking back to **Activity 2/1**, transaction (e), we can see that the the yacht which Eric bought does fit this description, huge as it might be. As Eric's

DEFECTIVE GOODS AND SERVICES: CLASSIFICATION OF TRANSACTIONS

consideration was money, the deal would have been a sale of goods. In **Activity 2/1**, transaction (f), Frank, by contrast, would not have made a contract of sale of goods. A lease of land (technically classified as 'chattels real') is not a personal chattel.

A thing in action is an intangible form of property which cannot be physically possessed. The owner of a thing in action can only claim or enforce the rights which the thing confers by taking legal action. (Hence the name thing in action.) Intellectual property rights, such as copyright, are things in action. The rights might be spelled out in a document, but that document is not the property. The property is the right to claim or enforce the copyright and, ultimately, this right can only be achieved by taking legal action. Debts, patents, shares and trade marks are other examples of things in action. In **Activity 2/1**, transaction (g), therefore, Gertrude's purchase of the shares is not a contract of sale of goods.

Emblements are annual crops and vegetable products which have been cultivated by human labour. Section 61(1) specifically includes emblements as goods. So when Henry, in **Activity 2/1**, transaction (h), pays £2 for a pound of 'pick your own' strawberries, this is therefore a sale of goods.

Whilst contracts to sell things which must be severed from the land are sales of goods, sales of an interest in land or to sell a part of the land are not. In *Morgan* v *Russell & Sons* [1909] 1 KB 357 the court decided that a contract to remove and sell cinders and slag which had lain on a piece of land for up to 50 years was not a sale of goods. The sale was of an interest in land. The relevant extracts from the judgments of Lord Alverstone CJ and Watson J can be read in *Cases and Materials* (2.1.1.1).

Contracts to supply services are not covered by the 1979 Act. When we examined the definition of a sale of goods given by s. 2(1) we saw that a contract can only be one of sale of goods if 'the seller transfers or agrees to transfer the property in goods to the buyer'. A contract to provide a service cannot fit within such a definition. A person who sells a service does not transfer ownership of a personal chattel, but agrees to perform some action. In **Activity 2/1**, transaction (i), therefore, Ian's contract to have his hair cut would not be covered by the 1979 Act. (The definition of a contract for the supply of services is examined below at **2.5.3**.)

Nor are contracts to supply work and materials covered by the 1979 Act. However, it must be said that it can be very difficult to distinguish contracts of sale of goods and contracts to supply work and materials. The Court of Appeal considered the distinction in *Robinson* v *Graves* [1935] 1 KB 579, in which the Court of Appeal had to decide whether or not a contract to have a portrait painted was a sale of goods.

ACTIVITY 2/3

Read Greer LJ's judgment in *Robinson* v *Graves* in *Cases and Materials* (2.1.1.1). Then write down:

(a) Why Greer LJ held that the contract was not a sale of goods.

(b) On what grounds *Lee* v *Griffin* (1861) 1 B & S 272 (where the contract was for the manufacture and supply of a set of false teeth) was distinguished.

(a) Greer LJ, giving the leading judgment of the Court of Appeal, held that the essence of the contract was not the purchase and sale of something created by the artist. It was rather that the artist would use what skill he had to paint a portrait which the client would ultimately have to accept and pay for.

(b) *Lee* v *Griffin* was distinguished on the grounds that the substance of the contract was the production of something to be sold by the dentist to the dentist's customer. It was therefore a sale of goods.

In **Activity 2/1**, transaction (j), therefore, Joan will not have made a contract of sale of goods by agreeing to commission the sculpture. However, if the sculpture had already been made when Joan agreed to buy it then this would have been a sale of goods. In **Activity 2/1**, transaction (k) Kevin will, on the other hand, have made a contract of sale of goods by agreeing to buy the spectacles. Although these two examples are reasonably easy to classify, it must be said that the distinction between contracts of sale of goods and contracts for work and materials can be very hard to draw. The court will make the distinction by looking for the substance of the contract.

One difficult question which has yet to be answered authoritatively is whether or not computer software can be regarded as goods. The disks on which the software is supplied are obviously goods, but what of the intellectual information contained on the discs? We shall see, in the following chapter, that when goods are sold by a business they must be of satisfactory quality and fit for the buyer's purpose. These requirements are strict, and so if software is to be classified as goods this will make software retailers strictly liable for faults which render the software unsatisfactory or unfit for the buyer's purpose. (On the question as to whether or not software constitutes goods, see the article by Elizabeth MacDonald, 'The Council, the Computer and the Unfair Contract Terms Act 1977', (1995) 58 MLR 588 in **Cases and Materials (2.1.1.1)**.) See also the opinion of Sir Iain Glidewell expressed in *St Albans City and District Council* v *International Computers Ltd* [1996] 4 All ER 481.)

2.3.2 TYPES OF GOODS

2.3.2.1 Sales and agreements to sell

Section 2 of the Sale of Goods Act 1979 makes a distinction between a sale and an agreement to sell.

Section 2(4) states: 'Where under a contract of sale the property in the goods is transferred from the seller to the buyer the contract is called a sale.'

Section 2(5) states: 'Where under a contract of sale the transfer of the property in the goods is to take place at a future time or subject to some condition later to be fulfilled the contract is called an agreement to sell.'

In later chapters we shall see why this distinction is important. Here it is enough to say that both sales and agreements to sell are covered by the 1979 Act.

2.3.2.2 Existing and future goods

The 1979 Act classifies goods in two ways. The first classification is between existing and future goods. Section 5 states:

(1) The goods which form the subject of a contract of sale may be either existing goods, owned or possessed by the seller, or goods to be manufactured or acquired by him after the making of the contract of sale, in this Act called future goods.
(2) There may be a contract for the sale of goods the acquisition of which by the seller depends on a contingency which may or may not happen.

DEFECTIVE GOODS AND SERVICES: CLASSIFICATION OF TRANSACTIONS

(3) Where by a contract of sale the seller purports to effect a present sale of future goods, the contract operates as an agreement to sell the goods.

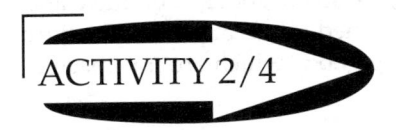

ACTIVITY 2/4

Steve, a retailer, sells the following goods:

(a) a bicycle which is in the shop window;

(b) a tricycle which he has taken 'on approval' from a dealer, but which he has not yet bought;

(c) 50 bicycle pumps which his business has yet to make;

(d) a racing bicycle which he intends to buy from another business;

(e) an antique bicycle, subject to a condition that he can persuade the current owner to sell it.

Complete the following chart, to indicate which of the contracts were for the sale of existing goods and which were for the sale of future goods.

Goods	Existing goods	Future goods
Bicycle		
Tricycle		
Bicycle pumps		
Racing bicycle		
Antique bicycle		

(a) The sale of the bicycle was a contract for the sale of existing goods. The bicycle did exist at the time of the contract and it was owned by Steve.

(b) The sale of the tricycle was a contract for the sale of existing goods. The tricycle did exist at the time of the contract, and it was possessed by Steve.

(c) The sale of the bicycle pumps was a contract for the sale of future goods as, at the time of the contract, they had yet to be manufactured.

(d) The sale of the racing bicycle was a contract for the sale of future goods (whether it had already been manufactured or not) because, at the time of the contract, Steve had yet to acquire it.

(e) The sale of the antique bicycle was a contract for the sale of future goods. The antique bicycle did in fact exist at the time of the contract, and both Steve and the buyer know which bicycle they meant, but Steve had yet to acquire ownership or possession of it.

Looking back to **Activity 2/1**, transactions (l) and (m), we can see that when Liza agrees to buy the sports car which has yet to be manufactured, and when Martin agrees to buy the painting if the antique dealer can acquire it, they both make contracts to buy future goods. Both are contracts of sale of goods, and both would be covered by the 1979 Act.

2.3.2.3 Specific and unascertained goods

The second classification of goods which the 1979 Act makes is between specific and unascertained goods. Specific goods are defined by s. 61(1) as: 'goods identified and agreed on at the time a contract of sale is made'. Unascertained goods are not defined by the 1979 Act. In effect, they are defined by default as being goods which are not specific.

SAQ 2/2

Having given it a test drive, Beryl agrees to buy her friend's car. The friend orders a new car from the garage.

(a) Does Beryl make a contract to buy specific or unascertained goods?

(b) Does Beryl's friend make a contract to buy specific or unascertained goods?

(a) Beryl made a contract to buy specific goods. The car in question was identified and agreed upon at the time when the contract was made.

(b) When Beryl's friend ordered a new car from a garage, this might have been a purchase of specific or unascertained goods. If the car to be sold was identified and agreed upon at the time of the contract, then the contract would have been for the sale of specific goods. If the car was not identified at the time of the contract, but merely described as being of a particular model and colour, then the contract would have been for the sale of unascertained goods.

We can see that Naomi, in **Activity 2/1**, transaction (n), would have made a contract of sale of goods when she ordered the new Ford Fiesta. The goods were unascertained, but contracts for the sale of both specific and unascertained goods are contracts of sale of goods.

It is not certain whether or not future goods can ever be regarded as specific. In **Chapter 5** we shall see that we need to know whether goods are specific or unascertained for two purposes; applying the statutory rules on when the property in the goods passes from the seller to the buyer, and deciding if the contract can be made void for mistake or voidable for frustration under the Act. Future goods can never be specific as far as the rules on the passing of the property are concerned. However, they possibly can be specific as regards the Act's rules on mistake and frustration.

By now, we have decided upon all the transactions listed in **Activity 2/1**. How many did you intuitively get correct?

3.4 Contracts of Hire-purchase

ACTIVITY 2/5

Harold visits a local garage store and agrees to take a car on hire-purchase over a three year period.

DEFECTIVE GOODS AND SERVICES: CLASSIFICATION OF TRANSACTIONS

(a) In one sentence, write down the effect of the agreement which Harold has made.

(b) Write down the parties to the agreement.

(a) Section 15 of the Supply of Goods (Implied Terms) Act 1973 defines a contract of hire-purchase:

> ... 'hire-purchase agreement' means an agreement, other than conditional sale agreement, under which—
> (a) goods are bailed ... in return for periodical payments by the person to whom they are bailed ..., and
> (b) the property in the goods will pass to that person if the terms of the agreement are complied with and one or more of the following occurs—
>   (i) the exercise of an option to purchase by that person,
>   (ii) the doing of any other specified act by any party to the agreement.
>   (iii) the happening of any other specified event.

If the option to purchase is exercised, the purchase price is usually a nominal sum. The customer does not agree to continue to hire the goods until the end of the period. If the goods are not hired until the end of the period the customer will lose the right to buy the goods. You might therefore have written something like, 'Harold is hiring the car for up to three years, and if he continues to hire it until the end of the period his last payment will buy the car for a nominal sum.'

(b) It is possible that Harold will be making the hire-purchase agreement with the garage, and that he and the garage will be the only two parties involved. It is more likely that there will be a triangular transaction, involving a finance company. If this is the case, the garage will have sold the car to the finance company, who will then have made the hire-purchase agreement with Harold. Harold might not be aware that this is what had happened.

ACTIVITY 2/6

Read the speeches of Lord Herschell LC and Lord Watson in *Helby* v *Mathews* [1895] AC 471 in *Cases and Materials* (2.2). Then write down why the Sale of Goods Act 1979 does not apply to contracts of hire-purchase.

You should have written that as a hire-purchase contract does not impose on the hirer any obligation to buy the goods, it is not a sale of goods. Therefore the provisions of the 1979 Act do not apply to such contracts. Under a contract of hire-purchase the hirer has an option to buy the goods, but has not agreed to buy them.

A conditional sale agreement is one under which the property in the goods is not transferred to the buyer until all the conditions of the contract have been fulfilled. Almost invariably these conditions relate to the payment of the price. If the price is to be paid by instalments then a conditional sale agreement can be very similar indeed to a hire-purchase agreement. (So much so that for certain purposes, including the one in issue in *Forthright Finance Ltd* v *Carlyle Ltd* considered immediately below, the Consumer

Credit Act 1974 regards them as the same thing.) However, as far as the statutory implied terms are concerned, a conditional sale is governed by the Sale of Goods Act 1979 whereas a hire-purchase agreement is governed by the implied terms in the Supply of Goods (Implied Terms) Act 1973. (As we shall see in **Chapter 3**, the terms implied by the two statutes are virtually identical. The distinction is only important because the correct statute must be applied.)

In the following case the Court of Appeal again considered the difference between hire-purchase and conditional sale.

Forthright Finance Ltd v *Carlyle Finance Ltd* [1997] 4 All ER 90
The plaintiff company owned a Ford car which it delivered to a dealer under an agreement described as a hire-purchase agreement. Under the agreement the dealer had an option to purchase the car and was to be taken as having exercised that option when all the instalments had been paid. The property in the car would then pass to the dealer unless the dealer elected not to take title. The dealer delivered the car to a customer who acquired good title to the car. This deal was financed by the defendant company to whom the dealer purported to transfer ownership of the car. In proceedings between the two parties the question arose as to whether the agreement between the plaintiffs and the dealer was a hire-purchase agreement or a conditional sale agreement. If the deal was a hire-purchase agreement then the defendants would be liable to the plaintiffs in conversion, because when the deal was made between the dealer and the defendants the car would still have belonged to the plaintiffs. (Title would not have passed from the plaintiffs to the dealer until the dealer exercised the option to purchase.) If the agreement was a conditional sale agreement the dealer would have agreed to buy the car. If this was the case then s. 25(1) of the 1979 Act would allow the dealer to pass good title to the defendants and so there would have been no conversion. (It is not necessary for you to understand why or how s. 25(1) has this effect.) Held: The agreement between the plaintiff and the dealer was a conditional sale agreement because the dealer was contractually obliged to pay all of the instalments. The term allowing him not to exercise the option to purchase would only be exercised in the most exceptional circumstances and did not therefore affect the true nature of the agreement. (It is worth noting that it was only because the conditional sale between the plaintiffs and the dealer was a commercial agreement, and therefore not a conditional sale within the meaning of the Consumer Credit Act 1974, that property could pass under s. 25 of the 1979 Act. In conditional sales to which the Consumer Credit Act 1974 applies s. 25(2) of the 1979 Act excludes the operation of s. 25(1).)

An extract from the judgment of Phillips LJ, in which he considered the decision in *Helby* v *Mathews*, can be read in *Cases and Materials* (2.2).

2.5 Contracts to Transfer the Property in Goods, Contracts of Hire and Contracts for the Supply of a Service

The Supply of Goods and Services Act 1982 implies terms very similar to those implied by the Sale of Goods Act 1979 into contracts for the transfer of the property in goods, and contracts of hire. Terms which have no equivalent in the 1979 Act are implied into contracts to supply a service.

2.5.1 CONTRACTS FOR THE TRANSFER OF THE PROPERTY IN GOODS

Section 1 of the Supply of Goods and Services Act 1982 defines the contracts concerned:

> (1) In this Act . . . 'contract for the transfer of goods' means a contract under which one person transfers or agrees to transfer to another the property in goods, other than an excepted contract.

DEFECTIVE GOODS AND SERVICES: CLASSIFICATION OF TRANSACTIONS

(2) For the purposes of this section an excepted contract means any of the following—
   (a) a contract of sale of goods;
   (b) a hire-purchase agreement;
   (c) a contract under which the property in goods is (or is to be) transferred in exchange for trading stamps on their redemption;
   (d) a transfer or agreement to transfer which is made by deed and for which there is no consideration other than the presumed consideration imported by the deed;
   (e) a contract intended to operate by way of mortgage, pledge, charge or other security.

The excepted contracts listed in s. 1(2)(a)–(c) are excluded because they are dealt with by other pre-existing statutes. (In the case of acquiring property in goods in exchange for trading stamps the statute in question is the Trading Stamps Act 1964, the effect of which is considered in **Chapter 3**. The types of contracts listed in s. 1(2)(d) and (e) are excluded on the grounds of policy.)

SAQ 2/3

Would the following be examples of contracts for the transfer of property in goods, as defined by s. 1?

(a) Anne visits a garage and barters her big old car for a new small car. (No money changes hands.)

(b) Anne visits a garage and buys a new car for £12,000. She trades in her old car for £4,000, and this amount is set off against the price.

(c) A garage advertises that customers who collect tokens when buying petrol will be able to exchange these tokens for certain goods. Bert collects tokens every time he buys petrol. When Bert has sufficient tokens he exchanges these for a set of wine glasses.

(d) As a valued customer of a certain garage, Charlene is given a free tankful of petrol.

(e) David pays a contractor to install central heating in his house.

(a) As a contract of barter this agreement would be a contract for the transfer of goods, within the meaning of s. 1 of the Supply of Goods and Services Act 1982. The agreement is one under which the garage agrees to transfer property in the new car to Anne, and Anne agrees to transfer property in the old car to the garage. Neither contract is a sale of goods as neither party paid a money consideration.

(b) This is likely to be a sale of goods, and therefore covered by the Sale of Goods Act 1979, rather than be within s. 1 of the 1982 Act. Earlier in this chapter we examined *Aldridge v Johnson* (1857) 7 E & B 885 in which 32 bullocks valued at £192 were exchanged for 100 quarters of barley, valued at £215, the balance of £23 being paid in cash. We saw that the court assumed that this amounted to two contracts of sale. In *G.J. Dawson (Clapham) Ltd* v *H & G Dutfield* [1936] 2 All ER 232 the plaintiff sold two lorries to the defendant for £475. The plaintiff was to be paid £250 cash and to receive two other lorries valued at £225 within one month. These two lorries were not delivered in the time stipulated. The plaintiff could therefore claim £225, as the balance of the purchase price, as Hilberry J held that this was a contract of sale of goods. (This judgment is reproduced in *Cases and Materials* (2.3).) Either way, Anne will be regarded as having bought the new car and the 1979 Act, rather than the 1982 Act, will govern the contract.

(c) This contract would be within s. 1 of the 1982 Act. The contract is one under which one person agrees to transfer to another the property in goods, and the contract is not a sale of goods. (See the decision of the House of Lords in *Esso Petroleum Ltd* v *Commissioners of Customs & Excise* [1976] 1 All ER 117, above at 2.3.1.)

(d) If this was a genuine gift then it would not be within the definition set out in s. 1 as it would not be a contract. An agreement cannot be a contract if one party supplies no consideration to the other.

(e) This contract to supply 'work and materials' would be a contract for the transfer of property in goods. The question to ask here is what the essence of the contract is. Earlier we saw that in *Lee* v *Griffin* the contract to make a set of false teeth was a contract of sale of goods, whereas the contract to paint a portrait in *Robinson* v *Graves* was not. A contract to paint a portrait would be classified by s. 1 of 1982 Act as a contract for the transfer of the property in the goods. Some of the old decisions as to whether or not contracts were sales of goods are hard to reconcile. (Often they were concerned with whether or not a contract was a sale of goods because until 1954 s. 4 of the Sale of Goods Act 1893 made a contract of sale of goods to the value of £10 unenforceable unless there was written evidence of it. There was no such rule for contracts other than sales of goods.) In the past a contract to print a book (*Clay* v *Yates* (1856) 1 H & N 73) and a contract for a vet to inject cattle (*Dodd* v *Wilson* [1946] 2 All ER 691) were not classified as sales of goods; contracts to buy a meal in a restaurant (*Lockett* v *Charles Ltd* [1938] 4 All ER 170) and to supply and fit a carpet (*Philip Head & Sons Ltd* v *Showfronts Ltd* [1970] 1 Lloyd's Rep 140) were classified as sales of goods.

It should be noticed that the 'work and materials' contracts, such as to install central heating in a house, have two sets of terms implied into them. As such a contract is one to transfer the property in goods, ss. 2–5 of the Supply of Goods and Services Act 1982 imply terms which are virtually identical to the terms implied by ss. 12–15 of the Sale of Goods Act 1979. As the contract could also be classified as a contract to supply a service, s. 13 of the 1982 Act implies a different term, that the supplier of the service will use reasonable care and skill. In order to prove that this latter term has been breached, the consumer will need to prove negligence. Liability under the 1979 Act, and under ss. 2–5 of the 1982 Act is strict. So for example in a contract to supply central heating, if the boiler supplied is not of satisfactory quality then liability will be strict as this is a contract to transfer the property in the boiler. If the central heating does not work as it should for reasons unknown, then the consumer will need to prove that the supplier did not install the central heating using reasonable care and skill.

2.5.2 CONTRACTS OF HIRE

ACTIVITY 2/7

In as simple a sentence as possible, describe a contract of hire.

DEFECTIVE GOODS AND SERVICES: CLASSIFICATION OF TRANSACTIONS

You might have written something like, 'A contract of hire is one under which a person gains possession of goods, but not ownership, in return for a payment of rent.' Such a definition would be essentially correct. The owner who gives up possession is best referred to as the bailor, while the person who pays for possession is best referred to as the bailee. (The word 'hirer' is inconvenient because it can apply equally to either the bailor or to the bailee.) The bailee has no option to purchase the goods. When the contract comes to an end the bailee is bound to return the goods to the bailor, or deal with them as the bailor directs. Section 6 of the 1982 Act gives the following definition:

(1) In this Act a 'contract for the hire of goods' means a contract under which one person bails or agrees to bail goods to another by way of hire, other than an excepted contract.
(2) For the purposes of this section an excepted contract means any of the following—
  (a) a hire-purchase agreement;
  (b) a contract under which goods are (or are to be) bailed in exchange for trading stamps on their redemption.

Section 6(3) of the 1982 Act provides that for the purposes of that statute a contract can be a contract of hire even if goods or services are also supplied under the contract and even if the bailee's consideration is not the payment of money. So again, a contract of hire may also be classified as a contract of service. If the goods hired are not of satisfactory quality then liability will be strict under s. 9 of the 1982 Act. If the service element of the contract is defective then the consumer will need to prove negligence in order to establish that s. 13 of the 1982 Act has been breached.

2.5.3 CONTRACTS TO SUPPLY SERVICES

Part II of the Supply of Goods and Services Act 1982, incorporating ss. 12–16, is headed 'supply of services'. Section 12 describes the contracts with which Part II is concerned:

(1) In this Act a 'contract for the supply of a service' means, subject to subsection (2) below, a contract under which a person ('the supplier') agrees to carry out a service.
(2) For the purposes of this Act, a contract of service or apprenticeship is not a contract for the supply of a service.
(3) Subject to subsection (2) above, a contract is a contract for the supply of a service for the purposes of this Act whether or not goods are also—
  (a) transferred or to be transferred, or
  (b) bailed or to be bailed by way of hire,
under the contract, and whatever is the nature of the consideration for which the service is to be carried out.

SAQ 2/4

David makes three contracts as follows:

(a) He has his watch repaired at a jeweller's shop. This involves the jeweller putting a new cog in the watch. After the repair is finished the watch soon ceases to work.

(b) He buys a new video and TV from a shop. The contract requires the shop to set the equipment up in David's house. A shop employee does this. The television cannot receive Channel 4.

(c) David has a central heating system installed in his house. Two of the radiators supplied under the contract do not heat up as they should.

Which, if any, of the three contracts are contracts to provide a service? Which statutes will imply terms into the various contracts?

The classification of contracts such as these is not an exact science. We are looking for the substance of the contract, but the borders between the different types of transactions are often blurred. My own views are as follows:

(a) The repair of the watch looks like a contract to supply a service. (Even though goods, the cog, were also transferred.) It would therefore be governed by the Supply of Goods and Services Act 1982. Section 13 of the 1982 Act would imply a term that the service be supplied using reasonable care and skill. Section 4 would imply a term of strict liability requiring the actual cog supplied to be of satisfactory quality.

(b) This would appear to be a contract of sale of goods, even though the shop has also to provide a service. The Sale of Goods Act 1979 would therefore govern the contract, s. 14(2) implying a term of strict liability as to the satisfactory quality of the television sold. The setting up of the television is a contract for the supply of a service and so s. 13 of the 1982 Act would imply a term that it was performed using reasonable care and skill. Section 12(3) of the 1982 Act makes it plain that the fact that a transaction has been classified as a sale of goods does not also prevent the transaction from being a contract for the supply of a service.

(c) This would seem to be both a contract for the transfer of goods and a contract for the supply of a service. Two sections of the Supply of Goods and Services Act 1982 would therefore imply terms into the contract. Section 13 would imply a term that the installation of the central heating was supplied using reasonable care and skill. Section 4 would imply a term of strict liability that the goods supplied under the contract were of satisfactory quality.

ACTIVITY 2/8

Earlier in this chapter we saw that parts (a), (b), (d), (f), (g), (i) and (j) of Activity 2/1 were not sales of goods. Write down whether any of these contracts would be governed by the Supply of Goods (Implied Terms) Act 1973 or by the Supply of Goods and Services Act 1982.

You should have written along the following lines. Transaction (a) is a contract of hire-purchase and is therefore governed by the 1973 Act. Transactions (b) and (d) are both contracts for the transfer of the property in goods and are therefore governed by the 1982 Act. Transaction (f) would not be within the ambit of either statute. It is a transfer of an interest in land rather than a contract for the transfer of the property in goods or a contract to supply a service. Transaction (g) would not be governed by either statute. Obviously the contract is not one of hire or to provide a service. Nor is it a contract for the transfer of the property in goods as the shares are not goods. Transaction (i) is obviously a contract to supply a service and is therefore governed by the 1982 Act. Transaction (j) would be a contract to supply a service, as the substance of the contract is the sculptor's use of skill to produce the sculpture. In that goods were also transferred, it would also be a contract to transfer the property in goods.

2.6 End of Chapter Assessment Question

Indicate whether the following transactions would be sales of goods, contracts of hire-purchase, contracts for the transfer of the property in goods, contracts of hire, contracts for the supply of a service or none of these. Where the transactions are sales of goods, indicate (whenever possible) whether the goods are specific or unascertained, and whether the goods are existing or future goods. You should indicate these matters by writing the type of transaction and the words 'specific', 'unascertained', 'existing' or 'future' in the space below the various transactions.

(a) Alice agrees to buy a house for £55,000.

(b) In a shop, Bill uses his credit card to pay £45 for a second-hand watch.

(c) Carol books a holiday for £220.

(d) Donald agrees to buy a car which has yet to be manufactured.

(e) Elaine pays a plumber £1,000 to install central heating in her flat.

(f) Fred pays £85 to have his car serviced.

(g) George buys four new car tyres, to be fitted by the seller.

(h) Harold agrees to pay a garage £24,000 for a second-hand Rolls Royce which is currently owned by another of the garage's customers. The sale is conditional on the garage itself being able to acquire the car.

(i) Ian hires a car for one week for £100.

(j) Jane exchanges her record player for a television.

(k) As part of a supermarket's advertising promotion, Keith is given a 'free' bottle of wine on account of having purchased £50 worth of beer.

A complete list of the answers can be found in *Cases and Materials* (2.5).

CHAPTER THREE

CONTRACT BASED REMEDIES: STATUTORY IMPLIED TERMS AS TO QUALITY AND FITNESS

3.1 Objectives

By the end of this chapter you should be able to:

- describe the circumstances in which goods are sold or supplied 'in the course of a business;

- recognise the circumstances in which the statutory terms as to satisfactory quality will not be implied into a consumer transaction;

- describe the terms as to 'satisfactory quality' which the Sale of Goods Act 1979, the Supply of Goods (Implied Terms) Act 1973 and the Supply of Goods and Services Act 1982 imply;

- evaluate how the new standard of 'satisfactory quality' has altered the old standard of 'merchantable quality';

- describe the terms as to 'fitness for purpose', which are implied by the 1979, 1973 and 1982 Acts;

- explain the circumstances in which the implied terms as to fitness for purpose will not be implied into consumer transactions;

- apply the requirements of satisfactory quality and fitness for purpose to problem situations;

- analyse the requirement that a person who supplies a service in the course of a business will carry out the service with reasonable care and skill.

3.2 Introduction

Sections 12–15 of the Sale of Goods Act 1979 imply five terms, which favour the buyer, into contracts of sale of goods. The buyer and the seller of the goods have no need to mention these terms, as the 1979 Act automatically incorporates them into their contract. Terms which are virtually identical to those in the 1979 Act are implied into contracts of hire, hire-purchase and contracts for the transfer of the property in goods by the Supply of Goods (Implied Terms) Act 1973 and the Supply of Goods and Services Act 1982.

STATUTORY IMPLIED TERMS AS TO QUALITY AND FITNESS

Terms which are different in their effect are implied into contracts under which a service is supplied in the course of a business. In **Chapter 2** we classified the types of contracts which consumers might make and identified which of the three statutes would imply terms into the various types of transactions. In this chapter and **Chapter 4** we examine the substance of the terms which are implied into consumer contracts.

SAQ 3/1

Let us assume that last week you went into a shop to buy a new printer for your computer. You gave the shop assistant details of your computer and explained that the printer was to be used with this computer. The assistant described a certain type of printer and said that it would suit your needs. Relying on the assistant, you bought the printer.

The Sale of Goods Act 1979 would imply four terms in your favour. What do you think these terms might be? Write down any which occur to you.

You might have known, or have guessed, that the Sale of Goods Act 1979 would imply the following terms: that the shop owned the printer and passed ownership to you (s. 12); that the printer corresponded with the description given by the assistant (s. 13); that the printer was of satisfactory quality, and would therefore work as well as a reasonable person would expect (s. 14(2)); that the printer was fit for your purpose and would therefore work well with your computer (s. 14(3)). If the sale had been a sale of goods by sample (which in this case it was not), s. 15 would have implied a term that the bulk of the goods would correspond with the sample.

Each of the five terms implied into contracts of sale and into analogous contracts needs to be considered in detail. However, some of the terms are more important to consumers than others, and it seems best to consider the terms in order of their importance to consumers. The simplest way to examine the implied terms is to consider in detail each of the terms implied by the Sale of Goods Act 1979 and then consider how, if at all, the corresponding terms implied by the Supply of Goods (Implied Terms) Act 1973 and the Supply of Goods and Services Act 1982 differ.

In this chapter we examine the three terms which are most important to consumers: that goods sold or supplied are of satisfactory quality; that goods sold or supplied are fit for the consumer's purpose; and that services supplied in the course of a business are carried out using reasonable care and skill. In **Chapter 4** we examine the three other implied terms.

3.3 Quality in Business Sales

When goods are sold otherwise than in the course of a business, then the Sale of Goods Act 1979 implies no term as to the quality of the goods (s. 14(1)). It may well be that the goods are sold by description, and if this is the case then the goods will have to match the description, as we shall see in **Chapter 4**. However, if there is no description, or if

STATUTORY IMPLIED TERMS AS TO QUALITY AND FITNESS

the description does not relate to the quality of the goods, then the buyer has no statutory guarantee of quality. For example, if a private seller sells a bicycle to a buyer, making it plain that what is being sold is the bicycle which they both can see, without any guarantee of quality, then the buyer will not be able to complain about the quality of the bicycle, no matter how poor this might be.

However, s. 14(2) and (3) of the Sale of Goods Act 1979 do imply terms as to the quality of the goods into sales made 'in the course of a business'. So first we must decide when a sale is made in the course of a business, then we must examine the terms which are implied into such sales. (In *Cases and Materials* (3.1), s. 14 is reproduced in full.)

3.3.1 WHEN ARE GOODS SOLD 'IN THE COURSE OF A BUSINESS'?

Both s. 14(2) and (3) begin with the words, 'Where the seller sells goods in the course of a business...'. The Sale of Goods Act 1979 does not go on to define exactly when a seller does sell goods in the course of a business, and until recently there was surprisingly little case law on the matter. A fairly narrow test evolved, based on the application of cases decided under the Trade Descriptions Act 1968 and the Unfair Contract Terms Act 1977. The 1968 Act imposes criminal liability on those who apply false trade descriptions 'in the course of a trade or business'. The 1977 Act defines a consumer as a person who, while not acting in the course of business himself, does deal with a person who makes the contract 'in the course of a business'. It was thought that cases decided on the meaning of words in the 1968 and the 1977 Acts could be applied to the meaning of 'in the course of a business' in the Sale of Goods Act 1979. The Court of Appeal considered the meaning of s. 14(2) and words 'in the course of a business' in the following case.

Stevenson v *Rogers* [1999] 1 All ER 613
The defendant sold a fishing boat to the plaintiff. The boat was not being used as stock in trade at the time of the sale. The plaintiff claimed that the boat was not of merchantable quality (the case arose before the requirement of merchantable quality was changed to a requirement of satisfactory quality). The trial judge ruled that the boat was not sold in the course of the defendant's trade or business and that s. 14(2) therefore did not apply.
Held: The boat was sold in the course of the defendant's business and therefore s. 14(2) did imply a term requiring the boat to be of merchantable quality.

ACTIVITY 3/1

Read the judgment of Potter LJ in *Stevenson* v *Rogers* in *Cases and Materials* (3.1.1) and answer the following questions:

(a) Why was the Court of Appeal free from any constraints imposed by *Havering LBC* v *Stevenson* [1970] 3 All ER 609, *Davies* v *Sumner* [1984] 3 All ER 831 and *R & B Customs Brokers Co. Ltd* v *United Dominions Trust Ltd* [1988] 1 All ER 847?

(b) In what way were the Sale of Goods Act 1893 and the Supply of Goods (Implied Terms) Act 1973 relevant?

(c) How should a consolidating Act be construed?

(d) What mischief in s. 14(2) of the Sale of Goods Act 1893 did the 1973 Act seek to remedy?

(e) How was this mischief discovered?

(f) Why was it a case of the tail wagging the dog to apply the decision in *R & B Customs Brokers Co. Ltd* to s. 14(2) of the Sale of Goods Act 1979?

(g) For the purposes of s. 14(2) of the 1979 Act, when is a sale made 'in the course of a business'?

(a) These cases could be distinguished. They were authorities on the meaning of words used in the Trade Descriptions Act 1968 and the Unfair Contract Terms Act 1977. The court could use the tools of construction available to it to construe the words of s. 14(2) of the 1979 Act at their face value.

(b) The Sale of Goods Act 1893 implied a term as to merchantable quality only where the seller was a dealer in the type of goods sold. The Supply of Goods (Implied Terms) Act 1973 changed the law so that the term was implied where the seller sold goods 'in the course of a business'. The Sale of Goods Act 1979 was a consolidating Act which made no material amendments to the statutes it consolidated.

(c) A consolidating statute should be construed in the same way as any other. But if real doubts remained about the meaning of words in a consolidating Act the words were to be construed as if they remained in the earlier Act. So the 1979 Act should be regarded as no more than the sum of its parts and the words in question could be construed as if they remained in the 1973 Act.

(d) The mischief in s. 14(2) of the 1893 Act which the 1973 Act sought to remedy was the restrictive effect of the requirement of satisfactory quality. It did not impose on every business seller the requirement of merchantable quality. It only imposed that requirement on those who habitually dealt in the goods sold.

(e) The mischief was discovered by reference to *Hansard* and the statement of the Minister who introduced the Bill which became the 1973 Act.

(f) It was a case of the tail wagging the dog because s. 14(2) was the primary provision in the overall scheme of increased protection for buyers which the 1973 Act initiated. *R & B Customs Brokers* was a decision on the meaning of s. 12 of the Unfair Contract Terms Act 1977, a much lesser provision conferring protection on buyers.

(g) For the purposes of s. 14(2) of the 1979 Act the words 'in the course of a business' should be taken at face value. Any sale made in the course of a business is within s. 14(2), without the need to prove any degree of regularity of such sales. So sporadic sales which are no more than incidental to the seller's business are included. By contrast, purely private sales outside the confines of the business carried on by the seller are not within s. 14(2).

Where an auctioneer sells on behalf of a private seller the auctioneer can free himself of liability under s. 14(2) and (3) but only if the buyer is aware that the auctioneer is selling on behalf of a private seller, or if reasonable steps have been taken to bring this to the buyer's notice (s. 14(5)).

STATUTORY IMPLIED TERMS AS TO QUALITY AND FITNESS

3.4 Satisfactory Quality (Section 14(2))

3.4.1 BUSINESS SALES TO WHICH SECTION 14(2) WILL NOT APPLY

We have already mentioned that s. 14(2) implies a term that goods sold in the course of a business are of satisfactory quality. However, s. 14(2) does not imply such a term into all sales made in the course of a business. Before examining the meaning of satisfactory quality, we must first identify the circumstances in which the term will not be implied.

Section 14(2C) states that the term implied by s. 14(2):

> ... does not extend to any matter making the quality of goods unsatisfactory—
> (a) which is specifically drawn to the buyer's attention before the contract is made, [or]
> (b) where the buyer examines the goods before the contract is made, which that examination ought to reveal ...

This section therefore mentions two instances where a seller of unsatisfactory goods will not incur liability under s. 14(2), even if the goods were sold in the course of a business. We need to consider each of these in turn.

3.4.1.1 Defects specifically drawn to buyer's attention

If the defects which make the goods unsatisfactory are specifically drawn to the buyer's attention before the contract is made, then the buyer will not be able to later claim that these particular defects made the goods unsatisfactory. To take an obvious example, if a department store sells a china tea set at a reduced price, pointing out that one of the teacups is cracked, then the buyer will not be able to reject the tea set as unsatisfactory merely because of the crack in that teacup.

Nor will the buyer be able to claim that the goods are of unsatisfactory quality merely because the defect which was specifically pointed out proves to be more costly to rectify than was at first imagined.

Bartlett v *Sydney Marcus Ltd* [1965] 1 WLR 1013
A second-hand Jaguar was sold by a garage. The seller pointed out that the car's clutch was defective, and said that the defect could be rectified by carrying out a minor repair. The dealer offered to sell the car as it was for £550, or to repair the clutch and then sell the car for £575. The buyer took the car as it was for £550. The repair to the clutch was a fairly major one and cost £84 7s 11d. The buyer claimed this sum from the seller as damages under s. 14(2). Held: The buyer could not claim damages under s. 14(2). The defect in the clutch had been drawn to the buyer's attention, and could not therefore render the car of unmerchantable (now unsatisfactory) quality.

You should notice that s. 14(2C) only gives protection as regards defects specifically drawn to the buyer's attention.

SAQ 3/2

Assume that the garage in *Bartlett* v *Sydney Marcus Ltd* had made no mention of the clutch, but had knocked £25 off the original asking price 'to take account of any repairs which might prove necessary'. Would it have been possible for the buyer to claim that the defective clutch made the car of unmerchantable (now unsatisfactory) quality?

Yes. The defective clutch would not have been specifically pointed out to the buyer, and s. 14(2C) would therefore not apply. If goods are sold as 'shop-soiled' this will not evade the requirement that they be of satisfactory quality. However, the words 'shop-soiled' will be part of the description referred to in the definition of satisfactory quality (i.e., 'taking account of any description of the goods' — s. 14(2A)).

3.4.1.2 Buyer examines the goods prior to sale

A buyer of goods has no duty to examine the goods before purchasing them. If a business sells goods which are obviously unsatisfactory, the business will not be able to escape liability on the grounds that the defects would have been quite apparent to any buyer who cared to look at the goods.

But as we have seen, s. 14(2C) says that a buyer who does make an examination will not be able to claim that the goods are unsatisfactory in respect of defects which that examination ought to have revealed.

SAQ 3/3

George buys a second-hand television from a shop which repairs, and occasionally sells, electrical goods. George spends a few minutes examining the exterior of the television, and then buys it for £65. The shopkeeper explains that the television's picture quality cannot be seen, as the shop's aerial has been blown down in a gale.

(a) Is this sale made in the course of a business?

(b) Could George claim that the television was of unsatisfactory quality on the grounds that:

  (i) The television could not get a proper picture?

  (ii) The screen was slightly cracked?

(a) This would clearly be a sale 'in the course of a business'.

(b) (i) George could claim that the poor picture made the television of unsatisfactory quality. His examination of the television in the shop could not have revealed that the picture was poor. Goods sold as second-hand are not required to reach the standard of goods sold as new, but obviously this television would not have been of satisfactory quality.

  (ii) George could not claim that the crack in the screen made the television of unsatisfactory quality. His examination in the shop should have revealed the crack.

3.4.2 GOODS 'SUPPLIED UNDER THE CONTRACT'

Section 14(2) requires goods 'supplied under the contract' to be of satisfactory quality. Case law has established that this means not only the goods being sold, but also any packaging within which the goods are contained. But what if if the packaging has to be returned to the seller?

STATUTORY IMPLIED TERMS AS TO QUALITY AND FITNESS

ACTIVITY 3/2

Read *Geddling* v *Marsh* [1920] 1 KB 668 in *Cases and Materials* (3.2.1). Then write down:

(a) Whether the bottle in which the mineral water was contained was sold.

(b) Whether the bottle was supplied under the contract of sale.

(c) Whether the buyer succeeded under s. 14 of the Sale of Goods Act 1893.

You should have written that:

(a) The bottle was not sold, it had to be returned to the manufacturer.

(b) The bottle was supplied under the contract of sale.

(c) The buyer did succeed under s. 14. The section covers not only what is sold, but also that which is supplied under the contract of sale.

3.4.3 THE REQUIREMENT OF SATISFACTORY QUALITY

The Sale and Supply of Goods Act 1994 amended s. 14(2) of the Sale of Goods Act 1979. Prior to this amendment, s. 14(2) required goods sold in the course of business to be of 'merchantable quality'. Previously, s. 14(6) provided that:

> Goods ... are of merchantable quality ... if they are as fit for the purpose or purposes for which goods of that kind are commonly bought as it is reasonable to expect having regard to any description applied to them, the price (if relevant) and all the other relevant circumstances.

As we shall see, the exact meaning of merchantable quality caused considerable difficulty. In the light of this, s. 1 of the Sale and Supply of Goods Act 1994 changed the requirement of merchantable quality to a requirement of satisfactory quality.

Section 14(2A) of the Sale of Goods Act 1979 now defines the meaning of satisfactory quality:

> For the purposes of this Act, goods are of satisfactory quality if they meet the standard that a reasonable person would regard as satisfactory, taking account of any description of the goods, the price (if relevant) and all the other relevant circumstances.

SAQ 3/4

Is the new test of satisfactory quality subjective or objective? There is some similarity between the definitions of merchantable and satisfactory quality. What is the difference between the old test and the new one?

The new test is objective. The standard required is that which the reasonable person, rather than the buyer and the seller, would regard as satisfactory. The old test of merchantable quality required the goods to be as fit for their commonly bought purposes as one could reasonably expect. The new test requires the goods to meet the standard that a reasonable person would regard as satisfactory. Under both tests regard may be had to the price, description and other relevant circumstances.

It must be said that the new definition of satisfactory quality does not appear to be all that different from the old definition of merchantable quality. However, s. 14(2B) of the 1979 Act now goes on to say:

> For the purposes of this Act, the quality of goods includes their state and condition and the following (among others) are in appropriate cases aspects of the quality of goods—
> (a) fitness for all the purposes for which goods of the kind in question are commonly supplied,
> (b) appearance and finish,
> (c) freedom from minor defects,
> (d) safety, and
> (e) durability.

This detailed description of 'aspects of the quality of goods' shows that the satisfactory quality test is stricter than the old merchantable quality test. To understand the new requirement, we must know something of the old merchantable quality test and the problems which it caused.

3.4.4 THE DIFFICULTIES WHICH THE TEST OF MERCHANTABLE QUALITY CAUSED

The requirement that goods sold in the course of a business be of satisfactory quality is, to consumers, the most important provision of the Sale of Goods Act 1979. However, it must be realised that in 1893, when the original Sale of Goods Act was passed, the concept of a 'consumer' would have been quite alien to both the judiciary and to Parliament. The original Act was designed to regulate the affairs of businessmen and merchants. The meaning of 'merchantable' was fairly clear, at least to the judiciary and to merchants. But over the years, the meaning of merchantable became less clear. (The definition of merchantable quality which used to be contained in s. 14(6) of the 1979 Act was only introduced in 1973.) When it is remembered that for over 100 years s. 14 imposed a term as to merchantable quality into every contract under which a business sold goods, it is hardly surprising that a mass of case law dealing with the meaning of the term evolved.

It is perhaps a little unfortunate that today's consumers have to rely on a statute which sought to make rules for Victorian merchants. (Of course the 1893 Act could always have been used by a Victorian 'consumer' who bought goods of unmerchantable quality.) Nevertheless, that is the state of affairs, and so we need to examine what the term as to merchantable quality meant, as it is so similar in definition to the requirement of satisfactory quality. As we shall see, most of the important cases on the meaning of 'merchantable' were not consumer cases. They were cases between two businesses. However, it is these cases we need to examine to discover the meaning of merchantable. If we were to concentrate solely on cases involving consumers then we would not fully understand the meaning of either merchantable or satisfactory quality.

Broadly speaking, in recent years the courts adopted two tests — the acceptability test and the usability test — to decide whether or not goods sold were merchantable. Unfortunately, it was never clear which test a court might use. Often the two tests would arrive at the same conclusion, but sometimes they would not.

STATUTORY IMPLIED TERMS AS TO QUALITY AND FITNESS

The *acceptability test* held that goods were merchantable if they were in such a state that a reasonable buyer would still have bought the goods at the same price, and without any special terms, if he or she had known of their actual condition, including any defects, when making the purchase.

The *usability test* held that the goods were merchantable if a reasonable buyer could have used the goods for any of the purposes for which goods of that contract description were commonly used.

ACTIVITY 3/3

The facts of four of the leading cases on the meaning of merchantable quality are summarised below. Read the extracts of the judgments from the four cases in *Cases and Materials* (3.2.2). In each case decide whether the court reached its decision on the basis of the acceptability test or the usability test. Then delete the 'Usability/ Acceptability' box as appropriate.

Kendall (Henry) & Sons v *William Lillico & Sons Ltd* [1969] 2 AC 31
The plaintiff, the owner of a game farm, bought foodstuff for his pheasants from S. The foodstuff contained Brazilian groundnut extract which had become slightly mouldy. The effect of this was that the plaintiff's pheasants died. S had bought the Brazilian nut extract from G who had bought it from K. S paid damages to the plaintiff and then claimed these damages from G, who in turn claimed them from K. Brazilian nut extract is an ingredient of foodstuffs for many animals such as cattle. The mould would not have injured animals such as cattle.
Held: S's claim failed. The groundnut extract was of merchantable quality because it could safely have been used as cattle food, one of its main purposes.

Usability/~~Acceptability~~   (Delete one)

Sumner Permain & Co. v *Webb & Co.* [1922] 1 KB 55
A dealer bought a large quantity of tonic water, intending to export it to Argentina. The Argentinian authorities refused to let the tonic water into the country as it contained salicylic acid. Other countries would not have been concerned about this acid, which is an ingredient of aspirin, but Argentinian law did not allow it to be present in drinks. The dealer rejected the tonic water on the grounds that it was not of merchantable quality. The dealer had told the seller that the tonic water was destined for Argentina. The seller did not know that Argentinian law prohibited the sale of drinks containing salicylic acid.
Held: The tonic water was of merchantable quality because it could have been used for just about any purpose other than the one for which the buyer intended to use it.

Usability/~~Acceptability~~   (Delete one)

Shine v *General Guarantee Corporation Ltd* [1988] 1 All ER 911
A motorist bought a second-hand specialist sports car which gave him few problems. However, when he discovered that the car had been involved in a crash and totally submerged in water he sought to reject it under s. 14(2).
Held: The car was not of merchantable quality. Bush J, at 915, said that no member of the public who was aware of the car's history 'would touch [it] with a barge pole unless they could get it at a substantially reduced price to reflect the risk they were taking'.

~~Usability~~/Acceptability   (Delete one)

Brown (BS) & Sons Ltd v *Craiks Ltd* [1970] 1 All ER 823
B ordered a quantity of fabric from S. This type of fabric could be used to make clothes or it could be used industrially. B intended to use the fabric to make dresses, but did not

say so. S thought the fabric was to be used industrially. The price B paid was slightly higher than was usual for industrial fabric. B rejected the cloth on the grounds that, as it was not fit to be made into clothes, it was not of merchantable quality.

Held: The cloth was merchantable. The cloth was perfectly fit for industrial use and the higher price had not indicated that it was to be used to make dresses.

Usability / Acceptability   (Delete one)

You should have calculated that the courts used the two tests as follows: *Kendall (Henry) & Sons*, the usability test; *Sumner Permain & Co.*, the usability test; *Shine*, the acceptability test; *Brown (BS) & Sons*, the usability test. The acceptability test, which is more favourable to the buyer, tended to be used more in cases where the buyer was a consumer, whereas the usability test tended to be used more in commercial contracts. However, there was no hard and fast distinction between commercial and consumer cases.

In order to determine the meaning of satisfactory quality it is necessary to look in turn at each of the five matters mentioned by s. 14(2B). First though, it should be appreciated that the five matters mentioned are only 'aspects' of the quality 'in appropriate cases'. The test of satisfactory quality primarily depends upon meeting the standard which a reasonable person would regard as satisfactory, having regard to the price, description and other relevant circumstances. For example, if a stock car racer while acting in the course of a business sells a car to another stock car racer, the car will most likely have a somewhat battered appearance and finish. 'Appearance and finish' is one of the aspects of quality mentioned by s. 14(2B). However, the battered appearance and finish are very unlikely to make the quality of the stock car unsatisfactory. The test of satisfactory quality is whether or not the car would meet the standard which a reasonable person would regard as satisfactory, having regard to the price, description and other relevant circumstances. Similarly, goods with minor defects which are sold at a reduced price on account of these defects might well be of satisfactory quality.

ACTIVITY 3/4

Read the report of the Law Commission on 'Sales and Supply of Goods', paras 3.1 to 3.27, in *Cases and Materials* (3.2.2). Then, on a separate sheet of paper, in one sentence or one paragraph, explain each of the matters listed below. (This Activity is likely to take between 30 minutes and one hour.)

(a) When the word 'merchantable' was used by Victorian judges, what in essence did the term mean?

(b) Why did the Law Commission feel that it was not possible to have a single formula defining the required quality of goods sold in the course of a business?

(c) Why did the Commission not think it appropriate to have different standards of quality for different types of goods or transactions?

(d) What problems would have been caused for retailers if consumers had been given a higher standard of protection, as regards quality, than other buyers?

(e) The Law Commission considered suggesting that goods should have to be of good quality. What problems would the use of such a qualitative adjective cause?

(f) In what circumstances did the Law Commission think that it would be necessary to have a list of aspects of quality?

STATUTORY IMPLIED TERMS AS TO QUALITY AND FITNESS

(g) What problems were envisaged if the quality requirement were to be based only on the expectations of a reasonable buyer?

You should have answered along the following lines:

(a) The word 'merchantable' meant to the Victorian judges that one merchant buying the goods from another would have regarded the goods as suitable.

(b) The possible circumstances are so varied that no one formula can define the required quality in every case.

(c) The Commission felt that it was not reasonably practicable to do this. If this were to be done, then in every case it would have to be ascertained what type of goods or transaction the case concerned. At the consultation stage the Law Commission had found little support for the idea of different standards.

(d) If consumers were given a higher standard of protection than others, then shopkeepers would often be the losers. Retailers would buy goods under one standard as to quality, and then sell the same goods on under a higher standard. Liability could not therefore always be passed down the line.

(e) The use of a qualitative adjective such as 'good' would cause problems where the expectations of buyer and seller were not that the quality would be good. 'Good' quality would cause problems, for example, where goods were sold as seconds or for scrap.

(f) The Commission thought that a list of aspects of quality would be necessary if the required standard was based on a single neutral adjective. The Commission considered 'proper', 'suitable' and 'appropriate.' In the event, 'satisfactory' was enacted.

(g) The Commission envisaged that the general public might not understand the requirements of such a term, and also that standards might drop if the expectations of a reasonable person became lowered in the face of sellers establishing that certain goods always had defects.

3.4.5 ASPECTS OF THE QUALITY OF GOODS

The Law Commission Report 160, 'Sale and Supply of Goods' 1987, recommended that the Sale of Goods Act 1979 should be amended to include the provisions now found in s. 14(2B). Section 14(2B) is set out above at **3.4.3**. Here we consider each of the five aspects of quality in turn. The relevant paragraphs from the Law Commission Report (paras 3.28–3.61) are set out in *Cases and Materials* (3.2.3). You should read these in conjunction with the text set out below.

3.4.5.1 'Fitness for all the purposes for which goods of the kind in question are commonly supplied'

This is a change from the requirement of the usability test that the goods be fit for any of the purposes for which goods of that kind are commonly used. This change might mean that the outcome of the following case, one of the leading cases on the meaning of merchantable quality, would now be different.

Aswan Engineering Establishment Co. v *Lupdine Ltd* [1987] 1 All ER 135
The plaintiffs bought a consignment of liquid waterproofing compound from the first defendants for shipment to Kuwait. The compound was contained in heavy duty plastic pails, and these were stored inside containers. On arrival at Kuwait the containers were

left outside in the sun in temperatures up to 70 degrees centigrade. The pails could only have tolerated these temperatures if they had been packed into the containers in a certain way. The pails melted and the compound was lost. Similar pails had been exported to other countries without any mishap. The plaintiffs sued the first defendants, claiming that the pails made the compound unmerchantable. In turn, the first defendants claimed against the second defendants, the manufacturers from whom they had bought, since the second defendants knew that the pails were to be exported to Kuwait. The contract between first and second defendants described the pails as 'heavy duty pails suitable for export'. The first defendants went into liquidation. The plaintiffs carried the case on against the second defendants (in negligence, alleging that the second defendants owed them a duty of care). Held: The pails were of merchantable quality.

The court reached its decision because the pails were fit for most of their normal purposes. At first sight it would seem that the outcome of the *Aswan* case would be different under the new test of satisfactory quality, because the pails were not fit for all of their purposes, i.e. they were not fit to be left out in the Kuwaiti sun. On the other hand, the outcome might well be the same today, because leaving the pails in the Kuwaiti sun is unlikely to be regarded as a purpose for which the pails would commonly be supplied.

3.4.5.2 'Appearance and finish'

The courts certainly considered matters of appearance and finish when considering whether goods were merchantable, as the following case shows.

Rogers v *Parish (Scarborough) Ltd* [1987] QB 933
A motorist bought a new Range Rover for over £14,000. The car had several minor defects and both parties agreed that another new Range Rover should be substituted for it. The substituted car had several problems. The motorist drove the car for six months, clocking up 5,500 miles. The sellers had made several attempts to rectify matters, but the car still had several defects. (Scratches on the paint work, leaking oil seals, and excessive engine noise.) The motorist rejected the car under s. 14(2).
Held: The car was not of merchantable quality. The way in which such cars were marketed conjured up very high expectations, and the car had failed to live up to them. Mustill LJ said, at 944, that new cars were bought not merely for 'the buyer's purpose of driving the car from one place to another but of doing so with the appropriate degree of comfort, ease of handling and reliability and, one might add, of pride of the vehicles' outward and interior appearance'.

Goods may now be regarded as unsatisfactory because of minor defects in their appearance and finish. However, it must be remembered that this will depend upon whether or not the defects would cause a reasonable person to regard the goods as unsatisfactory.

3.4.5.3 'Freedom from minor defects'

The requirement of merchantable quality was always a condition. Whenever the term was broken the buyer was therefore able to reject the goods. In some cases the courts were for this reason unwilling to regard goods as unmerchantable merely because they had minor defects which could easily be remedied. It was thought that rejection of the goods was too drastic a remedy to give to the buyer.

Millars of Falkirk Ltd v *Turpie* 1976 SLT 66
A new Ford Granada car was sold to the plaintiff by a dealer who took a Zodiac in part exchange. The Granada's power steering system leaked oil onto the plaintiff's garage floor. The defendants collected the car, repaired the leak and redelivered the car. However, the steering system again leaked oil onto the plaintiff's garage floor. This defect, which was obvious, should have been sorted out by the mere tightening of a nut and could certainly have been sorted out by installing a new power steering unit. Installing a new unit would have been quick and easy and would have cost under £25. The defendants wanted to effect this repair, but the plaintiff claimed to reject the car under s. 14(2).

STATUTORY IMPLIED TERMS AS TO QUALITY AND FITNESS

Held: The car was of merchantable quality, and so the buyer could not reject it under s. 14(2). The defect was easy to cure and it was unlikely that the car could be driven for long enough to create danger. In addition, such minor defects are relatively common in new cars.

SAQ 3/5

Would the case be decided differently under the new satisfactory quality test?

It is now plain that the approach taken in *Rogers v Parish (Scarborough) Ltd* is correct, and that when new consumer goods are bought even minor defects can make them unsatisfactory and give the buyer the right to reject. It seems likely therefore that *Millars of Falkirk Ltd v Turpie* would be decided differently under the test of satisfactory quality. (The Law Commission Report 160 thought that it should be differently decided.) The car would probably not meet the standard which the reasonable person would regard as satisfactory, (a) because it could not be driven, (b) because it was not properly finished, and (c) because it had minor defects.

The statutory implied terms remain conditions in sales where the buyer is a consumer, but can in certain circumstances be treated as warranties where the buyer is not a consumer. This matter is considered in **Chapter 4** at **4.7**.

When goods are sold second-hand, minor defects are less likely to render them unsatisfactory than if they were sold new.

3.4.5.4 'Safety'

Obviously, if goods are unsafe this is likely to mean that they do not meet the quality standard which a reasonable person would regard as satisfactory. Again though, the specific reference to safety is only an aspect of quality in appropriate cases. For example, if aluminium ladders are sold for scrap because they have been found to be unsafe, the buyer will not be able to reject on the grounds that the ladders cannot safely be used as ladders.

Many goods are safe if used properly, but unsafe if used improperly. Such goods will be regarded as unsatisfactory only if the seller fails to provide proper safety instructions.

SAQ 3/6

John buys a new gas cooker. As John has no heating in his house he uses the cooker as a heater, leaving all four gas rings burning for several hours. This causes the kitchen to become filled with carbon monoxide, because gas cookers do not have flues. John is injured by the fumes. Was the cooker unsafe?

The cooker was not unsafe. John misused it.

3.4.5.5 'Durability'

Section 14(2B) does not require the goods to remain durable for a reasonable time. Like the old requirement of merchantable quality, the new section only requires the goods to be reasonably durable when supplied. As Professor Goode puts it (*Commercial Law*, 2nd edn, Penguin, 1995, p. 325): 'As before, durability is a quality element which bites at the time of supply.' The Law Commission Report 160 took the same view. Although it is up to the buyer to prove that the goods were not reasonably durable when supplied, if a person buys goods which develop faults soon after they are supplied then there will be a strong presumption that the goods were not reasonably durable when supplied. The seller may be able to rebut this by showing that the buyer misused the goods, or failed to follow instructions, or that the goods were accidentally damaged. But if the seller cannot rebut the presumption, then the goods will be regarded as having been of unsatisfactory quality when supplied. The Law Commission Report 160 did not think it possible to provide a definite indication of how long goods should last or in what condition they should remain.

SAQ 3/7

Jane buys a new computer from a shop. One week later the computer ceases to work. At what time did the computer have to be reasonably durable? What would a court presume about the durability of the computer?

The computer would have had to have been reasonably durable when it was supplied. A court would presume that the computer was not reasonably durable when supplied, unless the shop could provide evidence of an accident or of misuse.

ACTIVITY 3/5

Re-read the four cases set out in Activity 3/3. In each case decide whether the decisions would have been the same if the new test of satisfactory quality had been applied. In particular, decide whether any of the matters ((a), (b), (c), (d) and (e)) specifically mentioned by s. 14(2B) would be relevant.

It is not possible to answer an activity such as this with any degree of certainty. (If in doubt you should argue both sides of the coin.) My own opinions are as follows. *Kendall (Henry) & Sons*: (a), (c) and (d) would seem to apply, and might make the quality of the

STATUTORY IMPLIED TERMS AS TO QUALITY AND FITNESS

goods unsatisfactory. *Sumner Permain & Co.*: assuming that tonic water is not commonly supplied to Argentina, none of the matters in s. 14(2B) would seem to make the quality of the goods unsatisfactory. There was nothing wrong with the tonic water. *Shine*: (a), (c), (d) and (e) would seem to make the quality of the goods unsatisfactory. *Brown v Craiks*: (a) might make the quality of the goods unsatisfactory.

Finally, it should be pointed out that liability under s. 14(2) is strict. The seller will be liable if the goods are unsatisfactory even though this is not in any way the seller's fault. Indeed, the seller will still be liable even if the buyer ordered goods which they both knew could be obtained only from one manufacturer (see *Wren v Holt* [1903] 1 KB 610 below).

3.4.6 SATISFACTORY QUALITY IN OTHER CONSUMER TRANSACTIONS

In **Chapter 2** we classified consumer transactions. We saw that the Supply of Goods (Implied Terms) Act 1973 implied terms into contracts of hire-purchase and the Supply of Goods and Services Act 1982 implied terms into contracts of hire and contracts for the transfer of the property in goods. If you are unclear as to the definitions of such contracts you should re-read **Chapter 2**. The terms as to satisfactory quality, in both s. 10(2) of the 1973 Act and ss. 4(2) and 9(2) of the 1982 Act, are identical to the term in s. 14(2) of the 1979 Act, except that in the 1982 Act the five aspects of quality are not set out. Therefore our interpretation of the meaning of the term satisfactory quality in the 1979 Act is equally applicable to the terms as to satisfactory quality which are implied by the other two statutes. (The relevant sections of the 1973 and 1982 Acts can be read in *Cases and Materials* (3.1).) It is also the case that the terms as to satisfactory quality in both the 1973 and the 1982 Acts do not apply in the same circumstances as the Sale of Goods Act 1979 term does not apply. That is to say, as regards defects specifically pointed out to the consumer or, if the consumer carried out an examination of the goods prior to sale, as regards defects which that examination ought to have revealed (Supply of Goods (Implied Terms) Act 1973, s. 10(2C) and Supply of Goods and Services Act 1982, ss. 4(3) and 9(3)).

3.5 Fitness for the Buyer's Purpose (Section (14(3))

Section 14(3) of the Sale of Goods Act 1979 states:

> Where the seller sells goods in the course of a business and the buyer, expressly or by implication, makes known . . . to the seller . . . any particular purpose for which the goods are being bought, there is an implied [term] that the goods supplied under the contract are reasonably fit for that purpose, whether or not that is a purpose for which such goods are commonly supplied . . .

Section 14(3) goes further than s. 14(2). We have seen that s. 14(2) requires goods to be of satisfactory quality, and that this means that they should meet the standard which a reasonable person would regard as satisfactory. Section 14(3) says that if a buyer lets a business seller know that the goods are to be used for any particular purpose, even an unusual purpose, then the goods must be reasonably fit for that purpose.

SAQ 3/7

Jill buys a racing bicycle from a shop and uses it to ride on country paths. The frame of the bicycle snaps when Jill rides over a bump. Can Jill reject the bicycle under either s. 14(2) or (3)? Would your answer be different if Jill had told the shopkeeper that she intended to use the bicycle to ride on country paths?

Jill would have no claim under either subsection. Section 14(2) would not help her because the bicycle was of satisfactory quality. Section 14(3) would not help her because she had not made it plain that she was going to ride the bicycle on rough ground. If Jill had told the shopkeeper that she intended to use the bicycle on country paths she would have a remedy under s. 14(3), on the grounds that the bicycle was not fit for the particular purpose which she had made known to the seller.

3.5.1 CIRCUMSTANCES IN WHICH SECTION 14(3) WILL NOT APPLY

At first sight it might seem that s. 14(3) imposes an impossible burden on the seller. But s. 14(3) goes on to say that it will not impose liability, 'where the circumstances show that the buyer does not rely, or that it is unreasonable for him to rely, on the skill or judgment of the seller'. Often the reliance on the seller will be implied. In *Cases and Materials* (3.3.1) you should read the speech of Lord Reid in *Kendall (Henry) & Sons v William Lillico & Sons Ltd*, which examines the difficulties caused in deciding whether or not reasonable reliance was placed on the seller's skill and judgment.

It can be difficult to say whether a buyer's reliance on a seller's skill and judgment is reasonable. However, it is reasonable to expect retailers to know the qualities of the goods which they sell. If a customer makes an inappropriate purpose known to a retailer, the retailer should advise that the goods are unsuitable for that purpose.

Where defective goods are to be used for their ordinary purpose, then in addition to suing under s. 14(2) the buyer will also be able to sue under s. 14(3), on the basis that the buyer would impliedly have made known the purpose for which the goods were to be used.

Grant v *Australian Knitting Mills Ltd* [1936] AC 85
G bought a pair of long woollen underpants in the defendant's shop. A chemical used in the manufacture of the pants had not been rinsed out properly, and as a consequence G suffered dermatitis which hospitalised him for several months.
Held: The terms as to merchantable quality and fitness for purpose had both been breached.

SAQ 3/8

There is an overlap between s. 14(2) and (3). Assume that goods which are of plainly unsatisfactory quality, and which are not suitable for the particular purpose which the buyer made known to the seller, are bought from a shop. Will s. 14(2) and (3) both, or neither, apply if:

(a) the buyer did not rely on the seller's skill and judgment; or

(b) the buyer used the goods for their usual purpose, without mentioning this purpose to the seller; or

(c) the buyer examined the goods and spotted the defect. Nevertheless the buyer bought the goods because the seller (wrongly) said that the defect would cause no practical problems?

STATUTORY IMPLIED TERMS AS TO QUALITY AND FITNESS

(a) Section 14(2) would apply, s. 14(3) would not.

(b) Both s. 14(2) and (3) would apply.

(c) Section 14(3) would apply, s. 14(2) would not.

Section 14(3) does not always impose liability where goods do not suit a buyer's purpose. The buyer must have made the purpose known and must reasonably have relied on the seller's skill and judgment.

ACTIVITY 3/6

In *Griffiths v Peter Conway Ltd* [1939] 1 All ER 685 the sellers made to order a tweed coat for the plaintiff. The coat gave the plaintiff dermatitis because she was abnormally sensitive to certain types of wool. The plaintiff did not reveal this fact to the sellers. The coat would not have affected a normal person. Clearly the coat was of merchantable quality. However, the plaintiff claimed that the coat was not fit for her purpose. Read the judgment of Sir Wilfrid Greene MR in *Cases and Materials* (3.3.1) and then write down why the plaintiff did not succeed.

You should have written that the plaintiff did not succeed because she did not make her allergy known to the seller. It was not enough for her to make known that she intended to wear the coat. She also had to make known her allergy. How otherwise could the seller exercise skill and judgment in deciding that the goods were fit for the plaintiff's purpose?

How can we tell whether or not a buyer did in fact rely on the skill and judgment of the seller, and whether or not such reliance was reasonable? The only short answer we can give is that it can be very difficult. Each case must be decided on its facts. However, it should be remember that s. 14(3) only imposes liability on business sellers, and that generally, as has been stated, if a consumer buys from a retailer it will be assumed that the retailer has knowledge about the goods sold. The relative degrees of expertise of the buyer and the seller will also be important. A buyer who claims special expertise about the goods bought is less likely to be able to rely on s. 14(3). A seller who makes it plain that he or she has little expertise is less likely to be liable.

ACTIVITY 3/7

Read the facts of the following case, and the extract from Lord Guest's speech in *Cases and Materials* (3.3.1), and then answer the following questions:

(a) If the case were to arise today, would the herring meal be of satisfactory quality? (The answer to this part of the question will not be found in Lord Guest's speech, but earlier in this chapter at 3.4.3.

(b) Did the buyer succeed under s. 14(3)?

(c) On what grounds did Lord Guest distinguish *Griffiths v Peter Conway Ltd*?

Ashington Piggeries Ltd v *Christopher Hill Ltd* [1971] 1 All ER 847
A manufacturer of animal feed stuffs was asked to make food for mink, according to a certain formula. One of the ingredients in the formula was herring meal. The manufacturer bought herring meal from S, who had never previously made food for mink. S knew that the herring meal was going to be used to feed mink. The meal was contaminated with a chemical (DMNA) and would have been poisonous to all animals, but it was only fatally poisonous to mink. The state of scientific and technical knowledge at the time was such that this contamination of the foodstuff could not have been suspected.

(a) The herring meal would not be of satisfactory quality because a reasonable person would not regard the meal as meeting a satisfactory standard. The following aspects of quality would be relevant:

  (i) that the meal was not fit for all the purposes for which herring meal is commonly supplied;

  (ii) that it was not safe; and

  (iii) that it had a defect.

  (The herring meal was held not to be of merchantable quality by a majority of 3:2.)

(b) The House of Lords decided that the buyer won under s. 14(3). The buyers made a partial reliance on the seller's skill and judgment. The buyer supplied the formula, but relied on the seller's skill and judgment to use wholesome materials.

(c) *Griffiths* v *Peter Conway Ltd* was distinguished on the grounds that the tweed coat would not have harmed a normal person, whereas all animals are sensitive to DMNA.

The above case demonstrates that business sellers must have extensive knowledge of the properties of any goods which they sell. This creates more of a problem for modern sellers than it did for sellers in the last century, when the original Act was passed. Four factors have contributed to this. First, in the previous century sellers probably stocked a much smaller range of goods. Second, goods in the last century were generally much less technical than modern goods. Third, business sellers in the last century often carried on the operation of a family business which had sold the same type of goods for a long time. Inevitably, such sellers acquired a detailed knowledge of the goods in which the business dealt. Modern shop assistants do not have such expertise. Fourth, the pace of technological change has meant that new types of goods are arriving on the market much more quickly than was the case 100 hundred years ago.

SAQ 3/9

In *Wren* v *Holt* [1903] 1 KB 610 the plaintiff was made ill by drinking beer which contained arsenic. The pub from which the plaintiff bought the beer was a tied house, and only sold one brewery's beer. The plaintiff knew that the pub could only sell this brewery's beer and drank in the pub because he liked the beer.

Was the beer of merchantable (now satisfactory) quality? Did the plaintiff win on the grounds that the beer was not fit for the purpose made known to the seller?

STATUTORY IMPLIED TERMS AS TO QUALITY AND FITNESS

The beer was not of merchantable quality. The jury decided that the plaintiff could not have relied on the seller's skill and judgment because he knew that the pub sold only the type of beer which had injured him. The Court of Appeal was not willing to rule that the jury's decision was incorrect.

3.5.2 FITNESS FOR PURPOSE IN OTHER CONSUMER TRANSACTIONS

Section 10(3) of the Supply of Goods (Implied Terms) Act 1973 and ss. 4(4) and (5) and 9(4) and (5) of the Supply of Goods and Services Act 1982 imply terms as to fitness for purpose. These terms are virtually identical to the terms implied by s. 14(3) of the Sale of Goods Act 1979 and can be read in *Cases and Materials* (**3.1**). As with the 1979 Act, the terms as to fitness for purpose implied by the 1973 and the 1982 Acts do not apply if the consumer does not rely, or if it is unreasonable for the consumer to rely, on the supplier's skill and judgment. (Supply of Goods (Implied Terms) Act 1973, s. 10(3) and Supply of Goods and Services Act 1982, ss. 4(6) and 9(6)). In trading stamp transactions the terms are implied by s. 4 of the Trading Stamps Act 1964, which can be read in *Cases and Materials* (**3.3.2**).

3.6 The Status of the Implied Terms

In consumer cases the terms as to satisfactory quality and fitness for purpose are conditions (Sale of Goods Act 1979, s. 15A; Supply of Goods (Implied Terms) Act 1973, s. 11A; Supply of Goods and Services Act 1982, ss. 5A and 10A). In consumer cases therefore breach of any of the implied terms as to satisfactory quality or fitness for purpose will give the consumer the right to terminate the contract and recover money paid. This is the case even if the breach of condition is slight. In sales of goods only, the right to reject is lost once the goods have been accepted, but the consumer still has a right to damages. (The circumstances in which goods have been accepted were examined in **Chapter 1**.)

3.7 Flexibility of Satisfactory Quality and Fitness for Purpose

SAQ 3/10

It is not possible to create an all-embracing test of satisfactory quality. Nor, when considering fitness for purpose, is it possible to define exactly what amounts to a reasonable reliance on the seller's skill and judgment. Why do you think this is so? In two or three lines, write down your answer.

You might have written sentences something like the ones which follow. The test of satisfactory quality applies to so many different types of goods that it would be impossible to encapsulate the test in a simple formula. Any attempt to do this would inevitably be expanded by case law. The current broad concept gives the judiciary the flexibility to do justice in each case, albeit at the expense of certainty. The same problems would be encountered when formulating an exact test of reasonable reliance on the seller's skill and judgment.

From a consumer's point of view, s. 14(2) and (3) of the 1979 Act, and the corresponding terms implied by the 1973 and the 1982 Acts, are the most important sources of consumer protection law. The change from merchantable quality to satisfactory quality is a major one, and the meaning of the new term will not be fully known until cases have interpreted it.

3.8 Terms Implied into Contracts for the Supply of a Service

3.8.1 IMPLIED TERM ABOUT CARE AND SKILL

Section 13 of the Supply of Goods and Services Act 1872 states:

> In a contract for the supply of a service where the supplier is acting in the course of a business, there is an implied term that the supplier will carry out the service with reasonable care and skill.

SAQ 3/11

Section 13 applies only to contracts where the supplier of the service is acting in the course of a business. It appears to be the rough equivalent of terms such as s. 14(2) of the Sale of Goods Act 1979, which imply that an end product sold in the course of a business should be of satisfactory quality.

(a) In what way is the term implied by s. 13 different from the terms which imply that an end product should be of satisfactory quality?

(b) Would any term be implied if the service was supplied otherwise than in the course of a business?

(c) Do you think that s. 13 of the 1982 Act was a codification of the common law?

(a) Section 13 adopts a tort standard, the standard of common law negligence. The terms which insist that goods, or an end product, will be of satisfactory quality adopt a contract standard. If a service is carried out to repair goods or to achieve a certain result, s. 13 does not necessarily guarantee that the goods will then work satisfactorily or that the result will be achieved. The requirement that goods be of satisfactory quality is quite different. Above, at **3.4**, we saw that liability under s. 14(2) of the 1979 Act is strict in that the seller of the goods will be liable for the goods not being of satisfactory quality, even if this is not at all his fault.

(b) If a service is carried out other than in the course of a business then the 1982 Act will not imply a term that the service is carried out using reasonable care and skill. However, the supplier of the service can be liable in negligence, even if no charge was made for the service. Lord Devlin in *Hedley Byrne* v *Heller & Co. Ltd* [1963] 2 All ER 575 stated, at 608: 'A promise given without consideration to perform a service cannot be enforced as a contract by the promisee; but if the service is in fact performed and done negligently, the promisee can recover in an action in tort.' This statement was quoted with approval by Lord Goff in *Henderson* v *Merrett Syndicates Ltd* [1994] 3 All ER 506 at 519. The fact that a service is supplied in the course of a business is a factor to be taken into account when considering the care and skill with which the service should be supplied.

STATUTORY IMPLIED TERMS AS TO QUALITY AND FITNESS

(c) The terms implied by the 1982 Act into contracts for the supply of a service were intended to be a codification of the position at common law. In respect of the supply of particular types of services there will also be extensive case law on the standard of performance required.

SAQ 3/12

X is making a product for Y, a consumer. The terms of the contract are such that this might be either a sale of goods or a contract for the supply of a service. Either way a term will be implied by a statute. Why might it be important to decide how the contract is classified?

It would be important to classify the term if the end product did not work as it should, but if this defect was not due a lack of reasonable care and skill on X's part. If the contract is classified as a sale of goods, or as a contract to transfer the property in goods, then X will be strictly liable if the end product is not of satisfactory quality and not fit for Y's purpose. If the contract is classified as the supply of a service, then X will only be liable if Y can prove that he failed to exercise reasonable care and skill. The fact that the contract is classified as a sale of goods or a contract for the transfer of the property in goods will not prevent it from also being classified as a contract for the supply of a service. (See **Chapter 2**, on the classification of contracts.)

SAQ 3/13

A surgeon contracts to perform a delicate heart by-pass operation. Is it reasonable to imply a term that the operation will be successful?

It does not seem particularly reasonable to imply a term that the operation will be successful. In *Greaves & Co. Contractors Ltd* v *Baynham, Meickle & Partners* [1975] 3 All ER 99 Lord Denning MR, at 103–104, said, 'The surgeon does not warrant that he will cure the patient. Nor does the solicitor warrant that he will win the case. But, when a dentist agrees to make a set of false teeth for a patient, there is an implied warranty that they will fit his gums.' In *Thake and another* v *Maurice* [1986] 1 All ER 497 a surgeon was not held liable for having performed a vasectomy which did not work. There was no suggestion that the surgeon had not performed the operation completely. (The effect of a very few vasectomies could be reversed naturally.) Kerr J held that a doctor would only be taken to guarantee the success of an operation if he expressly said as much in clear and unequivocal terms.

Bolam v *Friern Hospital Management Committee* [1957] 2 All ER 118
The plaintiff was mentally ill and on the advice of a consultant he went to the defendant hospital for electro-convulsive therapy. He signed a consent form which did not warn

him of the risk of fractures (a one in 10,000 risk). While undergoing the treatment the plaintiff suffered fractures. The use of relaxant drugs would have greatly reduced the risk of a fracture. There were two bodies of medical opinion about the use of relaxant drugs while undergoing the treatment. The plaintiff claimed that the defendants were negligent in administering the treatment without relaxant drugs and in not warning him of the risks of the treatment.

Held: A doctor is not negligent if he acts in accordance with the opinion of skilled medical men merely because there are other skilled medical men who take a contrary view. McNair J explained, at 121, the skill required of those who provide a service which involves the use of some special skill and competence:

> In an ordinary case it is generally said that you judge [whether an act was negligent] by the action of the man in the street.... But where you get a situation which involves the use of some special skill or competence ... the test is the standard of the ordinary skilled man exercising and professing to have that special skill. A man need not possess the highest expert skill at the risk of being found negligent. It is well established law that it is sufficient if he exercises the ordinary skill of an ordinary competent man exercising that particular art.

The full judgment of McNair J can be read in *Cases and Materials* (3.4).

In *Cases and Materials* (3.4) you should also read 'The Quality of Services Supplied: Guidance from the Court of Appeal' by Dr R G Lawson (1984) 134 NL 39). Dr Lawson reviews three cases involving the fitting of a carpet, the installation of central heating and the fitting of a kitchen. He concluded that 'if there is a common thread to these cases it is that consumers are not entitled to demand perfection.'

It is of course possible that the supplier of a service does expressly or impliedly guarantee the success of the service provided. In *Greaves & Co. Contractors Ltd v Baynham, Meikle & Partners* [1975] 1 WLR 1095 the plaintiffs had a contract to build a warehouse. The warehouse was to be used for the storage of oil drums. These were to be kept on the first floor and moved into place by fork lift trucks. The plaintiffs knew this and so did the defendants, a firm of consultant structural engineers, whom the plaintiffs employed to design the warehouse. The first floor of the warehouse cracked because of vibrations caused by forklifts. The plaintiffs were liable on their contract to build the warehouse. The defendants in turn were liable to the plaintiffs on two grounds. First, it was implied into the agreement between the plaintiffs and defendants an absolute warranty that the design would be fit for its intended purpose, as this was the common intention of the parties. Second, the defendants were in breach of their duty to use reasonable care and skill.

In *Midland Bank plc v Cox McQueen, The Times*, 2 February 1999, a firm of solicitors were asked by a bank to get a customer's wife to sign a legal charge. The solicitors thought that they had done this but in fact the signature was a forgery made by an impostor. The Court of Appeal held that the solicitors did not give a promise to answer for the fraud of the customer if that fraud could not be detected by exercising all reasonable care and skill. Such a promise would only be given if the language used compellingly indicated that it had been given.

SAQ 3/14

In *Luxmoore-May and another v Messenger May Baverstock* [1990] 1 All ER 1067 the defendants, a small firm of auctioneers who held themselves out as offering expert and specialist advice about paintings, agreed to 'research' two paintings given to them by the plaintiffs. The representative of the small firm thought it possible that the

STATUTORY IMPLIED TERMS AS TO QUALITY AND FITNESS

paintings might be by Stubbs and so they took them to Christie's for their opinion. Five to ten minutes after they were handed over, Christie's returned the paintings without saying anything favourable about them. The plaintiffs asked the small firm to auction the paintings, with a reserve price of £40. The paintings were sold for £840. Five months later Sotheby's sold the paintings as by Stubbs for £88,000. The plaintiffs sued the defendants claiming the difference in the two sale prices. Do you think that the plaintiffs won? Write down your views.

You might have deduced that the plaintiffs did not win. Slade LJ said, at 1076:

> The valuation of pictures of which the artist is unknown, pre-eminently involves an exercise of opinion and judgment, most particularly in deciding whether an attribution to any particular artist should be made. Since it is not an exact science, the judgment in the very nature of things may be fallible, and may turn out to be wrong. Accordingly, provided that the valuer has done his job honestly and with due diligence, I think that the court should be cautious before convicting him of professional negligence merely because he has failed to be the first to spot a 'sleeper' or the potentiality of a 'sleeper'.

A person who is just beginning to supply a service is expected to immediately reach the standard expected of any other supplier of that service. (In *Nettleship* v *Weston* [1971] 2 QB 691 the negligence of a learner driver caused a crash in which the knee-cap of the person teaching her to drive was broken. The Court of Appeal held that the duty of care which a learner driver owed to passengers and the public was the same objective and impersonal standard as every other driver owed.)

SAQ 3/15

Is it fair to impose stricter liability on the seller of goods than on the supplier of a service?

It hardly seems fair at all. A business seller of goods cannot be responsible for defects in goods manufactured by another, especially if the goods are hidden behind packaging. Of course, such a seller may be able to sue the person from whom he bought the goods, and so on down the line until the manufacturer is reached. However, if any of the sellers have become insolvent then the person who bought from that seller will be the loser. The supplier of a service on the other hand must necessarily play a part in the performance of the contract.

Another significant consequence of the term as to reasonable care and skill being tortious is that this may lead to a procedural advantage. Both claims in contract and claims in tort are statute barred after six years. But time starts to run against a claim in contract from the date of the breach of contract, whereas time starts to run against a claim in tort from the date of damage.

3.8.1.1 Exclusion of the term implied by s. 13

In consumer sales liability for breaches of the terms as to satisfactory quality and fitness for purpose can never be excluded (ss. 6(2) and 7(2) of the 1977 Act), whereas in non-consumer cases liability can be excluded by a term which satisfies the test of reasonableness (s. 6(3)). Section 13 of the Supply of Goods and Services Act 1982 is treated differently by the 1977 Act. Section 1(a) of the 1977 Act tells us that a breach of s. 13 of the 1982 Act is to be treated under the Act as negligence. Section 2(1) of the 1977 Act tells us that a person cannot by reference to any contract term exclude or restrict his liability for death or personal injury resulting from negligence. However, s. 2(2) says that a person can restrict or exclude liability for other loss or damage resulting from negligence if the term so doing satisfies the Act's requirement of reasonableness. So there is no rule of law that a term whereby a consumer agrees that a service shall not be supplied with reasonable care and skill is automatically invalid. Rather, the fact that the customer was a consumer will just be another factor to be decided in considering whether or not the exclusion clause satisfied the Act's test of of reasonableness.

3.8.1.2 Status of the term implied by s. 13

The term implied by s. 13 is not described as a condition or a warranty. It is an innominate term and whether or not the consumer can treat the contract as repudiated on account of it having been breached will depend upon whether or not the breach deprived the consumer of substantially the whole benefit which the contract was intended to confer. If the breach did deprive of substantially the whole benefit the consumer can treat the contract as repudiated. If the breach did not deprive of substantially the whole benefit the consumer is able only to claim damages.

3.8.2 IMPLIED TERM ABOUT TIME OF PERFORMANCE

Section 14 of the Supply of Goods and Services Act 1982 states:

(1) Where, under a contract for the supply of a service by a supplier acting in the course of a business, the time for the service to be carried out is not fixed by the contract, left to be fixed in a manner agreed by the contract or determined by the course of dealing between the parties, there is an implied term that the supplier will carry out the service within a reasonable time.

(2) What is a reasonable time is a question of fact.

In many contracts where a business supplies a service, no time for completion of the service is agreed. Section 14(1) therefore protects the customer by implying that the service shall be supplied within a reasonable time. In deciding what amounts to a reasonable time all the circumstances will need to be considered.

3.8.3 IMPLIED TERM ABOUT CONSIDERATION

Section 15 of the Supply of Goods and Services Act 1982 states:

(1) Where, under a contract for the supply of a service, the consideration for the service is not determined by the contract, left to be determined in a manner agreed by the contract or determined by the course of dealing between the parties, there is an implied term that the party contracting with the supplier will pay a reasonable charge.

(2) What is a reasonable charge is a question of fact.

Again it is commonplace for a contract for the supply of a service to be made without the price being fixed. Section 15(1) protects the customer by implying that the price will be a reasonable price. This section applies even if the service is not supplied in the course of a business.

When a person gives an estimate for the price of work to be carried out, this is taken to be only an approximate indication of the likelihood of the cost. A quotation on the other hand is taken as a definite price at which the service will be supplied.

STATUTORY IMPLIED TERMS AS TO QUALITY AND FITNESS

3.9 Summary

In this chapter we have covered the following:

- The statutory implied terms as to satisfactory quality and fitness for purpose are implied only into contracts which are made in the course of a business.

- The terms as to satisfactory quality will not apply as regards defects which were specifically pointed out to the consumer.

- A consumer has no obligation to examine the goods prior to the making of the contract, but a consumer who does examine the goods will not be able to claim that the goods were unsatisfactory as regards defects which the examination ought to have revealed.

- The new requirement of satisfactory quality requires the goods to meet the standard which a reasonable person would regard as satisfactory, taking account of any description of the goods, the price (if relevant) and all the other relevant circumstances.

- The following five matters are aspects of the quality of goods in appropriate cases:

    (a) fitness for all the purposes for which goods of the kind in question are commonly supplied,

    (b) appearance and finish,

    (c) freedom from minor defects,

    (d) safety, and

    (e) durability.

- Breach of a statutory implied term as to satisfactory quality of fitness for purpose gives a consumer the right to terminate the contract and receive back money paid. In contracts of sale of goods only, this right is lost once the goods have been accepted.

- Neither the definition of satisfactory quality, nor the five aspects of quality, are intended to formulate an exhaustive test.

- The implied terms as to fitness for the consumer's purpose will not apply where the circumstances show that the consumer does not rely, or that it is unreasonable for the consumer to rely, on the supplier's skill and judgment.

- Whether a consumer did rely on a supplier's skill and judgment, and whether it was reasonable for the consumer to do this, are questions of fact, depending on the circumstances of each particular case.

- There is a considerable overlap between the requirements of satisfactory quality and fitness for purpose.

- Section 13 of the Supply of Goods and Services Act 1982 implies a term that a business supplier of a service will supply the service using reasonable care and skill.

- Unlike the implied terms which apply when goods are supplied, s. 13 of the 1982 Act does not promise fitness for a particular purpose or the achievement of an end result. The standard imposed is the same standard as in the tort of negligence.

- Even where the customer is a consumer, the term implied by s. 13 of the 1982 Act can be excluded by a term which satisfies the requirement of reasonableness under the Unfair Contract Terms Act 1977. This is not the case if the supplier's negligence causes death or personal injury.

- Section 14 of the Supply of Goods and Services Act 1982 implies a term that a business supplier of a service will supply the service within a reasonable time. (Unless the time for carrying out the service is agreed or can be determined by a course of dealing between the parties.)

- Section 15 of the 1982 Act implies a term that a person to whom a service is supplied will pay a reasonable charge for the service. (Unless the consideration for the service has been agreed or can be determined by the course of dealing between the parties.)

CHAPTER FOUR

CONTRACT BASED REMEDIES: STATUTORY IMPLIED TERMS AS TO CORRESPONDENCE WITH DESCRIPTION AND AS TO TITLE

4.1 Objectives

By the end of this chapter you should be able to:

- analyse the circumstances in which goods are sold or supplied by description;

- describe the circumstances in which a failure to match a description will amount to breach of the statutory implied terms as to correspondence with description;

- describe the remedies available to a consumer if a statutory term as to correspondence with description is breached;

- explain the terms as to title etc. implied by the Sale of Goods Act 1979, the Supply of Goods (Implied Terms) Act 1973 and the Supply of Goods and Services Act 1982;

- describe the remedies available to a consumer if a term as to the right to sell, hire, etc. is breached;

- identify the circumstances in which a consumer transaction is made by sample;

- explain the statutory terms implied when a transaction is made by sample and the remedies available for breach of such terms.

4.2 Introduction

In **Chapter 3** we examined the terms as to satisfactory quality and fitness for purpose which are implied in the consumer's favour by the Sale of Goods Act 1979, the Supply of Goods (Implied Terms) Act 1973 and the Supply of Goods and Services Act 1982. In this chapter we examine the terms as to title and correspondence with description which those statutes imply. We also look briefly at the terms which are implied when a consumer relies on a sample when making a contract.

The implied terms in the 1973 and the 1982 Acts are virtually identical to the term set out in the 1979 Act. Almost all of the case law on the meaning of the terms and the circumstances in which they will apply concerns the Sale of Goods Act 1979. We therefore first examine the term implied by ss. 12, 13 and 15 of the 1979 Act and then see how, if at all, the corresponding terms implied by ss. 8, 9 and 11 of the 1973 Act and ss. 2, 3, 5, 7, 8 and 10 of the 1982 Act differ (see *Cases and Materials* (4.1)).

We conclude the chapter by considering the remedies available to a consumer if one of the implied terms is breached.

4.3 Correspondence with Description (Section 13(1))

Section 13 of the Sale of Goods Act 1979, s. 9 of the Supply of Goods (Implied Terms) Act 1973 and ss. 3 and 8 of the Supply of Goods and Services Act 1982 all imply a term that if goods are sold, hired, etc. by description then the goods will correspond with the description. These terms are implied into all sales, whether made in the course of a business or not.

Section 13(1) of the Sale of Goods Act 1979 states: 'Where there is a contract for the sale of goods by description, there is an implied [term] that the goods will correspond with the description.'

4.3.1 SALE OF GOODS BY DESCRIPTION

Section 13(1) is only to apply where there is a contract for the sale of goods by description. When deciding whether or not goods were sold by description, it is convenient to separate specific goods from unascertained goods.

ACTIVITY 4/1

Re-read the definitions of specific, future and unascertained goods in Chapter 2. Then, delete the words 'yes' or 'no' as appropriate.

(a) Are specific goods necessarily sold by description? (Yes/No.)

(b) Are unascertained goods necessarily sold by description? (Yes/No.)

(c) Are future goods necessarily sold by description? (Yes/No.)

You should have completed **Activity 4/1** to indicate that:

(a) Specific goods are defined as goods which were identified and agreed upon at the time of sale. This identification and agreement might or might not have been made by description.

(b) Unascertained goods were defined as goods which were not identified and agreed upon at the time of sale. Such goods can only be sold by description. How else are the parties able to identify what is being sold?

(c) Future goods are to be manufactured by or acquired by the seller after the contract of sale. Therefore the sale of future goods must be by description.

STATUTORY IMPLIED TERMS AS TO CORRESPONDENCE WITH DESCRIPTION

SAQ 4/1

Think back to the last time you shopped in a supermarket. Presumably, you selected items and took them to the checkout. The items selected would have been described by words, either on the packaging or on the supermarket shelves. If you selected the goods yourself, do you think that this would necessarily have prevented the sale of these goods from being a sale by description? Write down your opinion.

Section 13(3) caters specifically for this type of situation, stating: 'A sale of goods is not prevented from being a sale by description by reason only that, being exposed for sale or hire, they are selected by the buyer.'

Almost all goods bought from a retailer are described in some way or other. However, this does not automatically mean that s. 13(1) will apply to the sale of these goods. The fact that there is a description does not necessarily mean that the goods are sold *by* description.

Recently the courts have interpreted s. 13(1) as applying only when the description amounts to a term. (In **Chapter 1** we saw that statements made before the contract is formed can either be terms or they can be representations. If a term is broken then this is breach of contract. If a representation is broken then this is not breach of contract, although there might be a remedy for misrepresentation. If you have forgotten the distinction between terms and representations, it might pay you to refresh your memory.) Furthermore, if s. 13(1) is to apply, not only must the description have been a term of the contract, it must have been relied upon by the buyer.

Harlingdon & Leinster Enterprises Ltd v *Christopher Hull Fine Art Ltd* [1991] 1 QB 564
S sold a painting to B for £6,000 and said that the painting was by Munter, a German expressionist painter. Both S and B were art dealers. B was a specialist in German expressionistic painting, S was not. S made it plain to B that he had no expertise in this specialised field. It later came to light that the painting was a fake and was worth under £100. B rejected the painting under s. 13(1).
Held: B could not reject the painting under s. 13(1). S had clearly made a description, but B had not relied on this description when deciding to buy the painting. The description was not an essential term of the contract.

ACTIVITY 4/2

Read the judgment of Nourse LJ in *Cases and Materials* (4.2.1). Then write down:

(a) How important a term must the description be in order for s. 13 to apply?

(b) If Nourse LJ's judgment is correct, does s. 13 say anything at all?

92 STATUTORY IMPLIED TERMS AS TO CORRESPONDENCE WITH DESCRIPTION

(a) Nourse LJ said that the description must be influential in the sale, not necessarily alone, but so as to become an essential term, i.e. a condition, of the contract. He said that if this was not the case a description could be said to be one by which the contract for the sale of goods is made.

(b) If Nourse LJ's decision is correct then s. 13 appears to say nothing. Section 13 could be paraphrased as: 'Where a description can be classified as a condition of the contract, there is an implied condition that the goods will correspond with the description.'

Prior to 1973 the term as to merchantable quality was only implied if the sale was a sale by description. Courts therefore often strove to decide that a sale was a sale by description so as to be able to imply the term as to merchantable quality. Consequently, some of the older authorities seem at odds with the decision in the above case. (See **Chapter 1** at **1.5.1.6**.)

SAQ 4/2

Alan buys a new motorbike under a written contract of sale. One of the terms states that the bike should be fitted with an immobiliser. This term is breached because the bike is not fitted with an immobiliser. If any term of a contract is broken then the common law will always provide the injured party with a remedy. Alan has now decided that he does not want the motorbike. For what reason might he argue that this broken term is covered by s. 13(1)?

In consumer cases the term implied by s. 13(1) is a condition. So if the term is covered by s. 13(1), then Alan will be able to reject the car and get his money back. If the term is not covered by s. 13(1), then at common law the term might be classed only as a warranty, or as an innominate term which did not deprive Alan of substantially the whole benefit of the contract. If either of these two latter classifications were adopted, Alan would only gain a right to damages. If it is correct that s. 13(1) can only apply where the description was an essential term of the contract, then the only purpose in arguing s. 13(1) seems to be that it will always give the right to call the contract off, rather than giving a mere right to damages. (Later in this chapter, when we consider the status of the implied terms, we will see that a consumer can reject for any breach of a statutory implied condition, whether this is reasonable or not.)

4.3.2 BREACH OF SECTION 13(1)

The old cases on correspondence with description impose a very strict duty on the seller. These cases concerned commercial, rather than consumer, buyers and the courts took the attitude that the description must have been important to the parties, otherwise they would not have included it in their contract.

STATUTORY IMPLIED TERMS AS TO CORRESPONDENCE WITH DESCRIPTION

Arcos Ltd v E. A. Ronaasen & Son [1933] AC 470
S contracted to sell a quantity of wooden staves to be used for making cement barrels. The staves, which S described as staves 'half an inch thick' were to be shipped to England. Ninety per cent of the staves were between half an inch and five eighths of an inch, but ten per cent were over five eighths of an inch. B rejected all of the staves, even though they were perfectly fit for making barrels.
Held: B could reject the staves as they did not match the description. Lord Atkin stated, at 479, 'If the written contract specifies conditions of weight, measurement and the like, those conditions must be complied with. A ton does not mean about a ton, or a yard about a yard. Still less when you descend to minute measurements does ½ inch mean about ½ inch. If the seller wants a margin he must and in my experience does stipulate for it.'

Re Moore and Co. Ltd and Landauer and Co. Ltd [1921] 2 KB 519
A consignment of 3,100 tins of peaches was to be shipped from Australia to B in London. The shipment arrived late. B rejected the consignment on the grounds that whereas the peaches had been described as packed 30 tins to a case, about half of the tins were packed 24 to a case instead of 30. The correct number of tins was delivered.
Held: B could reject all of the tins. The goods were not as described. Scrutton LJ stated, at 524, 'The arbitrator finds that 24 tins to the case are as valuable commercially as 30 tins to the case. That may be so. Yet a man, who has bought under contract 30 tins to the case, may have sold under the same description, and may be put into considerable difficulty by having goods tendered to him which do not comply with the description under which he bought.'

If the failure to match the description is so microscopically small that it can be regarded as a trifle, then the rule *de minimis non curat lex* (the law is not concerned with trifles) will protect the seller. In both of the above cases it might seem that the failure to match the description was a trifle. There are probably two main reasons why the cases were decided as they were. First, these were commercial contracts where the buyer and seller were likely to think the description important. Second, the buyers were likely to have sold the goods on to other buyers under the same description. Neither of these matters is the case in a typical consumer purchase. Most consumers buy goods under an oral contract and intend the goods for their own or their family's consumption. This does not, however, mean that a less strict duty is imposed when the buyer is a consumer. The term as to correspondence with description applies to all sales, whether made to a commercial or to a consumer buyer.

In *Reardon Smith Line Ltd v Hansen-Tangen* [1976] 3 All ER 570 Lord Wilberforce said that some of the old authorities such as *Re Moore & Co. and Landauer & Co.* were excessively technical and due for a fresh examination by the House of Lords. The relevant extract, which can be read in **Cases and Materials (4.2.2)**, makes a distinction between words which identify an essential part of the description of the goods and words which identify the goods only in the sense that they let the buyer know which particular goods are being sold. This latter type of identifying words do not have any legal effect. In *Ashington Piggeries Ltd v Christopher Hill Ltd* [1972] AC 441, Lord Diplock stated, at 503–4:

> The 'description' by which unascertained goods are sold is, in my view, confined to those words in the contract which were intended by the parties to identify the kind of goods which were to be supplied. It is open to the parties to use a description as broad or narrow as they choose. But ultimately the test is whether the buyer could fairly and reasonably refuse to accept the physical goods proffered to him on the ground that their failure to correspond with that part of what was said about them in the contract makes them goods of a different kind from those he had agreed to buy. The key to section 13 is identification.

SAQ 4/3

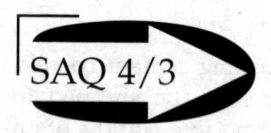

Billy intends to host a large party and buys a huge pack of smoked salmon. When Billy next visits the shop from where the salmon was bought he sees a notice explaining that the huge packs of salmon were incorrectly labelled. The packaging in which the salmon was wrapped had said that it was Norwegian salmon, whereas in fact the salmon was Scottish. Billy had noticed the label, but did not care whether the salmon was Scottish or Norwegian.

(a) Did the words on the packaging constitute a description?

(b) If Billy no longer wanted the salmon, because his party was cancelled, could he reject the salmon under s. 13(1)?

(a) The words on the packaging would have amounted to a description.

(b) Billy could not reject the salmon under s. 13(1). The description was not an essential term of the contract, and it did not matter to Billy where the salmon originated. (*Arcos Ltd* v *E. A. Ronaasen & Son* and *Re Moore and Co. Ltd and Landauer and Co. Ltd* could be distinguished on the grounds that both concerned commercial contracts in which the descriptions in question were deliberately inserted by the parties. The speech of Lord Atkin in *Arcos Ltd* v *E. A. Ronaasen & Son* can be read in *Cases and Materials* (4.2.2). It can be seen that Lord Atkin had a commercial buyer and a commercial seller firmly in mind.)

SAQ 4/4

In *Arcos Ltd* v *E. A. Ronaasen & Son* it was decided that the buyer of the staves could reject the staves even though they were perfectly fit for making barrels.

(a) Why should the buyer want to reject, when he would still need wooden staves with which to make barrels?

(b) From a public policy point of view, why do you think that Lord Atkin insisted that contract descriptions should be rigidly adhered to?

(c) If the case were to arise today, would the description 'half an inch thick' be covered by s. 13(1)?

(a) Presumably the buyer rejected the staves because he could buy similar staves cheaper elsewhere. Lord Atkin stated: 'No doubt in business men often find it unnecessary or inexpedient to insist on their strict legal rights. In a normal market, if they get something substantially like the specified goods, they may take them with or without grumbling and claim for an allowance. But in a falling market I find that buyers are often as eager to insist on their legal rights as courts

STATUTORY IMPLIED TERMS AS TO CORRESPONDENCE WITH DESCRIPTION 95

of law are ready to maintain them.' Consumers too might find that equivalent goods were available more cheaply elsewhere. They might also want to terminate the contract as they had changed their minds about wanting the goods in question.

(b) From a public policy point of view Lord Atkin's approach makes sense in a business context. First, it is certain. Second, it allows the buyer to resell the goods under the same description as he bought them. Third, a line must be drawn somewhere and it seems better and easier to draw it exactly at the contract description rather than to draw it elsewhere. However, this line might make less sense in a consumer context. Many consumers would not necessarily want to terminate the contract and reject the goods. They would be satisfied if goods which did match the description were substituted for those which did not. There is of course no reason why consumers should not come to such an agreement with the retailer. (In legal terms the consumer would have made a second contract with the retailer. Under this second contract the consumer gives up the right to reject the original goods in return for being supplied with the alternative goods which match the description.)

(c) A modern court might hold that s. 13(1) would not apply because it seems probable that the description 'half an inch thick' was not an essential term on which the buyer relied. In the light of more recent decisions, the old cases on when a sale was 'by description' must be viewed with some suspicion.

4.3.3 DESCRIPTIONS IN OTHER CONSUMER TRANSACTIONS

The terms as to description implied by s. 9(1) of the Supply of Goods (Implied Terms) Act 1973 and ss. 3(2) and 8(2) of the Supply of Goods and Services Act 1982 are virtually identical to the term implied by s. 13(1) of the Sale of Goods Act 1979. Therefore the case law we have considered on whether a sale of goods is made by description, and on whether the term as to correspondence with description has been breached, is equally applicable when considering these other statutes.

4.4 The Right to Sell (Section 12(1))

ACTIVITY 4/3

Impressed by the latest advertising campaign, you phone your local Toyota dealer and order a new Corolla. A contract is made, and your new car is to be delivered next week. In fact the Toyota dealer has run out of Corollas, but is confident that the Toyota Motor Company will supply one before next week. Read s. 12(1) of the Sale of Goods Act 1979 in *Cases and Materials* (4.1) and then write down whether or not the Toyota dealer has breached it.

You should have written that s. 12(1) has not been breached. This is an agreement to sell, rather than a sale. The dealer is therefore required to have the right to sell when the property is to pass, rather than when the contract is made. (If you have forgotten the difference between a sale and an agreement to sell, look again at the definitions in **Chapter 2**.)

96 STATUTORY IMPLIED TERMS AS TO CORRESPONDENCE WITH DESCRIPTION

The purpose of a contract of sale of goods is to pass ownership of the goods to the buyer. A seller who does not have the right to sell cannot pass ownership to the buyer (with certain exceptions, which are not important in this context). Section 12(1) therefore implies the fundamental term that in the case of a sale the seller has a right to sell the goods.

If the contract is an agreement to sell, then the seller must have the right to sell when the property is to pass to the buyer, rather than when the contract is made. This is common sense. Consumers commonly order goods which the retailer has yet to acquire, or which have yet to be manufactured. Obviously, in such sales the retailer will not have the right to sell when the contract is made.

4.4.1 MEANING OF A 'RIGHT TO SELL THE GOODS'

Section 12(1) of the Sale of Goods Act 1979 does not say that the seller must own the goods, although this is how the section is often summarised. What s. 12(1) does say is that the seller must have a right to sell the goods. In most cases a seller who breaks s. 12(1) will break it on account of not owning the goods. However, as the following case shows, a seller may own goods but still not have the right to sell them.

Niblett Ltd v *Confectioners Materials Co. Ltd* [1921] 3 KB 387
In August 1919 a contract was made for the sale of 3,000 tins of condensed milk. 1,000 of the 3,000 tins delivered were labelled 'Nissly Brand'. The Nestlé company discovered that tins bearing the 'Nissly Brand' label had been imported. They claimed that the word 'Nissly' was too similar to their trade mark (Nestlé), and threatened to sue if the tins were sold or disposed of while bearing the 'Nissly Brand' label. The buyers accepted that they would not be able to sell the tins without removing the labels. They therefore sued the sellers for damages on the grounds that the sellers had broken s. 12(1).
Held: Section 12(1) had been broken and the buyers were entitled to damages.

ACTIVITY 4/4

Read the judgments of Bankes and Atkin LJJ in the *Niblett* case in *Cases and Materials* (4.3.1). Then write down:

(a) Why the court held that s. 12(1) had been broken, even though the sellers did own the tins of milk when they sold them?

(b) If the case were to arise today, would the goods be of satisfactory quality? (To answer this part of the question you will need to refer to Chapter 3 at 3.3, rather than to the judgments of Bankes and Atkin LJJ.)

(a) The Court of Appeal held that the sellers did not have the right to sell the tins, even though they did own them, because they could have been restrained by an injunction from selling the tins. If you are prohibited by an injunction from selling something, or could be so prohibited, then you do not have the right to sell it.

(b) The goods would not be of satisfactory quality. Section 14(2B) of the 1979 Act says that the quality of the goods includes 'their state and condition' and the labels

STATUTORY IMPLIED TERMS AS TO CORRESPONDENCE WITH DESCRIPTION 97

would have reduced the goods to an unsatisfactory state. As Bankes LJ explained, the labels were part of the state and condition of the goods.

4.4.2 EFFECT OF BREACH OF SECTION 12(1)

Section 12(1) is a condition, and so if the section is breached the buyer therefore has the right to reject the goods and terminate the contract. A buyer who does this will regain all of the purchase price paid. As we shall see in **Chapter 1** at **1.9.1**, the goods must be rejected before they have been accepted. So it will not normally be open to a buyer to benefit by using the goods for a substantial time before rejecting them. A buyer who does use the goods for a substantial time will be deemed to have accepted the goods.

However, the leading case has decided that if the seller breaches s. 12(1) then this goes further than a mere breach of condition and amounts to a total failure of consideration. The logic is that the buyer made the contract to get title to the goods and, if title was not passed on, then the buyer acquired nothing at all for which the price was paid. This can seem unfair when the buyer had the use of the goods for some considerable time. The buyer gets all of the purchase price back, and no allowance is made for the use of the goods which the buyer enjoyed.

Rowland v *Divall* [1923] 2 KB 500
B, a garage owner, bought a car from S for £334. Unknown to both parties, the car had been stolen before S acquired it. B used the car for about two months and then sold it to a third party, for £400. Two months after this second sale the police seized the car and returned it to its owner. B refunded the £400 to the third party and then sued S for the return of the £334 which he had paid for the car. S admitted that he had broken s. 12(1). However, S argued that B was not entitled to a full refund of the purchase price because B had had the use of the car for some time.
Held: B won and got all of the purchase price back, despite the use of the car which he had had. Atkin LJ stated, at 506: 'It seems to me that in this case there has been a total failure of consideration, that is to say that the buyer has not got any part of that for which he paid the purchase money. He paid the money in order that he might get the property, and he has not got it. It is true that the seller delivered to him the de facto [actual] possession, but the seller had not got the right to possession and consequently could not give it to the buyer. Therefore the buyer, during the time that he had the car in his actual possession had no right to it, and was at all times liable to the true owner for its conversion . . . The whole object of a sale is to transfer property from one person to another.'

In *Karflex Ltd* v *Poole* [1933] 2 KB 251, the plaintiffs were hire-purchase dealers, who bought a car from K and who then made a hire-purchase agreement in respect of the car with the defendant. As is usual in hire-purchase agreements, the defendant had an option to purchase the car after paying all of the instalments. In fact the defendant defaulted on his very first payment. The plaintiffs sued to recover possession of the car. It was then discovered that K had never had the right to sell the car. The plaintiffs, however, paid off the true owner and continued with their action against the defendant. Although this was a contract of hire-purchase, rather than of sale, the court followed *Rowland* v *Divall*.

SAQ 4/5

(a) Did the plaintiffs in *Karflex Ltd* v *Poole* have the right to hire at the time when the contract of hire-purchase was made?

98 STATUTORY IMPLIED TERMS AS TO CORRESPONDENCE WITH DESCRIPTION

(b) If the contract had been one of sale rather than hire, would the plaintiffs have broken s. 12(1)?

(c) Was the defendant liable for instalments due?

(d) Did the defendant recover the deposit which he had put down when he made the hire-purchase agreement?

(a) The plaintiffs did not have the right to hire when they made the hire-purchase agreement. They subsequently acquired this right.

(b) If the contract had been one of sale, the plaintiffs would have broken s. 12(1).

(c) The defendant was not liable for any of the instalments, as there had been a total failure of consideration.

(d) For the same reason, the defendant could recover his deposit.

In the following case the Court of Appeal considered the effect of an express term in a conditional sale agreement which said that the property remained vested in the finance company until the consumer had paid the total cash price and all sums owing. Was this term a condition, a warranty or an innominate term? (If you refer back to s. 12(1) of the 1979 Act you will see that in the case of an agreement to sell, such as a conditional sale, the statutory implied term as to the right to sell is that the seller will have such a right at the time when the property is to pass. This term would not therefore have been breached.)

Barber v NWS Bank plc [1996] 1 All ER 906
The plaintiff bought a car from a dealer, K Ltd, for £7,995 under a conditional sale agreement. The plaintiff was allowed £3,800 against his old car by way of deposit and agreed to pay the balance to a finance company (the bank) to whom K Ltd assigned the car. The agreement stated that the property in the car would pass to the plaintiff when he paid the balance of the total cash price and all other sums owing, but that until then the property in the car would remain vested in the bank. The plaintiff continued to pay the instalments until he discovered that that the car was the subject of an earlier finance agreement with a different finance company, M Ltd. The bank were aware of this earlier finance agreement. The plaintiff claimed to rescind the agreement and demanded all of his money back, including the deposit. The bank accepted that it was an express term of their agreement with the plaintiff that they were the owners of the car at the time of the agreement. However, the bank claimed that the term was not a condition but only a warranty, or an innominate term, breach of which had not substantially deprived the plaintiff of the whole benefit of the contract. Either way, the bank argued, the plaintiff was only entitled to damages for proved damages.
Held: Where a term in a conditional sale agreement to buy a car stated that the property in the goods remained vested in the finance company until the hirer had completed all payments, this was an express condition that at the date of the agreement the finance company owned the car. The plaintiff was therefore entitled to treat the contract as repudiated and claim back all money paid under it, even though he had had the use of the car for a considerable time. (An extract from the judgment of Sir Roger Parker can be read in *Cases and Materials* (4.3.2).)

STATUTORY IMPLIED TERMS AS TO CORRESPONDENCE WITH DESCRIPTION

ACTIVITY 4/5

The unfair advantage gained by buyers in cases such as *Rowland* v *Divall* has been much criticised. Read Atkin LJ's judgment and the extract from the Law Commission Report 160 in *Cases and Materials* (4.3.2), and write down, on a separate sheet of paper, answers to the questions below. Your answers should be fairly brief, at most a short paragraph.

(a) How is it that the buyer in cases such as *Rowland* v *Divall* has not accepted the goods?

(b) Why did the Law Commission conclude that there was no reason why the buyer should pay the seller for the use of the goods? Were Atkin LJ's reasons the same?

(c) If, as in *Rowland* v *Divall*, there is a chain of buyers and sellers, none of whom had the right to sell, the buyers will sue each seller in turn. Generally the loser will be the buyer who bought from the thief. In what circumstances will one of the other buyers suffer loss?

(d) What two major complications would arise if the buyer had to pay the seller for the use and enjoyment of the goods?

(a) If there has been a breach of s. 12(1) this is regarded as a total failure of consideration. Therefore the rules on the loss of the right to reject through acceptance do not apply.

(b) There is no reason why the buyer should pay the seller for the use of someone else's goods. The goods were never the seller's to sell. Atkin LJ also made the point that the buyer never had legal possession of the car and was therefore at all times liable to its true owner in conversion.

(c) A buyer in the chain will suffer loss if the seller from whom he bought cannot be traced or is not worth suing.

(d) The first complication would be that it would be a difficult task to place a valuation on the use and enjoyment which the buyer had had. The second complication would be that the law of conversion would have to be altered. At the moment the true owner can sue either the seller or the buyer in conversion, claiming the full value of the goods.

4.4.3 CIRCUMSTANCES IN WHICH SECTION 12(1) WILL NOT APPLY

As we shall see in **Chapter 6**, a seller cannot use an exclusion clause to exclude liability under s. 12(1) of the Sale of Goods Act 1979. However, s. 12(3) says that s. 12(1) will not apply where 'there appears from the contract or is to be inferred from its circumstances an intention that the seller should transfer only such title as he or a third person may have'. By way of example, let us assume that Albert is the plaintiff in a case in which he is trying to establish that he, and not Bert, owns certain goods. It would be possible for Albert to sell to Charlene such ownership of the goods as he might have. Until the case between Albert and Bert was decided, nobody would know what ownership of the goods Albert had. In effect, Charlene would be taking a risk, and Albert could be regarded as insuring against losing the case.

100 STATUTORY IMPLIED TERMS AS TO CORRESPONDENCE WITH DESCRIPTION

4.4.4 WARRANTIES AS TO TITLE ETC.

All of the Sale of Goods Act 1979 implied terms are conditions, except for those contained in s. 12(2)(a) and 12(2)(b). Section 12(2)(a) implies a warranty that the goods are free, and will remain free, from any encumbrances not disclosed to or known to the buyer. Section 12(2)(b) implies a warranty that the buyer will enjoy quiet possession of the goods.

ACTIVITY 4/6

(a) Write down the significance of these terms being classified as warranties rather than conditions.

(b) Define an encumbrance. (You will probably need to look the word up in a dictionary.)

(c) Write down what you think is meant by the buyer's right to enjoy quiet possession of the goods.

(a) You should have written along the following lines. If a term is classified as a warranty then breach of the term only allows the buyer to sue for damages. Breach does not allow the buyer to terminate the contract.

(b) An encumbrance is a burden or charge on property, such as a mortgage or a lien.

(c) The buyer's right to quiet possession means that it is implied at the time of sale that no person has a right prevent the buyer from continuing to enjoy possession of the goods.

In *Microbeads AC and another* v *Vinhurst Road Markings Ltd* [1975] 1 All ER 529, the defendants bought road marking machines and accessories from the plaintiffs. The machines proved to be unsatisfactory and the defendants refused to pay the price. The plaintiffs sued for the price. Two years after the sale a third party, Prismo Universal Ltd, was granted a patent, which the road marking machines infringed. After Prismo Universal Ltd had brought an action against the defendants for breaching their patent, the defendants counterclaimed that the plaintiffs had breached s. 12(1) and 12(2).

ACTIVITY 4/7

Read the judgment of Lord Denning MR in the *Microbeads* case in *Cases and Materials* (4.3.3). Then write down:

(a) whether s. 12(1) was breached by the plaintiff;

(b) whether s. 12(2) was breached.

STATUTORY IMPLIED TERMS AS TO CORRESPONDENCE WITH DESCRIPTION

(a) You should have written that: Section 12(1) was not breached because the plaintiffs had a right to sell the goods at the time of the sale.

(b) Section 12(2) was breached because the defendants could not continue to enjoy quiet possession.

4.4.5 TERM AS TO TITLE IN OTHER CONSUMER TRANSACTIONS

Section 8(1) of the Sale of Goods (Implied Terms) Act 1973 and ss. 2(1) and 7(1) of the Supply of Goods and Services Act 1982 imply terms as to transfer of title or the right to possess which are virtually identical to the terms implied by s. 12(1) of the Sale of Goods Act 1979. The relevant terms are reproduced in *Cases and Materials* (4.1).

ACTIVITY 4/8

Re-read the facts of *Karflex Ltd* v *Poole*, which are set out above SAQ 4/5. Which section of which statute would now help the defendants?

As this was a contract of hire-purchase, the governing statute would be the Supply of Goods (Implied Terms) Act 1973. Section 8(1) of the Act does not imply a term that the creditor will have a right to hire the goods at the time when the goods are hired, but only that he will have a right to sell the goods at the time when the property is to pass. (This seems surprising in the light of s. 7 of the Supply of Goods and Services Act 1982 which applies to contracts of hire and which requires the bailor to have the right to transfer possession of the goods for the period of the hire.) It would seem therefore that s. 8(1) of the Sale of Goods (Implied Terms) Act 1973 has not been broken. However, it would also seem that s. 8(2)(b)(iii) of the 1973 Act has been broken because the true owner would have the right to disturb the defendant's quiet possession of the goods. Section 8(2) only implies a warranty, unlike s. 8(1) which implies a condition. However, it seems virtually certain that a hire-purchase agreement would contain an express term that the finance company remained the owner of the goods until the hirer had paid all of the instalments. We saw earlier in this chapter in *Barber* v *NWS Bank plc* [1996] 1 All ER 906 that the Court of Appeal classified such a term as a condition, breach of which would entitle the hirer to the return of all money paid under the contract. In *Barber* v *NWS Bank plc* Sir Roger Parker, giving the only judgment of the Court of Appeal, said that he regarded *Karflex* v *Poole* as 'plainly right'.

4.5 Sale by Sample (Section 15)

The final term which the Sale of Goods Act 1979 implies is contained in s. 15(2). It states:

In the case of a contract for sale by sample there is an implied [term]—
(a) that the bulk will correspond with the sample in quality; ...
(c) that the goods will be free from any defect, making their quality unsatisfactory, which would not be apparent on reasonable examination of the sample.

This section applies to all sales by sample, whether made in the course of business or not. Of course, the vast majority of sales by sample will be made by a business to another business. Consumers buy relatively few goods by sample, but it is necessary to understand the terms implied into contracts made on the basis of a sample to give a full picture of the implied terms.

4.5.1 WHEN IS A SALE 'BY SAMPLE'?

Section 15(1) of the Sale of Goods Act 1979 states that: 'A contract of sale is a contract for sale by sample where there is an express or implied term to that effect in the contract.'

When an express term of the contract states that the sale is by sample then this is straightforward. However, it is much more difficult to recognise an implied term which has the effect of making the sale by sample. Lord MacNaghten gave the classic description of an implied sale by sample in *Drummond* v *Van Ingen* (1887) 12 App Cas 284 at 297:

> The office [function] of a sample is to present to the eye the real meaning and intention of the parties with regard to the subject matter of the contract which, owing to the imperfection of language, it may be difficult or impossible to express in words. The sample speaks for itself.

SAQ 4/6

A consumer looks at a certain pair of shoes in a shop window. The consumer asks the shopkeeper for a pair of these shoes and the shopkeeper fetches an identical pair from the store room. The shopkeeper decided to stock these particular shoes because the manufacturer's salesman showed him a pair, to demonstrate the quality of the stitching and the thickness of the sole.

(a) Did the consumer buy the shoes by sample?

(b) Did the shopkeeper buy the shoes by sample?

(a) The consumer would not have bought the shoes by sample. There was no bulk and no sample.

(b) The shopkeeper would have bought the shoes by sample.

4.5.2 TERMS IMPLIED INTO A SALE BY SAMPLE

Section 15 of the 1979 Act implies two terms into a sale by sample. Section 15(2)(a) implies a term that the bulk will correspond with the sample in quality. This rule is similar to the rule in s. 13(1) which requires goods sold by description to match their description. The sample, in effect, is the description. Except as regards differences which would be regarded as trifles, the bulk of the goods must exactly match the sample. However, if the sample is given only for a visual examination, according to normal trade practice, then it is only as regards matters which a normal visual examination would have revealed that the bulk must match the sample in quality.

It is not a defence that a bulk which does not correspond with the sample in quality could easily be made to do so.

E & S Ruben Ltd v *Faire Bros & Co. Ltd* [1949] 1 All ER 215
The sellers sold 'Linatex', a type of vulcanised rubber, in rolls which were forty one feet long and five feet wide. The sale was by sample. The sample delivered was flat and soft, whereas the bulk delivered was crinkly and folded. These defects in the bulk could have been put right by warming the bulk and this would have been relatively easy to do.

STATUTORY IMPLIED TERMS AS TO CORRESPONDENCE WITH DESCRIPTION

Held: The sellers were in breach of s. 15(2)(a). (An extract from the judgment of Hilberry J is set out in *Cases and Materials* (**4.4**).)

Section 15(2)(c) requires the goods to be free from any defect, making their quality unsatisfactory, which a reasonable examination of the sample would not reveal. This is similar to s. 14(2), the requirement of satisfactory quality. However, under s. 14(2) the buyer has no obligation to examine the goods, whereas under s. 15(2)(c) the buyer is not protected as regards defects which a reasonable examination of the sample would have revealed. Nor can a buyer claim that goods are of unsatisfactory quality if the sale was by sample and the defects rendering the goods unsatisfactory would have been apparent on a reasonable examination of the sample (s. 14(2C)(c).) The presumption here is that the buyer will examine the sample to see that it is of satisfactory quality.

Section 15(2)(c) does not state that the bulk must in all cases be free of all defects which were not present in the sample. The defects which make the bulk unsatisfactory must also have been apparent on a reasonable examination of the sample.

Godley v *Perry* [1960] 1 All ER 36
A retailer bought a number of catapults from a wholesaler. The sale was by sample. The retailer sold one of the catapults to a young boy. This catapult snapped while the boy was using it, and this caused the boy to lose an eye. The boy recovered damages from the retailer under s. 14. The retailer sued the wholesaler under s. 15, claiming an indemnity for the damages paid to the boy. The retailer had tested the sample catapult, by pulling the elastic back. This had not revealed the defect which was in all of the catapults. The defect could only have been discovered by snapping a catapult or testing it to destruction.
Held: The wholesaler was liable under s. 15(2)(c). The defect which made the bulk of the catapults unsatisfactory was not apparent on a reasonable examination of the sample. (In *Cases and Materials* (**4.4**) the judgment of Edmund Davies J is set out. In this judgment the meaning of a 'reasonable examination' of the sample was considered in some depth.)

ACTIVITY 4/9

In the following case the sellers were not liable under s. 15. Read the facts of the case, and the judgment of Sellers J in *Cases and Materials* (4.4), and then write down:

(a) **Why the sellers were not liable under s. 15(2)(a).**

(b) **Why the sellers were not liable under s. 15(2)(c).**

Steels & Busks Ltd v *Bleecker Bik & Co. Ltd* [1956] 1 Lloyd's Rep 228
Under previous contracts S had bought pale crepe rubber from B. In the contract in dispute, S agreed to buy five tons of pale crepe rubber from B, 'quality as previously delivered'. This was a sale by sample. The bulk was the five tons to be delivered, the sample was the rubber previously supplied. The five tons were delivered, and S used this rubber to make corsets. However, the five tons delivered contained an invisible preservative, PNP, which had not been present in the rubber previously supplied. This preservative stained the fabric of the corsets.

(a) Sellers J held that the sellers were not liable under s. 15(2)(a) because the defect in the rubber would not have been apparent on a reasonable examination of the sample. Only a microscopic examination would have revealed the defect.

104 STATUTORY IMPLIED TERMS AS TO CORRESPONDENCE WITH DESCRIPTION

(b) Section 15(2)(c) had not been broken because the bulk was of merchantable (now satisfactory) quality. It could be used for any of its normal purposes once the dye had been washed out. Sellers J held that PNP was not a defect or an impurity, but a preservative the presence of which did not affect quality. (In the light of ss. 14(2A) and 14(2B) of the 1979 Act it is now possible that the rubber would be of unsatisfactory quality, in which case B would succeed under s. 15(2)(c).)

4.5.3 SALE BY SAMPLE AND DESCRIPTION

Section 13(2) of the Sale of Goods Act 1979 provides that:

> If the sale is by sample as well as by description it is not sufficient that the bulk of the goods corresponds with the sample if the goods do not also correspond with the description.

This section seems straightforward enough. If the sale is by sample and description then the goods must match both.

Nichol v *Godts* (1854) 10 Ex 191
B bought by sample oil which was described as 'foreign refined rape oil'. The bulk of the oil did correspond with the sample. However, neither the bulk nor the sample matched the description because the oil was in fact a mixture of rape and hemp oil. Held: The buyer could reject the oil.

4.5.4 THE BUYER'S RIGHT TO COMPARE THE BULK WITH THE SAMPLE

Section 34 of the Sale of Goods Act 1979 says that when tendering delivery of goods sold by sample the seller must, on request, afford the buyer a reasonable opportunity to compare the bulk with the sample. Section 35(2)(b), which replaces the repealed s. 15(2)(b), says that the buyer is not deemed to have accepted the goods until he has had a reasonable opportunity of comparing the bulk with the sample. (A buyer who is deemed to have accepted goods will no longer be able to reject them for breach of condition, but will still be able to claim damages.)

4.5.5 TERMS AS TO SAMPLE IN OTHER CONSUMER TRANSACTIONS

Terms which correspond to s. 15 of the Sale of Goods Act 1979 are implied by s. 11 of the Supply of Goods (Implied Terms) Act 1973 and ss. 5 and 10 of the Supply of Goods and Services Act 1982. These terms can be read in *Cases and Materials* (4.1).

4.6 No Implied Term in a Sale by Model

Consumers do not buy many goods by sample. Retailers, on the other hand, do. When a shopkeeper is deciding whether or not to stock a particular item, a sales representative will commonly produce a sample to demonstrate the qualities of the product.

It often happens that consumers try a product in a shop and then, satisfied with the model product they have tried, agree to make a purchase. Often the shop does not sell the actual model tested, but a different one which is assumed by both parties to be the same in every respect. (An example is given in **SAQ 4/6** above.) This is not a sale by sample, as there is no bulk. Nor is it a sale by description, unless the retailer made a description. Nor will s. 14 of the Sale of Goods Act 1979 provide any help unless the goods supplied are of unsatisfactory quality. It seems that in cases such as these there ought to be an implied term that the actual product bought should be identical to the model tested. If there is such an implied term it will arise as a matter of general contract law, rather than be implied by any of the sections of the 1979 Act.

STATUTORY IMPLIED TERMS AS TO CORRESPONDENCE WITH DESCRIPTION

4.7 The Status of the Implied Terms

In all three of the statutes which we have considered the terms as to the right to sell, hire, etc. are conditions. Breach of these particular terms, as we have seen, give the buyer, bailee, etc. the right to terminate the contract and receive the return of all money paid under the contract. This is the case even if a buyer of goods would ordinarily be regarded as having accepted the goods, or even if a person to whom goods were supplied otherwise than under a contract of sale of goods would be regarded as having affirmed the contract, because the terms implied are so fundamental that breach of them amounts to a total failure of consideration.

The terms as to correspondence with description, satisfactory quality, fitness for purpose, and correspondence by sample are, in all three statutes, conditions. If any of these conditions are broken then a consumer will have the right to terminate the contract and get his money back. (The right to terminate a contract of sale of goods, but not the right to claim damages, will be lost when the consumer accepts the goods. The right to reject in contracts other than sales of goods, but not the right to damages, will be lost once the contract has been affirmed. See **Chapter 1** at **1.9.1.1**.) The terms as to freedom from encumbrances and quiet possession are, in all three statutes, warranties. If one of the warranties is broken then the consumer will be entitled to damages only.

The consumer's right to reject for breach of one of the conditions is not affected by the breach being only very slight. This is made plain by s. 15A of the Sale of Goods Act 1979, which reads:

> (1) Where in the case of a contract of sale—
>   (a) the buyer would, apart from this subsection, have the right to reject goods by reason of a breach on the part of the seller of a term implied by section 13, 14, or 15, above, but
>   (b) the breach is so slight that it would be unreasonable for him to reject them,
> then, if the buyer does not deal as a consumer, the breach is not to be treated as a breach of condition but may be treated as a breach of warranty.
> (2) This section applies unless a contrary intention appears in, or is to be implied from, the contract.
> (3) It is for the seller to show that a breach fell within subsection (1)(b) above.

Terms identical in effect are contained in s. 11A of the 1973 Act and ss. 5A and 10A of the 1982 Act.

SAQ 4/7

(a) What is the status of s. 8 of the 1982 Act as regards consumer buyers?

(b) What is the status of s. 8 as regards non-consumer buyers?

(c) When is a buyer a consumer? (This matter was dealt with in the Introduction).

106 STATUTORY IMPLIED TERMS AS TO CORRESPONDENCE WITH DESCRIPTION

(a) As regards consumer buyers, all of the implied terms labelled as conditions give the consumer the right to reject the goods and terminate the contract.

(b) As regards non-consumer buyers, the terms are conditions unless the breach is so slight that it would be unreasonable for the buyer to reject the goods.

(c) Essentially, a buyer who buys goods otherwise than in the course of business, from a seller who sells such goods in the course of business, is a consumer buyer as long as the goods are of a type ordinarily supplied for private use or consumption.

SAQ 4/8

You might remember *Millars of Falkirk* v *Turpie* from Chapter 3 at 3.4.5.3). In that case, a Ford Granada was sold with a defective steering unit which meant that the car could not be driven. The court decided that the car was of merchantable quality (although it would not today be of satisfactory quality) because it felt that rejection of the car was too drastic a remedy for a relatively minor matter which could be put right fairly easily.

(a) Did the court in *Millars of Falkirk* v *Turpie* have the option of awarding damages to the buyer but not letting him call the contract off?

(b) Could the court now award the buyer (a solicitor) damages instead of allowing him to call the contract off?

(c) Would the garage which sold the car to the solicitor now be able to reject the car and return it to the manufacturer from whom it was bought?

(a) The court did not have the option of awarding the buyer only damages. It was all or nothing. Either the car was not of merchantable quality, in which case the buyer could reject it, or it was of merchantable quality, in which case the buyer had no remedy.

(b) The solicitor who bought the car was a consumer. The court would therefore be in the same position today. Either the car is not of satisfactory quality, in which case the solicitor can reject it; or it is of satisfactory quality, in which case the solicitor has no remedy.

(c) The garage might well be entitled only to damages, under s. 15A. This would depend upon whether or not the contract under which the garage bought the car showed an intention that the term should be a condition, and whether or not the breach was so slight as to make rejection of the car unreasonable.

4.8 The Supply of a Service

In **Chapter 3** we examined the effect of s. 13 of the Supply of Goods and Services Act 1982, and saw that it implies into contracts to supply a service in the course of a business a term that the service will be supplied using reasonable care and skill. You should remember this term when considering the types of contracts which we have considered in this chapter. It is possible for a contract to be classified as a contract for the supply of a service even though goods are also transferred or bailed by way of hire (s. 12(3) of the 1982 Act).

STATUTORY IMPLIED TERMS AS TO CORRESPONDENCE WITH DESCRIPTION

4.9 Summary

In this chapter we have covered the following points:

- When goods are sold, hired, etc. by description the various statutes imply a term that the goods will correspond with the description.

- Not all descriptions will take effect to mean that the sale, hire, etc. was made by description.

- When the term as to correspondence with description is breached a consumer will always have the right to terminate the contract and receive back money paid. In contracts of sale of goods only, this right will be lost once the goods have been accepted. In other contracts it will be lost once the contract has been affirmed.

- Implied terms as to the right to sell, hire, etc. are implied into all transactions under which a consumer acquires goods.

- If the term as to the right to sell, hire, etc. is breached this is regarded as a total failure of consideration. Hence the consumer is entitled to the return of all money paid, even in a sale of goods where the goods would ordinarily have been accepted and in other contracts where the contract would ordinarily have been affirmed.

- Warranties that the goods are free from encumbrances, and that the consumer will enjoy quiet possession, are implied into all transactions under which a consumer acquires goods.

- If one of the warranties is broken the consumer is entitled only to damages.

- Where a consumer acquires goods by sample two conditions are implied:

    (a) that the bulk of the goods will correspond with the sample in quality, and

    (b) that the goods will be free from defects which make their quality unsatisfactory if these defects would not be apparent on a reasonable examination of the sample.

- If either of the terms as to sample is breached then the consumer will be entitled to terminate the contract and receive back money paid. In contracts of sale of goods only, this right will be lost once the goods have been accepted; in other contracts, once the contract has been affirmed.

- In a sale by model there is no statutory implied term that the goods acquired will exactly match the model examined.

108 STATUTORY IMPLIED TERMS AS TO CORRESPONDENCE WITH DESCRIPTION

4.10 End of Chapter Assessment Questions

This question is concerned not only with the sections of the Sale of Goods Act 1979 which were covered in this chapter, but also with s. 14(2) and (3), which were covered in **Chapter 3**.

STATUTORY IMPLIED TERMS AS TO CORRESPONDENCE WITH DESCRIPTION

(1) Complete the following Table to indicate which sections of which statutes (Sale of Goods Act 1979, Supply of Goods (Implied Terms) Act 1973 or Supply of Goods and Services Act 1982) imply the terms indicated.

Term implied \ Type of transaction	Sale of goods	Hire-purchase	Transfer of property in goods	Hire of goods
The right to sell/transfer property				
Freedom from encumbrances and quiet possession				
Correspondence with description				
Satisfactory quality in business deals				
Fitness for purpose in business deals				
Correspondence with sample				

110 STATUTORY IMPLIED TERMS AS TO CORRESPONDENCE WITH DESCRIPTION

(2) One year ago Gazza, an ardent soccer fan, decided that he would need a better television to watch his team's progress in the European Cup, which was due to start in 12 months time. Gazza visited the premises of TeleHire Ltd and took a 24 inch SuperLuxe Television on HP over three years. Gazza then sold his old television to a friend. Last week, shortly before the first match of the European Cup, a police officer visited Gazza's flat and took the hired television away. The officer explained that, unknown to TeleHire Ltd, the television was one of a consignment which had been stolen from the manufacturer. The thief had sold the televisions on to the wholesaler from whom TeleHire Ltd had bought them.

Gazza felt that he needed a television urgently and hurried out to buy a new Widescreen Super Digital Soccerview Special TV from BestTellies Ltd, who were to install the television in Gazza's home. Shortly after the installer had gone, Gazza found that this television could not get any picture at all. He rang BestTellies Ltd who explained that there was nothing wrong with the television, but the installer found that Gazza's aerial connection was very unusual, and very difficult to connect to the television. It seems that the failure to attach the television to Gazza's aerial connection is the source of the problems with the picture. BestTellies Ltd say that they could fit a new aerial connection but that this would cost £15.

Gazza's team are eliminated from the European Cup in the first round. Gazza decides never to watch football again and becomes a fan of classical music. He visits BestSounds Ltd and buys a top of the range Hi-Fi set and arranges for a large aerial to be installed in his garden. BestSounds explain that Gazza will first need to have a specified area concreted to a depth of three feet. Gazza arranges for MacTar Ltd to do the concreting. The concreting is done and the aerial is installed. In a gale the aerial blows down and is badly damaged. BestSounds say that this is not their fault, it must have been due to the faulty concreting. MacTar Ltd say that there was nothing wrong with their work. As Gazza can no longer listen to his favourite station he has decided that he no longer wants the expensive Hi-Fi equipment which he bought.

Advise Gazza of any rights he may have against TeleHire Ltd, BestTellies Ltd, BestSounds Ltd or MacTar Ltd.

See *Cases and Materials* (4.6) for outline answers.

CHAPTER FIVE

MISCELLANEOUS ASPECTS OF THE SALE OF GOODS ACT 1979

5.1 Objectives

By the end of this chapter you should be able to:

- explain why it can be important to know when the ownership of goods passes to a consumer who is buying the goods;

- describe the rules relating to the transfer of the property in goods which are contained in ss. 16–20 of the Sale of Goods Act 1979;

- analyse when the property in the goods and the risk pass to the consumer in typical consumer sales;

- explain the circumstances in which the 1979 Act will make a contract void for mistake or avoided on the grounds of frustration;

- explain the ways in which a seller of goods can effect delivery, and how the place of delivery will be determined;

- explain the remedies available to a consumer if goods are delivered late or if the wrong quantity of goods is delivered;

- describe the circumstances in which an unpaid seller will have a lien over the goods or a right to resell the goods;

- analyse the legal position when a retailer sells the same goods to two different consumers;

- explain the protection given to a consumer who buys a motor vehicle which is the subject of a prior hire-purchase agreement;

- outline the effect of the Unsolicited Goods and Services Act 1971.

5.2 Introduction

In this chapter we examine several disparate sections of the Sale of Goods Act 1979 which can be of importance to consumers. Most of the matters dealt with by these sections do not have equivalents in contracts other than sales of goods, such as contracts to hire or to supply services. Where there is an equivalent this is also examined.

We begin by examining the precise time at which a consumer becomes the owner of the goods being bought, and why this might be of particular importance to the consumer.

Then we examine the Sale of Goods Act 1979 rules on delivery. How is the place of delivery determined? What does the seller's duty to deliver entail? What remedies are available if the wrong quantity of goods is delivered? What remedies are available if delivery is not made on time?

We move on to examine the ways in which the contract price can be determined, and the position of a seller who has not yet been fully paid. Has the seller the right to keep hold of the goods until payment? Has the seller the right to sell the goods to a second consumer?

Then we consider two exceptions to the *nemo dat* rule (that a person who does not own goods cannot pass ownership to someone else). We examine the position where the same goods are sold to two different consumers, and the position of a consumer who buys a motor vehicle which is subject to a prior hire-purchase agreement.

Finally, we examine the provisions of the Unsolicited Goods and Services Act 1971. We shall see that in certain circumstances this Act allows a consumer who has been sent goods without a prior request to treat the goods as a gift.

5.3 Sales of Goods: the Passing of the Property and the Risk

5.3.1 INTRODUCTION

In a typical consumer sale of goods the consumer takes the goods away immediately after the making of the contract and the payment of the price. In such situations there is no problem about when the property in the goods (ownership of them) and the risk pass to the consumer. However, as we shall see, the 1979 Act does not link the passing of the property to the payment of the price. There may be circumstances in which a consumer will have paid the price and yet not received ownership of the goods. There may also be circumstances in which a consumer will be the owner of the goods, even though the price has not yet been paid and possession of the goods has not yet been obtained. Both of these sets of circumstances could put the consumer into an unfortunate position.

SAQ 5/1

For what two reasons in particular might it be important to know whether or not the property in the goods had passed to a consumer who had bought them? (Need a hint? Think about: the goods being damaged; the seller becoming insolvent.)

You might have deduced that it might be important to determine exactly when the property and the risk pass for the following reasons:

    (a)   If the goods are damaged or destroyed before the property has passed to the consumer, the seller will have to bear the loss. (Generally, as we shall see, the risk

MISCELLANEOUS ASPECTS OF THE SALE OF GOODS ACT 1979

of loss or damage to the goods passes with the property). Whereas if the goods are damaged or destroyed after the property has passed to the consumer, it is the consumer who will have to bear the loss.

(b) If the seller becomes insolvent, the consumer will only be able to claim undelivered goods, or keep goods which have been delivered, if the property has passed. If the property has not passed the consumer will be reduced to making a claim against the liquidator or receiver as an unsecured creditor.

5.3.2 THE RULES CONTAINED IN THE SALE OF GOODS ACT 1979

Four sections of the Sale of Goods Act 1979 concern themselves with the passing of the property in the goods. Before we examine these sections in detail we need to understand the difference between specific goods, on the one hand, and unascertained or future goods, on the other.

Section 61(1) of the 1979 Act, the interpretation section, defines specific goods as 'goods identified and agreed on at the time a contract of sale is made'. For example, if I visited a garage and agreed to buy a particular used car then this would be a contract for the sale of specific goods. The car has been identified and agreed upon, and the garage would not be able to perform the contract by delivering any other car.

The 1979 Act provides no definition of unascertained goods. In effect, such goods are defined by default as being goods which are not specific. Unascertained goods are sold by description, rather than by being identified and agreed upon at the time of sale. So if, to extend the previous example, you had phoned a car dealer and ordered a new Nissan Primera, the contract would be for the sale of unascertained goods; you would not, at this stage, know exactly which car from the dealer's stock you were going to get. The dealer might have a particular car in mind, but would be under no obligation to deliver that car. The delivery of any new car which matched the contract description would fulfil the contract.

The Act also refers to 'future goods', which s. 61(1) defines as 'goods to be manufactured or acquired by the seller after the making of the contract of sale'. So if Nissan agree to supply a garage with 100 cars which have yet to be manufactured, then this would be a sale of future goods. It should be noticed that the goods can be future goods even if they do exist when the contract is made. Existing goods which the seller has yet to acquire are as much future goods as goods which have yet to be manufactured. As far as the rules on the passing of the property are concerned, future goods can never be specific. A specialist car dealer might agree to sell a vintage car to a consumer, knowing from where such a car could be obtained. This would be a sale of future goods, even though the car does exist when the contract is made.

ACTIVITY 5/1

The following cases were considered in Chapters 3 and 4. Remind yourselves of the facts of each case and then write down, next to the names of each case, whether the contract was for the sale of specific, ascertained or future goods.

Rowland v *Divall* (1923) (page 97)
Arcos v *Ronaasen* (1933) (page 93)
Bartlett v *Sydney Marcus Ltd* (1965) (page 67)
Kendall (Henry) & Sons v *William Lillico & Sons Ltd* (1969) (page 71)
Shine v *General Guarantee Corporation* (1988) (page 71)

Harlingdon & Leinster Enterprises Ltd v *Christopher Hull Fine Art Ltd* (1991) (page 91)
Grant v *Australian Knitting Mills Ltd* (1939) (page 78)
Brown & Son Ltd v *Craiks Ltd* (1970) (page 71)

Rowland v *Divall, Bartlett* v *Sydney Marcus Ltd, Shine* v *General Guarantee Corporation, Grant* v *Australian Knitting Mills Ltd,* and *Harlingdon & Leinster Enterprises Ltd* v *Christopher Hull Fine Art Ltd* were all sales of specific goods. *Arcos* v *Ronaasen, Kendall (Henry) & Sons* v *William Lillico & Sons Ltd,* and *Brown & Son Ltd* v *Craiks Ltd* were all sales of unascertained (and possibly future) goods.

Now that we know how to distinguish specific, unascertained, and future goods we can apply the rules contained in ss. 16–20 of the 1979 Act (see *Cases and Materials* (5.1.1)). First we shall consider the rules which apply to specific goods and then those which apply to unascertained and future goods.

5.3.2.1 Specific goods

Section 17 of the Sale of Goods Act 1979 states that:

> (1) Where there is a contract for the sale of specific or ascertained goods the property in them is transferred to the buyer at such time as the parties to the contract intend it to be transferred.
> (2) For the purpose of ascertaining the intention of the parties regard shall be had to the terms of the contract, the conduct of the parties, and the circumstances of the case.

This section must be the starting point for deciding when the property in specific goods is to pass. It tells us that the property is to pass when the parties intend that it should, and also makes it quite plain that this intention can be inferred. Obviously, if the terms of the contract state exactly when the property is to pass then the intention of the parties will be quite clear. But s. 17 tells us that the conduct of the parties and the circumstances of the case can also indicate the parties' intention.

We shall see shortly that s. 18 lays down five rules of presumed intention. These rules tell us when the property is to pass if the parties' intentions are not ascertainable from the terms, the parties' conduct and the circumstances of the case. It is quite plain that s. 18 is subservient to s. 17, and that s. 18 will only apply if no intention was expressly or impliedly indicated by the parties. However, if one of the rules in s. 18 has already passed the property to the buyer, then it will be too late for the parties to show a contrary intention as to when the property should pass.

Dennant v *Skinner and Collom* [1948] 2 All ER 29
B bought several cars at an auction. After the cars had been knocked down to him, B paid for them with a bad cheque. The auctioneer, the plaintiff, would not take the cheque until B signed a statement that the property in the cars should not pass until the cheque was honoured. B signed the statement and took the cars away. The defendant, acting innocently, subsequently bought one of the cars.

ACTIVITY 5/2

Read the extract from Hallett J's judgment in the *Dennant* case in *Cases and Materials* (5.1.1.1). What was the outcome of this case?

MISCELLANEOUS ASPECTS OF THE SALE OF GOODS ACT 1979

Hallett J held that this was clearly an unconditional contract of sale and, as there was no evidence of any different intention, the property in the car passed to B as soon as it was knocked down to him. Once the property had passed, any intention later shown by the parties was too late to have any effect.

Rules of presumed intention

Section 18 lays down five rules for deciding when the property in the goods should pass, to be used only when the intention of the parties has not been expressed and cannot be inferred. The first four rules in s. 18 apply to specific goods, the fifth to unascertained and future goods. Before considering the rules in s. 18 it must be re-emphasised that all of these rules are subservient to s. 17, as is made plain by the first sentence of s. 18:

> Unless a different intention appears, the following are rules for ascertaining the intention of the parties as to the time at which the property in the goods is to pass to the buyer.

Rule 1 states:

> Where there is an unconditional contract for the sale of specific goods in a deliverable state the property in the goods passes to the buyer when the contract is made, and it is immaterial whether the time of payment or the time of delivery, or both, be postponed.

Four requirements are essential if Rule 1 is to apply:

- The contract of sale must be unconditional.

- The goods must be specific goods.

- The goods must be in a deliverable state.

- The parties must have not indicated a contrary intention.

The first requirement of Rule 1 is that the contract of sale must be unconditional. This means that the contract of sale must not make the passing of the property subject to the fulfilment of any condition. Perhaps the most commonly imposed condition is that the property should remain with the seller until payment is made. However, such a condition would either have to be a term of the contract of sale, or would have to be inferred from the parties' conduct or the circumstances of the case. Rule 1 states that no such intention should be inferred merely because the time of delivery or of payment is deferred.

Tarling v Baxter (1827) 6 B & C 360
On 6 January a contract to sell a haystack was made. The price was to be paid on 4 February and the haystack was not to be moved before 1 May. On 20 January the haystack was destroyed by fire.

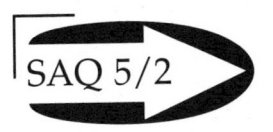

SAQ 5/2

The above case predates the 1979 Act. Would Rule 1 nowadays apply, and pass the property to the buyer when the contract was made?

The court held that the property had passed to the buyer on 6 January. Nowadays Rule 1 would apply, and the same conclusion would be reached.

The second requirement of Rule 1 is that the goods sold must be specific goods. We have already seen that specific goods are defined by s. 61(1) of the 1979 Act as goods identified and agreed on at the time the contract of sale is made.

This definition might seem to include future goods, as long as they were identified and agreed upon at the time of sale. However, common sense tells us that the property in future goods can hardly pass at the time of sale, as at that time the goods either do not yet exist or have yet to be acquired by the seller. Future goods, like unascertained goods, are dealt with by Rule 5.

The third requirement is that the goods should be in a deliverable state. Section 61(5) of the 1979 Act defines the meaning of this:

> Goods are in a deliverable state within the meaning of this Act when they are in such a state that the buyer would under the contract be bound to take delivery of them.

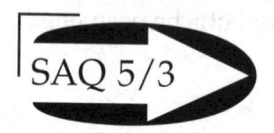

SAQ 5/3

Jane buys a new car from a garage. The car is not of satisfactory quality because its radiator has a leak. This breach would entitle Jane to reject the car. Was the car in a deliverable state, and therefore governed by s. 18 Rule 1? Read s. 18 Rule 1 and s. 61(5) and write down your opinion.

A literal interpretation of s. 18 Rule 1 and s. 61(5) might suggest that the car was not in a deliverable state. Jane would not have been bound to take delivery of the car as it was not of satisfactory quality. However, the courts have tended not to adopt this interpretation. Instead the courts have interpreted s. 61(5) to mean that goods are in a deliverable state if the terms of the contract do not still compel the seller to do something to the goods before the buyer would be bound to take delivery of them. So, unless a contrary intention could be inferred, Rule 1 would apply and the property in the car would have passed to Jane at the time when the contract was made.

Underwood Ltd v Burgh Castle Brick and Cement Syndicate [1922] 1 KB 343
The contract was for the sale of a 30 ton horizontal condensing engine which was bolted to, and embedded in, a concrete floor. It took two days to unbolt the engine and a further two weeks to remove it from the concrete to which it had become attached by its own weight. While the engine was being loaded onto a railway wagon it was accidentally damaged.
Held: Property had not passed to the buyer at the time of the accident.

MISCELLANEOUS ASPECTS OF THE SALE OF GOODS ACT 1979 117

ACTIVITY 5/3

Read the judgment of Bankes LJ in the *Underwood* case in *Cases and Materials* (5.1.1.1). On what two grounds did Bankes LJ hold that property had not passed?

Bankes LJ held either that Rule 1 did not apply because the risk and expense of dismantling the engine showed that the parties had evinced a different intention. Alternatively, Rule 1 did not apply because, as the engine had to be unfixed from the seller's premises, it was not in a deliverable state when sold. The mere fact that the goods had to be taken to bits before delivery would not have prevented the goods from being in a deliverable state. Rowlatt J, in the High Court, gave the example of a billiard table which on account of its size would have to be dismantled before the buyer could take it away, but said that this would not prevent the table from being in a deliverable state. Nor, he said, would the need to pack the goods. Bankes LJ, in the Court of Appeal, explained that in order for an item to be in a deliverable state 'it must have everything done to it that the sellers had to do to it as an article'.

The final requirement of Rule 1 is that, like all the Rules, it will only apply if the parties do not show an intention as to when the property is to pass. We have already seen that the parties may agree that the sale is subject to a condition precedent such as that the property is not to pass until the price is paid. We have also seen that Rule 1 says that it is immaterial whether the time of payment or the time of delivery, or of both, be postponed.

Does section 18 Rule 1 apply to a typical consumer purchase of goods?

The wording of s. 18 Rule 1 seems straightforward enough, yet the Rule seems to be clearly out of line with the expectations of modern consumers. In *R.V. Ward Ltd v Bignall* [1967] 1 QB 534 Diplock LJ at 545 said: 'The governing rule, however, is in section 17, and in modern times very little is needed to give rise to the inference that the property in specific goods is to pass only on delivery or payment.' *R.V. Ward Ltd v Bignall* was not a consumer case. The defendant, a car dealer, agreed to buy two cars from the plaintiff, another car dealer, for £850. The defendant paid a £25 deposit but left both cars with the plaintiff pending payment of the balance of the price. In the Court of Appeal both Sellers and Diplock LJJ were of the opinion that s. 17 would operate so as to prevent the operation of s. 18 Rule 1. Applying s. 17, the property in the goods did not pass to the buyer on the making of the contract.

It is fairly well settled that in supermarket sales the courts will imply an intention that the property is not to pass until the price is paid. The contract may be made at the till, and the goods which the cashier rings up are specific goods in a deliverable state, but it is presumed that the parties do not intend the property to pass until the price is paid. However, in some circumstances the shopper at the supermarket and the management of the supermarket might show that they intend the property to pass even though the full price has not been paid.

Lacis v Cashmarts [1969] 2 QB 400
The defendant, a shopper in a cash and carry store, loaded a basket with £185 worth of goods. At the cash desk an assistant removed the goods from the defendant's basket and put them into a wire trolley. The assistant called out the prices of the goods and the

manager rang the prices up on a till. The till could not ring up amounts over £100, so the manager therefore first rang up £100 and then rang up £85. The manager forgot about the £100 and only asked for £85. The shopper paid, knowing that he had been undercharged by £100. The defendant was convicted of stealing £100 worth of the goods and appealed to the Divisional Court.

Held: The defendant's appeal was allowed because the defendant had taken the goods with the consent of the manager. Generally, the property in goods bought in supermarkets and cash and carry stores will only pass on payment of the price because that is the intention of the parties. But when the defendant paid the price of £85, property in all of the goods passed because the manager handed them to the defendant. (It should be noticed that the defendant was charged under the Larceny Act 1916. This Act is now repealed. The defendant would now be guilty of an offence under the Theft Act 1968.) The judgment of Lord Parker CJ is set out in *Cases and Materials* (5.1.1.1).

Davies v *Leighton* [1979] Crim LR 575

The defendant was charged with theft. In a supermarket she had asked an assistant for a quantity of apples and tomatoes. The assistant had weighed and bagged the goods and handed them to the defendant, who had left the supermarket without paying for the goods. The defendant argued that property in the goods passed at the time she received them from the assistant, and at that time there was no evidence of theft because at that time she had not intended to appropriate property belonging to another.

Held: The Divisional Court convicted the defendant, holding that it was well settled that in supermarket sales the property was not intended to pass until payment of the price. The assistant had no authority to deal with the transfer of the property and so could not change this general rule. If the person handing over the weighed, bagged goods had been in a managerial position the case might have been different.

A more difficult question to answer is whether in a non-self-service shop the property also passes only on the payment of the price? Support for that view can be found in the well known case of *Ingram* v *Little* [1960] 1 QB 31. In that case a rogue, having been taken for a ride in a car offered for sale by private vendors, agreed to buy the car. When the rogue produced a cheque book the vendors made it plain that they would not take a cheque. Subsequently the vendors, having been taken in by the rogue's false claims as to his identity, did accept a cheque which proved to be worthless. Dealing with the position as it was when the rogue produced the cheque book, Sellers LJ, at 49, drew the inference that, 'the property would not have passed until cash had been paid'. Sellers LJ thought that this view could be reached either on the basis that there was no contract made until the vendors agreed to accept a cheque or on the basis that the failure to pay cash was a repudiation of the contract, that this repudiation was immediately accepted by the vendors, and that this therefore ended the contract. As retailers are no less keen to be paid for their goods than other sellers, either of these points of view could be applied when a consumer buys goods in a non-self-service shop. Let us assume that a consumer buys expensive specific goods from a shop where he is not known, perhaps a Persian rug for £1,500, and then offers to pay by cheque. It seems very unlikely that the shopkeeper will agree to the consumer immediately taking the goods away. (If the price of the goods was under £50 and the cheque and was backed up by a cheque guarantee card the position would of course be quite different.) The most obvious way in which this conclusion might be reached would seem to be that the shopkeeper, like the vendors of the car in *Ingram* v *Little*, would not intend property to pass until a satisfactory method of payment had been agreed. (Alternatively, the shopkeeper who had been given a cheque could be regarded as an unpaid seller within the meaning of s. 39 of the 1979 Act, and be entitled to a lien over the goods. The unpaid seller's lien is considered below at **5.5.2**.)

Let us now remind ourselves of why it is likely to matter whether or not the property in specific goods bought in a shop, but to be delivered later, passes at the time of the contract. If the property does pass immediately is this in the consumer's favour or to the consumer's detriment? Answer the two following SAQs and you will have reached an answer.

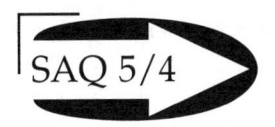

MISCELLANEOUS ASPECTS OF THE SALE OF GOODS ACT 1979

SAQ 5/4

A consumer buys specific goods, a Persian carpet, from a shop for £950. The consumer pays with a cheque. The shopkeeper says that the goods cannot be taken away before the cheque is cleared. The following day the shop's entire stock is destroyed in a fire. The consumer does not know of the fire. The cheque is cashed.

(a) Upon what basis will it be decided whether or not the consumer can claim back the purchase price?

(b) Had the property passed at the time of the fire?

(c) What if the consumer had paid cash, but agreed to collect the carpet the following week by which time it had been destroyed in the fire?

(a) If at the time of the fire the property in the goods had not passed to the consumer, then he will be entitled to claim back the price as the property and the risk would not have passed. (And so the contract would have become frustrated under s. 7 of the 1979 Act, see frustration below at **5.3.2.6**.) If the property in the goods had passed to the consumer then prima facie the consumer would not be entitled to any refund of the price. (However, if the goods were insured by the shopkeeper the consumer might well be entitled to the proceeds of the insurance. See risk below at **5.3.2.4**. If the fire was the fault of the shopkeeper then the shopkeeper would be liable for having failed to take reasonable care of the consumer's goods. See s. 20(3) of the 1979 Act below at **5.3.2.4**.)

(b) Section 18 Rule 1 would appear to state that the property in the goods passed to the consumer upon payment of the price. However, the intention of the parties appears to be that the property would not pass until the cheque was cleared. As s. 17 takes precedence over s. 18, it seems likely that the the property would not have passed.

(c) It the consumer had paid cash it would seem that the property in the goods would probably have passed, under s. 17, when the cash was paid. This reasoning seems in line with decision in *Lacis* v *Cashmarts* and with the judgment of Sellers LJ in *Ingram* v *Little*. Sellers LJ said, at 48: 'If [the rogue] had paid cash for the car, then it seems clear that there would have been a concluded and unimpeachable transaction.' In that case the property in the car would have passed to the rogue upon payment of cash as this is what the parties would have intended. (Again, the injustice that would seem to be caused to the consumer might be avoided if the shop's stock was insured (see risk below **5.3.2.4**) or if the fire was the fault of the shop.) An alternative view, applying the dicta of Diplock LJ in *R.V. Ward Ltd* v *Bignall*, is that the parties might have demonstrated an intention that the property was to pass only on delivery. However, in *Underwood Ltd* v *Burgh Castle Brick and Cement Syndicate* Bankes LJ said:

> In many sales of specific articles to be delivered the property passes on the making of the contract. A man may select and agree to buy a hat and the shopman may agree to deliver it at the buyer's house. There notwithstanding the obligation to deliver the hat, the property passes at the time of the contract.

Diplock's dictum seems to suggest that in modern times (post 1967?) this would be incorrect. However it is hard to know on what basis, other than a policy of increased consumer protection, it can be assumed that the intentions of shopkeepers and consumers have changed in this regard.

SAQ 5/5

A consumer buys specific goods, a Persian carpet, from a shop for £950. The consumer pays with a cheque. The shopkeeper says that the goods cannot be taken away before the cheque is cleared. The following day a winding-up petition is presented, but the consumer remains unaware of this. The cheque is cashed by the company liquidator.

(a) Upon what basis will it be decided whether or not the consumer is entitled to delivery of the goods?

(b) Had property passed at the time when the winding-up petition was presented?

(a) If at the time when the winding-up order was presented the property in the goods had already passed to the consumer, then the consumer will own the goods and they will therefore have to be delivered to him. If the property has not passed, then the consumer will not own the goods. The consumer will not therefore be entitled to delivery of the goods, but will be reduced to claiming a refund of the price as an unsecured creditor. (The contract would not become frustrated as the goods did not perish — see s. 7 below at **5.3.2.6**.)

(b) As in **SAQ 5/4**, it would seem that the parties' intention was that the property should not pass until the cheque was cleared.

The two SAQs just considered show that whether or not it will favour the consumer that the property passed upon the making of the contract will depend upon the nature of the problem which later arose. However, it is the intention of the parties at the time of the contract which bring s. 17 into play. At the time of the conclusion of the contract, the facts of **SAQs 5/4** and **5/5** are identical. As regards the passing of the property, it would not be possible for a court to adopt the outcome most favourable to the consumer without allowing their judgment as to what the parties intended at the time of the contract to be coloured by what the consumer would later prefer the court to decide. (The subsequent *behaviour* of the parties can of course indicate what they intended at the time of the contract. For example, in *R.V. Ward Ltd* v *Bignall* Sellers LJ, at 541, said: 'I would hold that the property had not passed to the buyer; all that has happened since [the date of the contract] fits in with that view, and is not in harmony with the two vehicles having been transferred to the buyer when the bargain was made.' However, the rules on the passing of the risk, considered below at **5.3.2.4** might help the consumer.)

Section 18 Rule 2 states:

> Where there is a contract for the sale of specific goods and the seller is bound to do something to the goods for the purpose of putting them into a deliverable state, the property does not pass until the thing is done and the buyer has notice that it has been done.

Rule 2 only applies where the seller must do something to specific goods 'for the purpose of putting them into a deliverable state'. We have already seen that Bankes LJ explained

MISCELLANEOUS ASPECTS OF THE SALE OF GOODS ACT 1979

that in order for an item to be in a deliverable state 'it must have everything done to it that the sellers had to do to it as an article'. (Although there is some authority that in a deliverable state refers to the physical moveability of the goods, see *Philip Head & Sons Ltd* v *Showfronts Ltd* [1970] 1 Lloyd's Rep 170 in **Cases and Materials (5.1.1.1)**.)

Note also that under Rule 2 the property does not pass as soon as the goods are put into a deliverable state. It passes only when the buyer has notice of this. In *Underwood Ltd* v *Burgh Castle Brick and Cement Syndicate* the contract for the sale of condensing engine was not governed by Rule 1 because the engine was not in a deliverable state when the contract was made. The contract would have been governed by Rule 2, and under this Rule the property would only have passed when the buyer had notice that the engine had been put into a deliverable state.

SAQ 5/6

A consumer buys a second-hand car from a garage. It is a term of the contract that the car is to be re-sprayed by the garage prior to delivery. At what time does the property in the car pass to the consumer?

The car would not be in a deliverable state as the seller had to re-spray it before the consumer would be bound to take delivery of it. Therefore the sale would be governed by s. 18 Rule 2 and the property would not pass until the garage had re-sprayed the car and the consumer had notice of this. (If in a deliverable state is taken to refer to the physical moveability of the goods, then the best approach seems to be to regard this sale as conditional, so that none of the s. 18 Rules apply. If this interpretation were adopted the same outcome would be reached under s. 17 — the parties would not have intended the property to pass until the seller had re-sprayed the car. In *Anderson* v *Ryan* [1964] IR 34 Henchy J considered a case where a customer visited a garage and agreed to buy a Mini car for £225 plus £22 for panel repairs which were to be made to it. The customer wrote out a cheque for £244, representing £225 for the Mini and the remainder for panel beating which the defendant had previously done for the plaintiff. Henchy J held that this was a mere agreement to sell, rather than a sale, and that the property did not pass. The parties did not intend the property to pass until the panel repairs had been done and paid for.

Rule 3 states:

> Where there is a contract for the sale of specific goods in a deliverable state but the seller is bound to weigh, measure, test, or do some other act or thing with reference to the goods for the purpose of ascertaining the price, the property does not pass until the act or thing is done and the buyer has notice that it has been done.

This Rule seems relatively straightforward. However, two points should be noted. First, Rule 3 is only to apply where the weighing etc. is to be done in order to ascertain the price. If it is done for some other reason, such as to check the quality of the goods, then Rule 3 will not apply. Second, Rule 3 will only apply if the weighing etc. is to be done by the seller.

When buying food consumers often ask for a particular item (such as a piece of meat or cheese) which is sold at a certain price per pound. Rule 3 might apply to these transactions in a non-self-service shop. However, earlier in this chapter we saw that in a supermarket, goods will not pass until the parties pay for them, as this is presumed to be the intention of the parties (*Davies* v *Leighton*). We also saw that the same reasoning might well apply to goods sold in non-self-service shops.

Rule 4 states:

When goods are delivered to the buyer on approval or on sale or return or other similar terms the property in the goods passes to the buyer:—
(a) when he signifies his approval or acceptance to the seller or does any other act adopting the transaction;
(b) if he does not signify his approval or acceptance to the seller but retains the goods without giving notice of rejection, then, if a time has been fixed for the return of the goods, on the expiration of that time, and, if no time has been fixed, on the expiration of a reasonable time.

The delivery of goods on approval or sale or return, within the meaning of Rule 4, does not amount to a sale or even to an agreement to sell. The 'buyer' is under no obligation at all to buy the goods. He can exercise his option to do so, or not, as he pleases. Until the 'buyer' does exercise his option to buy there is only an offer to sell on the part of the 'seller'.

It is not always easy to state when goods are delivered on approval or sale or return or other similar terms. The Sale of Goods Act 1979 does not define 'on approval' or 'sale or return' and the two phrases are thought to have much the same meaning, as the words 'or other similar terms' seems to apply to both. What is certain is that the buyer is under no obligation to buy. Shops commonly state that customers who are not completely satisfied with goods they have bought can return the goods within a certain time. These transactions are sales, with an express term as to returning the goods, rather than delivery of the goods on approval. If, however, a mail order company sends goods to a consumer on the understanding that they are delivered on approval then Rule 4 would govern the transaction. The position will depend upon the intention of the parties. Perhaps the easiest way to find this intention is to ask whether or not the parties would think that the 'seller' could call the whole deal off before the buyer was deemed to have accepted the offer in one of the ways set out in Rule 4. If the parties would think that the seller could do this then only an offer to sell would have been made and the transaction would be governed by Rule 4. If the parties would not think that the seller could do this then a contract would have been concluded, with an express term allowing the buyer to return the goods. If goods are ordered from a mail order company without an approval period being agreed then the sale is of unascertained goods.

SAQ 5/7

A consumer buys a bicycle from a shop. The shopkeeper agrees that if the consumer is not satisfied with the bicycle he can return it within one week. The consumer rides the bicycle into town and chains it up outside a shop. The bicycle is stolen.

(a) What would be the position if this was a sale from the outset?

(b) What would be the position if the contract was governed by s. 18 Rule 4?

(c) Would this be a sale from the outset?

MISCELLANEOUS ASPECTS OF THE SALE OF GOODS ACT 1979

(a) If the agreement was a sale from the outset the property would have passed (defeasibly) to the consumer. The loss would therefore have to be borne by the consumer.

(b) If the transaction were governed by s. 18 Rule 4 the property in the goods would not have passed. The loss would therefore be that of the shop (assuming that the consumer had not broken the duties of a bailee).

(c) The agreement looks very like a sale from the outset. The parties would not think that the shopkeeper had merely made an offer to sell (which he could of course revoke before the property passed).

When goods are delivered to a consumer on approval the property will pass under Rule 4 on the happening of various events. First, the property is to pass when the consumer signifies approval or acceptance to the seller. An obvious example of this would be that the consumer writes to the seller to say that the goods are accepted.

Second, the property passes when the consumer does any other act adopting the transaction. Any act which would prevent the goods from being returned to the seller would be an act adopting the transaction. Commonly this act will be that the consumer resells or pledges the goods.

Kirkham v *Attenborough* [1895–9] All ER Rep 450
K, a jewellery manufacturer, delivered jewellery to W on sale or return. Shortly afterwards, W pledged the jewellery to several pawnbrokers. W died, having never paid K for the jewellery. K sued the various pawnbrokers for the return of the jewellery. The pawnbrokers refused to return the goods unless K paid what they were owed.
Held: K did not get the jewellery back. When W pledged the jewellery to the pawnbrokers this was an act which adopted the transaction, because W no longer had control of the goods and the power to return them to K. At that time the property in the goods therefore passed to W under Rule 4, and K could not therefore get the return of the jewellery. (The full judgment of the Court of Appeal is set out in *Cases and Materials* (**5.1.1.1**.)

Third, the property will pass after the expiry of a fixed time. A fixed time might be stipulated by the terms of the contract. For example, S might sell goods to B on the understanding that if B does not return them by the end of the month, then B will have agreed to buy them.

Finally, if no time has been fixed, the property will pass if the consumer retains the goods for more than a reasonable time.

Poole v *Smith's Car Sales (Balham) Ltd* [1962] 2 All ER 482
In August 1960 S sold a four year old car to B, a car dealer, on 'sale or return'. The car was not returned by October 1960, so S wrote to B saying that if the car was not returned by 10 November, the car would be deemed to have been sold to B. The car was not returned until the end of November.
Held: The property had passed because the buyer had retained the car for more than a reasonable time. (An important factor was that the value of such a second-hand car was likely to fall fairly rapidly.)

The word 'retains' implies that the buyer must have some responsibility for failing to return the goods. If the failure to return is caused by actions beyond the buyer's control he will not be deemed to have retained the goods.

MISCELLANEOUS ASPECTS OF THE SALE OF GOODS ACT 1979

SAQ 5/8

Mary joins a book club. She receives several free books and in return agrees that thereafter she will be sent one book per month on approval. She further agrees that if she does not return such books within 21 days she will have to pay for them. There is no obligation to buy any books. Mary receives a book the day before she is due to go on a four week holiday. She has no time to return the book. After her holiday Mary sends the book back but the seller insists that she is too late. Will she have to pay for the book?

It would seem that Mary will have to pay for the book, which was delivered on approval. A time was fixed for the return of the good and that time has expired. (Many Book Clubs which operate this type of scheme agree that even if the fixed time has expired the book can still be returned.)

It is important to note that s. 18 Rule 4 will only apply where the goods are delivered in response to a request from the consumer. If the goods are delivered without such a request, the consumer can treat the goods as a gift. (See the Unsolicited Goods and Services Act 1971, at the end of this chapter.)

5.3.2.2 Unascertained goods

Consumers often buy unascertained goods. For example a consumer who orders a ton of coal to be delivered to his house or who fills his car with petrol at a filling station makes a contract to buy unascertained goods.

The transfer of the property in unascertained goods is governed by ss. 16, 17 and 18 Rule 5 of the Sale of Goods Act 1979. These rules are hierarchical and must be applied in the correct order. Section 16 takes precedence over s. 17, which takes precedence over s. 18 Rule 5.

So the starting point is s. 16, which states:

> [Subject to section 20A below] Where there is a contract for the sale of unascertained goods no property in the goods is transferred to the buyer unless and until the goods are ascertained.

This section does not tell us when the property is to pass. It merely prohibits the passing of the property until the goods are ascertained. Unascertained goods become ascertained when the goods are identified as the goods to be used in the performance of the contract. (The fact that the goods become ascertained does not mean that we now apply one of the four earlier rules. If the goods are unascertained at the time of the contract, ss. 16, 17 and 18 Rule 5 apply.)

Once the goods have become ascertained, s. 17 is the next section to consider. You should remember that this section says that the property in ascertained goods passes when the parties intend that it should pass, and that their intention can be ascertained from the terms of the contract, the conduct of the parties and the circumstances of the case.

So if, in a contract for the sale of unascertained goods, one of the terms states that the property should pass as soon as the goods become ascertained, then this term would apply and that is when the property would pass.

If the intention of the parties cannot be ascertained from the terms of the contract, or from the parties' conduct, or from the circumstances of the case, then s. 18 Rule 5 will apply.

Rule 5 states.

> Where there is a contract for the sale of unascertained or future goods by description, and goods of that description and in a deliverable state are unconditionally appropriated to the contract, either by the seller with the assent of the buyer or by the buyer with the assent of the seller, the property in the goods then passes to the buyer; and the assent may be express or implied, and may be given either before or after the appropriation is made.

SAQ 5/9

Unascertained goods are sold. What four conditions must be fulfilled before the property in the goods will pass to the buyer under Rule 5?

The four conditions are: that the goods match the contract description; that the goods are in a deliverable state; that the goods are unconditionally appropriated to the contract; and that assent to the appropriation is given by the party to the contract who did not appropriate the goods to the contract.

Goods of that description and in a deliverable state

The property is only transferred under Rule 5 when goods which match the description and which are in a deliverable state are unconditionally appropriated to the contract by either the buyer or the seller. The description will define the essential characteristics of the goods. We have examined the meaning of 'in a deliverable state' already, when considering Rules 1 and 2, and the words have the same meaning here. If necessary, you should look back to Rules 1 and 2, to remind yourself of the meaning of 'in a deliverable state'.

Unconditionally appropriated

The property passes when (with the other party's assent) goods matching the contract description and in a deliverable state are unconditionally appropriated to the contract. In this context, the meaning of 'unconditionally appropriated' has caused considerable difficulty. Generally, goods are unconditionally appropriated to the contract when they are irrevocably earmarked as being the particular goods for the contract in question. If the goods are in a warehouse or a store, this would mean more than that the seller separating the goods from others and attaching the buyer's name to them. At this stage the seller would have the power to change his mind and would still be able to deliver those goods to a different buyer. Goods are irrevocably earmarked when one of the parties to the contract does an act which shows an irrevocable intention that those particular goods will be used to perform that particular contract. Sometimes an appropriation is obvious enough, for example when the seller delivers goods matching the contract description to the buyer. Section 18 Rule 5(2) confirms that such a delivery is an unconditional appropriation, and adds that delivery to a carrier or bailee for transmission to the buyer is also to be regarded as an unconditional appropriation (unless the seller reserves a right of disposal).

However, as the Rules in s. 18 are subservient to s. 16, even delivery to a carrier will not pass the property unless the goods have become ascertained.

Healy v Howlett and Sons [1917] 1 KB 337
S, a fish exporter in Ireland, agreed to sell 20 boxes of mackerel to B in London. S sent 190 boxes of mackerel to Holyhead. The fish were consigned to S's own order, but S sent a telegram instructing railway officials at Holyhead to deliver 20 boxes to B, 20 boxes to C and 150 boxes to D. The train on which the 190 boxes were carried to Dublin was delayed. This meant that a boat to Holyhead was missed. At Holyhead a railway official picked out and earmarked 20 boxes for B, 20 for C and 150 for D. Because of the delay, the mackerel were not merchantable when they reached B. B refused to accept the goods and S sued for the price.

ACTIVITY 5/4

Read the judgments of Ridley and Avory JJ in *Healy v Howlett* in *Cases and Materials* (5.1.1.2). At what time were the 20 boxes appropriated to B?

It was held that there was no appropriation of the goods to B until the railway official at Holyhead earmarked and picked out the 20 boxes delivered to B. (By this time the fish had already deteriorated and become unmerchantable. B was therefore entitled to reject the goods because at the time when the property passed to him the goods were unmerchantable.)

So if a wine retailer delivered 100 cases of a particular wine to a carrier, with instructions that ten cases were to be delivered to consumer A, three cases to consumer B etc., the goods would not at this stage have become ascertained or appropriated and so property would not have passed. (If each box had been marked with the name of the buyer then property would have passed on delivery to the carrier — see Ridley J in *Healy v Howlett*.)

The exact meaning of unconditionally appropriated has caused considerable difficulty. In *Carlos Federspiel & Co. SA v Charles Twigg & Co. Ltd* [1957] 1 Lloyd's Rep 240 Pearson J thoroughly reviewed the old cases on the meaning of appropriation. The relevant extract from Pearson J's judgment is set out in *Cases and Materials* (5.1.1.2). You will see that the buyer setting the goods aside, expecting to use them in the contract is not enough:

> To constitute an appropriation of the goods to the contract, the parties must have had, or be reasonably supposed to have had, an intention to attach the contract irrevocably to those goods, so that those goods and no others are the subject of the sale and become the property of the buyer.

Section 18 Rule 5(3) allows for appropriation 'by exhaustion' in certain circumstances:

> (3) Where there is a contract for the sale of a specified quantity of unascertained goods in a deliverable state forming part of a bulk which is identified either in the contract or by subsequent agreement between the parties and the bulk is reduced to (or to less than) that quantity, then, if the buyer under that contract is the only buyer to whom goods are then due out of the bulk—

MISCELLANEOUS ASPECTS OF THE SALE OF GOODS ACT 1979

    (a) the remaining goods are to be taken as appropriated to that contract at the time when the bulk is so reduced; and
    (b) the property in those goods then passes to that buyer.

SAQ 5/10

Anne orders three cases of wine from a wine retailer. At this time the retailer has 12 cases of this wine. The company sells nine cases to a different customer. Does s. 18 Rule 5(3) pass the property in the three remaining cases to Anne?

Section 18 Rule 5(3) would not pass the property in the three cases of wine to Anne. The goods were not part of a bulk which was identified in the contract or by subsequent agreement.

Even if there is a definite appropriation, the 'property will not pass unless the appropriation is unconditional. A common condition would be that the property is not to pass to the buyer until the goods have been paid for in full.

Section 19(1) clearly allows for such a condition, stating that:

> Where there is a contract for the sale of specific goods or where goods are subsequently appropriated to the contract, the seller may, by the terms of the contract or appropriation, reserve the right of disposal of the goods until certain conditions are fulfilled; and in such a case, notwithstanding the delivery of the goods to the buyer . . . the property in the goods does not pass to the buyer until the conditions imposed by the seller are fulfilled.

Terms which reserve title until payment has been made in full are not unusual in commercial contracts of sale, but are less commonly found in consumer sales.

ACTIVITY 5/5

When a motorist drives into a garage and asks an attendant to fill the car with petrol, the contract is for the sale of unascertained goods. At what stage is the petrol unconditionally appropriated to the contract? Read the judgment of Croom-Johnson J in *Edwards v Dinn* [1976] 1 WLR 943 in *Cases and Materials* (5.1.1.2). Then write down your answer.

The Divisional Court held that the petrol is unconditionally appropriated, with the assent of the garage, when the petrol is put into the tank of the car. (Common sense leads us to this answer as it would be very difficult, if not impossible, for the seller to get the petrol sold, and only the petrol sold, back out of the tank.)

The facts of *Re London Wine Co. (Shippers) Ltd* 1986 PCC 121 were as follows. The company sold wine to customers who paid the price. The company continued to store the wine for the customers, but the customers were given 'certificates of title' to the wine they had bought. The wine was described as 'lying in bond' but no wine was ever physically separated from other wine held by the company. The company charged the customers for insurance and storage. The company went into liquidation and three classes of customers argued that the wine they had bought belonged to them. The first class of customers had bought what happened to be the whole of the company's stock of the type of wine in question at the date of the contract. The second class of customers had between them bought what happened to be the whole of the company's stock of the type of wine in question at the date of the contract. The third class of customers had not bought all of the company's stock of a particular wine, but the company had acknowledged that an appropriate quantity was being held for the customers. The company could, without undue difficulty, have acquired more of all three types of wine sold.

SAQ 5/11

Do you think that the property in the wine in *Re London Wine Co.* had passed to the three classes of customers? Write down your thoughts.

Property had not passed to the first class of customers as the customers had not bought specific goods (they had not agreed to buy whatever bottles of wine the company had on the day the contract was made, they had merely happened to order the exact amount then held by the company). The goods were therefore unascertained at the time of the contract and remained unascertained as the company had never ascertained which goods were to be covered by the contract. It might have intended to deliver all of the wine of a particular type which it held at the date of the contract, but could have changed its mind and sold more of this type of wine which it subsequently acquired. As the wine had not been ascertained, the parties' intentions as to the passing of the property could not have passed the property. Therefore the certificates of title could not pass the property. Nor had the wine passed 'by exhaustion' as the wine had not been sold as part of a bulk which was identified either in the contract or by subsequent agreement. A similar argument defeated the second class of buyers. The third class were defeated because the goods had never become ascertained.

Assent

The property only passes when the party who does not do the appropriating assents to the appropriation. This assent can be express or implied and can take place before the appropriation. A consumer who orders goods to be delivered to him impliedly assents to the appropriation of those goods.

5.3.2.3 Undivided shares in goods forming part of a bulk

Sections 20A and 20B were added to the Sale of Goods Act 1979 by the Sale of Goods (Amendment) Act 1995. Before the amendments, in cases such as the one below, ss. 16–18 could operate very unfairly against a buyer who had paid in advance for goods forming part of an undivided bulk. If the seller became insolvent before property had passed to

MISCELLANEOUS ASPECTS OF THE SALE OF GOODS ACT 1979

the buyer then the buyer had no rights, other than as an unsecured creditor. (In *Cases and Materials* (5.1.1.3) paras 2.1–2.15 of the Law Commission Report No. 215 are reproduced. These paragraphs examine the law as it was before ss. 20A and 20B were enacted.)

Re Wait [1927] 1 Ch 606
By a c.i.f. contract of 20 November 1925, W bought 1000 tons of wheat. By a c.i.f. contract of 21 November, W sold 500 tons of this wheat to sub-buyers. The 1,000 tons was loaded on board ship and the bill of lading sent to W. The sub-buyers paid W for their 500 tons. W became bankrupt before the ship arrived.
Held: The sub-buyers could not have specific performance of the contract because the goods were not specific or ascertained. The sub-buyers' 500 tons had never been identified or appropriated and therefore remained unascertained goods. The consequence of this was that the sub-buyers did not own the 500 tons and had no beneficial interest or lien in respect of the goods.

ACTIVITY 5/6

Read ss. 20A and 20B of the Sale of Goods Act 1979 in *Cases and Materials* (5.1.1.3). Then write your answers to the following questions:

(a) If the facts in *Re Wait* were to happen today, what interest in the wheat would the sub-buyers have?

(b) When would this interest have been created?

(c) Would the sub-buyers' interest in the wheat prevent W from delivering wheat to other sub-buyers?

(a) The sub-buyers would have been owners in common of all of the bulk (50% share).

(b) The sub-buyers would have become owners in common when they paid for the wheat.

(c) The sub-buyers would be deemed to have consented to delivery to other sub-buyers.

It would appear then that ss. 20A and 20B might help consumers who pay the price for unascertained goods to retailers who become insolvent before delivery is made. However, this help might be very much more limited than is first supposed.

SAQ 5/12

Gerald, a wine lover, visits a shop and buys two cases of 1997 Chilean Special Reserve Cabinet Sauvignon. Gerald pays the price, £96, cash. The shop agrees to deliver the wine to Gerald's house the following week. Delivery is not made as agreed. Gerald discovers that the shop is insolvent and that a liquidator has been called in.

(a) Why can s. 17 not help Gerald?

(b) Why does s. 20A not help Gerald?

(a) Section 17 cannot help Gerald because s. 17 is subservient to s. 16. Gerald probably did intend that he should become the owner of the wine when he paid for it. But unless the wine was ascertained property in it cannot have passed (subject to ss. 20A and 20B).

(b) Section 20A will not help Gerald as the wine he bought did not form part of a bulk which was identified in the contract or identified by subsequent agreement between the parties. It would not be enough that both parties had in mind that the wine should come from whatever stock the shop then had. Either the contract must identify the bulk or the parties must subsequently agree to it.

Section 20A will only help a consumer who has paid the price for some or all of the goods which form part of the identified bulk. It would not allow a consumer who had not paid any of the price to insist that a liquidator performs the contract. (Although a liquidator might well be quite happy to do this.)

A 'bulk' is defined by s. 61 of the Sale of Goods Act 1979 as:

> ... a mass or collection of goods of the same kind which—
> (a) is contained in a defined space or area; and
> (b) is such that any goods in the bulk are interchangeable with any other goods therein of the same number and quantity ...

So, to go back to **SAQ 5/12**, s. 20A could operate in Gerald's favour if:

(a) Gerald paid the price or part of it;

(b) there was a bulk of bottles of 1997 Chilean Special Reserve Cabinet Sauvignon, that is to say, a collection of such bottles which was contained in a definite space or area and not mixed with any other types of wine;

(c) the contract identified the bulk from which the goods were being bought, or after the contract was made the parties agreed upon it. It can therefore be seen that ss. 20A and 20B would not help any of the three classes of buyers in *Re London Wine Co. (Shippers) Ltd*.

5.3.2.4 Risk

Meaning of risk

In this context, risk means the risk of damage to, or deterioration of, the goods. If the goods which form the subject matter of the contract are damaged or deteriorate, the party who has the risk will remain liable to perform the contract despite the damage or deterioration. So if goods are damaged while at the consumer's risk, then the consumer will remain liable to pay the full price for the goods. This is so, even if the consumer never received possession of the goods.

If the goods are damaged to the extent of becoming unsatisfactory while the seller has the risk, then the seller will not be able to perform the contract by delivering the

MISCELLANEOUS ASPECTS OF THE SALE OF GOODS ACT 1979

damaged goods. If the contract was for the sale of specific goods, then the seller will not be able to perform unless the goods can be repaired. The seller will therefore be in breach of contract, subject to the rules on mistake and frustration explained below. The buyer will not be liable for the price of the goods and, if he has suffered additional loss, will have an action for non-delivery. If the contract was for the sale of unascertained goods, then the seller will have to find replacement goods in order to perform the contract. Failure to supply such replacement goods will again put the seller in breach of contract. It follows that the party who bears the risk ought to insure the goods.

Section 20(1) of the Sale of Goods Act 1979 states that:

> Unless otherwise agreed, the goods remain at the seller's risk until the property in them is transferred to the buyer, but when the property in them is transferred to the buyer the goods are at the buyer's risk whether delivery has been made or not.

ACTIVITY 5/7

Write down the effect of s. 20(1) in a short sentence.

You might have written something like: 'Risk goes with ownership, unless otherwise agreed.'

Strangely then, risk is transferred with ownership rather than with possession. Of course, if there is an agreement to the contrary this will not be the case. But usually the parties do not concern themselves with risk when making the contract. In most of the cases which we have examined in this chapter risk passed with the property because there was no agreement to the contrary. Often, as in *Tarling* v *Baxter* (1827) 6 B & C 360, the risk passed to a buyer who did not yet have possession.

Section 20(1) can seem to lead to some very surprising consequences. Let us take as an example a consumer who visits a garage and buys a second-hand caravan. The garage is to deliver the caravan the following day. Before the caravan is delivered, the garage and all of its stock are destroyed in a fire. As the caravan was specific goods in a deliverable state, the property would have passed to the consumer as soon as the contract was made. (It is possible that a court might infer an intention that the property was not to pass until delivery. See the discussion of s. 18 Rule 1 above.) Unless there was an agreement to the contrary, the caravan would therefore have been at the consumer's risk when it was destroyed. The consumer would therefore be liable to pay for the caravan.

The consequence that the consumer would be liable for the price of the caravan is even more surprising when it is realised that the garage would almost certainly be able to claim for the caravan on its insurance. The consumer would be most unlikely to have insured the caravan from the moment when the contract was made. (Although the consumer could have insured the goods. A person who has ownership, possession or the risk has a sufficient interest to insure the goods.) In practice, of course, it is likely that the garage would claim on its insurance and then return the price to the consumer. However, the consumer would seem to be the loser where: the garage claims on its insurance and refuses to return any money to the consumer; the garage has not insured the goods; or the garage is in liquidation and an overzealous liquidator refuses to refund any of the consumer's money. It is also the case that once the seller's insurer has paid the seller, the insurer company will become subrogated to the seller's right to obtain the price from the consumer.

SAQ 5/13

Can you see anything in s. 20(1) which might enable the court to help a consumer in circumstances such as these?

The first words of s. 20(1) 'Unless otherwise agreed' might allow a court to help a consumer. To avoid injustice in situations such as this, a court might look hard to discover an agreement indicating a contrary intention. Such an agreement does not need to be express and can be found in different ways. The fact that the caravan was insured by the garage and was not insured by the customer might well be enough to mean that the parties had shown an intention that the property was not to pass until the consumer had taken possession of the caravan.

Section 20(2) provides a possible exception to the general rule in s. 20(1), by stating:

> But where delivery has been delayed through the fault of either buyer or seller the goods are at the risk of the party at fault as regards any loss which might not have occurred but for such fault.

An example of this can be seen in the following case.

Demby Hamilton & Co Ltd v *Barden* [1949] 1 All ER 435
S agreed to sell 30 tons of apple juice, which was to be delivered in weekly truckloads, to B. S crushed the last of that season's apples and put the juice in casks. After 20.5 tons of juice had been delivered, B asked S to hold up delivery. S did hold up delivery for several months, by which time the apple juice was found to have deteriorated.
Held: The property in the undelivered juice had not passed to B. However, applying s. 20(2), B had to bear the risk because the deterioration would not have happened but for his delay. (The relevant extract from Sellers J's judgment is set out in **Cases and Materials (5.1.1.4)**.)

The buyer in the above case was not a consumer, but the case demonstrates the working of s. 20(2). If it is a consumer's fault that delivery of goods is delayed then, as regards any loss caused by this fault, the risk will be with the consumer.

Section 20(3) spells out the duties of the party who has possession of the goods but who does not bear the risk. It states:

> Nothing in this section affects the duties or liabilities of either seller or buyer as a bailee or custodier of the goods of the other party.

A seller who has parted with the property but retained possession of the goods will be a bailee, as will a buyer who has gained possession of the goods but not the property. For example, in *Tarling* v *Baxter* the property and the risk passed to the buyer as soon as the contract was made. The seller was therefore a bailee, in that he retained possession of the haystack. (However, as it was not the seller's fault that the haystack was destroyed, s. 20(3) would not fix him with liability.)

Section 20(3) merely means that the party who finds himself in the position of a bailee has all the duties normally associated with being a bailee. The main duties of a bailee are not to cause loss through negligence, and to have the goods available for delivery.

MISCELLANEOUS ASPECTS OF THE SALE OF GOODS ACT 1979

Risk while goods are in transit

Section 32(1) of the Sale of Goods Act 1979 states:

> Where, in pursuance of a contract of sale, the seller is authorised or required to send the goods to the buyer, delivery of the goods to a carrier (whether named by the buyer or not) for the purpose of transmission to the buyer is prima facie deemed to be delivery of the goods to the buyer.

In effect this section makes the carrier the agent of the buyer, so that the risk is with the buyer as soon as the goods are delivered to the carrier. The subsection only applies to identified goods, and will not override s. 16. The property in unascertained goods, whether delivered to a carrier or not, cannot pass until the goods have been ascertained. Nor will the subsection apply if the carrier used is the seller's agent or employee. The seller must make a reasonable contract with the carrier, having regard to the nature of the goods and the circumstances of the case. If this is not done, and the goods are lost or damaged in transit, the buyer can decline to treat delivery to the carrier as delivery to himself, or may hold the seller responsible in damages (s. 32(2)). If the goods to be sent are unascertained, s. 18 Rule 5(2) provides that delivery to the carrier for the purpose of transmission to the buyer in pursuance of the contract is to be taken as an unconditional appropriation of the goods to the contract if the seller does not reserve the right of disposal.

Let us assume that a consumer orders a washing machine from a shop and asks the shop to deliver the machine to his house. The shop gives a washing machine to a carrier who is to deliver it to the consumer. The washing machine is damaged. Risk is on the consumer, who will be liable for the price of the goods. However, if the shop had delivered four identical washing machines to the carrier, for delivery to four customers, then the property and the risk could not pass to the individual consumers until their washing machines were ascertained (s. 16). If it was the carrier's fault that the machines were damaged then the carrier would be liable for the damage, either on the contract made with the shop or for having broken the duty of a bailee.

5.3.2.5 Mistake and frustration

If a retailer agrees to sell goods, ignorant of the fact that they have perished at the time of the contract, then the position varies depending upon whether the goods were unascertained or specific.

If the goods were unascertained then the seller will have to deliver other goods matching the contract description or be in breach of contract.

If the goods were specific and they perished, unknown to the seller, before the contract was made then s. 6 of the Sale of Goods Act 1979 will apply. Section 6 states:

> Where there is a contract for the sale of specific goods, and the goods without the knowledge of the seller have perished at the time when a contract is made, the contract is void.

The goods must perish

Asfar & Co Ltd v *Blundell* [1896] 1 QB 123
A cargo of dates was sold. The ship sank and the dates were submerged in the river Thames. The owner claimed on his insurance, arguing that the dates had perished. The insurers argued that the dates had not perished because they were still in existence and still retained the appearance of dates. They were covered in sewage and quite inedible, but could be used for distilling into alcohol.

ACTIVITY 5/8

Read the judgment of Lord Esher MR in *Asfar* v *Blundell* in *Cases and Materials* (5.1.1.5). Had the dates perished? What was Lord Esher's test to see if goods had perished?

The Court of Appeal held that the dates had perished. Lord Esher thought that goods had perished if the nature of the goods was so altered that for business purposes they became something else and unmerchantable as what they were sold as. Goods will also be regarded as having perished if they have been stolen and are therefore unavailable at the time fixed for delivery (*Barrow, Lane and Ballard Ltd* v *Phillip Phillips & Co Ltd* [1929] 1 KB 574).

Section 6 will only apply where the goods have perished before the contract was made, 'without the knowledge of the seller'. Section 6 will not protect a seller who expressly warrants that the goods exist. But if the terms of the contract are that the buyer takes a risk on the existence of the goods then s. 6 will not protect the buyer by making the contract void. If s. 6 applies it will make the contract void. If s. 6 does not apply, then the ordinary common law rules on mistake will apply.

Section 7 of the 1979 Act deals with frustration and states that:

> Where there is an agreement to sell specific goods and subsequently the goods, without any fault on the part of the seller or buyer, perish before the risk passes to the buyer, the agreement is avoided.

SAQ 5/14

What is the difference between s. 6 and s. 7?

Section 6 deals with the situation where the goods do not exist at the time when the contract is made. Section 7 deals with the situation where the goods do exist at the time when the contract is made, but cease to exist before the risk passes to the buyer.

Like s. 6, s. 7 only applies to specific goods. It avoids the contract where the goods perish after the contract has been made but before risk has passed to the buyer. If the perishing was the fault of either party then s. 7 will not apply.

MISCELLANEOUS ASPECTS OF THE SALE OF GOODS ACT 1979

SAQ 5/15

Assuming that the parties have not agreed to separate the passing of the risk and the passing of the property, can s. 7 apply to contracts governed by s. 18:

Rule 1?

Rule 2?

Rule 3?

Rule 4?

Rule 5?

Section 7 can apply only to contracts governed by Rules 2 and 3. If the contract is governed by Rule 1 the property (and risk) would pass at the time of the contract. Rule 5 is concerned with unascertained and future goods, and s. 7 does not apply to such contracts. Earlier in this chapter we saw that when Rule 4 applies there is neither a sale nor an agreement to sell when the goods are delivered to the buyer. When the buyer is deemed to have accepted the seller's offer in one of the ways set out in Rule 4 then the property and the risk will pass simultaneously.

If s. 7 does apply then the contract is avoided. This means that:

- the seller will have no obligation to deliver the goods and will not be in breach of contract for failure to deliver;

- the buyer need not pay the price and can recover any amount of the price already paid;

- other losses lie where they fall.

If a contract is frustrated at common law, rather than under s. 7, then the Law Reform (Frustrated Contracts) Act 1943 will apply. You will have studied this Act in the Contract Programme. You might remember that under the 1943 Act the loss does not lie where it falls. Instead the court is given wide powers to apportion the loss between buyer and seller by awarding expenses and by requiring a party who has received a valuable benefit to pay for it.

ACTIVITY 5/9

Section 7 will not apply to the following contracts. In each case, write down why it should not apply.

(a) A orders a best-selling novel from a Book Club. Before the novel is posted the Book Club's entire stock is destroyed in a fire.

(b) B visits an antique shop and buys an oak table. B pays the full price in cash. The shop agrees to deliver the table the following day. Before delivery is made the table is destroyed by vandals who break into the shop.

(c) C visits a builders merchant and agrees to buy a heap of barbecue charcoal lying in the yard. The builders merchant is to weigh the charcoal to ascertain the price. Before the weighing is done the Government outlaws the sale of this type of charcoal.

(d) D visits a wood yard and agrees to buy a specific pile of wood which the wood yard is to saw up into lengths of one metre before delivery. Before the wood has been sawed up it is destroyed in a fire, caused by one of the yard's employees who was playing a practical joke on another employee.

(a) The contract is for the sale of unascertained goods. Section 7 only applies to contracts for the sale of specific goods. The Book Club would therefore remain liable to perform the contract.

(b) The contract is for the sale of specific goods in a deliverable state and therefore risk would have passed to B as soon as the contract was made. (If risk or property had not passed on account of the parties' intentions, then s. 7 would frustrate the contract.)

(c) Section 7 only applies where the goods perish. It does not apply where the contract is frustrated on the grounds that it has become illegal. (A contract which becomes illegal after it was made but before it was performed will be frustrated at common law. The Law Reform (Frustrated Contracts) Act 1943 will therefore apportion the loss.)

(d) Section 7 will not apply because the loss is the seller's fault.

If the goods have perished after the property and the risk have passed to the consumer, then the consumer will have to bear the loss.

5.4 The Seller's Duty to Deliver

Section 27 of the Sale of Goods Act 1979, which is headed 'Duties of seller and buyer', states:

> It is the duty of the seller to deliver the goods, and of the buyer to accept and pay for them, in accordance with the terms of the contract of sale.

We shall see that delivery need not necessarily amount to a physical transfer of the goods, and that the seller's duty to deliver does not necessarily mean that the seller must take the goods to the buyer.

Section 28 says that the seller's duty to deliver, and the buyer's duty to accept and pay, are concurrent conditions. This means that both parties must be ready and willing to perform their respective duties. If the buyer is not ready and willing to pay, then the seller can refuse to deliver. Similarly, if the seller is not ready and willing to deliver, then the buyer can refuse to pay.

As we have seen, s. 27 says that it is the seller's duty to deliver the goods in accordance with the terms of the contract. Delivery is defined by s. 61 as 'voluntary transfer of possession from one person to another'. Already in this chapter we have seen that ownership and possession are often separated when goods are sold. It is important to remember that delivery is concerned with the transfer of possession rather than with the transfer of ownership.

MISCELLANEOUS ASPECTS OF THE SALE OF GOODS ACT 1979

The terms of the contract will determine whether the goods were specific or unascertained. If the contract was to sell specific goods, then it is the goods specified which must be delivered. If the contract was to sell unascertained goods, then the seller must deliver goods which correspond with the contract description.

5.4.1 WAYS OF EFFECTING DELIVERY

Delivery can either be actual delivery, in which case the goods are physically delivered to the buyer, or it can be constructive delivery. A constructive delivery is a symbolic delivery. It is achieved by the seller delivering the means to control the goods rather than by delivering the goods themselves.

ACTIVITY 5/10

(a) In hire-purchase contracts the consumer hires the goods for a fixed time before finally buying them with the final payment. Let us assume that Jim has taken a washing machine on hire-purchase. When Jim finally buys the washing machine this is a sale, and so the seller has a duty to deliver the washing machine. Write down whether you think the seller would need to regain possession of the washing machine in order to deliver it.

(b) Billy buys a car from S Ltd, a local garage. The car is parked in S Ltd's car park, which is outside the showroom where Billy makes the contract. Write down how you think S Ltd might most easily deliver the car.

You might have written that:

(a) the seller would not have to regain possession of the washing machine. A notional delivery would take place, by the fact of Jim's continuing to possess the washing machine.

(b) S Ltd could effect delivery by handing over the means of controlling the car. The easiest way to achieve this would be by giving Billy the car keys. (Both of these forms of constructive delivery are explained immediately below.)

5.4.1.1 Actual delivery

Actual delivery will occur when the goods are physically transferred to the consumer. This is the most common form of delivery in domestic sales.

5.4.1.2 Constructive delivery

As we have seen, a constructive delivery is a symbolic delivery. There are several ways in which constructive delivery might be effected in a consumer contract.

Delivering the means of control

A seller can deliver goods by delivering an object which gives the buyer the means to control the goods. We saw an example of this in **Activity 5/10**, where S could effect delivery of the car by giving B the keys to the car. Similarly, where goods are held in a warehouse a seller can deliver by giving the buyer the keys to the warehouse.

Buyer continues in possession

If the buyer is already in possession of the goods as a bailee, then constructive delivery can be effected by the buyer continuing to be in possession with the seller's consent. We saw an example of this in **Activity 5/10**. Jim was hiring the washing machine until the end of the hire-purchase agreement when he finally bought it. There was no need for a physical delivery of the washing machine, so a notional delivery took place.

Delivery to a carrier

We have already seen that s. 32(1) of the 1979 Act states that if the seller is authorised or required to send the goods to the buyer, delivery to a carrier is prima facie to be regarded as delivery to the buyer. This is not the case if the carrier is the seller's employee or agent. Section 32(2) requires that the seller make a reasonable contract, having regard to the nature of the goods and the circumstances of the case, with the carrier. If the seller does not make a reasonable contract the buyer may decline to treat delivery to the carrier as delivery to himself, or may hold the seller responsible in damages (s. 32(2)).

5.4.2 THE PLACE OF DELIVERY

ACTIVITY 5/11

Let us assume that you buy a washing machine from a shop and that no mention of delivery is made. We have seen that it is the seller's duty to deliver the washing machine. Write down what you think this duty would entail.

You might well have written that the seller's duty to deliver would mean that the seller would have physically to bring the washing machine to your house, having arranged a time at which you would be there. Surprisingly, perhaps, the seller's duty to deliver would probably not oblige the seller to do this. To find out why, read on.

Section 29 of the Sale of Goods Act 1979 states:

> (1) Whether it is for the buyer to take possession of the goods or for the seller to send them to the buyer is a question depending in each case on the contract, express or implied, between the parties.
> (2) Apart from any such contract, express or implied, the place of delivery is the seller's place of business if he has one, and if not, his residence; except that, if the contract is for the sale of specific goods, which to the knowledge of the parties when the contract is made are in some other place, then that place is the place of delivery.

Section 29(1) shows us that the seller's duty to deliver does not mean that the seller must dispatch the goods to the consumer. Whether the seller is to send the goods, or whether

MISCELLANEOUS ASPECTS OF THE SALE OF GOODS ACT 1979

the consumer is to collect them, will depend upon the terms of the contract, express or implied. We have already seen that delivery is defined as voluntary transfer of possession from one person to another. If the consumer is to collect, the seller would deliver merely by allowing the consumer to take the goods away.

Section 29(2) begins by making it plain that, unless there has been an agreement to the contrary, the place of delivery will be the seller's place of business, or if the seller has no place of business, the seller's home. But then s. 29(2) makes an exception in the case of specific goods which both parties know to be elsewhere. In contracts to sell these goods the place of delivery will be the place where both parties know the goods to be.

SAQ 5/16

Think back to the washing machine in Activity 5/11.

(a) Was there an express term that the shop would deliver the machine to your house?

(b) Was there an express term as to where the place of delivery would be?

(c) Applying s. 29(2), where would the place of delivery be?

(a) No express term stated that the seller would deliver the machine to your house.

(b) Nor did an express term fix a place of delivery.

(c) We can see that as the goods were not specific goods which both parties knew to be elsewhere, the place of delivery would be the seller's place of business. It is possible that the courts would imply a term that a bulky item such as a washing machine should be delivered to a consumer's home. However, it must be said that this seems very unlikely. Generally, retailers charge if they are to make physical delivery, or advertise that 'delivery is free' or included in the price.

ACTIVITY 5/12

Re-read the facts of the following cases, which were considered above. Then, in each case, decide (a) where the place of delivery would have been, and (b) how delivery would have been effected. (Assume that no express term decided these matters.)

Dennant v Skinner and Collom [1948] 2 All ER 29   (a)   (b)

Lacis v Cashmarts [1969] 2 QB 400   (a)   (b)

In *Dennant v Skinner and Collom*, (a) the place of delivery would have been the auctioneer's place of business, where both parties knew the specific goods (the car) to be. (b) Delivery would have been effected by handing over the car keys, the means of controlling the car. In *Lacis v Cashmarts*, (a) the place of delivery would have been at the supermarket checkout, where both parties knew the specific goods to be. (b) The goods would have been physically delivered by the checkout operator running the items through the till and placing them where the shopper could pick them up.

5.4.3 THE TIME OF DELIVERY

The time at which the goods are to be delivered may be fixed by a term of the contract. If no time is fixed then the goods must be delivered within a reasonable time.

What amounts to a reasonable time will depend upon all the circumstances of the case.

A seller who fails to deliver on time commits a breach of contract. Consequently, the buyer will always be able to claim damages for any foreseeable loss which the delay has caused. Frequently though, a buyer will want to go further and call the contract off. Whether or not the buyer can do this will depend upon whether time was 'of the essence'.

SAQ 5/17

A buyer can call the contract off for late delivery if time was 'of the essence'. If time was not 'of the essence' then the buyer can only claim damages. Is this the same as saying that the buyer can call the contract off for late delivery if the time of delivery was a condition of the contract, whereas the buyer cannot call the contract off if the time of delivery was only a warranty?

It amounts to the same thing. Section 10(2) of the 1979 Act states that whether or not time is of the essence depends upon the intentions of the parties.

In commercial contracts terms which fix the time of delivery are generally regarded as a condition, but in consumer contracts the courts might well treat terms as to the time of delivery as a warranty.

When a reasonable time is implied into the contract, then initially time is not of the essence, and would therefore be a warranty. However, when the time of delivery is only a warranty it can become of the essence if the buyer gives notice that the goods must be delivered within a certain (reasonable) date.

McDougall v *Aeromarine of Emsworth Ltd* [1958] 3 All ER 431
B ordered a new pleasure yacht which was to conform to certain specifications. S agreed to use their best endeavours to deliver by 1 May 1957. However, a term of the contract provided that 'owing to the effect of delays and shortages such delivery date cannot be guaranteed'. The yacht was not delivered on 1 May, and on 19 September 1957 B called the contract off because 4/5 of the yachting season was over.

ACTIVITY 5/13

Read the judgment of Diplock J in *McDougall* v *Emsworth* in *Cases and Materials* (5.2.1). Then write down your answers to the following questions:

(a) Could B call the contract off?

(b) How was the time of delivery fixed?

MISCELLANEOUS ASPECTS OF THE SALE OF GOODS ACT 1979

(c) Was the term as to the time of delivery a condition or a warranty?

(a) Diplock J held that B was entitled to call the contract off.

(b) As no time of delivery was definitely fixed by the contract, delivery had to be made within a reasonable time.

(c) More than a reasonable time had expired since the formation of the contract, and therefore a term of the contract had been broken. According to s. 10, this term could either be a condition or a warranty depending upon the terms of the contract. Looking at the facts of the case, the term was a condition. (In *Cases and Materials* (5.2.1), see also the judgment of Denning LJ in *Charles Rickards Ltd* v *Oppenheim* [1950] 1 All ER 420.)

When a seller delivers late, and breaks a condition by so doing, the contract is not automatically terminated. The buyer certainly has the right to terminate but must let the seller know that he now regards the contract as terminated. If the buyer leads the seller to believe that the contract is not to be called off then the buyer may waive the right to terminate.

A tender of delivery may be treated as ineffectual unless it was made at a reasonable hour, and what is a reasonable hour is a question of fact (s. 29(5)).

5.4.4 DELIVERY OF THE WRONG QUANTITY

If the seller delivers a smaller quantity of the goods than the contract stipulated, then s. 30(1) gives the buyer two choices:

- accept the goods and pay for them at the contract rate, or

- reject the whole delivery.

If the seller delivers a greater quantity than the contract stipulated, then s. 30(2) and (3) give the buyer three choices:

- accept the right quantity and reject the excess, or

- reject the whole delivery, or

- accept the whole amount delivered and pay for the excess at the contract rate.

A consumer is always therefore entitled to reject the delivery if the wrong quantity of goods is delivered, unless the deviation from the contract can be regarded as a trifle within the rule *de minimis non curat lex*.

A consumer can always reject a delivery of the wrong quantity, but this does not mean that the consumer is entitled to repudiate the contract. If the consumer does reject a delivery on the grounds that it was of the wrong quantity, then it is up to the seller to collect the rejected delivery. But having collected it, the seller can still perform the contract by delivering the correct quantity, as long as the time for delivery has not expired. What the seller cannot do is to top up a short delivery. This would amount to delivery by instalments and the buyer is not required to accept this, unless it was what had been agreed (see below at 5.4.5).

Section 30(2A) of the 1979 Act now provides that a buyer who does not deal as a consumer cannot reject the goods on account of delivery of the wrong quantity if the shortfall or excess is so slight as to make rejection unreasonable. The rights of buyers who deal as consumers are not affected. Consumer buyers can therefore reject on account of the wrong quantity having been delivered, even where this is unreasonable (subject to the *de minimis* rule).

5.4.5 DELIVERY BY INSTALMENTS

Section 31(1) of the Sale of Goods Act 1979 states that: 'Unless otherwise agreed, the buyer of goods is not bound to accept delivery of them by instalments.'

This section is quite straightforward and makes it plain that the seller can only deliver by instalments if this is what was agreed in the contract. We have already seen that if too few goods are delivered, then the consumer has the option to reject the delivery. If the seller were to be allowed to make up the shortfall, then this would amount to a delivery by instalments.

5.4.6 THE IMPORTANCE OF DELIVERY

The fact that delivery has taken place has several important consequences for the consumer and the seller. We have seen that delivery is concerned with possession of the goods rather than with ownership. Once delivery has been made:

(a) the consumer must accept the goods or face the prospect of paying damages for non-acceptance;

(b) the seller can demand payment;

(c) an unpaid seller can no longer have a lien over the goods. (The unpaid seller's lien is considered below at **5.5.2**.)

A seller who does not deliver will break a term of the contract. The consumer will be entitled to damages for non-delivery and possibly also to specific performance. If the failure to deliver amounts to a repudiation of the contract then the consumer may terminate the contract.

5.5 The Duty to Pay the Price

The most fundamental obligation of a consumer is to pay the price. Usually of course the price will be agreed but this is not always the case.

ACTIVITY 5/14

Parties can make a contract for the sale of goods without expressly fixing the price, as long as they intend to make a contract, and as long as the terms of the contract are reasonably certain. There are three ways in which the price can be fixed if the parties do not fix it in the contract. Write down any of the three ways which occur to you.

MISCELLANEOUS ASPECTS OF THE SALE OF GOODS ACT 1979

First, you might have guessed that the previous dealings of the parties can fix the price. For example, if B frequently buys goods from S at a certain price then there is no need to mention this price every time a contract is made. Second, you might have guessed that the price can be fixed in 'a manner agreed by the contract'. This might involve the parties to the contract agreeing that a third party, such as a named valuer, should fix the price. Third, you might also have guessed that if the contract does not fix the price, or determine how it is to be fixed the buyer must pay a reasonable price. These rules can be found in s. 8 of the Sale of Goods Act 1979, which states:

> (1) The price in a contract of sale may be fixed by the contract, or may be left to be fixed in a manner agreed by the contract, or may be determined by the course of dealing between the parties.
> (2) Where the price is not determined as mentioned in subsection (1) above the buyer must pay a reasonable price.
> (3) What is a reasonable price is a question of fact dependent on the circumstances of each particular case.

In contracts to supply a service s. 13 of the Supply of Goods and Services Act 1982 is in effect identical to s. 8 of the 1979 Act. If the consideration for the service is not determined by the contract, or left to be determined in a manner agreed by the contract, or determined by a course of dealing between the parties, there is an implied term that the party contracting with the supplier will pay a reasonable price. What is a reasonable price is a question of fact.

When there is a dispute as to whether or not a given price was fixed as the contract price everything will depend on the intentions of the parties. When a supplier gives an estimate then this is not regarded as the definite contract price, but only as an indication of what the price is likely to be. A quotation on the other hand is regarded as a definite offer to perform the contract at the price quoted.

5.5.1 LATE PAYMENT

Section 10(1) of the Sale of Goods Act 1979 states that:

> Unless a different intention appears from the terms of the contract, stipulations as to time of payment are not of the essence of a contract of sale.

We saw earlier in this chapter that if the consumer does not pay the price at the agreed time then this amounts only to a breach of warranty. However, s. 28 of the 1979 Act makes plain that the time of delivery and payment are concurrent conditions:

> Unless otherwise agreed, delivery of the goods and payment of the price are concurrent conditions, that is to say, the seller must be ready and willing to give possession of the goods to the buyer in exchange for the price and the buyer must be ready and willing to pay the price in exchange for possession of the goods.

Section 28 states that both parties must be ready and willing to perform the contract. If one or other party is not ready and willing to perform the contract then the other party has no obligation to fulfil his contractual obligations. The section does not say that actual delivery and actual payment must be made at the same time. The section is talking about willingness to pay and deliver. So, unless there has been an agreement to the contrary, if the consumer is not ready and willing to pay the price the retailer will not need to be ready and willing to deliver the goods. It should also be noticed that the rule in s. 28 applies 'unless otherwise agreed'. It is of course very commonly the case in consumer contracts that the consumer will be given some form of credit.

5.5.2 LIEN

A seller who has a lien over goods has a right to retain possession of the goods, even though property may have passed to the buyer. Section 41 of the Sale of Goods Act 1979 explains the unpaid seller's lien:

(1) Subject to this Act, the unpaid seller of goods who is is possession of them is entitled to retain possession of them until payment or tender of the price in the following cases:—
   (a) where the goods have been sold without any stipulation as to credit;
   (b) where the goods have been sold on credit but the term of credit has expired;
   (c) where the buyer becomes insolvent.

(2) The seller may exercise his lien or right of retention notwithstanding that he is in possession of the goods as agent or bailee or custodier for the buyer.

An unpaid seller is defined by s. 38 of the 1979 Act as a seller to whom the whole of the price has not been paid or tendered, or who has taken a bill of exchange or negotiable instrument as conditional payment and the condition has not been fulfilled. (Generally, in consumer contracts this second category would mean that the seller has taken a cheque which has been dishonoured.)

SAQ 5/18

(a) How is the unpaid seller's lien affected by the granting of credit to the consumer?

(b) A seller who unconditionally sells specific goods in a deliverable state will often, for some time at least, be in possession of the goods as the consumer's bailee. Why is this so?

(a) If the consumer has been granted credit, then the unpaid seller cannot exercise his lien unless either the credit has expired or the consumer has become insolvent.

(b) Unless otherwise agreed, property in specific goods in a deliverable state will pass to the consumer when the contract is made. If the seller retains possession for any time after the contract, for example until delivery can be effected, the seller will retain possession as the consumer's bailee.

Section 43(1) of the 1979 Act says than an unpaid seller will lose the lien:

(a) when he delivers the goods to a carrier or other bailee or custodier for the purpose of transmission to the buyer without reserving the right of disposal of the goods;
(b) when the buyer or his agent lawfully obtains possession of the goods;
(c) by waiver of the lien or right of retention.

The seller's lien presupposes that the property in the goods has passed to the consumer s. 39(1)). If the property has not passed to the consumer, s. 39(2) grants an unpaid seller a similar right to withhold possession of the goods.

MISCELLANEOUS ASPECTS OF THE SALE OF GOODS ACT 1979

Example

A consumer buys a second-hand car for £3,200. The consumer gives the seller a cheque. The seller is most unlikely to let the consumer take the car away. The seller will be an unpaid seller as the whole of the purchase price has not been paid or tendered. (Offering a cheque would not amount to a tender of the price — the exact sum of money in cash would have to be offered.) The seller could therefore exercise a lien over the goods. (The same conclusion could be reached on the basis that the parties would not have intended the property to pass until the cheque was cleared. See above at **5.3.2.1**.)

5.5.3 THE RIGHT OF RESALE

In certain circumstances an unpaid seller has the right to resell the goods to a second buyer. Clearly this will not be the case in all circumstances. Let us assume, for example, that S sells goods to consumer B and that B does not pay immediately. S is an unpaid seller, even though B might have been granted credit. If S, at this stage, sold the goods to a second consumer then this would clearly be a breach of contract.

The unpaid seller's exercise of his right of lien does not of itself rescind the contract (s. 48(1) of the 1979 Act). However, if an unpaid seller who has exercised the right of lien resells the goods, the second buyer acquires a good title as against the original buyer (s. 48(2)). Unless the seller has a right of resale, this second sale would amount to a breach of the first contract.

ACTIVITY 5/15

There are four circumstances in which an unpaid seller has the right of resale. Write down any of the circumstances which occur to you.

It is not easy to predict the circumstances, even though they are obvious enough once explained. Despite this, you might have written that the right of resale would arise: if the buyer repudiates the contract; if the goods are perishable and the buyer does not pay within a reasonable time (s. 48(3)); if the seller gives the buyer notice of an intention to resell and the buyer does not pay within a reasonable time (s. 48(3)); if the contract itself gives the seller a right to resell in the event of the buyer defaulting.

If the seller does effect the right to resell, the contract with the original buyer is terminated.

ACTIVITY 5/16

S Garage Ltd sells a car to Billy for £3,000. Billy consistently refuses to pay the price and S Ltd take this as a repudiation of the contract and resell the car to Brenda. Assuming that Billy's behaviour did amount to a repudiation, write down what you think the position between S Ltd and Billy would be if:

(a) Brenda bought the car for £3,100;

(b) Brenda bought the car for £2,550.

(a) If Brenda paid £3,100, S Ltd would be able to keep all of the money and would have no liability to Billy. The contract with Billy was terminated and Billy would have no interest in the goods.

(b) S Ltd has suffered a loss of £450 as a result of Billy's breach of contract. As long as this loss was foreseeable, and could not have been mitigated by getting a higher price from a different buyer, S Ltd will be able to claim damages in respect of the loss.

5.6 Sale by a Seller in Possession after a Sale

When a consumer buys specific goods but does not take them away, the situation occasionally arises that the retailer mistakenly sells the same goods to a second consumer. As the retailer has made two contracts in respect of the same goods, obviously one of the consumers will not be entitled to the goods. Section 24 of the Sale of Goods Act 1979 deals with this problem:

> Where a person having sold goods continues or is in possession of the goods, or of the documents of title to the goods, the delivery or transfer by that person, or by a mercantile agent acting for him, of the goods or documents of title under any sale, pledge, or other disposition thereof, to any person receiving the same in good faith and without notice of the previous sale, has the same effect as if the person making the delivery or transfer were expressly authorised by the owner of the goods to make the same.

Section 8 of the Factors Act 1889 is virtually identical except that it is slightly wider, in that it also applies to a person who takes the goods 'under any agreement for sale, pledge, or other disposition thereof'. The Factors Act 1889 is still in force and in many judgments it is s. 8 of the Factors Act 1889, rather than s. 24 of the Sale of Goods Act 1979, which the judge considers.

In essence, s. 24 provides that if a seller sells goods to one buyer but then sells the same goods to another buyer who acts in ignorance of the first sale, the second buyer will get title to the goods as long as the seller still had possession of the goods when making the second sale and as long as the second buyer took the goods away.

SAQ 5/19

A garage has a vintage Rolls Royce for sale. The owner of the garage goes to visit Anne and sells the Rolls Royce to her. A large deposit is paid and a date for delivery is fixed. The owner tries to ring the garage to say that the Rolls Royce has been sold, but the phone is engaged. Then the garage's star salesman sells the Rolls Royce to Bill, who drives it away.

(a) When Anne made the contract with the garage owner, did she get either ownership or possession of the Rolls Royce?

(b) When Bill made the contract with the garage did he get either ownership or lawful possession of the Rolls Royce?

(a) When she made the contract, Anne would immediately have gained ownership of the Rolls Royce (s.18 Rule 1 of the 1979 Act). Anne never got possession, although immediately after the contract she would have been entitled to it. (If the property did not pass to Anne under s. 18 Rule 1, on account of the operation of s. 17 of the 1979 Act, then the garage would only have made an agreement to sell. As the garage would still own the goods at the time of selling to Bill, there would be no need to invoke s. 24 to pass ownership to Bill. Anne would be able to sue the garage for damages for non-delivery.)

(b) When Bill made the contract he would have got ownership of the Rolls Royce, even though ownership had earlier passed to Anne. Bill therefore gained lawful possession of the Rolls Royce, as owner of it.

Where a seller sells the same goods twice, then either the first buyer or the second buyer will get title to the goods. The buyer who fails to get title will not be left without a remedy, but will be able to sue the seller for damages for breach of contract. Usually this will be a satisfactory remedy, but not if the goods were unique, as in the example above. Nor will damages be an effective remedy if the seller has gone into liquidation. In such a case, the buyer entitled only to damages will be left without an effective remedy.

SAQ 5/20

In SAQ 5/19 Bill got the car. Why is it better to let the second buyer get title and leave the first buyer only with the right to sue for damages? What is the policy here?

You might have written along the following lines. When a seller sells the same goods twice, then one of two innocent buyers must lose title. It is true that title usually passes to the first buyer and that it might therefore be logical to let that buyer retain title. However, s. 24 will only apply if the seller retained possession of the goods after the first sale, and if the second buyer took delivery of the goods or of documents of title to them. As the first buyer did not take delivery of the cars, and as the second buyer did, it is easier to let the second buyer keep title. To do otherwise would involve unnecessary complications (Buyer 2 having to pass the goods on to Buyer 1; Buyer 1 claiming that they had been damaged; Buyer 2 might have consumed the goods, etc.).

5.7 Sale of a Motor Vehicle Obtained on Hire Purchase

A debtor under a hire-purchase agreement does not own the goods being hire-purchased until the final payment is made. Up until that time the debtor is merely hiring the goods. If the debtor sells the goods to a third party, without revealing that the goods are subject to the hire-purchase agreement, the third party will generally get no title. *Nemo dat quod non habet*; the debtor cannot give what he has not got.

The Hire-Purchase Act 1964, part III, makes an exception in the case of motor vehicles. It states that where a debtor sells a motor vehicle which is subject to a hire-purchase or conditional sale agreement, then a private purchaser who buys the motor vehicle in good faith will get title to the vehicle.

An example might make this clearer. Daley has taken a car on hire-purchase from Motorhire Co. Ltd. Daley does not therefore own the car, it is owned by Motorhire Co. Ltd. Daley sells the car to Terry, who buys it in good faith and without knowledge of the hire-purchase agreement. Terry will get ownership of the car, even though Daley did not have ownership to give.

You should notice the following requirements:

(a) The 1964 Act only applies to motor vehicles. Motor vehicle is defined by s. 29(1) of the Hire-Purchase Act 1964 as 'a mechanically propelled vehicle adapted or intended for use on roads to which the public has access'.

(b) The innocent purchaser must be a private purchaser. Such a purchaser can be in business but must not be in business as a motor dealer or finance company. If the motor vehicle is first sold to a non-private purchaser (who ought to be able to check that the vehicle is not the subject of a hire-purchase agreement) then the first private purchaser to buy the vehicle is still protected.

(c) The innocent private purchaser must agree to buy the motor vehicle or take it on hire-purchase. Those who acquire the motor vehicle in other ways, such as taking them as security for a loan, are not protected.

(d) This exception to the *nemo dat* rule only applies to a motor vehicle which is subject to a hire-purchase agreement or bought under a consumer conditional sale. (A conditional sale is very similar to hire-purchase, except that the buyer does agree to pay all of the instalments, and does therefore agree at the outset to buy the goods.)

(e) If the first private purchaser does not act in good faith then neither that purchaser nor any subsequent purchaser is protected.

The relevant sections of the Hire-Purchase Act 1964 are set out in *Cases and Materials* (5.3).

5.7.1 EXTENT OF THE TITLE PASSED UNDER THE HIRE-PURCHASE ACT 1964

Section 27(2) of the Hire-Purchase Act 1964 tells us that if this exception to *nemo dat* applies, 'that disposition [by the debtor] shall have effect as if the creditor's title to the vehicle has been vested in the debtor immediately before that disposition'.

This makes it plain that the title acquired by the private purchaser is only the title of the creditor (the finance company which made the hire-purchase agreement with the debtor). If the creditor had no title then no title is passed to the private purchaser.

5.8 Unsolicited Goods and Services Act 1971

Section 1 of this Act provides that a person who receives unsolicited goods may treat them as an unconditional gift in certain circumstances, namely that: the goods were sent

MISCELLANEOUS ASPECTS OF THE SALE OF GOODS ACT 1979

to the recipient with a view to his acquiring them; the recipient has no reasonable cause to think that they were sent with a view to being acquired for a trade or business purpose; and the recipient has neither returned nor agreed to return the goods. Goods are unsolicited if they are delivered without any prior request made by the recipient or by someone on his behalf. The recipient can treat the goods sent as an unconditional gift six months after the date on which they were received, provided that the sender did not take possession of the goods and the recipient did not unreasonably prevent them from being collected. If the recipient gives written notice to the sender saying from where the goods can be collected the period is reduced to 30 days from the day on which the notice was given. Section 2 of the 1971 Act makes it an offence to demand payment for unsolicited goods. (The relevant sections of the 1971 Act can be read in *Cases and Materials* (5.4).)

5.9 Summary

This chapter has covered the following:

- A consumer becomes the owner of goods bought when the property in the goods passes to him.

- The rules on the transfer of the property in contracts for the sale of specific goods are set out in ss. 17 and 18 of the Sale of Goods Act 1979; s. 17 provides that the property passes when the parties intend it to pass; the Rules in s. 18 are only to be used when the intention of the parties cannot be ascertained.

- Section 18 Rule 1 provides that where there is an unconditional sale of specific goods in a deliverable state, the property passes at the time of the contract; however, in many such consumer sales a court might infer that the parties did not intend the property to pass until payment and delivery.

- Section 18 Rule 2 provides that where there is a contract for the sale of specific goods and the seller is bound to do something to the goods for the purpose of putting them into a deliverable state the property in the goods does not pass until the thing is done and the buyer has notice that it has been done.

- Section 18 Rule 3 provides that where there is a contract for the sale of specific goods in a deliverable state but the seller is bound to weigh, measure, test, or do some other act or thing with reference to the goods for the purpose of ascertaining the price, the property does not pass until the act or thing is done and the buyer has notice that it has been done.

- Section 18 Rule 4 provides that when goods are delivered to the buyer on approval or other similar terms the property in the goods passes to the buyer:

    (a) when he signifies his approval or acceptance to the seller or does any other act adopting the transaction;

    (b) if he does not signify his approval or acceptance to the seller but retains the goods without giving notice of rejection, then, if a time has been fixed for the return of the goods, on the expiration of that time, and, if no time has been fixed, on the expiration of a reasonable time;

- The rules on the transfer of the property in contracts for the sale of unascertained goods are set out in ss. 16–18 of the Sale of Goods Act 1979.

- Section 16 tells us that the property in unascertained goods cannot pass until the goods have become ascertained (subject to ss. 20A and 20B).

- Once s. 16 has become satisfied, s. 17 will pass the property in unascertained goods at the time when the parties intend it to pass.

- If the parties' intention cannot be discerned, then s. 18 Rule 5 will pass the property in unascertained goods when goods matching the contract description and in a deliverable state are unconditionally appropriated to the contract by one of the parties to the contract with the assent of the other party.

- Section 20A will make a consumer who pays the price (or part of it) for a specified quantity of goods which form part of an identified bulk an owner in common of the bulk.

- Unless the parties agree otherwise, goods sold are at the risk of the party who has the property in the goods.

- Section 6 makes a contract for the sale of specific goods void if, without the knowledge of the seller, the goods had perished at the time when the contract was made.

- Section 7 avoids an agreement to sell specific goods, on the grounds of frustration, if the goods perished after the contract was made but before the risk passed to the consumer.

- The seller's duty to deliver the goods to the consumer does not entail taking the goods to the consumer's house.

- In a consumer sale the place of the delivery will be the seller's place of business unless the contract is for the sale of specific goods which both of the parties know to be elsewhere (in which case that place will be the place of delivery).

- An unpaid seller may have a lien over the goods; such a lien will entitle him to retain possession of the goods even if the property in the goods has passed to the buyer; an unpaid seller might also have the right to resell goods already sold to another buyer in certain circumstances.

- If a seller sells the same goods to two different consumers, the second buyer will gain ownership of the goods if the seller retained possession of the goods after the sale to the first consumer and if the second consumer acted in good faith and took delivery of the goods.

- The first private purchaser of a motor vehicle which is the subject of a hire-purchase agreement will gain the title of the creditor provided he buys the car in good faith.

- In certain circumstances the Unsolicited Goods and Services Act 1971 allows a consumer to treat unsolicited goods as an unconditional gift.

MISCELLANEOUS ASPECTS OF THE SALE OF GOODS ACT 1979

5.10 End of Chapter Assessment Question

John and Jane Consumer go shopping in the January sales. John buys an ex-demonstration model sofa from AB Stores Ltd, getting a 10 per cent reduction on the price by paying cash. AB agree to deliver the sofa the following Tuesday. John also visits a wine merchant and agrees to buy 12 cases of 1987 Special Reserve Cabernet Sauvignon. The wine is to be delivered one case at a time over the next 12 months. John pays the full price with a cheque for £360 and is given a certificate of title.

Jane visits an antique shop and agrees to buy a painting. The sale is concluded, but when Jane begins to write a cheque the shopkeeper says that she cannot take the painting away until the cheque is cleared. Jane goes to her bank to withdraw cash, but when she returns to the shop the dealer explains that he has sold the painting to a customer who came in after Jane left, as this customer paid cash. Jane is an expert on paintings and is sure that the painting is worth £800, whereas she had agreed to buy it for £200. Jane threatens legal action and the shop owner says that he will respond once he has taken legal advice.

Jane then bought a new washing machine, having inspected a demonstration model in CD Stores Ltd. After the contract is made CD agree to deliver the washing machine to Jane's house on Tuesday. Jane pays on her credit card.

Finally, Jane visits EF Cycles Ltd to see if her new modified racing bicycle is ready for collection. Jane ordered the bicycle in March. EF said they could not give an exact delivery date but that it should be delivered within about two months. Jane has visited the shop in May, July, August and November, but on each occasion the bicycle has not been ready. In November she said that if the bicycle was not ready by Christmas she would refuse to take it and demand her deposit back. The bicycle is not ready when Jane visits the shop, but the manager says it will be ready within two days. Jane refuses to accept this and demands a return of her money.

On Tuesday John and Jane encounter the following problems. First, they receive a letter from AB Stores saying that their entire stock of sofas, including the one bought by the Consumers, was destroyed in a fire on Sunday night.

Second, they receive a letter from the liquidator of the wine store, saying that as the store has gone into liquidation goods ordered will not be delivered, and those who ordered goods have become unsecured creditors of the company.

Third, Jane receives a letter from the antique shop saying that the shop owner has taken legal advice and that Jane has no rights in respect of the painting she bought as a cheque is not legal tender and he was not obliged to take a cheque.

Fourth, CD Stores phone to say that the carrier delivering the washing machine to Jane had been in an accident and that the washing machine intended for delivery to Jane was one of three on board the carrier's lorry, all of which had been destroyed. The accident was caused by a stolen car, the driver of which was not apprehended. CD Stores are refusing to refund any of the price.

Fifth, the manager of the bicycle shop rings up to say that the bicycle is ready for collection. Jane explains that she has now bought a different bicycle and therefore no longer wants the one which she ordered.

Finally, on Saturday morning John and Jane receive a bill for £40.00 from their book club. The letter accompanying the bill explains that a book was sent on approval four months ago. As the book has not been returned within the 28 day period of approval the book club is demanding payment for it. John and Jane never received the book in question and it seems likely that it was lost in the post.

See *Cases and Materials* (5.6) for an outline answer.

CHAPTER SIX

EXCLUSION AND LIMITATION CLAUSES

6.1 Objectives

By the end of this chapter you should be able to:

- identify whether or not an exclusion clause is a term of a consumer contract;

- explain the common law approach to the interpretation of exclusion clauses;

- analyse the extent to which a business can exclude or restrict liability for negligence;

- explain the circumstances in which an exclusion clause which is a term of a consumer contract will be rendered ineffective by the Unfair Contract Terms Act 1977;

- explain the circumstances in which an exclusion clause in a consumer contract will be effective only if it satisfies the requirement of reasonableness set out in the Unfair Contract Terms Act 1977;

- analyse the requirement of reasonableness under the 1977 Act;

- outline the effect of the Unfair Terms in Consumer Contracts Regulations 1994;

- apply the law on exclusion and limitation clauses to consumer problems.

6.2 Introduction

The doctrine of freedom of contract gives sane adults the freedom to contract on whatever terms they choose. This freedom gives consumers the 'right' to agree to exclusion clauses which try to exclude or limit liability for breach of contract. Until the Unfair Contract Terms Act 1977 came into force the common law approach to exclusion clauses was to uphold them. As long as the clause was a term of the consumer's contract, and as long as the wording of the clause was such that it excluded liability for a breach which subsequently occurred, then the consumer would have no remedy for that breach of contract. Notices or signs which were not part of a contract could also take effect to deny a consumer a remedy for breach of a tortious duty. The unfairness which resulted, particularly in consumer contracts, led to the passage of the Unfair Contract Terms Act 1977. As we shall see in this chapter, the 1977 Act now gives considerable protection to consumers faced with exclusion clauses. The 1977 Act is supplemented by the Unfair Terms in Consumer Contracts Regulations 1994, which apply only to consumer contracts.

EXCLUSION AND LIMITATION CLAUSES

6.3 Freedom of Contract

We have seen in previous chapters that the concept of a consumer was quite unknown to the Victorian judges who developed the law of contract. Laissez-faire was the predominant economic philosophy of the time, and the courts demonstrated their support for this by showing a marked unwillingness to interfere with bargains freely made. In *Printing and Numerical Registering Co. v Samson* (1875) LR 19 Eq 462 Sir George Jessel MR at 465 doubtless spoke for the judiciary as a whole when he said:

> If there is one thing more than another which public policy requires it is that men of full age and competent understanding shall have the utmost liberty of contracting, and that their contracts when entered into freely and voluntarily shall be held sacred and shall be enforced by Courts of Justice. Therefore, you have this paramount public policy to consider — that you are not lightly to interfere with this freedom of contract.

This attitude seems reasonable enough when considering the affairs of merchants contracting with each other at arm's length. A merchant who does not wish to be bound by a particular term should ensure that the term is not included in the contract. As explained in earlier chapters, the law of contract was developed very much with the merchant contractor, rather than the consumer, in mind. In a consumer context, as several of the cases considered in this chapter demonstrate, Jessel MR's words look much less reasonable.

With one or two notable exceptions the twentieth century judiciary adhered to the doctrine of freedom of contract, even in consumer cases. This led to some patently unfair results. Exclusion clauses were common in consumer contracts. These clauses did not become incorporated as a result of bargaining between the consumer and the seller. Most consumers pay little attention to the wording of the contracts which they make and in any case are often compelled to deal on the seller's standard terms. If they do not like these terms then they cannot make the contract. Only when the consumer is injured by the product, or when the product proves to be defective, are the terms of the contract read. If an exclusion clause denied the consumer any redress then the courts would uphold the clause. (See the extract from Lord Denning MR in *George Mitchell Ltd v Finney Lock Seeds Ltd* [1983] 1 QB 296 in *Cases and Materials* (6.1).)

This imbalance between the rights of the consumer and the retailer has been radically altered by the Unfair Contract Terms Act 1977 and the Unfair Terms in Consumer Contracts Regulations 1994. Sir George Jessel's view is now redundant in consumer contracts.

6.4 The Common Law Approach to Exclusion Clauses

It might be thought that since the coming into force of the 1977 Act and the 1994 Regulations the common law has little relevance to exclusion clauses. However, the common law on exclusion clauses is still important in three ways. First, it is the common law which makes the rules on whether or not an exclusion clause should be considered a term of a particular contract or not. Second, the common law approach on how exclusion clauses should be interpreted can still be relevant in some consumer cases. Third, the common law has developed the Unfair Contract Terms Act 1977, by deciding how sections of the Act should be interpreted. We shall therefore consider each of these three aspects of the common law in turn.

6.4.1 IS THE EXCLUSION CLAUSE INCORPORATED INTO THE CONTRACT?

The first step when considering whether an exclusion clause will be effective against a consumer is to ask whether or not the clause was incorporated into the contract which the consumer has made.

SAQ 6/1

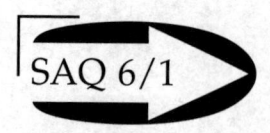

Later in this chapter we shall see that it is unlikely that an exclusion clause can take away the contractual rights of a consumer. Why then do we bother with analysing whether or not the exclusion clause was incorporated into the contract?

We first analyse whether or not the exclusion clause was incorporated into the contract because if it was not so incorporated then it cannot be effective as a term of the contract. Despite the 1977 Act and the 1994 Regulations, it is still possible that an exclusion clause which was incorporated into a consumer contract can exclude or restrict the liability of the business for breach of contract. If the clause was not incorporated into the contract which the consumer made, then it is not possible that the clause can have this effect.

ACTIVITY 6/1

This Activity will take quite a long time. First, the basic rules on the circumstances in which an exclusion clause will be incorporated into a contract are stated. Then the facts of eight of the leading cases are set out. As regards each of the cases, you should indicate whether or not the clause in question was incorporated as a term of the contract. You should also state briefly the reasons for your decision. The rules on incorporation of exclusion clauses into contracts are as follows:

- A party who has signed a contract containing an exclusion clause will generally be bound by the clause.

- If a consumer was induced to sign the contract because the effect of the exclusion clause was misrepresented to him, then the clause will be restricted to the meaning represented.

- An exclusion clause which is not signed by the consumer can be incorporated into the contract if the consumer has actual notice of its existence. This actual notice might be communicated by a sign or other notice. If the consumer has notice of the existence of the exclusion clause it is not necessary that he knows exactly what it said.

- A notice can also prevent liability in tort from arising if it is brought to the consumer's attention clearly enough.

- An exclusion clause will only be incorporated into a contract if it was contained in a document which the reasonable person would regard as a part of the contract. Generally, tickets may be regarded as a part of the contract, whereas receipts will not usually be regarded as part of the contract.

- An exclusion clause can become incorporated into a contract on account of a course of dealing between the parties. However, in consumer cases this course of dealing

EXCLUSION AND LIMITATION CLAUSES

would have to be very well-established, and the exclusion clause consistently applied.

Chapelton v Barry UDC [1940] 1 KB 532
The plaintiff wanted to hire a deck chair on a beach. Deck chairs belonging to the defendants were piled up near a notice which read: 'Barry Urban District Council. Cold Knap. Hire of chairs 2d per session of 3 hours.' The notice also stated that those wishing to hire deck chairs should get tickets from the attendant and that these tickets should be retained for inspection. The notice did not exclude any liability for breach of contract. The plaintiff paid 4d to hire two deck chairs, getting two tickets from the attendant. The plaintiff put the tickets in his pocket without reading them. On the reverse of the tickets it stated that the council would 'not be liable for any accident or damage arising from the hire of the chair'. Due to the defendant's negligence the canvas came away from the chair on which the plaintiff was sitting and this caused the plaintiff injury.
Held:

Curtis v Chemical Cleaning and Dyeing Co. [1951] 1 All ER 631
The plaintiff took a white satin wedding dress, which was decorated with beads and sequins, to the defendant's dry cleaning shop. The plaintiff was asked to sign a piece of paper, headed 'Receipt'. The plaintiff asked what the piece of paper said and was told that it excluded the defendants from certain types of liability, including damage to beads and sequins. The plaintiff signed the piece of paper which contained the following exclusion clause: 'This article is accepted on condition that the company is not liable for any damage howsoever arising.' The dry cleaners stained the dress and, when sued by the plaintiff, attempted to rely on the exclusion clause.
Held:

Hollier v Rambler Motors (AMC) Ltd [1972] 2 QB 71
The defendant's garage had repaired the plaintiff's car three or four times in the previous five years. On at least two of these occasions the plaintiff had signed a form, without reading it, which contained the words: 'The company is not responsible for damage caused by fire to customer's cars on the premises.' The plaintiff made an oral contract for his car to be repaired by the defendants. Whilst the defendants had the car it was damaged by a fire caused by the defendant's negligence. The plaintiff claimed damages for breach of an implied term that the defendants would take reasonable care of the car. The defendants relied on the exclusion clause which, they argued, had become incorporated into the contract by a course of dealing between the parties.
Held:

L'Estrange v F. Graucob Ltd [1934] 2 KB 394
The plaintiff, who owned a cafe, signed a form when ordering a cigarette vending machine. In ordinary sized print the form contained the essential terms of the contract. In small print a term stated: 'Any express or implied condition, statement, or warranty, statutory or otherwise not stated herein is expressly excluded.' The plaintiff did not read the form or know what the exclusion clause said. The vending machine did not work properly. The plaintiff sued claiming damages for breach of what is now s. 14(3) of the Sale of Goods Act 1979, the implied term that the goods would be fit for her purpose. The defendants claimed that the exclusion clause which the plaintiff had signed expressly excluded all implied warranties.
Held:

McCutcheon v David MacBrayne Ltd [1964] 1 All ER 430
The plaintiff's brother-in-law, M, arranged for the defendant's ferry to ship the plaintiff's car from Islay to the mainland of Scotland. The ship carrying the car sank, owing to the defendant's negligence. The plaintiff sued for damages for negligence. The defendants relied on their exclusion clauses. These were exhibited in their office, where M had made

the contract, and on the ship itself. On the invoice on which the receipt was written there was a statement that the goods were carried subject to conditions specified on sailing bills and notices. Usually the person consigning goods was asked to sign a risk note, incorporating an exclusion clause, but due to an oversight M had not been asked to sign it. Both M and the plaintiff had shipped goods with the defendants before, sometimes signing the risk note, sometimes not. Neither M nor the plaintiff had ever read any of the notices or the risk notes which they had signed. The defendants argued that their exclusion clauses were incorporated into the oral contract of carriage which had been made by a previous course of dealings between the parties.
Held:

Olley v Marlborough Court Hotel Ltd [1949] 1 KB 532
A married couple paid for a week's board and residence at a residential hotel and paid the bill in advance. As a consequence of the hotel's negligence, furs belonging to the wife were stolen from the hotel bedroom. A notice in the hotel bedroom stated: 'The proprietors will not hold themselves responsible for articles lost or stolen, unless handed to the manageress for safe custody. Valuables should be deposited for safe custody in a sealed package and a receipt obtained.' The hotel sought to rely on the notice in the bedroom.
Held:

Thompson v London, Midland and Scottish Railway Co. [1930] 1 KB 41
The plaintiff could not read. Her niece bought her a ticket for a train excursion. On the front of the ticket it said, 'Excursion. For conditions see back'. The back of the ticket stated that the ticket was issued subject to the conditions in the defendant's time tables and excursion bills. The time table, which could be bought for 6d, stated that the defendants could not be liable in respect of injury however caused. The plaintiff was injured by the defendant's negligence. A special jury found that the defendants had not done enough to bring the conditions to the attention of the plaintiff. The defendants appealed arguing that there was no evidence on which the jury could come to this finding.
Held:

Thornton v Shoe Lane Parking Ltd [1971] 1 All-ER 686
The plaintiff parked his car in the defendant's car park. A notice outside the car park stated: 'All cars parked at owner's risk.' Inside the car park the plaintiff stopped at a red light. When this turned to green a ticket was issued from a machine. The ticket stated that it was issued subject to the conditions which were displayed inside the premises. To find what these conditions said it would have been necessary to drive into the car park and walk around. The conditions inside the car park exempted liability for personal injury as well as liability for damage to cars. The plaintiff was badly injured, partly due to the negligence of the defendants. The defendants relied on the exclusion clause inside the car park to which the ticket referred.
Held:

- *Chapelton v Barry UDC*: the exclusion clause did not protect the defendants. The ticket was a mere voucher or receipt for the money paid for the hire of the chair. The terms on which the deck chairs were hired were set out on the notice, which contained no exclusion clause.

- *Curtis v Chemical Cleaning and Dyeing Co.*: the defendants could not rely on the exclusion clause as they had misrepresented its effect.

- *Hollier v Rambler Motors (AMC) Ltd*: the course of dealing was not sufficiently well established to incorporate the exclusion clause into the oral contract which was made.

EXCLUSION AND LIMITATION CLAUSES

- *L'Estrange* v *F. Graucob Ltd*: the plaintiff had signed the exclusion clause and so she was bound by it. It did not matter at all that she had not read it and did not know what it said.

- *McCutcheon* v *David MacBrayne Ltd*: liability for negligence was not excluded. The fact that the plaintiff had not always been asked to sign the risk note meant that the terms therein had not been established by a previous course of dealings between the parties.

- *Olley* v *Marlborough Court Hotel Ltd*: the notice could not protect the hotel as it was not part of the contract made between the hotel and the couple. The contract had already been made before the guests could see the notice.

- *Thompson* v *London, Midland and Scottish Railway Co.*: the exclusion clause was binding on the plaintiff. When she accepted the ticket the plaintiff was bound by the contract. At this time she had sufficient notice of the special conditions in the time table. The fact that the plaintiff could not read made no difference.

- *Thornton* v *Shoe Lane Parking Ltd*: the defendants were not saved by the exclusion clause to which the ticket referred, because the defendant neither knew of it, nor had sufficient steps been taken to draw it to his attention, at the time of contracting. The plaintiff's act in causing the machine to issue the ticket was an irrevocable act concluding the contract, and so conditions could not afterwards be incorporated into the contract. The notice outside the car park did not exclude liability for personal injury.

6.4.1.1 Is the exclusion clause a term of a collateral contract?

In **Chapter 7** we shall examined the doctrine of privity of contract, which holds that a contract is a private bargain between the parties who made it. Those who did not make the contract can neither enforce it nor become liable under it. In **Chapter 1** we considered *Webster* v *Higgin*, and you might remember that in that case the court found that the exclusion clause in the written contract was no part of the collateral contract, which was made when the consumer purchased the car in reliance on the defendant's guarantee that it was in good condition. Even where there is no collateral contract, an exclusion clause will not be able to protect a party who did not make the contract, even if the clause expressly states that it should have this effect.

Adler v *Dickson and Another* [1955] 1 QB 158
A shipping company issued the plaintiff with a ticket for a cruise around the Mediterranean. An exclusion clause, which was a part of the contract, protected the company from liability for negligence, whether the same shall arise from or be occasioned by the negligence of the company's servants . . . in the discharge of their duties, or whether by the negligence of other persons directly or indirectly in the employment or service of the company . . . under any circumstances whatsoever'. The plaintiff was injured when mounting the gangway of the ship. She brought an action in negligence against the master and the boatswain of the ship.
Held: The contract did not expressly or impliedly deny the plaintiff the right to sue the defendants in tort. However, even if it had done so Jenkins LJ said that the two defendants could not have relied upon it as they were not parties to the contract.

6.4.2 COMMON LAW CONSTRUCTION OF EXCLUSION CLAUSES

The *contra preferentum* rule holds that exclusion clauses should be interpreted narrowly, against the wishes of the party trying to rely on them. Any ambiguity in the clause will be interpreted in favour of the consumer. The rule has become significantly less important since the Unfair Contract Terms Act 1977 took effect. In *George Mitchell* v *Finney Lock Seeds* [1983] 2 AC 803 Lord Denning MR said, at 297, that the courts used the rule 'so as to depart from the natural meaning of the words of the exemption clause and to put upon them a strained and unnatural construction'. At 299 he said that he thought that the arrival of the 1977 Act would mean that the courts would no longer have to go through all kinds of gymnastic contortions to get around exclusion clauses. The *contra preferentum* rule is undoubtedly of less importance than it was before, but it can still help a consumer. We shall see shortly that even in the light of the 1977 Act some exclusion clauses are binding upon consumers if they are reasonable. So a reasonable clause, which strictly interpreted did not apply on the facts of the case, could still be ineffective under the *contra preferentum* rule. The following case shows an example of the rule being applied.

Houghton v Trafalgar Insurance [1954] 1 QB 247
A motor insurance policy contained a clause excluding liability for damage 'caused or arising whilst the car is conveying any load in excess of that for which it was constructed'. The car only had seating capacity for five people but at the time of the accident there were six people in the car. Consequently, the insurers denied liability under the policy.
Held: The exclusion clause did not help the insurers as the load referred to only covered cases where there was a specified weight which must not be exceeded, as in the case of lorries and vans. Somervell LJ said, at 249: 'If there is any ambiguity, since it is the defendant's clause, the ambiguity will be resolved in favour of the assured.'

Andrews Bros Ltd v Singer & Co. Ltd [1934] 1 KB 17
The plaintiffs agreed to buy 'new Singer cars' from the defendants. One of the cars delivered was not new. The plaintiffs claimed damages. The defendants relied on an exclusion clause which stated, 'all conditions, warranties and liabilities implied by common law, statute or otherwise are excluded'.

SAQ 6/2

In the above case the *contra preferentum* rule operated so as to prevent the exclusion clause from being effective. Can you spot why this was so?

You might have spotted that the clause did not work because the term that the cars should be new was an express term of the contract rather than an implied term. The defence had argued that the description was within s. 13 of the Sale of Goods Act 1893, and was therefore a statutory implied term. This argument was rejected as 'very strained' by Scrutton LJ.

In the light of the cases which we have examined so far in this chapter, it might be thought that exclusion clauses were commonly defeated by the courts prior to the introduction of legislation in this area. This would be far from true. The cases we have examined were very much the exception rather than the rule. Furthermore, in the cases where the clauses were held ineffective this only saved the particular plaintiff who brought the action. The businesses which sought unsuccessfully to rely on the clauses in question would have been very likely to have rendered their exclusion clauses effective in future by ensuring that they were incorporated into future contracts and that they were sufficiently clearly worded to exclude liability.

EXCLUSION AND LIMITATION CLAUSES

6.5 The Unfair Contract Terms Act 1977

The Unfair Contract Terms Act 1977 regulates exclusion clauses in two ways. First, some exclusion clauses are declared invalid. Second, other exclusion clauses are effective only if they satisfy the Act's requirement of reasonableness. Despite its name, the Act deals not only with unfair contract terms but also with the exclusion of liability for the tort of negligence. The Act does not create new duties.

6.5.1 SCOPE OF THE ACT

The important sections of the 1977 Act (ss. 2 to 7) do not apply to all types of liability, but only to business liability.

ACTIVITY 6/2

Read s. 1 of the 1977 Act in *Cases and Materials* (6.2.1). What is meant by 'business liability'?

Section 1(3) tells us that 'business liability' under the Act means liability for breach of obligations arising in one of two ways. First, for liability arising from things done or to be done by a person in the course of a business (whether his own business or another's). Second, liability arising from the occupation of premises used for business purposes of the occupier. An occupier who allows access to premises for recreational or educational purposes is not liable for the dangerous state of the premises unless the provision of the educational or recreational facilities was part of the business activities of the occupier (s. (3)(b)). The Act does not give a definition of 'business' but s. 14 says that 'business' includes a profession and the activities of any government department or local or public authority.

Curiously, the 1977 Act also applies to the exclusion of liability for breach of the terms implied by s. 13 of the Sale of Goods Act 1979 and s. 9 of the Supply of Goods (Implied Terms) Act 1973 (the implied terms as to correspondence with description in contracts of sale of goods and hire-purchase) and for misrepresentations, even if the description or misrepresentation was not made in the course of a business (s. 6(4) and s. 3 of the Misrepresentation Act 1967, as substituted by s. 8 of the 1977 Act).

6.5.2 NEGLIGENCE LIABILITY

Section 2 of the Unfair Contract Terms Act 1977 deals with the exclusion of negligence liability. Section 1(1) defines negligence as:

> ... the breach—
> (a) of any obligation, arising from the express or implied terms of a contract, to take reasonable care or exercise reasonable skill in the performance of the contract;

(b) of any common law duty to take reasonable care or exercise reasonable skill (but not any stricter duty);
(c) of the common law duty of care imposed by the Occupier's Liability Act 1957 ...

This statutory definition of negligence plainly includes breaches of duty which would amount to the tort of negligence or give rise to liability under the Occupier's Liability Act 1957. It would also seem to include any other tort the commission of which depended upon a duty to take reasonable care having been broken. However, the definition also makes it plain that breach of a duty imposed by a tort of strict liability, such as the duty imposed under *Rylands* v *Fletcher* (1866) LR 1 Ex 265, is not to be regarded as negligence. Section 2 of the 1977 Act will therefore not apply to such a breach of duty. Breach of contract will amount to negligence if the breach consists in failing to take reasonable care and skill in performing the contract.

Both intentional and inadvertent breaches of duty are included, whether arising directly or vicariously (s. 1(4)).

Section 2 of the Unfair Contract Terms Act 1977 states:

(1) A person cannot by reference to any contract term or to a notice given to persons generally or to particular persons exclude or restrict his liability for death or personal injury resulting from negligence.

(2) In the case of other loss or damage, a person cannot so exclude or restrict his liability for negligence except in so far as the term or notice satisfies the requirement of reasonableness.

(3) Where a contract term or notice purports to exclude or restrict liability for negligence a person's agreement to or awareness of it is not of itself to be taken as indicating his voluntary acceptance of any risk.

SAQ 6/3

Assume that the cases of *Olley* v *Marlborough Court Hotel Ltd* and *Chapelton* v *Barry UDC* were to arise today. Assume also that Mrs Olley had regularly stayed at the hotel in the same room and that Mr Chapelton was aware of the exclusion clause when he hired the deck chair. How would the cases now be decided?

In *Olley's* case the first point to make is that if the notice in the room was not brought to the consumer's attention before the contract was made then the case would be decided exactly as it was in 1949, because the notice would not have been a term of the contract which Mrs Olley made. However, assuming that the notice in the room was incorporated into the contract by a course of dealing between the parties (because Mrs Olley stayed regularly at the hotel), we would then consider the effect of the 1977 Act. It would be an implied term of the contract that the hotel should take reasonable care to see that Mrs Olley's property was safe in her room (Supply of Goods and Services Act 1982, s. 13). Failure to take such care would amount to 'negligence' as defined by s. 1(1) of the 1977 Act. Liability for the loss of Mrs Olley's fur coat could therefore only be excluded or restricted so far as this satisfied the test of reasonableness (s. 2(2) of the 1977 Act.) (The requirement of reasonableness is examined below at **6.5.9**.)

EXCLUSION AND LIMITATION CLAUSES

The exclusion clause in *Chapelton* would be a term of the contract if Mr Chapelton was aware of it when he made the contract. (If the clause was not a term of the contract then the case would have been decided as it was in 1940.) The hirers of the deck chair would be under a duty to provide the service using reasonable care and skill (s. 13 of the 1982 Act). Failure to take such care would amount to negligence under the 1977 Act. The personal injury resulting from the hirer's negligence could not be restricted or excluded by any contract term (s. 2(1) of the 1977 Act).

Section 2 deals only with the exclusion or restriction of liability for negligence. It does not prevent an exclusion clause from doing away with a duty of care where such a duty would otherwise exist. However, s. 13(1) does have this effect: '[sections 2, 5, and 7 of the Act] also prevent excluding or restricting liability by reference to terms and notices which exclude or restrict the relevant obligation or duty'.

6.5.3 CONTRACTS OF SALE AND OF HIRE-PURCHASE (SECTION 6)

Section 6(1) of the Unfair Contract Terms Act 1977 states that liability arising under s. 12 of the Sale of Goods Act 1979 or the corresponding term implied by s. 8 of the Supply of Goods Implied Terms) Act 1973 cannot be excluded by any contract term. Section 6(2) states that as against a person dealing as a consumer, liability for breach of ss. 13–15 of the 1979 Act and ss. 9–11 of the 1973 Act cannot be excluded by reference to any contract term. The effect of s. 6 then is that liability for breach of any of the implied terms contained in the 1979 Act or the 1973 Act cannot be excluded where the buyer is dealing as a consumer. (We studied the effect of these terms in **Chapters 3** and **4**. There we saw that the 1979 Act, ss. 12–15, implied terms as to the right to sell, correspondence with description, satisfactory quality, fitness for purpose and correspondence with sample. Sections 8–11 of the 1982 Act implied virtually identical terms into contracts of hire-purchase.) Obligations other than those contained in the statutory implied terms, such as the obligation to deliver goods on time, are not affected by s. 6, but will be affected by s. 3, which is considered below.

Liability for breach of the terms implied by ss. 13–15 of the 1979 Act and ss. 9–11 of the 1973 Act can be excluded where the buyer/hirer is not a consumer, if the terms excluding or restricting liability satisfy the Act's requirement of reasonableness. We therefore need to be clear about the Act's definition of 'dealing as a consumer' in the 1977 Act.

ACTIVITY 6/3

Read s. 12 of the 1977 Act in *Cases and Materials* (6.2.1) and then answer the following questions. Assume that John is a teacher, Mark an accountant, Jane a solicitor and Fred a policeman.

(a) Are the following buyers dealing as consumers for the purposes of s. 6:

(i) John, a teacher, buys a new car from a garage?

(ii) The garage orders six new cars from the manufacturer?

(iii) The garage buys Mark's car?

(iv) Mark buys another car at an auction? (The car was put into the auction by a car dealer.)

(v) Jane buys an antique penny-farthing bicycle from a bicycle retailer.

(vi) A taxi driver sells his old car to Fred. This is the first such sale made by the taxi driver.

(vii) George, a retired builder, decides to build an extension to his house. When buying a large quantity of building materials, he gets trade discount from the builders merchant by pretending that he is still in business.

(b) If there is a dispute as to whether or not John is dealing as a consumer in his dealings with the garage, must John prove that he is dealing as a consumer, or must the garage prove that he is not?

You should have answered along the following lines:

(a)(i) John is dealing as a consumer. The garage does make the contract in the course of business and John does not.

(ii) As both parties are acting in the course of their respective businesses, the garage is not dealing as a consumer.

(iii) The garage is not dealing as a consumer. The garage does make the contract in the course of its business and Mark does not make it in the course of a business.

(iv) At a sale by auction the buyer is not in any circumstances to be regarded as a dealing as a consumer (s. 12(2)). Mark is not therefore dealing as a consumer.

(v) Jane is not dealing as a consumer because the goods passing under the contract are not of a type ordinarily supplied for private use or consumption (s. 12 (1)(c)).

(vi) Fred is not dealing as a consumer because the taxi driver is not acting in the course of a business (see *R & B Customs Brokers Co. Ltd* v *United Dominions Trust Ltd*, below).

(vii) George is not dealing as a consumer as he is holding himself out to be acting in the course of a business. In addition, the fact that the goods are not of a type ordinarily supplied for private use or consumption might also mean that George is not a consumer.

(b) The burden of proof is on the garage to show that John is not dealing as a consumer (s. 12(3)).

R & B Customs Brokers Co. Ltd v *United Dominions Trust Ltd* [1988] 1 WLR 321
The plaintiff was a freight forwarding company. One of the plaintiff's directors organised that the company should buy a car for his own use. This was the second or third time in the five years of the company's existence that it had bought a car. The car was bought from a third party car dealer and the deal was financed by the defendant finance company. The plaintiff company traded in its existing car in part-exchange. The defendant company's terms excluded all liability for any term as to description, quality or fitness for purpose unless the buyer was dealing as a consumer. The car leaked badly and this amounted to a breach of s. 14(3) of the Sale of Goods Act 1979.

EXCLUSION AND LIMITATION CLAUSES

Held: The company was dealing as a consumer within the meaning of s. 12 of the 1977 Act and therefore the term implied by s. 13 of the Sale of Goods Act 1979 could not be excluded.

It might seem strange that the company did not buy the car in the course of its business. (If a company buys anything other than in the course of its business would the contract not be ultra vires?) However, the Court of Appeal decided the case as it did because the plaintiff company had not held itself out as making the contract in the course of its business and because the necessary degree of regularity in making such contracts had not been shown. The Court applied the decision in *Davies v Sumner* [1984] 1 WLR 1301, a case on the meaning of 'in the course of a trade or business' in the Trade Descriptions Act 1968. Dillon LJ stated, at 330:

> This reasoning leads to the conclusion that, in the Act of 1977 also, the words 'in the course of a business' are not used in what Lord Keith [in *Davies v Sumner*] called 'the broadest sense'. I also find helpful the phrase used by Lord Parker CJ, and quoted by Lord Keith, 'an integral part of the business carried on'. The reconciliation between that phrase and the need for some degree of regularity is, as I see it, as follows: there are some transactions which are clearly integral parts of the businesses concerned, and these should be held to have been carried out in the course of those businesses; this would cover, apart from much else, the instance of a one-off adventure in the nature of trade, where the transaction itself would constitute a trade or business. There are other transactions, however, such as the purchase of the car in the present case, which are at highest only incidental to the carrying on of the relevant business; here a degree of regularity is required before it can be said that they are an integral part of the business carried on, and so entered into in the course of that business.

ACTIVITY 6/4

Read ss. 6 and 12 of the 1977 Act in *Cases and Materials* (6.2.1) and apply them to the following problem.

John, a teacher, buys a car from Mark, an accountant. The sale is by description and the car does not correspond with the description. An exclusion clause excludes all liability for failure to correspond with description. Is John a consumer? What is the effect of the exclusion clause?

John is not a consumer because Mark does not make the contract in the course of a business (s. 12(1)). Section 6 does apply even though the liability arising is not business liability (s. 6(4)). Therefore the liability which Mark would incur under s. 13 of the Sale of Goods Act 1979 can only be excluded so far as this satisfies the requirement of reasonableness (s. 6(3)).

6.5.4 MISCELLANEOUS CONTRACTS UNDER WHICH GOODS PASS

Section 7 applies to contracts, other than contracts of hire-purchase or sale of goods, under which possession or ownership of goods pass. This would encompass contracts for the transfer of property in goods (into which the statutory terms are implied by ss. 2–5 of the Supply of Goods and Services Act 1982) and for the hire of goods (into which the statutory terms are implied by ss. 7–10 of the 1982 Act.) In both such classes of contracts s. 7 of the Unfair Contract Terms Act 1977 makes rules similar to those found in s. 6 of the 1977 Act. That is to say that, as against a person dealing as a consumer, liability in respect of the goods' correspondence with description or sample, or their quality or fitness for any particular purpose, cannot be excluded or restricted by reference to any term. The only material difference between ss. 6 and 7 is that s. 7 does not contain any subsection which is the equivalent of s. 6(4). So the liabilities referred to in s. 7 are only the business liabilities defined by s. 1(3). If in **Activity 6/4**, above, John had been hiring the car from Mark then Mark's exclusion clause would not have been touched by the 1977 Act as Mark's liability would not have been business liability.

In **Chapter 4** we saw that s. 13 of the Supply of Goods and Services Act 1982 implies a term into a contract for the supply of a service by a business that the service will be supplied using reasonable care and skill. Sections 6 and 7 of the 1977 Act do not apply to the exclusion of liability arising under s. 13. However, ss. 2 and 3 of the 1977 Act will apply. We have already seen that s. 2(1) of the 1977 Act prevents the exclusion or restriction of liability for death or personal injury caused by negligence, and that s. 2(2) prevents the exclusion of other loss or damage caused by negligence unless the requirement of reasonableness is satisfied. Section 1(1)(a) of the 1977 Act classifies failure to take reasonable care or exercise reasonable skill in the performance of a contract as negligence for the purposes of the Act. Therefore when s. 13 of the 1982 Act is breached s. 2 of the 1977 Act will ensure that liability for death or personal injury so caused can never be excluded and liability for damage to property can only be excluded if this is reasonable. Section 3 of the 1977 Act would also be relevant, as we shall now see.

6.5.5 LIABILITY ARISING IN CONTRACT

ACTIVITY 6/5

Read s. 3 of the Unfair Contract Terms Act 1977 in *Cases and Materials* (6.2.1). In the light of the protection conferred by ss. 2, 6 and 7, in what circumstances is s. 3 likely to be of use to a consumer?

Section 3 provides that where a party deals as a consumer the other party to the contract cannot by reference to any contract term (a) restrict or exclude any liability for breach of contract, or (b) perform the contract in a manner which is substantially different from that expected, or (c) wholly or partly refuse to perform the contract at all, unless the term satisfies the requirement of reasonableness. (The s. 3 provisions also apply when one party deals on the other's written standard terms of business, whether the contract was a consumer contract or not.)

First, s. 3 can be useful to a consumer who has made a contract under which the ownership or possession of goods does not pass. Sections 6 and 7 provide no help to a consumer in respect of such contracts. Section 2 will provide help to the consumer where the loss or injury to the consumer was caused by the supplier's negligence, but not otherwise. So in a contract to provide a service, where liability arises otherwise than through the supplier's negligence, s. 3 might be useful to a consumer.

Second, s. 3 can be useful in contracts under which goods are supplied as regards breaches other than breaches of the statutory implied terms. (Sections 6 and 7 of course provide that in consumer contracts liability for breach of the statutory implied terms cannot be excluded by any contract term.)

A couple of examples might make this clearer. First, let us suppose that Mrs Smith makes a contract to have her house painted by a firm of painters. The firm's exclusion clause, which Mrs Smith signs, says that the firm cannot be liable for failure to perform the contract on time. The firm do not paint the house on time, but this cannot be attributed to the firm's negligence. Sections 6 and 7 provide no help to Mrs Smith as the contract is not one under which goods pass. Section 2 provides no help as the failure to paint the house on time was not caused by negligence. Section 3 may well help Mrs Smith as it provides that liability for breach of contract cannot be excluded unless the term excluding the liability satisfies the Act's requirement of reasonableness. Second, let us assume that Mr Smith ordered a new car from a garage. A term of the contract states that if the car cannot be delivered for reasons beyond the control of the seller the seller cannot incur any liability for this breach. This is a contract of sale of goods, but s. 6 of the 1977 Act will provide no help to Mr Smith as the breach of contract was not a breach of one of the statutory implied terms. Section 2 will provide no help as no-one has been harmed, and no other loss or damage has been caused, by negligence. Section 3 will render the exclusion clause invalid unless it satisfies the requirement of reasonableness under the 1977 Act.

166 EXCLUSION AND LIMITATION CLAUSES

The 1977 Act and consumer contracts

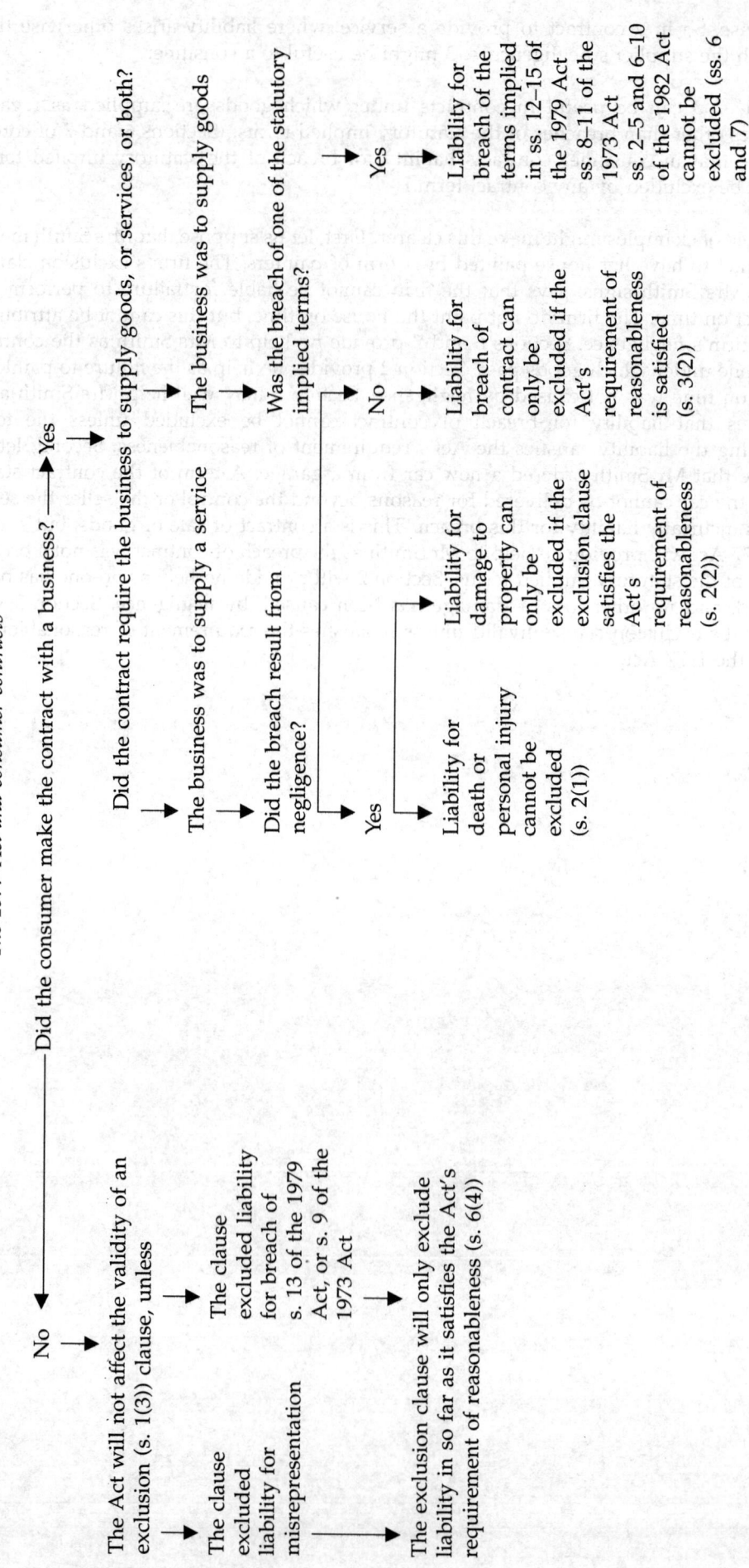

Did the consumer make the contract with a business?

Yes →

Did the contract require the business to supply goods, or services, or both?

- The business was to supply goods → Was the breach of one of the statutory implied terms? → **Yes** → Liability for breach of the terms implied in ss. 12–15 of the 1979 Act ss. 8–11 of the 1973 Act ss. 2–5 and 6–10 of the 1982 Act cannot be excluded (ss. 6 and 7)

- The business was to supply a service → Did the breach result from negligence?
  - **No** → Liability for breach of contract can only be excluded if the Act's requirement of reasonableness is satisfied (s. 3(2))
  - **Yes** →
    - Liability for death or personal injury cannot be excluded (s. 2(1))
    - Liability for damage to property can only be excluded if the exclusion clause satisfies the Act's requirement of reasonableness (s. 2(2))

No →

The Act will not affect the validity of an exclusion (s. 1(3)) clause, unless

→ The clause excluded liability for misrepresentation

→ The clause excluded liability for breach of s. 13 of the 1979 Act, or s. 9 of the 1973 Act

→ The exclusion clause will only exclude liability in so far as it satisfies the Act's requirement of reasonableness (s. 6(4))

EXCLUSION AND LIMITATION CLAUSES

6.5.6 UNREASONABLE INDEMNITY CLAUSES

Section 4 of the 1977 Act states that:

(1) A person dealing as a consumer cannot by reference to any contract term be made to indemnify another person (whether a party to the contract or not) in respect of liability that may be incurred by the other for negligence or breach of contract, except in so far as the contract term satisfies the requirement of reasonableness.

(2) This section applies whether the liability in question—

(a) is directly that of the person to be indemnified or is incurred by him vicariously;

(b) is to the person dealing as consumer or to someone else.

SAQ 6/4

(a) What does it mean when one person indemnifies another?

(b) Can a contract term which requires a consumer to indemnify another for breach of contract or negligence ever be effective?

(a) A person who indemnifies another agrees to assume the contractual liability of another. (Unlike a guarantee, a contract of indemnity does not need to be in writing.)

(b) A contract term requiring a consumer to indemnify another for breach of contract or negligence can be effective if it satisfies the requirement of reasonableness.

6.5.7 GUARANTEE OF CONSUMER GOODS

ACTIVITY 6/6

Read s. 5 of the Unfair Contract Terms Act in *Cases and Materials* (6.2.1). Then answer the following questions.

(a) How does s. 5 affect the relationship between the retailer and the consumer?

(b) What is the purpose of s. 5?

(a) Section 5 does not affect the relationship between the retailer and the consumer (s. 5(3)).

(b) Section 5 is trying to prevent the abuse of guarantees whereby they reduce the consumer's rights rather than increase them. Before the 1977 Act came into force a manufacturer's guarantee could not only reduce the consumer's rights against the manufacturer in negligence, it could also reduce the consumer's rights against the retailer. Section 5 now provides that where loss or damage to consumer goods arises while the goods are in consumer use, and this loss was caused by the negligence of the manufacturer or distribution of the goods, no notice or term operating by reference to a guarantee can exclude or restrict liability for the loss. It is interesting to note that for the purposes of this section goods are regarded as 'in consumer use' unless they are used or intended to be used exclusively for the purposes of a business. So if a doctor bought a vacuum cleaner for the surgery, but also cleaned his car with it, the vacuum cleaner would be regarded as in consumer use for the purposes of s. 5. The guarantee needs to be in writing, but is otherwise widely defined (s. 5(2)(b)).

6.5.8 EXCLUSION OF LIABILITY FOR MISREPRESENTATION

Section 3 of the Misrepresentation Act 1967, as substituted by s. 8 of the Unfair Contract Terms Act 1977, says:

> If a contract contains a term which would exclude or restrict—
> (a) any liability to which a party to a contract may be subject by reason of any misrepresentation made by him before the contract was made; or
> (b) any remedy available to another party to the contract by reason of such a misrepresentation,
> the term shall be of no effect except in so far as it satisfies the requirement of reasonableness as stated in section II(1) of the Unfair Contract Terms Act 1977; and it is for those claiming that the term satisfies that requirement to show that it does.

So this section makes no distinction between those who deal as consumers and those who do not. Exclusions or restrictions of liability for misrepresentations can only be effective if the person claiming that they are effective can prove that they satisfy the requirement of reasonableness under the 1977 Act.

6.5.9 THE REQUIREMENT OF REASONABLENESS

ACTIVITY 6/7

Read s. 11 of the Unfair Contract Terms Act 1977 in *Cases and Materials* (6.2.1). Then answer the following questions.

(a) In relation to a contract term, what is the general requirement of reasonableness?

(b) If the breach of contract transpires to be unexpectedly serious, does this have a bearing on whether the term was fair and reasonable?

(c) In what circumstances are the matters specified in sch. 2 of the Act relevant?

(d) What is the test of reasonableness as regards non-contractual notices?

(e) What two additional factors are to be considered as regards limitation clauses?

EXCLUSION AND LIMITATION CLAUSES

(f) **In a dispute as to whether or not a term satisfies the requirement of reasonableness, on which party is the burden of proof placed?**

(a) The general requirement of reasonableness is that the term shall have been a fair and reasonable one to be included in the contract having regard to the circumstances which were, or ought reasonably to have been, known to or in the contemplation of the parties when the contract was made (s. 11(1)).

(b) The consequences of breach will not have an effect on whether the term was fair and reasonable unless they were contemplated by the parties before the contract was made (s. 11(1)).

(c) Section 11(2) states that the matters specified in sch. 2 are relevant only as regards exclusion of the statutory implied terms in contracts to supply goods. However, the courts have not stuck to this approach. (In *Cases and Materials* (6.2.2) see the extract from the judgment of Slade LJ in *Phillips Products Ltd* v *Hyland* [1987] 2 All ER 620.)

(d) Non-contractual notices satisfy the requirement of reasonableness if it would be fair and reasonable to allow reliance on them, having regard to all the circumstances obtaining when the liability arose or (but for the notice) would have arisen (s. 11(3)).

(e) As regards limitation clauses, regard should also be had to the resources available to the person trying to rely on the exclusion clause and also to how far it was open to him to cover himself by insurance (s. 11(4)). Whereas limitation clauses, which try to limit the amount of damages payable, are covered by the Act (see s. 13(1)(b), considered below) clauses which fix the amount of damages payable are probably not. Such clauses will either be effective as liquidated damages, or ineffective as penalties under general contract principles.

(f) The burden of proof is on the party claiming that the term or notice does satisfy the requirement of reasonableness (s. 11(5)).

An appellate court is likely to treat the decision of the original court with the utmost respect when considering whether or not a term was fair and reasonable. (In *Cases and Materials* (6.2.2) see the extract from the judgment of Slade LJ in *Phillips Products Ltd* v *Hyland*.)

6.5.10 SCHEDULE 2

Theoretically, sch. 2 of the 1977 Act is of no importance to consumers. Schedule 2 lists five matters to which particular regard should be had in deciding whether a term was reasonable, but as we have seen, s. 11(2) states that the schedule is only to be used for the purposes of ss. 6 and 7 of the Act. Earlier in this chapter we saw that ss. 6 and 7, insofar as they apply to consumer contracts, dictate that no term can exclude or restrict liability for breach of the statutory implied terms. However, as we have seen, the courts have tended to extend the guidelines in sch. 2 to purposes other than those in ss. 6 and 7 of the Act, and so it is important to know what these guidelines are. We have seen that liability for loss or damage to property caused by negligence can be excluded in consumer cases where this is reasonable (s. 2(2)), and that liability in respect of breach of contract which is not caused by negligence can be excluded in consumer cases if reasonable (s. 3). It seems likely that in deciding what is reasonable the courts will consider the factors mentioned in sch. 2, along with other factors.

Schedule 2 lists the following guidelines: the relative bargaining strength of the parties and whether or not an alternative supplier could be found; whether or not the customer received any inducement to agree to the term or could have made a similar contract without agreeing to such a term; whether or not the customer knew or ought reasonably to have known of the existence and extent of the term; if the term applies unless some condition was complied with, whether it was reasonably practicable to comply with the condition; whether the goods were manufactured, processed or adapted to the special order of the customer.

6.5.11 PROVISIONS AGAINST EVASION OF LIABILITY

Section 10 of the 1977 Act provides that a person is not bound by any contract term prejudicing or taking away rights which arose under, or in connection with the performance of, another contract. So, for example, if a consumer bought a washing machine and signed a service contract, this service contract could not exclude or restrict the supplier's liability under the main contract.

Section 13(1) of the 1977 Act states that:

> (1) To the extent that this Part of the Act prevents the exclusion or restriction of any liability it also prevents:
> (a) making the liability or its enforcement subject to restrictive or onerous conditions;
> (b) excluding or restricting any right or remedy in respect of the liability, or subjecting a person to any prejudice in consequence of his pursuing any such right or remedy;
> (c) excluding or restricting any rules of procedure;
> and (to that extent) sections 2 and 5 to 7 also prevent excluding or restricting liability by reference to terms and notices which exclude or restrict the relevant obligation or duty.

An example might make it more clear how the three paragraphs of s. 13 might protect a consumer. Let us assume that Joe Consumer has bought a packet of cabbage seeds. Section 6 would prevent the exclusion or restriction of the seller's liability for breach of the Sale of Goods Act 1979 statutory implied terms. In addition, the three paragraphs of s. 13(1) would have the following effect:

- paragraph (a) of s. 13(1) would prevent a term or notice from making liability subject to a restrictive or onerous condition, such as that notice of defects in the seed would have to be notified within seven days of purchase;

- paragraph (b) would prevent a term or notice from denying Joe particular rights, such as the right to rescind the contract or treat it as repudiated; it would also prevent a term or notice from limiting the amount of damages payable, for example to the cost of the seed;

- paragraph (c) would prevent a term or notice from insisting that Joe's signature was absolute proof that the seeds conformed with the contract description.

Section 13(2) makes it plain that written agreements to submit disputes to arbitration are not to be treated as excluding or restricting any liability.

6.6 The Unfair Terms in Consumer Contracts Regulations 1994

These Regulations, which overlap the provisions of the Unfair Contract Terms Act 1977 apply only to consumer contracts. The definition of a consumer under the Regulations is wider than that of the 1977 Act and the Regulations can invalidate any unfair contract

EXCLUSION AND LIMITATION CLAUSES

term. The Regulations came into force in 1995 and implement an EC Directive. The Directive was based on German legislation.

6.6.1 TERMS TO WHICH THE REGULATIONS APPLY

Regulation 3(1) of the 1994 Regulations states that:

(1) Subject to the provisions of Schedule 1, these Regulations apply to any term in a contract concluded between a seller or supplier and a consumer where the said term has not been individually negotiated.

The Regulations are not therefore confined to exclusion and limitation clauses, but can consider the effect of any term in a consumer contract which is unfair (other than a 'core' term which is written in plain and intelligible language (reg. 3(2)).

ACTIVITY 6/8

Read sch. 1 and reg. 2, the interpretation Regulation in *Cases and Materials* (6.3). Then answer the following questions.

(a) What types of contracts are excluded by sch. 1?

(b) What is the definition of a consumer?

(c) Do the sellers or suppliers have to be acting in the course of a business?

(a) Schedule 1 excludes any contract relating to employment, succession rights, rights under family law, the incorporation and organisation of companies and partnerships or any term incorporated to comply with UK legislation or international conventions.

(b) A consumer is defined as a natural person who, in making the contract to which the Regulations apply, is acting for purposes which are outside his business. This definition makes it plain that a company cannot be a consumer within the Regulations. So the buyer in *R & B Customs Brokers Co. Ltd* v *United Dominions Trust Ltd* would not be within the Regulations. (Although this does not of course change the decision in that case. A company can still be a consumer for the purposes of the 1977 Act.) A person who buys goods partly for his own personal use and partly for the use of his business would seem to be a consumer for the purposes of the Regulations. (As well as acting for purposes which are within his business, he is also acting for purposes which are outside his business.) The Regulations do not prevent a person who holds himself out as acting in the course of a business from being a consumer, as the 1977 Act does.

(c) A seller or supplier must be acting 'for purposes relating to his business'. This may be wider than the requirement under the 1977 Act that, if the buyer is to be a consumer, the seller must make the contract 'in the course of a business'.

The Regulations will apply only to terms which have not been 'individually negotiated'. The burden of proof is on the seller or supplier to show that a term was individually negotiated (reg. 3(5)). A term shall always be regarded as not having been individually negotiated where it has been drafted in advance and the consumer has not been able to influence the substance of the term (reg. 3(3)). Even if one or more terms have been individually negotiated, the Regulations will apply to the rest of the contract if an overall assessment indicates that it is a pre-formulated standard contract (reg. 3(4)). So the fact that the price or the quantity have been individually negotiated will not prevent the Regulations from applying to other terms in a standard form contract.

The Regulations will not assess the validity of any term in plain, intelligible language, which (a) defines the subject matter of the contract, or, (b) concerns the adequacy of the price (reg. 3(2)). So the Regulations do not go so far as to ensure that the consumer is making a good bargain. However, a term as to the adequacy of the price or as to what the consumer is getting under the contract will have to be written in plain, intelligible language in order to escape assessment under the Regulations.

6.6.2 UNFAIR TERMS

An 'unfair term' is defined by reg. 4(1) of the 1994 Regulations 'as any term which contrary to the requirement of good faith causes a significant imbalance in the parties' rights and obligations under the contract to the detriment of the consumer.'

Regulation 4(2) states that:

> An assessment of the unfair nature of a term shall be made taking into account the nature of the goods or services for which the contract was concluded and referring, as at the time of the conclusion of the contract, to all circumstances attending the conclusion of the contract and to all the other terms of the contract or of another contract on which it is dependent.

So not only are all the relevant circumstances to be considered, but so are the other terms of the contract.

6.6.2.1 The requirement of good faith

Regulation 4(3) of the 1994 Regulations refers us to the matters specified in sch. 2 of the Regulations to determine whether a term satisfies the requirement of good faith. Schedule 2 reads:

> In making an assessment of good faith, regard shall be had in particular to—
> (a) the strength of the bargaining position of the parties;
> (b) whether the consumer had an inducement to agree to the term;
> (c) whether the goods or services were sold or supplied to the special order of the consumer; and
> (d) the extent to which the seller or supplier has dealt fairly and equitably with the consumer.

The first three of these have their equivalents in Schedule 2 of the Unfair Contract Terms Act 1977, and there is therefore some authority as to their meanings. The final one has no such equivalent.

Schedule 3 of the Regulations specifies an indicative and illustrative list of terms which may be regarded as unfair. These are important and should be read in *Cases and Materials* (6.3) and include: terms which attempt to exclude liabilty for death or personal injury caused by negligence (para. 1(a)), agreements which are binding on consumers whereas the seller or supplier's obligations are subject to a condition which he can choose to realise (para. 1(c)), authorising the seller or supplier to dissolve the contract on a discretionary basis, where the same facility is not granted to the consumer (para. 1(f)) allowing the seller or supplier to terminate a contract of indeterminate duration without reasonable notice or serious grounds for determination (para. 1(g)), using hidden terms to irrevocably bind the consumer (para. 1(i)), variation clauses unless there is a valid

EXCLUSION AND LIMITATION CLAUSES

reason specified in the contract (para. 1(j), (k) and (l)), and compulsory reference to arbitration not covered by legal provisions (para. 1(q)).

The Regulations do not specify that it is up to the seller or supplier to prove good faith. It is not clear upon whom the burden of proof will fall.

6.6.2.2 Detriment of the consumer

A term is only unfair if it causes a significant imbalance in the parties' rights and obligations to the detriment of the consumer.

6.6.3 CONSEQUENCES OF INCLUSION OF UNFAIR TERMS IN CONTRACTS

Regulation 5 of the 1994 Regulations tells us that an unfair term shall not be binding on the consumer, but that the contract shall continue to bind the parties if it is capable of continuing in existence without the unfair term. This would seem to imply a sort of 'blue pencil' test, that is to say that the rest of the contract should stand if can do so unaffected once the unfair term has been crossed out with a blue pencil.

6.6.4 CONSTRUCTION OF WRITTEN CONTRACTS

ACTIVITY 6/9

Read Regulation 6 of the 1994 Regulations in *Cases and Materials* (6.3). What common law rule of interpretation of exclusion clauses does this reiterate?

Regulation 6 reiterates the *contra preferentum* rule, explained earlier in this chapter.

6.6.5 PREVENTION OF CONTINUED USE OF UNFAIR TERMS

Regulation 8(1) places a duty on the Director-General of Fair Trading to consider any complaint made to him that a term drawn up for general use is unfair, unless the Director considers the complaint frivolous or vexatious. If the Director thinks that the term is unfair he may bring proceedings for an injunction to prevent the use of the term (reg. 8(2)). If given sufficient undertakings about the continued use of an unfair term the Director may choose not to seek an injunction (reg. 8(3)). An injunction may prevent not only the use of the particular unfair term, but also of any term having similar effect (reg. 8(6)).

The Office of Fair Trading have taken up this right to apply for an injunction zealously. One unfortunate effect of this success is that there are very few, if any, reported cases on the interpretation of the Regulations.

6.7 Summary

This chapter covers the following topics:

- An exclusion clause will not be able to restrict or limit liability for breach of contract unless the clause was incorporated into the contract.

- A notice or sign can prevent liability in tort from arising if it is brought to the consumer's attention clearly enough.

- At common law any ambiguity in an exclusion clause will be interpreted against the party trying to rely on the clause.

- The Unfair Contract Terms Act 1977 operates to make some exclusion clauses invalid and so as to make others valid only if they satisfy the requirement of reasonableness under the Act.

- The 1977 Act is concerned only with business liability (except for liability arising for misrepresentation or for breach of terms as to correspondence with description in sales of goods and hire-purchase contracts).

- Section 2(1) of the 1977 Act prevents the exclusion of liability for death or personal injury resulting from negligence; s. 2(2) prevents the exclusion of liability for other loss or damage resulting from negligence unless the exclusion satisfies the requirement of reasonableness.

- In contracts to supply a consumer with goods, the statutory implied terms in the consumer's favour cannot be excluded by any contract term (ss. 6 and 7 of the 1977 Act).

- In a contract to supply a service to a consumer, where liability arises other than through negligence, a contract term cannot exclude or restrict liability for breach of contract unless the term satisfies the requirement of reasonableness under the 1977 Act (s. 3).

- A contract term requiring a consumer to indemnify another for breach of contract or negligence can only be effective if it satisfies the requirement of reasonableness (s. 4).

- Where loss or damage to consumer goods arises while the goods are in consumer use, and this loss was caused by a person concerned in the manufacture or distribution of the goods, no notice or term operating by reference to a guarantee can exclude or restrict liability for the loss (s. 5 of the 1977 Act).

- Any term which seeks to exclude liability for a misrepresentation will only be effective if it satisfies the requirement of reasonableness under the 1977 Act (s. 3 of the Misrepresentation Act 1967, as substituted by s. 8 of the 1977 Act).

- The general requirement of reasonableness is that the term shall have been a fair and reasonable one to be included in the contract having regard to the circumstances which were, or ought reasonably to have been, known to or in the contemplation of the parties when the contract was made (s. 11(1)).

- The Unfair Terms in Consumer Contracts Regulations 1994 apply only to consumer contracts and run alongside the 1977 Act.

- The 1994 Regulations apply to any term which was not individually negotiated (reg. 3(1)).

- The 1994 Regulations define an unfair term as one which contrary to the requirement of good faith causes a significant imbalance in the parties' rights and obligations to the detriment of the consumer (reg. 4(1)).

- Schedule 2 of the 1994 Regulations lists four matters to which regard should be had when assessing good faith.

EXCLUSION AND LIMITATION CLAUSES

- Schedule 3 of the 1994 Regulations lists 17 types of terms which may be regarded as unfair.

- If a term is unfair under the 1994 Regulations, it is invalid but the rest of the contract may stand.

- The Office of Fair Trading has a duty to consider complaints about unfair terms and may seek injunctions to prevent their use.

6.9 End of Chapter Assessment Question

Finding that the brakes on his car are becoming ineffective, John, a shop assistant, takes the car to the AB Garage. A mechanic examines the car and says that the brake shoes and cylinders need to be replaced. John leaves the car at the garage so that the work on the brakes can be done and also agrees that the car should be serviced. John signs the AB Garage's standard terms and conditions which state, among other things, that 'neither the AB Garage nor its employees can be held liable for any injury, loss or other damage arising from a breach of this contract'. Shortly after getting his car back John is injured when the brakes fail completely. In addition, his car is a write-off. The AB Garage denies any liability on account of its exclusion clause.

John decides to buy a new car. He visits the showroom of CD Car Dealers and agrees to buy a new car, signing a set of standard terms and conditions, which include the following term: 'As the car you have bought is new and has never previously been registered, the vendors cannot accept any responsibility for any defects in the car which could not reasonably have been discovered by them, or for any loss, damage or injury caused by such defects. All terms, conditions, warranties and liabilities expressed or implied by statute or otherwise are hereby expressly excluded.'

On the third day of use the new car's engine seizes up due to a manufacturing fault which CD Car Dealers could not reasonably have discovered. John contacts CD Car Dealers to demand his money back, but he is told that the exclusion clause prevents any liability on the part of the vendors from arising.

Advise John of the legal effect of the two exclusion clauses contained in the contracts which he had made.

See *Cases and Materials* (6.5) for an outline answer.

CHAPTER SEVEN

PRODUCT LIABILITY (SAFETY)

7.1 Objectives

By the end of this chapter you should be able to:

- explain the principle of privity of contract;

- explain the extent to which a manufacturer's guarantee will provide a remedy in respect of unsatisfactory goods;

- explain the extent to which a purchaser of goods or services will be able to gain a remedy in respect of the product proving disappointing to a third party for whose benefit the contract was made;

- explain the circumstances in which a party to a contract will be able to enforce that contract in favour of a third party;

- outline the extent to which the law of tort protects consumers who buy defective products;

- analyse the effect of the reforms to privity proposed in the Bill drawn up by the 1996 Law Commission Report 242;

- outline the effect of the Consumer Protection Act 1987, Part 1;

- define a 'producer' and a 'product' for the purposes of the Part I of the Act;

- explain what is meant by a product being defective;

- outline the defences under Part I of the Act;

- explain the damages which can be recovered under Part I of the Act;

- explain the effect of the General Safety Requirement set out in Part I of the Act;

- list the powers given to the Secretary of State and to enforcement authorities by Part II of the Act;

- compare the general safety requirement of the General Product Safety Regulations 1994 with that of Part II of the 1987 Act;

- outline the ways in which the General Product Safety Regulations 1994 have changed the law.

7.2 Introduction

In this chapter we examine the civil and criminal law on product safety. First, we examine the remedies available to a person injured by a defective product. The law in this area comes from three main sources: the law of contract (including the terms implied by the Sale of Goods Act 1979 and related statutes), the law of tort, and Part I of the Consumer Protection Act 1987. As this book is written for LLB students, it can safely be assumed that you will already have studied the law of contract and the law of tort, and so the general principles of these subjects will not be re-examined in any detail. The terms implied by the Sale of Goods Act 1979, and related statutes, were studied in **Chapters 3 and 4** and so, again, there is no need for a re-examination in this chapter. However, in **Chapters 3 and 4** we did not examine the position of a consumer who is disappointed by a defective product which he did not buy. Privity of contract, which you will have studied in the contract programme, complicates the law here. We therefore begin this chapter by examining the effect of privity in some detail. Then we move on to the Consumer Protection Act 1987, Part I, which imposes strict civil liability on producers of unsafe products.

In the second half of this chapter we examine the criminal law on product safety. The law is to be found in the Consumer Protection Act 1987, Part II and in the General Product Safety Regulations 1994. We first examine the 1987 Act and then examine the different approach taken by the 1994 Regulations.

7.3 Product Liability in Contract and Tort

7.3.1 LIABILITY UNDER A CONTRACT

As mentioned in the introduction to this chapter, it is not proposed to examine the general principles of the law of contract in any detail. Contract is a foundation subject, and the basic principles should be familiar to students who opt to study consumer law. To recap as briefly as possible, the principles with which you should have a working knowledge are as follows. A contract is formed through the medium of offer and acceptance. Both sides must provide some consideration and there must be an intention to create legal relations. No special form is generally needed. If any of the terms of the contract are broken then the injured party will always have a remedy. (As we have seen in previous chapters, the Sale of Goods Act 1979 and related statutes, imply powerful terms into contracts. We also saw that in consumer contracts these terms cannot be excluded or diminished by exclusion clauses.) A consumer who is induced to enter into a contract by a misrepresentation will have the power to rescind the contract. However, this right to rescind can easily be lost. Damages for breach are designed to put the injured party in the position which he would have been in if the contract had been performed. Damages for breach are only awarded in respect of losses which were reasonably foreseeable at the time of breach.

SAQ 7/1

(a) Jim buys an electric iron which explodes in use. Jim and his flatmate, Pete, are both injured. Jim's best suit is destroyed and Pete's television is broken by the blast. How far does the law of contract protect (i) Jim? (ii) Pete?

PRODUCT LIABILITY (SAFETY)

(b) Jim buys his father a new watch for his birthday. The watch does not work. Can Jim's father sue the retailer in contract?

(c) Jim says that he is going to London the following day. Jim's father asks Jim to buy him a clock while he is in London. Jim buys the clock for his father. The clock turns out to be faulty.

(a)(i) The law of contract allows Jim to recover damages against the retailer of the iron. (Obviously, s. 14(2) of the Sale of Goods Act 1979 has been breached.) These damages will compensate Jim for his injuries, the damage to his suit and his not having been supplied with an iron of satisfactory quality.

(ii) The law of contract offers no protection to Pete. In respect of the iron, Pete has not made a contract with anyone. Privity of contract prevents Pete from suing the retailer on the contract made by Jim.

Daniels v White and Tarbard [1938] 4 All ER 258
Mr Daniels bought a bottle of lemonade which he and his wife drank. The lemonade inside the bottle was contaminated with 38 grains of carbolic acid. Drinking the contaminated lemonade injured both Mr and Mrs Daniels. They sued the manufacturers in negligence and Mr Daniels sued the retailer in contract.
Held: The manufacturers were not liable in negligence as they had taken all reasonable care to see that no injury was caused to the consumer or ultimate purchaser. (The manufacturers showed that they operated a 'fool-proof' system to see that their product was safe.) The lemonade was not of merchantable (now satisfactory) quality. Mr Daniels could therefore recover damages from the retailer in respect of his own injuries. However, Mrs Daniels could not claim from the retailer in respect of her injuries as there was no privity between her and the retailer.

(We shall see later in this chapter that Pete can sue the manufacturer of the iron under the Consumer Protection Act 1987, Part I. Pete will be able to recover damages for his injuries and, perhaps, damages to compensate for the destruction of his television.)

(b) Privity prevents Jim's father from suing the retailer in contract.

(c) Jim was acting as agent for his father. Therefore his father could sue the retailer on the contract as an undisclosed principal.

SAQ 7/2

What is the purpose of the privity rule?

A contract has always been regarded as a bargain, in which each of the parties to the contract provides consideration to the other contracting party or parties. A contractor's right to receive the consideration of the other party is conditional upon providing consideration to that other party. If this were not the case a person entering into a contract would not know to whom he might become liable on that contract. Crompton J in *Tweddle* v *Atkinson* (1861) 1 B & S 393 said of this notion: 'It would be a monstrous proposition to say that a person was a party to the contract for the purpose of suing upon it for his own advantage, and not a party to it for the purpose of being sued.' The privity rule has been approved several times by the House of Lords and remains the law to this day. (In *Cases and Materials* (7.1.1) see the extract from Lord Haldane's judgment in *Dunlop Pneumatic Tyre Company Limited* v *Selfridge and Company Limited* [1915] AC 847.)

The Law Commission Consultation Paper No. 121, 'Privity of Contract; Contracts for the Benefit of Third Parties' lists seven factors upon which the rule rests. None were found to be a convincing justification of the rule.

7.3.2 MANUFACTURERS' GUARANTEES

Sometimes manufacturers of goods include a guarantee with the goods. Usually, 'such a guarantee sets out the rights which it confers on a cardboard form which has to be completed by the purchaser of the goods.

SAQ 7/3

Let us assume that Jane buys a new television. Included with the television is a guarantee card. This card states that if the television should develop any faults within two years of the date of purchase the manufacturer will replace the television free of charge, as long as the purchaser completes the guarantee card and returns it to the manufacturer within 14 days of purchasing the television. (Other minor terms are also included.) Jane completes the guarantee card as requested and posts it back to the manufacturer. Write your answers to the following questions.

(a) The television is faulty, not being able to receive a good picture. What is Jane's best means of redress?

(b) Assuming that she still owns the television when the fault is discovered, in what circumstances will Jane want to take the manufacturer up on the guarantee?

(c) Jane gives the television to her daughter as a wedding present, and shortly afterwards flies back to her home in New Zealand. Jane's daughter discovers the fault as soon as she tries to use the television. How useful is the guarantee?

(d) The television explodes, injuring Jane's daughter. How useful is the guarantee?

(e) The television explodes, injuring Jane. How useful is the guarantee?

(a) Jane's best means of redress is to claim her money back from the retailer under s. 14(2) and (3) of the Sale of Goods Act 1979. The rights conferred by the guarantee are less potent than her Sale of Goods Act rights. (As Jane is a consumer, the terms implied by s. 14 are conditions, breach of which give Jane an

PRODUCT LIABILITY (SAFETY)

absolute right to terminate the contract and claim damages. The manufacturer's guarantee merely said that a replacement television would be supplied. Depending upon the other terms of the guarantee, Jane might find herself liable for the cost of returning the television etc.)

(b) If the television developed a fault 18 months after it was bought then it would be unlikely that this would cause a court to infer that the television was not of satisfactory quality at the time of sale. As the manufacturer's guarantee lasted for two years it might be very useful to Jane. The manufacturers' guarantee would also be likely to be useful to Jane if the retailer of the television has become insolvent by the time the fault in the television was discovered. Without the guarantee there would be no privity of contract between Jane and the manufacturer. The guarantee does create privity between Jane and the manufacturer, but only on the terms set out in the guarantee. (The rights conferred by a manufacturer's guarantee will only be those rights which the guarantee spells out. The contract created by the guarantee is not a contract of sale, and so the Sale of Goods Act 1979 will imply no terms into it.)

(c) At first sight it would appear that this is just the type of situation in which a manufacturer's guarantee is particularly useful. As regards the purchase of the television from the retailer, there is of course no privity of contract between the retailer and Jane's daughter. Unfortunately, neither is there privity of contract between Jane's daughter and the manufacturer on the contract of guarantee. The guarantee created a contract between Jane and the manufacturer but these two were the only parties to the contract. If Jane had been available to do so, then she could have rejected the television under the Sale of Goods Act 1979, s. 14(2). (On the assumption that the television had not been retained for a long enough time to be regarded as having been accepted by Jane.) Alternatively, Jane could have returned the television under the manufacturer's guarantee. (Although Jane's daughter is not a party to either the contract with the retailer or the contract of guarantee, neither the retailer nor the manufacturer is likely to make much of this. Consequently, if Jane's daughter returns the television to the shop, with the receipt, she is likely to be afforded the same remedies which Jane would have been afforded. Similarly, if she returns the television to the manufacturer under the guarantee, the manufacturer is likely to give her the same remedies as would have been given to Jane. Theoretically, however, these remedies are not available to Jane's daughter.)

(d) We shall see later in this chapter that a person injured by a defective product has the right to sue the producer, and others, under Part I of the Consumer Protection Act 1987. There is no requirement that the person injured was a party to any contract. There would therefore be no need to try and gain rights under the guarantee. (Which is just as well, as the privity rule would prevent the guarantee from conferring any contractual rights on Jane's daughter, and negligence on the part of the manufacturer might be difficult to prove.)

(e) Jane would not need the guarantee. First, she could recover for her injuries against the retailer under the Sale of Goods Act 1979. Second, if the retailer had become insolvent then she could recover against the manufacturer, and possibly others, under the Consumer Protection Act 1987, Part I.

SAQ 7/4

To be effective, a manufacturer's guarantee must create a contract between the consumer and the manufacturer. George buys a new washing machine. He fills in the manufacturer's guarantee card and returns it to the manufacturer.

(a) Where is the offer to be found?

(b) Where is the acceptance to be found?

(c) What consideration is supplied by each of the parties?

(d) Would the guarantee confer rights on anyone other than the person who completed it?

(a) The guarantee card is itself an offer.

(b) The precise basis on which a manufacturer's guarantee is accepted is a matter of some conjecture. It seems likely that the customer accepts by filling in the guarantee card and returning it to the manufacturer. Alternatively, if the consumer knew of the guarantee before purchasing the product, it might be possible to say that a collateral contract was formed between the consumer and the manufacturer.

(c) The manufacturer's consideration consists of the rights given to the consumer under the guarantee. The consumer's consideration consists of filling in the card and returning it. If the consumer knew of the guarantee before purchasing the product then a collateral contract might exist, as explained in (b) above. If this were the case then the consumer's consideration to the manufacturer would be purchasing the product from the retailer, filling in the guarantee card and complying with any other requirements set out in the guarantee. The manufacturer's consideration to the consumer would again consist of the rights granted by the guarantee.

(d) As the guarantee forms a contract between purchaser and manufacturer, no rights would be conferred on other parties.

Section 5 of the Unfair Contract Terms Act 1977 ensures that manufacturers' guarantees are not used to reduce a consumer's right to sue in negligence. This section provides that in the case of goods of a type ordinarily supplied for private use or consumption, liability for loss or damage arising from the goods proving defective while in consumer use, and resulting from the negligence of a person concerned in the manufacture or distribution of the goods, cannot be excluded or restricted by reference to any guarantee of the goods. Goods are to be regarded as 'in consumer use' when a person is using them, or has them in his possession for use, otherwise than exclusively for the purposes of a business. Section 5 does not apply between retailer and consumer purchaser because in that case the rights conferred on the consumer by the Sale of Goods Act 1979 and related statutes cannot be excluded by reference to any contract term (ss. 6 and 7 of the Unfair Contract Terms Act 1977).

It should be noticed that s. 5 is concerned with a manufacturer or distributor's liability in negligence. The section gives no rights to sue in contract and does not create any new rights in tort. It merely prevents a consumer from contracting out of his right to sue in tort. Before the Unfair Contract Terms Act 1977 became effective it was possible for a consumer to complete a guarantee in such a way that his rights to sue in tort were lost.

7.3.3 CONTRACT DAMAGES

The purpose of this section is not to reiterate the rules on remoteness and quantification of contract damages. You will already have considered these matters when studying the

PRODUCT LIABILITY (SAFETY)

law of contract. However, it is necessary to consider two matters. First, can a purchaser of faulty goods or services recover damages for his own personal injury, or for damage to his own property, which is caused by the faulty goods or services? Second, to what extent can a purchaser of faulty goods or services claim damages for losses suffered by another?

The first matter is relatively straightforward. A purchaser of goods or services will be able to claim damages for personal injury or for damage to property if this damage or injury was caused by breach of the contract and comes within one of the two rules in *Hadley* v *Baxendale* (1854) 9 Exch 341. There is no need to explore this further except to say that in several cases considered in earlier chapters a purchaser of goods gained damages in respect of foreseeable injuries or in respect of foreseeable damage to property caused by the goods bought (*Grant* v *Australian Knitting Mills Ltd*, *Godley* v *Perry*, *Ashington Piggeries Ltd* v *Christopher Hill Ltd* etc.).

To what extent can a purchaser of goods or services claim for a loss suffered by another? If the other person is physically injured, or suffers damage to property of more than £275, then, as we shall see later in this chapter, the Consumer Protection Act 1987 Part I will give the injured person a remedy against the producer and others. If the faulty goods or services merely disappoint the other person because they are of inferior quality, then it seems that there is little that can be done.

SAQ 7/5

Arthur buys Bill a new computer for Christmas. The computer does not work at all. Bill explains to the retailer that Arthur bought the computer as a Christmas present. The retailer refuses any remedy.

(a) Why can Bill not sue the retailer for breach of the terms implied by Sale of Goods Act 1979?

(b) Why can Arthur not claim substantial damages to reflect his lost expenditure?

(c) Can Arthur reject the computer under s. 14(2) of the Sale of Goods Act 1979?

(a) As we have seen, privity prevents Bill from suing on this contract which he did not make. Bill will therefore have no contractual rights against the retailer.

(b) It would seem to be that Arthur has suffered only nominal damages and that he will therefore only be entitled to recover a nominal sum. (This matter is considered in more detail immediately after this **SAQ**.)

(c) Arthur will be able to reject the computer as long as he has not accepted it. By virtue of s. 35(6)(b) the mere fact of delivery of the goods to another is not in itself enough to mean that the goods have been accepted. Arthur could therefore return the goods. If Arthur had accepted the goods then he would not be able to reject them.

SAQ 7/5 shows that little hardship is likely to arise when defective goods are bought on behalf of another and where the goods have not yet been accepted. However, when defective services are bought then the privity rule causes far more difficulty.

Jackson v *Horizon Holidays Ltd* [1975] 1 WLR 1468

Mr Jackson booked a holiday in Ceylon for himself, his wife and his three small children. The holiday company committed several bad breaches of contract so that the holiday was disastrous for all the Jackson family. The trial judge awarded damages of £1,100. He said that he could not award Mrs Jackson damages for her discomfort and vexation, but he could consider the effect that this would have upon Mr Jackson.

Held: The Court of Appeal held that the award of £1,100 should stand, but gave different reasons. Lord Denning MR held that Mr Jackson could recover damages on behalf of his family, to take account of their discomfort and vexation because the contract was made for their benefit. It did not matter that there was no privity between the members of the family and the holiday company. Orr LJ concurred. James LJ thought that the figure of £1,100 was correct because Mr Jackson had received no benefit from the family holiday which had cost £1,200. (An extract from the judgment of Lord Denning MR is set out in *Cases and Materials* (7.1.2).)

Lord Denning's judgment was severely criticised in *Woodar Investment Developments Ltd v Wimpey Construction UK Ltd* [1980] 1 WLR 277. Extracts from the five House of Lords' judgments are set out in *Cases and Materials* (7.1.2). It can be seen that Lord Wilberforce said that, while he could not agree with Lord Denning's reasoning, he was not prepared to dissent from the actual decision in *Jackson*:

> It may be supported either as a broad decision on the measure of damages (per James LJ) or possibly as an example of a type of contract — examples of which are persons contracting for family holidays, ordering meals in restaurants for a party, hiring a taxi for a group — calling for special treatment . . . there are many situations of daily life which do not fit neatly into conceptual analysis, but which require some flexibility in the law of contract. *Jackson's* case may well be one.

Lord Russell thought that substantial damages could not be recovered on behalf of third parties:

> I do not criticise the outcome of that case [*Jackson*]: the plaintiff had bought and paid for a high class family holiday: he did not get it, and therefore he was entitled to substantial damages for the failure to supply him with one.

Lord Keith agreed that third parties who stood to gain indirectly by virtue of a contract could not sue for breach in their own right:

> . . . but yet it may be proper to take into account in assessing the damages recoverable by the contracting party an element in respect of expenses incurred by him in replacing by other means benefits of which the third parties have been deprived or in mitigating the consequences of that deprivation.

Lord Keith quite plainly did not agree with Lord Denning's view in *Jackson*:

> That case [*Jackson*] is capable of being regarded as rightly decided upon a reasonable view of the measure of damages due to the plaintiff as the original contracting party, and not as laying down any rule of law regarding the recovery of damages for the benefit of third parties.

Lord Scarman seemed ready to abolish privity altogether. He ends his speech by saying that the law calls for review and 'now, not 40 years on'. Nearly 20 years on the law has yet to be changed. However, the Bill proposed by the Law Commission is currently working its way through Parliament and is highly likely to become law early in the year 2000. We therefore examine the effect of the Bill below at **9.2.5**.

PRODUCT LIABILITY (SAFETY)

It is not therefore possible to state with much certainty what the position now is as regards claiming damages on behalf of a third party disappointed by a consumer purchase made for the benefit of the third party.

It is worth noting that in the context of package holidays the injustice caused by cases such as *Jackson* v *Horizon Holidays* has been removed by the Package Travel, Package Holidays and Package Tours Regulations 1992 (SI 1992 No. 3288). These Regulations apply only to package holidays and do not detract from the principles of *Jackson* v *Horizon Holidays* in cases involving a purchase, other than a package holiday, made on behalf of a third party. Regulation 2(1) defines a package holiday as:

> ... the pre-arranged combination of at least two of the following components when sold or offered for sale at an inclusive price and when the service covers a period of more than twenty-four hours or includes overnight accommodation—
> (a) transport;
> (b) accommodation
> (c) other tourist services not ancillary to transport or accommodation and accounting for a significant proportion of the package,
> and
> (i) the submission of separate accounts for different components shall not cause the arrangement to be other than a package;
> (ii) the fact that a combination is arranged at the request of the customer and in accordance with his specific instructions (whether modified or not) shall not of itself cause it to be treated as other than pre-arranged ...

The 1992 Regulations set out the remedies of consumers in the case of defective packages and reg. 2(2) states that:

> ... in these Regulations, 'consumer' means, as the context requires, the principal contractor, any person on whose behalf the principal contractor agrees to purchase the package ('the other beneficiaries') or any person to whom the principal contractor or any of the other beneficiaries transfers the package ('the transferee').

7.3.4 SPECIFIC PERFORMANCE

In certain circumstances it may be possible for a contracting party to gain an order of specific performance of a contract made to benefit a third party. Once the order of specific performance has been made by the court the third party may enforce the order.

Beswick v *Beswick* [1968] AC 58
A coal merchant assigned his business to his nephew. In return the nephew agreed to employ the coal merchant as a consultant, at £6, 10 shillings a week, for the rest of his life and after the coal merchant's death to pay his widow an annuity of £5 per week for the rest of her life. After the coal merchant died the nephew made one payment of £5 to the widow, but then refused to make any more payments to her. The widow sued for £175 arrears and for an order of specific performance of the continuing obligation to pay the annuity. The widow sued in her personal capacity and as administratrix of her husband's estate.
Held: In her personal capacity the widow was not entitled to sue on the contract. In her capacity as administratrix of her husband's estate she could sue, but would only be entitled to nominal damages as her husband's estate had suffered no loss. However, to avoid injustice the House of Lords allowed the widow, in her capacity as her husband's administratrix, to specifically enforce the contract (because in effect she was suing as her husband).

In the light of this decision there may be circumstances in which it is possible for the contracting party to enforce a contract on behalf of a third party. This would of course oblige the contracting party to take legal action, something which he or she might be unwilling or unable to do. In addition, it must be remembered that specific performance is rarely ordered and there are so many circumstances in which it will not be available that this is unlikely to be of much use in many consumer cases. (You should be aware of the limitations on specific performance from your study of the contract programme. These limitations would include that it will not be ordered where damages would be an adequate remedy or where the contract is one the execution of which the court cannot supervise. These two limitations would prevent its use to enforce a contract for the sale of everyday goods or to provide a holiday where the holiday company refused to perform the contract.)

7.3.5 THE LAW COMMISSION BILL ON PRIVITY

The 1996 Law Commission Report 242, 'Privity of Contract: Contracts for the Benefit of Third Parties' found a good number of reasons for the reform of the law on privity. Already in this chapter we have seen that the intentions of the original contracting parties may be thwarted by the privity rule, that injustice may be caused to a third party, that the person who has suffered the loss cannot sue whereas the person who has suffered no loss can sue and that even if the contracting party can gain a remedy for the third party he may not want to or may not be able to do this. The Law Commission agreed with all of these criticisms and also noted that the rule is complex, artificial and uncertain and is subject to widespread criticism across the world.

ACTIVITY 7/1

Read the proposed Bill on privity of contract in *Cases and Materials* (7.1.3) and then answer the following questions. It is likely that this Activity will take some time, perhaps half an hour to an hour.

(a) In which of the two circumstances set out in clause 1(1) would a consumer be likely to be gain the right to sue on a contract made by another person?

(b) In what circumstances will a contract purporting to confer a benefit on a third party not be enforceable by the third party?

(c) To what extent must the third party be identified?

(d) What remedies will be available to the third party?

(e) Will third parties be able to avail themselves of exclusion and limitation clauses in the contract?

(f) In what circumstances can the parties to the contract not vary or cancel the contract?

(g) To what extent are defences against the third party available to the promisor?

(h) What does clause 4 mean?

(i) What does clause 5 mean?

(a) Few consumer contracts are likely to have an express term to the effect that a third party consumer can sue on the contract. However, many consumer contracts purport to confer a benefit on a third party. Therefore clause 1(1)(b) is more likely to be of use to a consumer than clause 1(1)(a).

(b) Even where the contract does intend to confer a benefit on a third party, the third party will not be able to enforce the contract if the proper construction of the contract shows that the contracting parties did not intend the contract to be enforceable by the third party (clause 1(2)).

(c) Clause 1(3) requires that the third party must be expressly identified in the contract. This identification might be by name, or by membership of a class or by description. If expressly identified, the third party does not need to be in existence at the time of the contract. Rights might therefore be conferred on a future spouse or on an unborn child.

(d) The third party will have available all the normal remedies available to a plaintiff suing for breach of contract (clause 1(4)).

(e) Third parties will be able to avail themselves of exclusion and limitation clauses in a contract (clause 1(5)).

(f) The parties to the contract cannot vary or cancel a contract which is enforceable by a third party under clause 1, without the consent of the third party, in three circumstances: first, if the third party has accepted the contract; second, if the promisor is aware that the third party has relied on the contract; third, if the third party has relied on the contract and the promisor can reasonably be expected to have foreseen that he would rely on it (clause 2(1) and (2)). However, the contract may expressly provide that it can be cancelled or varied without the consent of the third party or can stipulate that the consent be required in specific circumstances specified in the contract (clause 2(3)).

(g) The promisor will have the same defences against the third party that would have been available to him against the contracting party (clause 3(2)). These defences would include that the contract was void or unenforceable.

(h) Clause 4 allows the contracting party to enforce the contract. This right is in addition to the third party's right to enforce the contract.

(i) Clause 5 prevents the promisor from double liability. A court can reduce an award to a third party if there has already been a payment to the other contracting party in respect of the third party's loss or in respect of the cost of making good to the third party the promisor's default.

SAQ 7/6

To what extent would the decision in *Beswick* v *Beswick*, and SAQ 7/5(a) and (b) be changed by the Bill?

Beswick v *Beswick* would clearly be changed. Mrs Beswick was clearly named as the beneficiary of the contract and could therefore enforce it in her own right. This right would only be denied her if, as seems very unlikely, the proper construction of the contract was that her husband and the nephew did not intend her to have the right to enforce it. The onus of proving this would be on the nephew. SAQ 7/5(a) and (b) would probably not be changed. At paras 7.41 and 7.42 the Law Commission gave the following examples of how they thought the proposed law might work.

14. On Mr and Mrs C's marriage, their wealthy relative B buys an expensive 3 piece suite as a wedding gift from A Ltd, a well known Central London department store with a reputation for quality. She makes it clear when purchasing the 3 piece suite that it is a gift for friends and indeed the delivery slip and instructions show that it is to be sent to Mr and Mrs C's home and should be left with the housekeeper as it is a gift. After two weeks of wear the fabric on the suite wears thin and frays, and after three weeks, two castors collapse. Subject to rebuttal by A Ltd under the proviso to the second limb, Mr and Mrs C can sue A Ltd for breach of an implied term in the contract that the goods be of satisfactory quality. A Ltd have promised to confer a benefit (the suite of satisfactory quality) on Mr and Mrs C, who have been expressly identified by name.

(A footnote states that 'if there is to be no delivery to a third party it will normally be difficult to argue that a contract of sale purports to confer a benefit on a third party'.)

15. Again, the above example, save that A Ltd are entirely unaware that the suite is a gift for anyone, and it is delivered to B's home. Mr and Mrs C could not sue A Ltd, since the contract between B and A Ltd does not purport to confer a benefit on Mr and Mrs C, who have not been expressly identified.

These two examples make it plain that the problems which privity can present to consumers have not been entirely removed. (In *Cases and Materials* (7.1.3), see paras 7.54–7.56 'A Special Test of Enforceability for Consumers?')

7.4 The Law of Tort

As you will already have studied the law of tort as a subject in its own right, there is no point in reinvestigating the subject here. You will have seen that in order to establish the tort of negligence the claimant must prove three things: that the defendant owed him a duty of care, that the defendant broke that duty, and that as a consequence the claimant suffered damage which was not too remote.

The tort of negligence will provide no help in respect of mere defects in quality. *Donoghue v Stevenson* [1932] AC 562 was a case of product liability, but it and the line of cases it has produced have established that a manufacturer's duty of care to a product user is limited to not causing injury or damage to property. If this were not enough, two more obstacles stand in the path of a consumer suing a manufacturer in negligence. First, the manufacturer will not have broken any duty of care owed unless he failed to take reasonable care (see *Daniels v White and Tarbard*, above). Second, even if negligence is established it is generally the case that mere economic loss cannot be recovered.

Until the Consumer Protection Act 1987 came into force a person injured by a defective product which had been bought by another would only have an action against the manufacturer in negligence, as was the case in *Donoghue v Stevenson*. (Privity of contract would, of course, not prevent such an action as the claim would be in tort rather than in contract.) Now the Consumer Protection Act 1987, Part I, considered immediately below, would provide a more suitable basis of action.

It should be noted that the Consumer Protection Act 1987, Part I is only concerned with product liability, 'product' being defined by the Act as goods or electricity. Therefore a consumer who is injured while a service is being provided, such as a customer in a

PRODUCT LIABILITY (SAFETY)

restaurant who is poisoned by the food, will have to sue either in contract or, if privity prevents this, in tort. A consumer suing in contract is likely to rely on s. 13 of the Supply of Goods and Services Act 1982, which implies a term where the supplier is acting in the course of a business that the service shall be carried out with reasonable care and skill.

7.5 The Consumer Protection Act 1987, Part I

Part I of the Consumer Protection Act 1987 imposes strict civil liability on those who produce unsafe products. The statute is not concerned with product quality, nor is it designed to replace common law rules. Any person injured by an unsafe product has a claim against its producer, a definition which can include anyone involved in the chain of supply. The Act also gives a claim in respect of damage to other property (i.e. not the unsafe goods in question) if this amounts to at least £275. The Act was passed to comply with an EC Directive and this has a bearing on its construction. Section 1(1) of the Act states that Part I of the Act 'shall have effect for the purpose of making such provision as is necessary in order to comply with the product liability Directive and shall be construed accordingly'. In some areas the language of the Act differs from that of the Directive, and in these areas the effect of the Directive also needs to be considered.

Part I of the Act is reproduced in *Cases and Materials* (7.2).

7.5.1 WHO CAN BE LIABLE UNDER THE ACT?

ACTIVITY 7/2

Read s. 2 of the 1987 Act in *Cases and Materials* (7.2). Then answer the following questions.

A tin of baked beans contains a strong acid and consequently a customer who buys the beans in a supermarket is severely poisoned.

(a) Which, if any, of the following people could be liable under the Act: the farmer who grew the beans (assuming that they were the source of the problem), the manufacturer of the beans, the supermarket who sold the beans?

(b) Is it necessary that the person injured by the beans also bought the beans from the supermarket?

(c) Could a supermarket which imported the beans from Belgium be liable under the Act?

(a) Section 2(4) rules out liability on the part of the farmer, even if the beans were themselves the source of the problem, as long as the farmer supplied the beans before they had undergone any industrial process. A person who supplies game or agricultural produce before it has undergone an industrial process is not liable under the Act. If the farmer had industrially washed the beans, or industrially processed them, then he could be liable under the Act. The manufacturer is clearly made liable by s. 2(2)(a) as 'the producer of the product'. Section 1(2)(a) says that 'producer' in relation to a manufactured product means the person who manufactured it. (In the case of a product which is won or abstracted, rather than manufactured, the producer is the person who won or abstracted it. In the case of a product which is neither manufactured, won or abstracted but essential characteristics of which are attributable to an industrial or other process having been carried out, the producer is the person who carried out that process.) The supermarket will not normally be liable. The Act is not designed to make retailers liable. However, the supermarket could be made liable by s. 2(2)(b) if it was an 'own brand' tin of beans which had been sold. By selling 'own brand' products supermarkets use distinguishing marks to hold themselves out as the producer of the product.

(b) Any consumer injured by the goods can sue. This Act is not concerned with contractual liability and therefore the concept of privity has no bearing upon it.

(c) A supermarket which imported the beans from Belgium could not be liable under the Act (unless it own-branded the beans or refused to name others in the chain of supply, as explained immediately below this Activity). Importers are only liable under s. 2(2)(c) if they import a product into an EC member State from a State outside the EC, in the course of a business, to supply it to another. Belgium is, of course, an EC member State.

Section 2(3) allows any person involved in the chain of supply, which runs from the producer to the person who suffered the damage, to be sued if the supplier in question refuses to name a party who would be liable under s. 2(2). (That is to say, producers, own-branders or importers into the EC.) The person suffering the damage must request the supplier to identify one or more persons liable under s. 2(2). (Whether that person is still in existence or not.) This request must be made within a reasonable period after the damage occurs and at a time when it is not reasonably practicable for the person making the request to identify all those primarily liable under s. 2(2). Section 5(5) tells us that damage or loss to property shall be regarded as having occurred at the earliest time at which a person with an interest in the property had knowledge of the material facts about the loss or damage. The Act does not tell us when 'damage' consisting of personal injury is to be regarded as occurring. Presumably this would be at the time when the extent of the personal injury becomes known. The supplier who is asked to supply the information will be liable if he does not within a reasonable time either comply with the request or identify the person who supplied the product to him. The Act does not provide a definition of a reasonable time, which will depend upon all of the circumstances.

Where two or more persons are liable under the Act liability is joint and several (s. 2(5)). Each person liable is therefore liable for the full amount of the damage suffered.

The 1987 Act does not preclude a person from bringing an action arising otherwise than by virtue of the Act, (s. 2(6)), so common law rules are supplemented rather than replaced.

Before completing this section it is necessary to consider who a 'producer' might be in the case of a product which is neither manufactured, won or abstracted. Section 1(2)(c) tells us that if essential characteristics of such a product are attributable to an industrial or other process having been carried out (for example in relation to agricultural produce) the producer is the person who carried out that process. We have already seen that a farmer who grows defective produce is not to be held liable if at the time of supply the produce had not undergone an industrial process (s. 2(4)). Section 1(2)(c) would make a farmer who industrially washed vegetables liable, as this would change the characteristics of the vegetables in that they become washed. Canning of vegetables would also be included. Whether or not the mere packaging of vegetables would change their essential characteristics is hard to say.

PRODUCT LIABILITY (SAFETY)

7.5.2 WHAT IS A PRODUCT?

Section 1(2)(c) tells us that 'product, means any goods or electricity and . . . includes a product which is comprised in another product, whether by virtue of being a component part or raw material or otherwise'. Section 45 states that '"goods" includes substances, growing crops and things comprised in land by virtue of being attached to it and any ship, aircraft or vehicle'.

So in the case of a car, the car itself is a product, the car tyres are a product and the rubber from which the tyres are manufactured is a product.

As we have already see, s. 2(4) excludes game or agricultural produce at a time when it has not undergone an industrial process.

SAQ 7/7

A new car is sold. The driver is injured because one of the tyres explodes at high speed. This fault is caused because the raw material from which the tyres were made is found to have been treated in a dangerous way. From the list below, who is liable under Part I of the 1987 Act?

(a) the retailer of the car,

(b) the tyre manufacturer,

(c) the producer of the rubber, (who sold to the tyre manufacturer), or

(d) the manufacturer of the car.

(a) The car retailer is not a producer of the car and is therefore not liable under the Act. (He would of course be liable to the purchaser of the car under the Sale of Goods Act 1979.)

(b) The manufacturer of the tyre is liable as a 'producer', because he manufactured the faulty component.

(c) The producer of the rubber would be liable under s. 1(2)(b). (Unless the rubber was sold in its raw, unprocessed state — s. 2(4).)

(d) The manufacturer of the car is liable as he is a 'producer', as defined by s. 1(2)(a).

7.5.3 MEANING OF DEFECT

Section 3(1) tells us that a product is defective if its safety is not such as persons generally are entitled to expect, and that safety embraces not only risks of death or personal injury, but also the risk of damage to property.

Furthermore, s. 3(1) tells us that safety in relation to a particular product shall include safety with respect to products comprised in that product. (Making it plain that the car itself, as described in **SAQ 7/7**, is to be regarded as a defective product on account of the unsafe component, the tyre.)

Section 3(2) tells us that in determining what standards of safety persons are generally entitled to expect in relation to a product all the circumstances are to be taken into account. Three such circumstances are specifically mentioned:

(a) the manner in which, and purposes for which, the product has been marketed, its get-up, the use of any mark in relation to the product and any instructions for, or warnings with respect to, doing or refraining from doing anything with or in relation to the product;

(b) what might reasonably be expected to be done with or in relation to the product; and

(c) the time when the product was supplied by its producer to another.

The mere fact that subsequently supplied products are more safe does not by itself infer that earlier products were not safe.

The burden of proof is on the injured consumer to prove that the product was defective and that this defect caused the damage suffered. Thus the type of causation problems faced by those suing manufacturers in negligence might become equally familiar to those suing under the Act.

It is plain that warnings can make what would otherwise be a defective product 'safe'. Just as the lack of warnings may render a product unsafe. Advertisements may also affect the safety or otherwise of a product. It will be relevant to examine not only what the advertisement said, but also the market it was aimed at, particularly if it was aimed at children. Some products are of course inherently unsafe. The Act does not make producers of these products automatically liable to anyone they injure. As long as there are sufficient warnings and instructions, inherently dangerous products such as caustic soda will not be defective. Warnings and instructions may also be necessary where a product is known to be widely abused.

7.5.4 DEFENCES

A person sued under Part I of the 1987 Act in respect of a defect in a product is given six defences by the Act. In each of these the burden of proof is on the defendant to prove the defence. The defences are as follows.

7.5.4.1 That the defect is attributable to compliance with any requirements imposed by or under any enactment or with any Community obligation

It seems unlikely that this defence will apply very often. However, if the producer can show that the defect in the product is attributable to a mandatory requirement of either domestic or Community law then this will be a defence.

7.5.4.2 That the defendant did not at any time supply the product to another

A person who produces a dangerous product, perhaps a prototype car component, cannot be liable under Part I of the Act if the product was never supplied to another. If this were not the case then obviously research and design would be greatly limited. 'Supply' is defined by s. 46 in very wide terms. It includes selling, hiring, lending, hire-purchasing, contracts for work and materials, bartering and giving the product away as a promotional gift or prize. In a hire-purchase triangular transaction it is the dealer in the goods, (rather than the finance company which legally supplies), who is to be regarded as the supplier for the purposes of the Act.

PRODUCT LIABILITY (SAFETY)

7.5.4.3 That the product was supplied otherwise than in the course of business

The 1987 Act does not make liable those who act otherwise than in the course of business or any producers who do not seek to make a profit. So liability would not be imposed on a person who made and sold a pot of dangerous jam in order to raise money for a charity.

7.5.4.4 That the defect did not exist in the product at the relevant time

It is a defence for a defendant to show that the defect in the product did not exist at the time when he supplied the product to another. This defence will not be of any help as regards latent defects which exist, but which have not yet manifested themselves, at the time of supply to another. As the burden of proof as regards these defences is on the defendant it is up to him to show that the defect did not exist at the relevant time. It may, for example, be possible to show that misuse by the consumer has caused the defect.

7.5.4.5 That the state of scientific and technical knowledge was not such that the producer might be expected to have discovered the defect

This is the most controversial defence. It would mean that, (under the wording of the 1987 Act), those injured by Thalidomide would not have a claim under the Act, as a producer of Thalidomide could not, at the relevant time, have been expected to have discovered the defect while the drug was under his control. The wording of the Directive is different. Article 7(e) makes it a defence for the defendant to prove 'that the state of scientific and technical knowledge at the time when he put the product into circulation was not such as to enable the existence of the defect to be discovered'. This wording might also provide a defence to the manufacturers of Thalidomide, but it is narrower than the defence set out in the Act. Under the defence set out in the Directive, the state of scientific and technical knowledge must be such that nobody (not merely producers of that type of product) would be able to discover the existence of the defect. This is a different matter from producers of the product in question being expected to discover the defect.

7.5.4.6 That in the case of a component, the defect constitutes a defect in the ultimate product, and was wholly due to the faulty design of the ultimate product or to compliance with instructions given by the producer of the ultimate product

For example, if a car manufacturer designed a car in such a way that an otherwise safe component, such as a battery, became defective the producer of the battery would have a defence if the defect was wholly attributable to the faulty design of the car or to compliance with the car producer's instructions.

Section 6(4) makes it plain that contributory negligence can reduce a plaintiff's damages.

7.5.5 DAMAGE GIVING RISE TO LIABILITY

Section 5(1) defines 'damages' for the purposes of Part I of the Act as 'death or personal injury or any loss of or damage to property (including land)'.

Damage to the defective product itself is not recoverable under the Act. Nor is damage to the whole or part of any product which was supplied with the defective product comprised in it (s. 5(2)). So if a car battery exploded, destroying the car in which it was comprised, then the Act would provide no remedy in respect of damage to the battery or the car. (However, the Sale of Goods Act 1979 would provide the person who purchased from the retailer with a remedy under s. 14. Again, privity could cause problems. What if the person who purchased from the retailer had sold the car on? If this sale was made otherwise than in the course of business then s. 14 of the Sale of Goods Act 1979 would provide no remedy to the subsequent purchaser. The sub-purchasers only hope would be to sue the car or battery manufacturer in negligence.)

Section 5(3) excludes liability for loss or damage caused to business property. A claim can only be made in respect of property which, at the time it is lost or damaged, is 'of a description of property ordinarily intended for private use, occupation or consumption; and intended by the person suffering the loss or damage mainly for his own use, occupation or consumption'.

It is not necessary that the property is exclusively used privately. Damage to a mobile phone used mainly privately, but occasionally for business purposes, would seem to be included.

Perhaps the most important limitation is that on claims for trivial damage to property. No damages are to be awarded for any loss or damage to property if the amount recoverable does not exceed £275. This does not mean that each individual item of property destroyed must give rise to a claim of at least £275, but rather that the whole claim for property lost or damaged must amount to at least £275.

Liability under the Act cannot be limited or excluded by any contract term, by any notice or other provision (s. 7).

SAQ 7/8

John buys a new rotavator for cultivating his large garden. (For a small fee John tends the gardens of two of his neighbours.) While being correctly used, the rotavator explodes. In the explosion John and his wife are injured, the rotavator is destroyed, John's garden shed and everything in it is destroyed and his garden is polluted by oil. Which if any of these matters will be classed as 'damages' and therefore be recoverable under the Act?

First, the injuries to both John and his wife are clearly included. The loss of the rotavator itself is not included. Assuming that the shed, its contents and the land give rise to a claim of at least £275 then damages will be awarded to compensate for these losses. (Assuming also that the contents of John's shed were intended mainly for his own private use and not for business purposes.)

7.5.6 LIMITATION OF ACTIONS

ACTIVITY 7/3

Read s. 11A of the Limitation Act 1980 in *Cases and Materials* (7.2.1). Within what time span must an action under the Act be brought?

Section 11A(3) gives a long-stop limit of ten years from the relevant time (the time at which the product was supplied). Damages for personal injuries and loss of or damage to property must be claimed within three years of the date of damage or injury or three years from when the defendant knew or reasonably should have known of the claim s. 11A(4)).

7.6 Criminal Liability for Unsafe Products

Criminal liability as regards unsafe products is imposed by the Consumer Protection Act 1987, Part II, and by the General Product Safety Regulations 1994 (see *Cases and Materials* (7.3)). First we look briefly at Part II of the 1987 Act, then we consider the 1994 Regulations.

7.6.1 THE CONSUMER PROTECTION ACT 1987, PART II

Part II of the 1987 Act introduced the 'general safety requirement' which made it an offence to supply consumer goods which are not reasonably safe. This aspect of the Act has become significantly less important in the light of the General Product Safety Regulations 1994. Part II of the Act also gives the Secretary of State the power to make safety regulations, to serve prohibition and warning notices and to require a person to furnish information. Enforcement authorities can issue suspension notices and order the forfeiture of goods.

7.6.1.1 The general safety requirement

Section 10(1) of the 1987 Act sets out the general safety requirement:

> A person shall be guilty of an offence if he—
>   (a) supplies any consumer goods which fail to comply with the general safety requirement;
>   (b) offers or agrees to supply any such goods; or
>   (c) exposes or possesses any such goods for supply.

The 'general safety requirement' is objective. Section 10(2) tells us that goods fail to comply with it if they are not reasonably safe having regard to all of the circumstances, including:

(a) the manner in which, and purposes for which, the goods are being or would be marketed, the get-up of the goods, the use of any mark in relation to the goods and any instructions or warnings which are given with respect to the keeping, use or consumption of the goods;

(b) any relevant published safety standards;

(c) the existence of any means by which it would have been reasonable (taking into account the cost, likelihood and extent of any improvement) for the goods to have been made safer.

The meaning of 'safe' in this context is explained by s. 19(1):

> 'safe' in relation to any goods, means that there is no risk, or no risk apart from one reduced to a minimum, that any of the following will (whether immediately or after a definite or indefinite period) cause the death of, or any personal injury to, any person whatsoever, that is to say—
>   (a) the goods;
>   (b) the keeping, use or consumption of the goods;
>   (c) the assembly of any of the goods which are, or are to be supplied unassembled;
>   (d) any emission or leakage from the goods or, as a result of keeping, use or consumption of the goods, from anything else or;
>   (e) reliance on the accuracy of any measurement, calculation or other reading made by or by means of the goods,
> and 'safer' and 'unsafe' shall be construed accordingly.

Factor (a) contemplates that the goods are inherently unsafe. Examples of the four factors (b) to (e) might be as follows. (b) A firework explodes whilst in storage; (c) self-assembly furniture contains very sharp edges which injure a consumer who is assembling the furniture; (d) a battery leaks corrosive acid onto a consumer; (e) a faulty tyre pressure gauge which leads a consumer to falsely believe that his car tyres are correctly inflated.

> **SAQ 7/9**
>
> **Why could the definition of 'safe' not insist that there was no risk in relation to goods, rather than accepting that there might be a risk which is reduced to a minimum?**

If the regulations insisted that there was no risk in relation to goods then a huge number of goods could not be supplied. (Cars, cookers, aeroplanes etc. are all inherently unsafe to some degree or other.) Therefore it is necessary to allow that the risk should be allowed to be reduced to a minimum rather than insist that it be non-existent.

'Consumer goods' are defined by s. 10(7) as any goods ordinarily intended for private use or consumption, not being growing crops or things comprised in land by virtue of being attached to it, water, food, feeding stuff, fertilisers, gas from an authorised supplier, aircraft, motor vehicles, controlled drugs, licensed medicinal products or tobacco. (These products are excluded because they are covered elsewhere by more detailed regulations.)

The word 'supply' is defined widely by s. 46 to include sale, hire, loan, hire-purchase, but it must be made in the course of a business (whether or not a business dealing in the goods in question) and can be made either as principal or agent.

Three special defences are set out in s. 10(4). First it is a defence for a retailer to show that at the time he supplied the goods or offered or agreed to supply them or exposed or possessed them for supply, he neither knew nor had reasonable grounds for believing that the goods failed to comply with the general safety requirement (s. 10(4)(b)).

It is also a defence for a defendant to show that he reasonably believed that the goods would not be used or consumed in the United Kingdom (s. 10(4)(a)) or that the goods were not supplied or to be supplied as new goods (s. 10(4)(c)).

Sections 39(1) provides a defence of due diligence. It is up to the defendant to show that he took all reasonable steps and exercised all due diligence to prevent the commission of the offence. If the defendant alleges that the commission of the offence was due to the act or default of another or to reliance on information given by another then to rely on the due diligence defence the defendant must give the prosecution seven days' clear notice of information to identify the person whose fault it was. That person may then be prosecuted under the by-pass provision in s. 40. (The defence of due diligence and prosecution under the by-pass provision are examined in detail in **Chapter 14** in relation to the Trade Descriptions Act 1968.)

7.6.1.2 Power to make regulations (section 11)

Part II of the 1987 Act also empowers the Secretary of State to make such regulations as he sees appropriate to ensure that goods are safe, that unsafe goods are not made generally available, and that appropriate information is supplied with goods.

PRODUCT LIABILITY (SAFETY)

7.6.1.3 Prohibition and warning notices (section 13)

The Secretary of State may also serve 'prohibition notices' and 'warning notices' under the 1987 Act. Prohibition notices prohibit a particular person from supplying, offering to supply or possessing for supply goods which the Secretary of State considers to be unsafe (s. 13(1)(a)). The Secretary of State may also serve a 'notice to warn' requiring the person upon whom it is served to publish a warning at his own expense. The warning must, in the form and manner specified in the notice, and on occasions specified in the notice, give a relevant warning about goods which the Secretary of State considers unsafe which the person supplies or has supplied (s. 13(1)(b)). Notices to warn are most appropriate when unsafe goods have already been supplied to the public. Many manufacturers and importers voluntarily publish such notices in the national press.

7.6.1.4 Suspension notices (section 14)

Where an enforcement authority has reasonable grounds for believing that any safety precaution has been contravened in relation to any goods, the authority may serve a suspension notice prohibiting the person upon whom it is served, for a period of up to six months, from supplying the goods, offering to supply them, agreeing to supply them or exposing them for supply without the consent of the authority. Any person having an interest in any goods in respect of which a suspension order is in force may appeal against the order (s. 15).

7.6.1.5 Forfeiture (section 16)

An enforcement authority can apply under s. 16 for an order for the forfeiture of any goods on the grounds that that there has been a contravention in relation to the goods of a safety provision.

7.6.1.6 Power to obtain information (section 18)

The Secretary of State may serve a notice on a person requiring that person to furnish him with information to help him decide whether to make, vary or revoke safety regulations or serve, vary or revoke prohibition or warning notices. It is an offence to refuse to supply this information without reasonable cause.

7.6.2 THE GENERAL PRODUCT SAFETY REGULATIONS 1994

These Regulations are quite separate from the Consumer Protection Act 1987, Part II. An offence under the 1994 Regulations is not necessarily an offence under the Act, and vice versa. Often, however, an offence under one will be an offence under the other. For the purposes of the Regulations, s. 10 of the 1987 Act, is disapplied (reg. 5). This means that the general safety requirement of the Act is of no effect where the Regulations apply. However, s. 10 is not wholly redundant because in certain circumstances it will apply where the Regulations will not.

7.6.2.1 The general safety requirement

Regulation 7 states that: 'No producer shall place a product on the market unless the product is a safe product.'

This is the main offence created by the 1994 Regulations and is one of strict liability.

7.6.2.2 Meaning of producer

Regulation 2(1), the interpretation regulation, defines a 'producer' as:

(a) the manufacturer of the product, when he is established in the Community, and includes any person presenting himself as the manufacturer by affixing to the product his name, trade mark or other distinctive mark, or the person who reconditions the product;

(b) when the manufacturer is not established in the Community—

(i) if the manufacturer does not have a representative established in the Community, the importer of the product;

(ii) in all other cases, the manufacturer's representative; and

(c) other professionals in the supply chain, insofar as their activities may affect the safety properties of a product placed on the market . . .

SAQ 7/10

Is the definition of a producer wider or narrower than the definition of a person who could be guilty of breaching the general safety requirement under the 1987 Act?

Section 10 of the 1987 Act made it an offence to supply, offer or agree to supply or expose of possess for supply unsafe goods. The definition of a producer under the 1994 Regulations includes manufacturers, own-branders, people who recondition the product and other professionals in the chain of supply (insofar as their activities may affect the safety of a product placed on the market). This definition does not include retailers, (unless their activities affect the safety properties of a product placed on the market), who could of course be guilty of an offence under s. 10 of the 1987 Act, subject to the defence in s. 10(4)(b). (As we shall see shortly, distributors can commit two separate offences under the Regulations.) Also included, in the definition of a producer under the 1994 Regulations, where the manufacturer is not established in the EU, is the manufacturer's representative or the importer of the product.

7.6.2.3 Meaning of product

Regulation 2(1) of the 1994 Regulations defines 'product' as:

> . . . any product intended for consumers or likely to be used by consumers, supplied whether for consideration or not in the course of a commercial activity and whether new, used or reconditioned; provided, however, a product which is used exclusively in the context of a commercial activity even if it is used for or by a consumer shall not be regarded as a product for the purposes of these Regulations provided always and for the avoidance of doubt this exception shall not extend to the supply of such a product to a consumer.

SAQ 7/11

(a) How does the definition of a product differ from the type of goods to which the general safety requirement could apply under the 1987 Act?

PRODUCT LIABILITY (SAFETY)

(b) A barber's shop uses a hair dryer on customers' hair. Is the hair dryer a product for the purposes of the 1994 Regulations? What about a washing machine used by a consumer in a self-service launderette? What if a consumer bought a hair dryer previously used on customers in a barber's shop?

(a) Both the 1987 Act and the 1994 Regulations are concerned only with consumer goods, supplied in the course of a commercial activity. The most important differences seem to be that the Regulations apply to products which are not new and to products intended for export. The Regulations could also apply to those goods (tobacco etc.) outside the definition of consumer goods under the Act.

(b) Neither the hair dryer nor the washing machine would be regarded as a product. Both are used by consumers, but they are used exclusively in the context of a commercial activity. If a consumer bought a hair dryer previously used in a barber's shop then the hair dryer would be a product as it would have been supplied to a consumer.

7.5.2.4 Meaning of safe product

Regulation 2(1) of the 1994 Regulations states:

'"safe product" means any product which, under normal or reasonably foreseeable conditions of use, including duration, does not present any risk or only the minimum risks compatible with the product's use, considered as acceptable and consistent with a high level of protection for the safety and health of persons, taking into account in particular—
 (a) the characteristics of the product, including its composition, packaging, instructions for assembly and maintenance;
 (b) the effect on other products, where it is reasonably foreseeable that it will be used with other products;
 (c) the presentation of the product, the labelling, any instructions for its use and disposal and any other indication or information provided by the producer; and
 (d) the categories of consumers at serious risk when using the product, in particular children,
and the fact that higher levels of safety may be obtained or other products presenting a lesser degree of risk may be available shall not of itself cause the product to be considered other than a safe product.

As was the case with the definition of safety under Part II of the 1987 Act, it is accepted that the use of some products can never be free from all risk. Again, the product's characteristics, its use in combination with other products, the way it is marketed and the type of people who might use the product should all be taken into account. The fact that later products are safer does not automatically make an earlier product unsafe.

7.6.2.5 Application of the Regulations

The 1994 Regulations do not apply to antiques (reg. 3(a)). Nor do they apply to products supplied for repair or reconditioning before use, provided that the supplier clearly informs the person to whom he supplies the product to that effect (reg. 3(b)). Nor to products where there are specific EC laws governing all aspects of the safety of the product (reg. 3(c)).

7.6.2.6 Requirement to provide information

Regulation 8(1) of the 1994 Regulations requires a producer to provide consumers with information so that they can assess the risks inherent in a product throughout the normal or foreseeable period of its use, where such risks are not immediately obvious without adequate warnings, and to take precautions against those risks, and to adopt measures to ascertain the dangers of the product. These measures would include marking of the products or product batches in such a way that they can be identified, sample testing of marketed products, investigating complaints and keeping distributors informed of such monitoring. If necessary, the producer should withdraw the product from the market to avoid risks discovered.

7.6.2.7 Requirements of distributors

Regulation 9 of the 1994 Regulations requires distributors to act with due care in order to help ensure compliance with the requirements of reg. 7, the general safety requirement. In particular, a distributor must not supply products to any person which he knows, or should have presumed, on the basis of the information in his possession and as a professional, are dangerous products, and must, within the limits of his activities, participate in monitoring the safety of products placed on the market, in particular by passing on information on the product risks and cooperating in the action taken to avoid those risks.

Distributors who fail to comply with reg. 9 commit an offence, but the offence is fault based and not one of strict liability. A distributor is defined by reg. 2(1) as 'any professional in the chain of supply whose activity does not affect the safety of the product'. (A professional in the chain of supply whose activity did affect the safety of the product would be a producer. See **7.5.2.2** above.)

7.6.2.8 Preparatory acts

Regulation 13 of the 1994 Regulations states:

No producer or distributor shall—
    (a) offer or agree to place on the market any dangerous product or expose or possess any such product on the market; or
    (b) offer or agree to supply any dangerous product or expose or possess any such product for supply . . .

This regulation creates an offence of strict liability. It is necessary because reg. 7 relates only to placing an unsafe product on the market.

7.6.2.9 Defence of due diligence

Regulation 14 creates the standard defence of due diligence, and reg. 15 contains a by-pass procedure under which another person whose fault the offence was committed may be prosecuted.

7.7 Summary

A purchaser of an unsafe or defective product will be able to sue the retailer of the product under the Sale of Goods Act 1979. A third party for whose benefit the contract was made will not be able to sue on the contract. Nor will the purchaser of the product be able to claim substantial damages on behalf of a third party.

A purchaser of a product who completes a manufacturer's guarantee will make a separate contract with the manufacturer. This contract is not a contract of sale and so the Sale of Goods Act 1979 will not govern it. The terms of the contract will be those set out in the guarantee. Privity of contract may prevent a third party from enforcing the guarantee.

PRODUCT LIABILITY (SAFETY)

Where a defective service, such as a holiday, is bought on behalf of a third party a strict application of the privity rule would prevent the contracting party from recovering damages on the third party's behalf if the service should prove to be of unsatisfactory quality. However, following the House of Lords decision in *Woodar Investment Developments Ltd v Wimpey Construction UK Ltd*, the law in this area is unclear.

In limited circumstances it may be possible for a contracting party to specifically enforce a contract on behalf of a third party.

The law of negligence will not provide a remedy in respect of qualitatively defective products.

7.7.1 THE CONSUMER PROTECTION ACT 1987, PART I

This Act imposes strict civil liability on producers of unsafe products. The Act is not concerned with product quality. Manufacturers, own-branders and importers into the EC are all regarded as producers. Agricultural products which have not been subjected to an industrial process are not covered by the Act. Otherwise, products includes goods and electricity. There are several defences under the Act, the most important of which are that the defendant did not supply the product to another in the course of business, that the defect did not exist in the product at the relevant time or that the state of scientific and technical knowledge was not such that the producer might be expected to have discovered the defect. A claim can only be made in respect of death, personal injury or damage to other property amounting to more than £275. Damage to the defective product itself is not recoverable under the Act. Liability under the Act cannot be excluded by any contract term. A claim for damage or personal injury must be brought within three years of the damage or personal injury becoming apparent and within ten years of the product being supplied.

7.7.2 PRODUCT SAFETY UNDER THE CRIMINAL LAW

Part II of the Consumer Protection Act 1987 introduced a 'general safety requirement' which made it an offence to supply consumer goods which are not reasonably safe. The Act also gave the Secretary of State the power to make safety regulations, to serve prohibition and warning notices and to require a person to furnish information. Part II of the Act gives enforcement authorities the power to issue suspension notices and order the forfeiture of goods.

The General Product Safety Regulations 1994 were passed to give effect to an EC directive on product safety. The Regulations create a new 'general safety requirement', making it a strict liability offence for a producer to place an unsafe product on the market. Where the 1994 Regulations apply, the general safety requirement under the 1987 Act is of no effect. The Regulations also require producers to provide safety information and require distributors to act with due care to help ensure compliance with the regulations.

7.8 End of Chapter Assessment Question

Gazza and Lavinia were married last year. Gazza's mother paid for the couple to go on an an expensive holiday to Crete. The hotel at which the couple were staying was still under construction, and the building work was so noisy that neither Gazza nor Lavinia could sleep for their entire holiday. At the end of the holiday they both felt more in need of a holiday than they had when they had departed. (You should assume that the Package Travel, Package Holidays and Package Tours Regulations 1992 do not apply as Gazza and Lavinia are to drive to Crete, and all that was included in the price of the holiday was the price of the hotel accommodation.)

Lavinia's aunt bought the couple a kettle as a wedding present. The kettle exploded whilst in use, damaging the couple's kitchen. Fortunately no-one was injured. The retailer who sold the kettle had had several returned to him, on account of their having burst in use. He had mentioned this to the manufacturer but had not considered failing to stock such kettles. Lavinia had completed the manufacturer's guarantee card and returned it to the manufacturers. The card stated that if it was returned to the manufacturers within 14 days, the manufacturers would supply a replacement product if the defective product was sent to them within five days of the defect being discovered.

Explain any civil liability of the holiday company with whom Gazza's mother made the contract. Explain also what civil remedies may be gained, against whom and by whom, in respect of the kettle. Explain also the extent of any criminal liability as regards the unsafe kettle.

(You are not expected to consider the Trade Descriptions Act 1968. Nor are you expected to analyse the meaning of 'satisfactory quality' in any detail. Nor should you consider the remedies available to the retailer of the kettle.)

See *Cases and Materials* (7.5) for an outline answer.

CHAPTER EIGHT

THE CONSUMER CREDIT ACT 1974: HISTORY, STRUCTURE AND DEFINITIONS

8.1 Objectives

By the end of this chapter you should be able to:

- outline the history and structure of the Consumer Credit Act 1974;

- define a regulated agreement;

- differentiate between running-account credit and fixed-sum credit; between restricted-use credit and unrestricted-use credit; and between debtor-creditor-supplier agreements and debtor-creditor agreements;

- define non-commercial and small transactions;

- define a credit token agreement;

- recognise a linked transaction.

8.2 Introduction

In this chapter we look briefly at the history and structure of the Consumer Credit Act 1974 and then examine the definitions contained in the Act. It is necessary to master these definitions, which can be complex, in order to understand the substantive provisions of the Act.

8.3 The History and Structure of the 1974 Act

The Consumer Credit Act 1974 was passed in response to the Crowther Committee Report 1971. The previous law, which was to be found in several other statutes, was considered excessively technical and was ill suited to the needs of the modern commercial world. The Act enjoyed the support of all political parties and received the Royal Assent in 1974. However, due to the technicality and wide scope of the Act, it was only fully implemented in 1985. It is a lengthy Act, divided into 12 parts, but nevertheless it only provides a framework of the law. The details are left to be filled in by regulations and orders made under the Act. The Act is set out as follows:

204 THE CONSUMER CREDIT ACT 1974: HISTORY, STRUCTURE AND DEFINITIONS

- Part I of the Act sets out the duties and functions of the Director General of Fair Trading.

- Part II sets out the definitions of the different types of agreements to which the Act applies. We examine these definitions later in this chapter.

- Part III deals with the licensing of credit and hire businesses. A regulated agreement made by an unlicensed dealer is unenforceable. It is beyond the scope of this book to examine the licensing requirements in any detail.

- Part IV deals with advertising credit and canvassing credit. Part V deals with entry into credit or hire agreements. Parts IV and V are examined in **Chapter 9**.

- Part VI deals with matters arising during the currency of credit or hire agreements. In this part of the Act important rights are conferred on creditors and hirers and we examine these rights in **Chapter 10**.

- Part VII covers default and termination and we examine these matters in **Chapter 11**.

- Part VIII deals with securities, pledges, negotiable instruments and mortgages of land. It is beyond the scope of this book to examine these matters.

- Part IX deals with judicial control of credit agreements, a matter examined in **Chapter 11**.

- Part X deals with ancillary credit businesses, a matter beyond the scope of this book.

- Part XI deals with enforcement of the Act and Part XII supplemental matters.

Section 189(1) of the 1974 Act provides an extremely comprehensive list of definitions. Well over a hundred words and phrases are defined and s. 189(1) must be referred to constantly when considering any other section. Even words with which you might be familiar in a legal or a social context might have a different meaning under the Act. To take an example, the definition of the word 'creditor' is a very long way from the definition which would be found in any dictionary. There is no doubt that several key definitions must be mastered before the Act can be understood, and the mastery of these definitions is the main objective of this chapter. But this in itself causes difficulty. For example, in attempting to define the first important concept, a 'regulated agreement' we immediately need to consider three other definitions given by the Act. Unfortunately, these three definitions themselves lead us on to still more definitions. Despite these difficulties, the task of mastering the important definitions is not impossible.

Schedule 1 of the Act lists the 35 offences created by the Act. It also sets out the penalty for each of the offences.

Schedule 2 of the Act is unusual, but helpful. It sets out 24 examples which demonstrate the use of the terminology within the Act. Thirty-one of the more important terms within the Act are demonstrated in these examples. Schedule 2 begins with a table which shows in which sections of the Act the definitions of the 31 terms can be found, and which of the 24 examples demonstrate the use of each of the terms.

Both schedules 1 and 2 are reproduced in *Cases and Materials* (11.1).

8.4 The Definitions contained in the 1974 Act

In this chapter we examine the most important definitions in the Consumer Credit Act 1974. These are considered in order of their importance rather than in alphabetical order.

THE CONSUMER CREDIT ACT 1974: HISTORY, STRUCTURE AND DEFINITIONS

You will need to understand these definitions to understand the other provisions of the Act.

8.4.1 REGULATED AGREEMENTS

Apart from the rules on extortionate credit bargains, the 1974 Act directly controls only those agreements which can be classified as 'regulated agreements'. First, therefore, it is necessary to identify such agreements.

Section 189(1) defines a regulated agreement as 'a consumer credit agreement, or consumer hire agreement, other than an exempt agreement, and "regulated" and "unregulated" shall be construed accordingly'.

Section 189(1) also tells us where to find the definitions of a 'consumer credit agreement' (s. 8), a 'consumer hire agreement' (s. 15) and an 'exempt agreement' (s. 16). In order to understand the meaning of a 'regulated agreement' we therefore need to consider each of these other three definitions in turn. (See also the diagram below.)

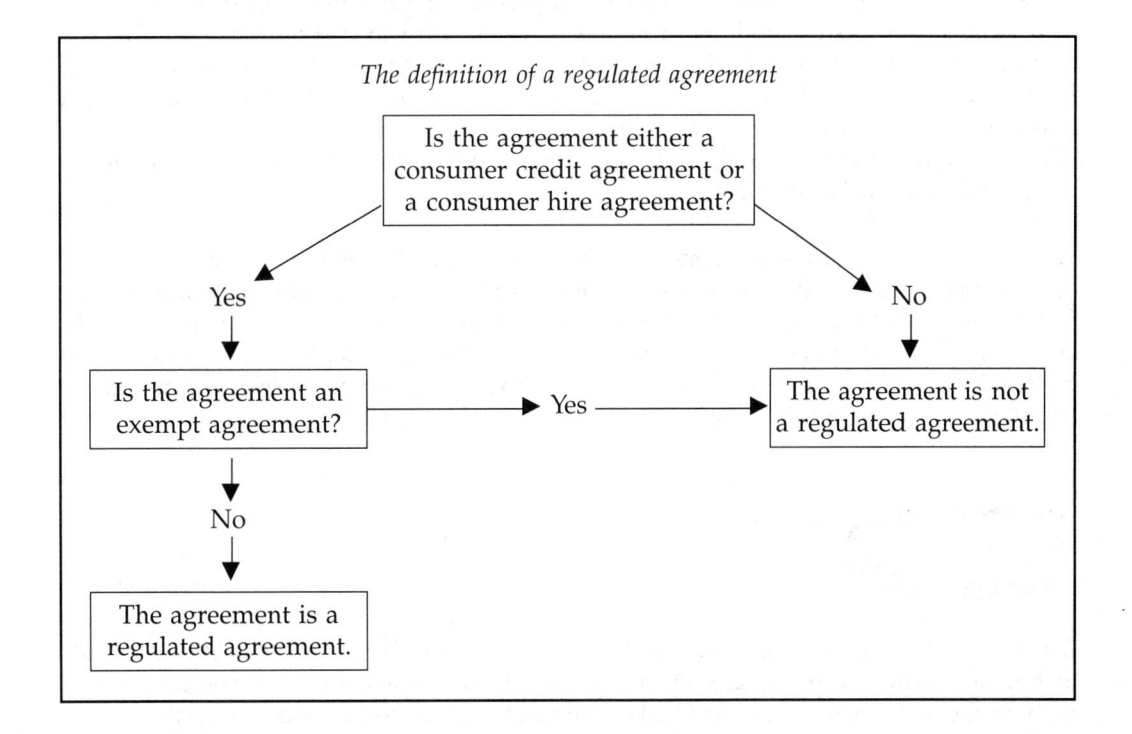

The definition of a regulated agreement

```
            Is the agreement either a
           consumer credit agreement or
            a consumer hire agreement?
           /                           \
         Yes                           No
          ↓                             ↓
   Is the agreement an  ──Yes──→   The agreement is not
   exempt agreement?               a regulated agreement.
          ↓
         No
          ↓
   The agreement is a
   regulated agreement.
```

8.4.1.1 Consumer credit agreements

Section 8(2) of the 1974 Act defines a consumer credit agreement as 'a personal credit agreement by which the creditor provides the debtor with credit not exceeding [£25,000]'.

Credit is defined by s. 9(1) as including 'a cash loan, and any other form of financial accommodation'.

A 'personal credit agreement' is defined by s. 8(1) as 'an agreement between an individual (the "debtor") and any other person ("the creditor") by which the creditor provides the debtor with credit of any amount'.

There is no requirement that the creditor is carrying on a business. However, if the creditor does not provide the credit in the course of a business then the agreement may be a 'non-commercial agreement', in which case several of the provisions of the Act will not apply to it. (The definition of 'non-commercial' agreements is examined below at **8.4.3**.)

ACTIVITY 8/1

Read s. 189(1) of the 1974 Act in *Cases and Materials* (8.1) to find the definition of 'individual', and then write down whether the following are 'individuals' within the meaning of s. 8(1).

(a) Mr Jones, a postman.

(b) A firm of doctors.

(c) A tennis club run as an unincorporated association.

(d) A private limited company.

Section 189(1) states: '"individual" includes a partnership or other unincorporated body of persons not consisting entirely of bodies corporate'. It can therefore be seen that the firm of doctors and the tennis club are both 'individuals' within the Act. Obviously, Mr Jones is an individual. A private limited company is not an individual and nor would a partnership consisting entirely of companies be an individual. It is perhaps a little surprising (given the name of the Act) that a business which is not incorporated qualifies as an individual in this context.

Not all 'personal credit agreements' are 'regulated agreements'. Only 'personal credit agreements' which are also 'consumer credit agreements' are 'regulated agreements'. The factor which distinguishes a 'consumer credit agreement' from other 'personal credit agreements' is that the credit provided is not more than £25,000. It is important here to realise that the figure of £25,000 relates only to the credit provided. It does not include any deposit paid or any interest payable.

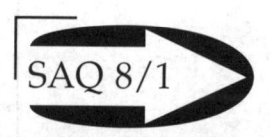

SAQ 8/1

Alice, a partner in a firm of hauliers, buys a lorry from Bertha Motors Ltd on behalf of her firm. Alice is to pay £33,000 altogether. This is made up of £3,000 down, and then 15 monthly instalments of £2,000. The total interest to be paid is £5,000.

(a) Is this a 'personal credit agreement'?

(b) Is this a 'consumer credit agreement'?

(c) Is this a regulated agreement?

(a) This is a 'personal credit agreement'. Alice is an individual to whom a creditor has provided credit.

(b) This agreement is also a 'consumer credit agreement'. To find the amount of credit given, both the £3,000 deposit and the £5,000 interest must be deducted from the total sum of £33,000. Once this has been done, it can be seen that the credit provided is £25,000. Therefore the agreement is a 'consumer credit agreement'.

THE CONSUMER CREDIT ACT 1974: HISTORY, STRUCTURE AND DEFINITIONS

(c) Section 8(3) tells us that a consumer credit agreement is a regulated agreement as long as it is not an 'exempt agreement'. Therefore the agreement will be a regulated agreement. (The definition of an exempt agreement is examined below at **8.4.1.3**. See also the diagram below.)

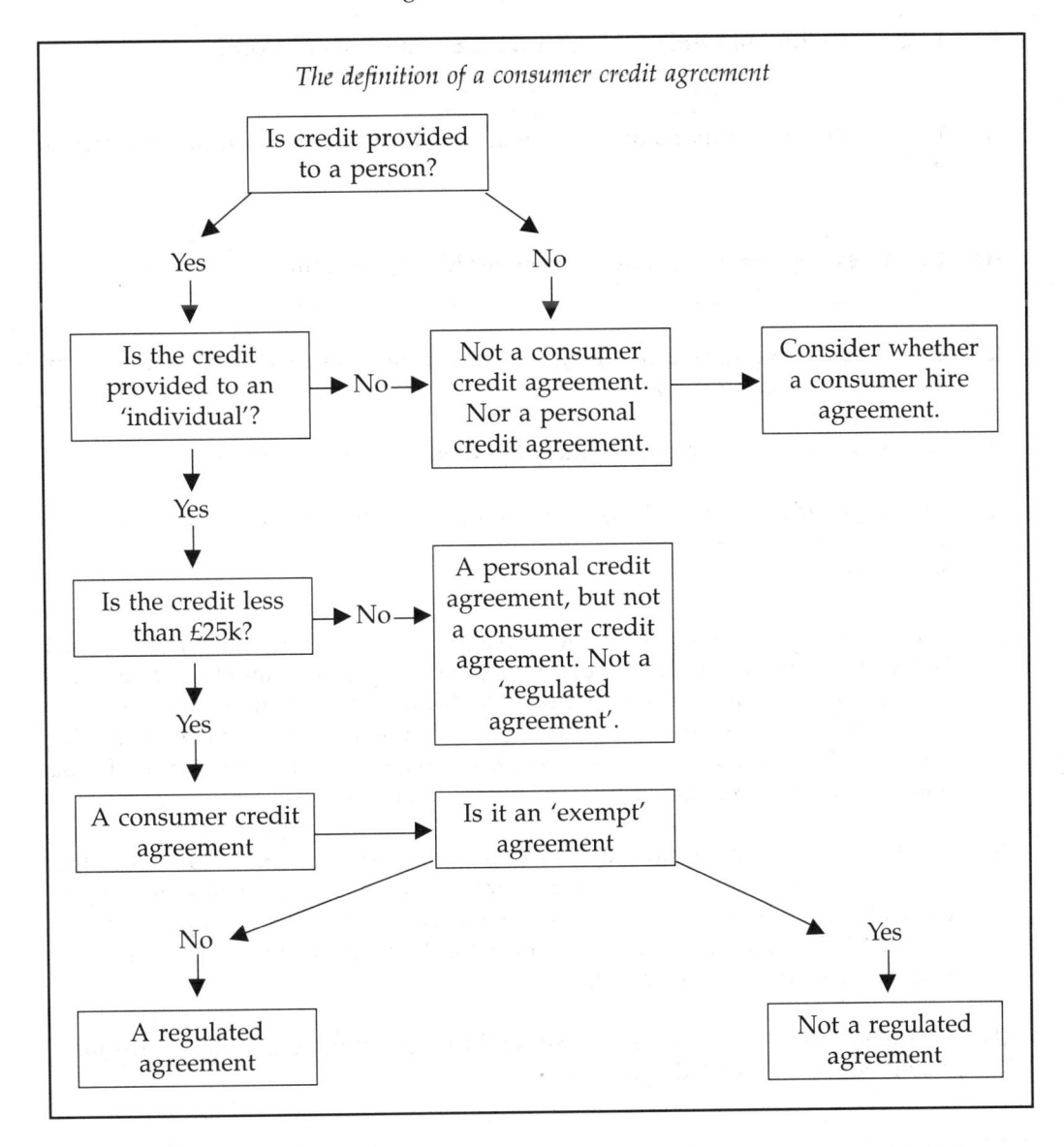

The definition of a consumer credit agreement

```
                    Is credit provided
                       to a person?
                    /                 \
                  Yes                  No
                   ↓                    ↓
         Is the credit          Not a consumer           Consider whether
         provided to an  →No→   credit agreement.   →    a consumer hire
         'individual'?          Nor a personal            agreement.
                   ↓            credit agreement.
                  Yes
                   ↓
                                A personal credit
         Is the credit less     agreement, but not
         than £25k?      →No→   a consumer credit
                   ↓            agreement. Not a
                  Yes           'regulated
                   ↓            agreement'.
         A consumer credit  →   Is it an 'exempt'
         agreement              agreement
              /                        \
             No                         Yes
              ↓                          ↓
         A regulated               Not a regulated
         agreement                 agreement
```

8.4.1.2 Consumer hire agreements

ACTIVITY 8/2

Read s. 15 in *Cases and Materials* (8.1). There are six requirements of a consumer hire agreement. If you answer the following six questions correctly you will have understood all of them. (Some of the answers are rather obvious, but others are not.)

(a) What legal status must the hirer possess?

(b) What legal status must the owner of the goods possess?

(c) A contract of hire states that if the hirer continues to hire the goods until the end of the agreed period then the goods will become the hirer's property when the final payment of hire is made. Is this a consumer hire agreement?

(d) Is there a minimum time for which the agreement should run?

(e) What is the maximum amount of payment which the hirer can be required to make?

(f) Can an exempt agreement be a consumer hire agreement?

(a) You should have answered along the following lines. The hirer must be an 'individual', as defined above.

(b) The owner must be a 'person', and could therefore be a company.

(c) Such an agreement would be one of hire-purchase and would not therefore be a 'consumer hire agreement'. (A hire-purchase agreement is a 'consumer credit agreement'.)

(d) There is no minimum time for which the agreement should run. What is required is that it should be capable of running for more than three months. Only a hire agreement for a term of less than three months, with no option to renew by either side, will fail this requirement. This requirement as to being capable of running for more than three months was inserted to exclude the short-term hire of tools and cars etc. as these agreements are not credit agreements at all.

(e) The hirer cannot be required to make payments exceeding £25,000. Notice that here we are concerned not with the maximum amount which the hirer might pay, but with the maximum amount which the hirer can be required to pay. If this is less than £25,000, the agreement is a 'consumer hire agreement'. It does not matter that the hirer may end up paying more.

(f) An exempt agreement can be a consumer hire agreement, but such an agreement would not be a regulated agreement.

SAQ 8/2

Helen hires an aeroplane from Jet Co. Ltd. The hire period is two months, at £8,000 per month. The contract of hire gives Helen the option of extending the hire period by another two months. Is this a consumer hire agreement?

To find the answer to this SAQ we need to work our way through the definition of a consumer hire agreement in s. 15(1). Helen is an individual and Jet Co. Ltd is a person.

THE CONSUMER CREDIT ACT 1974: HISTORY, STRUCTURE AND DEFINITIONS

The contract is not one of hire-purchase. The agreement is initially for only two months, but it is capable of subsisting for more than three months. If Helen had the jet for the full four months she would be required to pay £32,000, and would thus exceed the £25,000 limit. However, Helen cannot be required to have the jet for more than two months. The amount payable for two months' hire of the jet would be £16,000. The agreement is therefore a consumer hire agreement. (See the diagram below.)

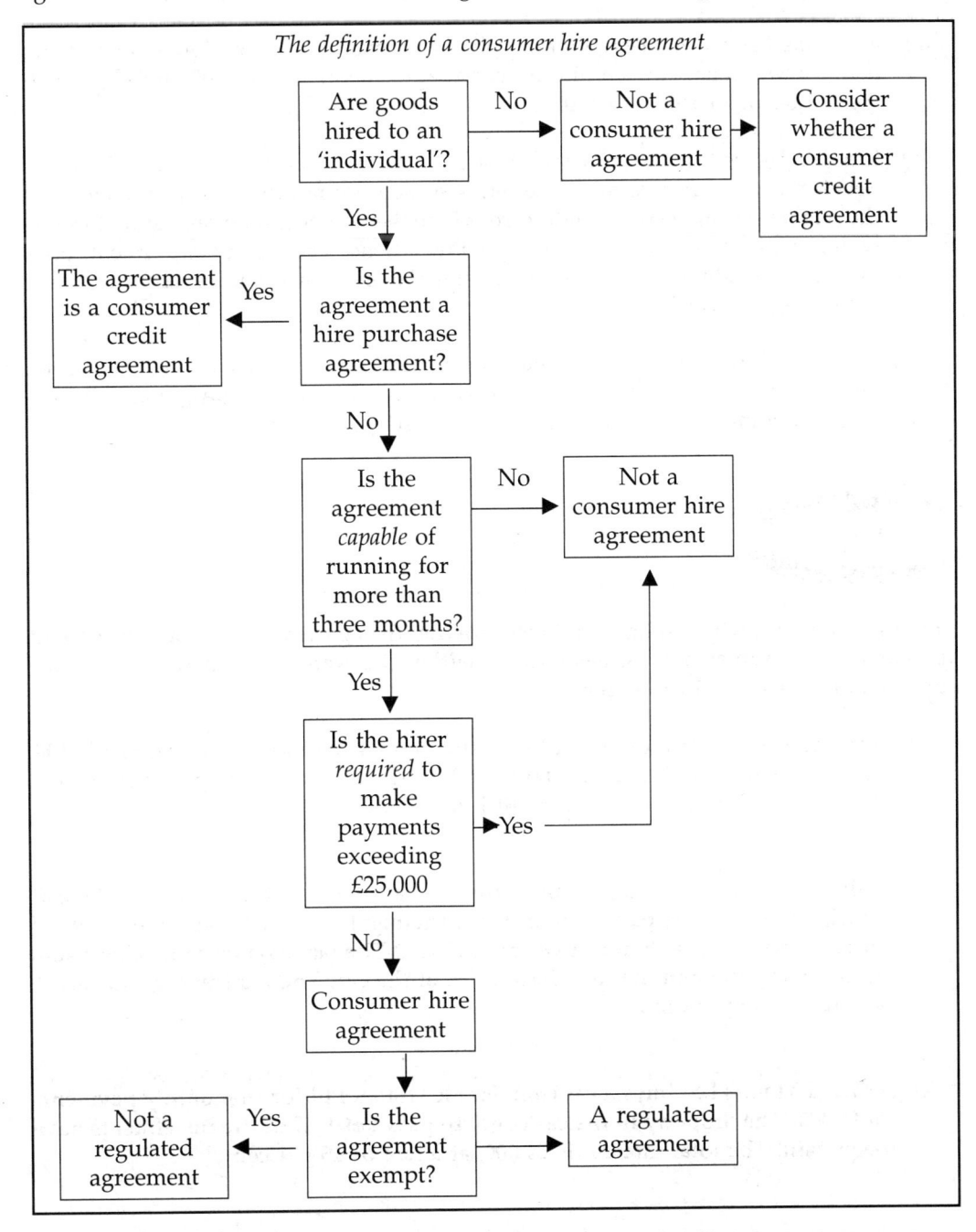

The definition of a consumer hire agreement

```
                    ┌─────────────┐   No   ┌─────────────┐   ┌─────────────┐
                    │ Are goods   │───────▶│ Not a       │──▶│ Consider    │
                    │ hired to an │        │ consumer    │   │ whether a   │
                    │ 'individual'│        │ hire        │   │ consumer    │
                    │     ?       │        │ agreement   │   │ credit      │
                    └─────────────┘        └─────────────┘   │ agreement   │
                           │                                 └─────────────┘
                           │ Yes
                           ▼
┌─────────────┐  Yes  ┌─────────────┐
│ The         │◀──────│ Is the      │
│ agreement   │       │ agreement a │
│ is a        │       │ hire        │
│ consumer    │       │ purchase    │
│ credit      │       │ agreement?  │
│ agreement   │       └─────────────┘
└─────────────┘              │
                             │ No
                             ▼
                    ┌─────────────┐   No   ┌─────────────┐
                    │ Is the      │───────▶│ Not a       │
                    │ agreement   │        │ consumer    │
                    │ *capable* of│        │ hire        │
                    │ running for │        │ agreement   │
                    │ more than   │        └─────────────┘
                    │ three months│               ▲
                    └─────────────┘               │
                           │ Yes                  │
                           ▼                      │
                    ┌─────────────┐               │
                    │ Is the hirer│               │
                    │ *required*  │               │
                    │ to make     │               │
                    │ payments    │── Yes ────────┘
                    │ exceeding   │
                    │ £25,000     │
                    └─────────────┘
                           │ No
                           ▼
                    ┌─────────────┐
                    │ Consumer    │
                    │ hire        │
                    │ agreement   │
                    └─────────────┘
                           │
                           ▼
┌─────────────┐  Yes  ┌─────────────┐       ┌─────────────┐
│ Not a       │◀──────│ Is the      │──────▶│ A regulated │
│ regulated   │       │ agreement   │       │ agreement   │
│ agreement   │       │ exempt?     │       └─────────────┘
└─────────────┘       └─────────────┘
```

8.4.1.3 Exempt agreements

Section 16 defines exempt agreements. The significance of an agreement being exempt is that it will not be a regulated agreement. The definition provided by s. 16 is extremely lengthy, and involves delegated legislation made by the Secretary of State. The delegated legislation currently in force is the Consumer Credit (Exempt Agreements) Order 1989 (SI 1989 No. 869). For our purposes we can summarise s. 16 to say that an agreement is an exempt agreement if:

(a) it is a mortgage given on land by a local authority or other non profit-making organisation such as a building society or a friendly society; or

(b) it is a debtor-creditor agreement (see definition below) where the rate of interest is lower than either 13 per cent or 1 per cent above the base rate of the London Clearing Banks; or

(c) it is a fixed-sum debtor-creditor-supplier agreement (see definitions below), other than a conditional sale or hire-purchase agreement, where the number of payments does not exceed four; or

(d) it is a purchase made on a credit card, such as American Express, where the debtor must within a certain time settle the account in full with one payment. (If the purchase is made on a credit card where the debtor has no obligation to settle within a given period then the agreement is not an exempt agreement. So a purchase would not be an exempt agreement merely on account of its being made with an Access card.)

The SAQ which follows will probably take you about half an hour to complete. However, it is an important one. If you correctly work your way through the SAQ you will have a good understanding of what constitutes a regulated agreement.

SAQ 8/3

In the six examples which follow, indicate whether the agreement is a consumer credit agreement, a consumer hire agreement, or neither. Indicate also whether or not the agreement is a regulated agreement.

(a) Alan agrees to sell a car to Bill in return for 24 monthly instalments of £100, payable in arrears. The total interest to be paid, at a rate of 14 per cent, is £600. The property in the car passes to Bill immediately.

(b) Celia takes a car on hire-purchase from Delia Motors Ltd. Celia pays a deposit of £4,000. She is to pay 36 monthly instalments of £750 each. (Total of all instalments payable therefore equals £27,000.) The last payment includes a sum representing the nominal purchase price of the car. The total interest is £6,000, at a rate of 19 per cent.

(c) Edward Motors Ltd buys a car from Frank Motors Ltd for 16 monthly payments of £1,000. The property in the car is not to pass until all of the instalments have been paid. The total interest is £4,000, at a rate of 15 per cent.

(d) Geraldine, a partner in a firm of doctors, engages a builder to extend the surgery. To pay the builders, the firm borrows £14,000 from the bank at 12 per cent interest. This loan is to be repaid in 12 monthly instalments.

(e) Harry is extending his house and hires a JCB excavator for a fixed period of ten weeks, at £350 a week.

(f) Ian decides to hire a car, rather than to purchase one. The hire charge is £100 a month for 36 months.

THE CONSUMER CREDIT ACT 1974: HISTORY, STRUCTURE AND DEFINITIONS

(a) This is a consumer credit agreement. An individual has been provided with credit not exceeding £25,000. The agreement is also a regulated agreement, as it is not an exempt agreement.

(b) This is a consumer credit agreement. An individual has been provided with credit not exceeding £25,000. The amount of credit provided is £21,000 (£31,000 total payments − £10,000 in deposit and interest charges.) The agreement is a regulated agreement, as it is not an exempt agreement.

(c) This is not a consumer credit agreement. The debtor is a company and is not therefore an 'individual', within the meaning of the Act. Nor, obviously enough, is the agreement a consumer hire agreement. Therefore the agreement is not a regulated agreement.

(d) This is a consumer credit agreement even though the debtor makes the contract in the course of a business. Despite the name of the Act, it does not distinguish between consumers and non consumers in the way that the Unfair Contract Terms Act 1977 does. The agreement is an exempt agreement, and therefore not a regulated agreement, because it is a debtor-creditor agreement with an interest rate below 13 per cent.

(e) This is not a consumer credit agreement because Harry has not been given any credit. Nor is it a consumer hire agreement because the agreement is not capable of subsisting for more than three months. As the agreement is not a consumer credit agreement nor a consumer hire agreement, it cannot be a regulated agreement.

(f) This is a consumer hire agreement. An individual has hired goods. The agreement is capable of running for more than three months and the hirer cannot be required to make payments exceeding £25,000. As the agreement is not an exempt agreement it is also a regulated agreement.

8.4.2 TYPES OF CONSUMER CREDIT AGREEMENTS

We have already examined the definition of a consumer credit agreement under the 1974 Act. We now need to consider such agreements further, and to make three further distinctions:

(a) between running-account credit and fixed-sum credit;

(b) between restricted-use credit and unrestricted-use credit; and

(c) between debtor-creditor-supplier agreements and debtor-creditor agreements.

8.4.2.1 Running-account credit and fixed-sum credit

ACTIVITY 8/3

In one sentence only, write down your opinion as to the likely difference between running-account credit and fixed-sum credit.

You probably wrote something like: 'Running-account credit allows the debtor to receive credit as and when desired, up to a certain limit, whereas fixed-sum credit is the loan of a definite amount.' Such a definition would be essentially correct. Fixed-sum credit can be taken or repaid in instalments, but the amount of credit is fixed at the beginning of the agreement or can be calculated by reference to the terms of the agreement. Once the credit has been repaid the agreement will be discharged. The rate of interest may be fixed, or the terms of the contract may allow it to be varied. (For example, the rate of interest is often variable.) Running-account credit can continue indefinitely. There is a 'master' agreement at the outset and this allows for separate contracts to be made under it. As all of the contracts are separate, the amount of APR cannot be determined in advance. There will be a credit limit which cannot be exceeded, and the debtor will make payments periodically. These will be deducted from the amount of credit outstanding. All credit other than running-account credit is fixed-sum credit. (In *Cases and Materials* (8.1) see s. 10 for the full definitions given by the Act.)

A fixed-sum credit agreement will be regulated if the credit is less than £25,000. A running-account credit agreement will be regulated if the credit limit is fixed at £25,000 or less (s. 10(3)(a).) A running-account agreement will still be a regulated agreement if a term of the agreement allows the maximum to be exceeded merely temporarily (s. 10(2)). If there is no credit limit, or if the limit is over £25,000, a running-account credit agreement will still be a regulated agreement if:

(a) the debtor is not able to draw at any one time an amount exceeding £25,000; or

(b) the rate of interest goes up, or some other condition favourable to the creditor applies, on account of the credit balance having exceeded a figure of £25,000 or less; or

(c) it is probable that the amount of credit will not exceed £25,000 (s. 10(3)).

ACTIVITY 8/4

David has arranged to borrow £12,000 from Credit Co. Ltd. £1,000 is to be borrowed on the first day of each month of the year. Read the definitions in s. 10 of the Act in *Cases and Materials* (8.1), and then write down whether this is running-account credit or fixed-sum credit.

You should have written that this is fixed-sum credit. The amount to be borrowed is fixed. The essence of running-account credit is that although there will be a maximum amount which can be borrowed, the amount actually borrowed is fluid, and there is no definite date at which the account must be settled in full. Fixed-sum credit is usually borrowed over a fixed length of time, although this is not always the case.

ACTIVITY 8/5

Indicate, by deleting the inappropriate term, whether the following types of transaction involve running-account or fixed-sum credit.

(a) A bank overdraft, allowing the account to be overdrawn up to a limit of £2,000.   (Running-account/fixed-sum.)

THE CONSUMER CREDIT ACT 1974: HISTORY, STRUCTURE AND DEFINITIONS

(b) A bank loan of £2,000.   (Running-account/fixed-sum.)

(c) A bank credit card (such as an Access card).   (Running-account/fixed-sum.)

(d) A store charge card, allowing credit of up to £2,000.   (Running-account/fixed-sum.)

(e) A contract of hire-purchase.   (Running-account/fixed-sum.)

(f) A conditional sale.   (Running-account/fixed-sum.)

(g) A credit sale.   (Running-account/fixed-sum.)

You should have indicated that (a), (c) and (d) involve running-account credit. Transactions (b), (e), (f) and (g) involve fixed-sum credit.

8.4.2.2 Restricted-use credit and unrestricted-use credit

ACTIVITY 8/6

In as simple a sentence as possible, write down your opinion as to the distinction between restricted-use and unrestricted-use credit.

You probably wrote something like: 'Unrestricted-use credit may be used by the debtor for any purpose, whereas restricted-use credit must be used for a particular purpose.' Such an answer would be essentially, but not quite, correct. Where credit is restricted-use the funds are transferred from the credidtor to the supplier of the goods or services, as happens where goods are bought with a credit card, or in a contract of hire-purchase. Where the creditor and the supplier are the same person, as in hire-purchase or conditional sale, the credit is also restricted-use. If money passes into the debtor's hands then the credit will not be restricted-use, even if the money is earmarked for some particular purpose, and even if the debtor would be in breach of contract if he did not use it for this particular purpose (s. 11(3)). For example, if a debtor borrows money from a creditor in order to pay off his overdraft, the credit will be restricted-use if the money is handed over to the bank, but the credit will be unrestricted-use if given to the debtor, because the debtor could, in breach of his contract with the creditor, use the money for some other purpose, such as to buy a new car. (Section 11 of the Act distinguishes between restricted-use credit and unrestricted-use credit, and can be read in *Cases and Materials* (8.1).)

8.4.2.3 Debtor-creditor-supplier and debtor-creditor agreements

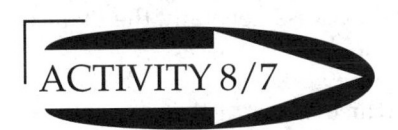

ACTIVITY 8/7

In as simple a sentence as possible, write down your opinion as to the difference between a debtor-creditor-supplier agreement and a debtor-creditor agreement.

214 THE CONSUMER CREDIT ACT 1974: HISTORY, STRUCTURE AND DEFINITIONS

You probably wrote along the following lines: 'In a debtor-creditor supplier agreement there are three parties: the debtor, the creditor and a third party who supplies goods or services, whereas in a debtor-creditor agreement there are only two parties: the debtor and the creditor.' Unfortunately, as we shall see, this common-sense answer is not correct.

The 1974 Act has substituted the term 'debtor-creditor-supplier' credit for the Crowther Committee's term a 'connected' loan. Both mean the same thing, that the creditor is either himself the legal supplier of the goods or services, or has an existing or contemplated future connection with the supplier. The term 'connected' loan seems a better way to describe what the Act calls 'debtor-creditor-supplier' agreements. The reason for making the distinction between debtor-creditor and debtor-creditor-supplier agreements is that where there is no connection between the legal supplier and the creditor, the contract between supplier and debtor should be treated in the same way as any other contract. But where there is a connection between the creditor and the supplier, even the contract of supply is influenced by the contract to supply credit.

Section 12 defines three types of debtor-creditor-supplier agreements. The first definition, set out in s. 12(a), is a regulated restricted-use credit agreement to finance a transaction between the debtor and the creditor, whether forming part of the agreement or not. This therefore means agreements where the creditor and the supplier are the same person. An example of this would be a contract of hire-purchase where the goods are let by the finance company. (It might be thought that there are three parties here; the debtor, the finance company and the supplier of the goods. However, under s. 12 supplier means the legal supplier not the physical supplier. In a typical contract of hire-purchase it is the finance company, not the dealer in the goods, which legally supplies the goods to the debtor.) Credit sales and conditional sales would fall within the definition under s. 12(a). Store 'charge cards' under which retailers themselves provide the credit would also be debtor-creditor-supplier agreements under s. 12(a).

Sections 12(b) and 12(c) cover loans to the debtor (or payments to the supplier at the debtor's request) made under a pre-existing arrangement, or in contemplation of future arrangements, between the creditor and the supplier. In such cases there are of course three parties: the debtor, the creditor, and the supplier with whom the creditor has or will have a connection. The main difference between the two is that s. 12(b) applies to restricted use agreements, whereas s. 12(c) applies to unrestricted-use agreements. Another difference is that under s. 12(c) the pre-existing arrangements between creditor and supplier must have been made in the knowledge that the credit is to be used to finance a transaction between the debtor and the supplier, whereas s. 12(b) applies where there are either pre-existing arrangements between creditor and supplier or where such arrangements are merely contemplated.

Examples of s. 12(b) debtor-creditor-supplier agreements include payments for goods or services with a credit card, the use of trading vouchers and loans from finance companies paid direct to suppliers who have an arrangement with the finance company and who introduced the debtor to the company. Examples of s. 12(c) debtor-creditor-supplier agreements are hard to find, but would include cases where a debtor receives a loan from a finance company to purchase from a supplier, the finance company having a pre-existing arrangement with the supplier and knowing that the loan is to finance a transaction with the supplier. Such a situation is unusual because generally the finance company would hand the money direct to the supplier.

A debtor-creditor agreement is any credit agreement which is not a debtor-creditor-supplier agreement. That is to say, it is a credit agreement where the creditor and the supplier are not the same person, and where there is no pre-existing arrangement between creditor and supplier, and no contemplation of such an arrangement. Regulated credit card agreements can be both debtor-creditor-supplier agreements (where the card is used to buy goods from a shop which has agreed to accept the card) and debtor-creditor agreement (where the card is used to withdraw money from the bank which issued it.)

THE CONSUMER CREDIT ACT 1974: HISTORY, STRUCTURE AND DEFINITIONS

ACTIVITY 8/8

Delete as necessary to indicate whether the following agreements are debtor-creditor-supplier agreements (DCS) or debtor-creditor agreements (DC).

(a) A typical contract of hire-purchase, under which a dealer sells goods to a finance company which makes a hire-purchase agreement with the debtor.   DCS/DC

(b) A typical conditional sale, under which the price is to be paid in instalments and the property is to remain in the seller until all the instalments are paid.   DCS/DC

(c) A bank loan.   DCS/DC

(d) A purchase made on a credit card, such as Access.   DCS/DC

(e) An overdraft facility.   DCS/DC

(a) This is a DCS agreement, within s. 12(a), as the legal supplier of the goods and the creditor are the same person.

(b) This is a DCS agreement, within s. 12(a), as the legal supplier and the creditor are the same person.

(c) This is a DC agreement, unless the loan is to be used for a specific purpose, and the bank has a business arrangement with the supplier.

(d) This is a DCS agreement, within s. 12(b), as the credit company has a pre-existing arrangement with suppliers who accept the card. Cheque guarantee cards and debit cards such as Switch and Delta do not give rise to a DCS agreement as they do not involve the granting of credit. They are excluded even when the card holder's use of them puts his account into debit (s. 187(3) and (3A)).

(e) This is a DC agreement. (See also the diagram below.)

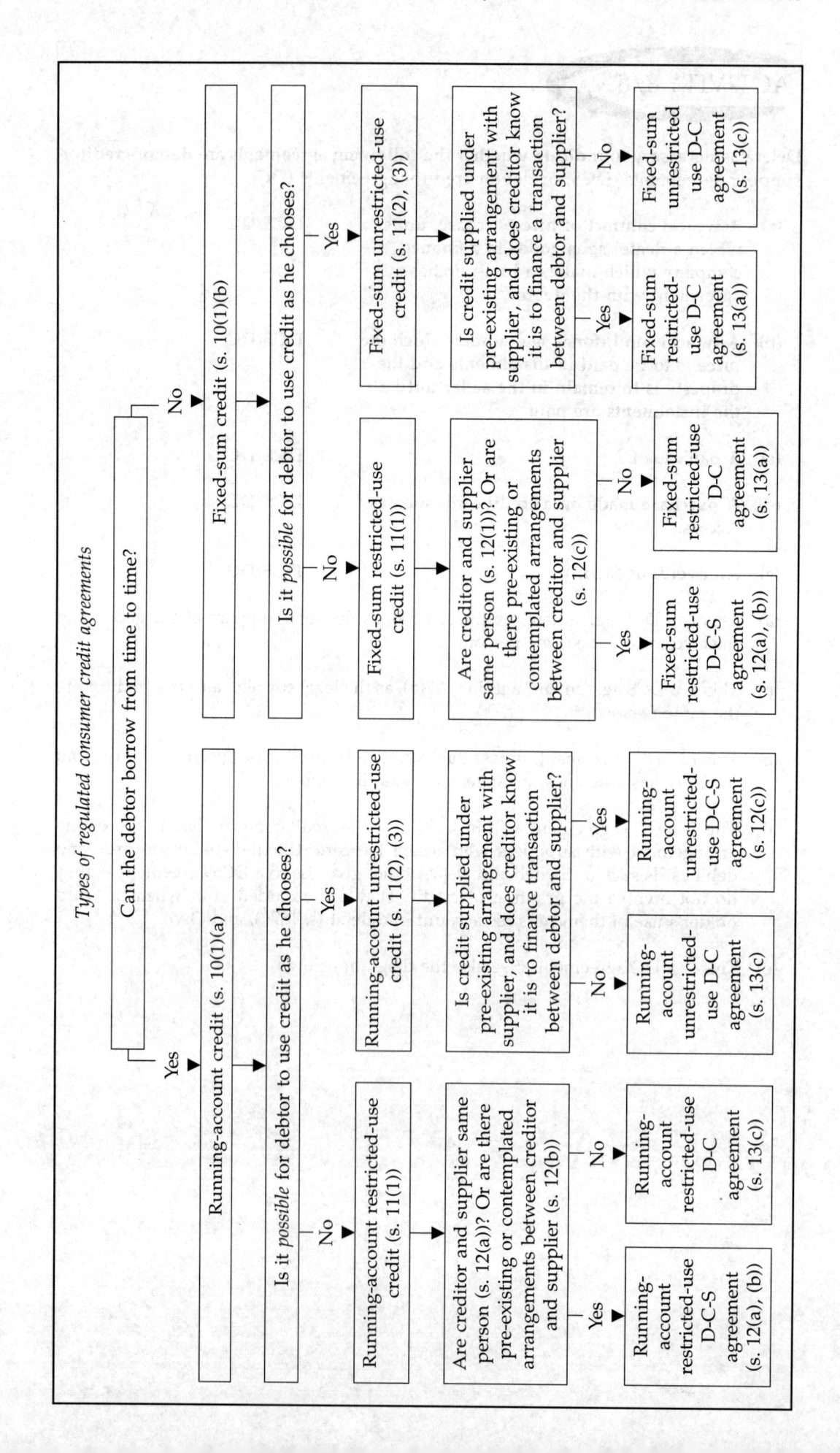

216 THE CONSUMER CREDIT ACT 1974: HISTORY, STRUCTURE AND DEFINITIONS

Types of regulated consumer credit agreements

Can the debtor borrow from time to time?

- **Yes** → Running-account credit (s. 10(1)(a))
- **No** → Fixed-sum credit (s. 10(1)(b))

Running-account branch:

Is it *possible* for debtor to use credit as he chooses?

- **Yes** → Running-account unrestricted-use credit (s. 11(2), (3))

  Is credit supplied under pre-existing arrangement with supplier, and does creditor know it is to finance a transaction between debtor and supplier?
  - **Yes** → Running-account unrestricted-use D-C-S agreement (s. 12(c))
  - **No** → Running-account unrestricted-use D-C agreement (s. 13(c))

- **No** → Running-account restricted-use credit (s. 11(1))

  Are creditor and supplier same person (s. 12(a))? Or are there pre-existing or contemplated arrangements between creditor and supplier (s. 12(b))?
  - **Yes** → Running-account restricted-use D-C-S agreement (s. 12(a), (b))
  - **No** → Running-account restricted-use D-C agreement (s. 13(c))

Fixed-sum branch:

Is it *possible* for debtor to use credit as he chooses?

- **Yes** → Fixed-sum unrestricted-use credit (s. 11(2), (3))

  Is credit supplied under pre-existing arrangement with supplier, and does creditor know it is to finance a transaction between debtor and supplier?
  - **No** → Fixed-sum unrestricted-use D-C agreement (s. 13(c))
  - **Yes** → Fixed-sum restricted-use D-C agreement (s. 13(a))

- **No** → Fixed-sum restricted-use credit (s. 11(1))

  Are creditor and supplier same person (s. 12(1))? Or are there pre-existing or contemplated arrangements between creditor and supplier (s. 12(c))
  - **No** → Fixed-sum restricted-use D-C agreement (s. 13(a))
  - **Yes** → Fixed-sum restricted-use D-C-S agreement (s. 12(a), (b))

THE CONSUMER CREDIT ACT 1974: HISTORY, STRUCTURE AND DEFINITIONS

8.4.3 NON-COMMERCIAL AND SMALL AGREEMENTS

A non-commercial agreement is defined by s. 189 as 'a consumer credit agreement or consumer hire agreement not made by the creditor or owner in the course of a business carried on by him'. This would therefore include loans from friends and relatives. You should notice that although a commercial loan must be made in the course of a business, the business carried on does not need to be a consumer credit business.

A 'small agreement' is either a consumer credit agreement where the credit or is less than £50, or a consumer hire agreement which does not require the hirer to make payments exceeding £50. In either case the agreement must be unsecured or secured only by a guarantee or an indemnity (s. 17(1)). A hire-purchase or conditional sale agreement cannot be a small agreement.

Non-commercial and small agreements are regulated by the Act, but are exempt from certain of its provisions. (Mainly the provisions which relate to entry into credit arrangements.)

If the same parties make several small agreements, where it appears probable that they have done so with the intention of avoiding the provisions of the Act, then the small agreements are regarded as regulated agreements other than small agreements (s. 173(b)).

Non-commercial and small agreements occupy a half-way house between regulated and exempt agreements.

8.4.4 CREDIT TOKENS AND CREDIT TOKEN AGREEMENTS

The Act does not use the term 'credit card' but does refer to 'credit-tokens', and 'credit-token agreements'.

Section 14(1) defines a credit-token:

> A credit-token is a card, check, voucher, coupon, stamp, form, booklet or other document or thing given to an individual by a person carrying on a consumer credit business, who undertakes—
> (a) that on the production of it (whether or not some other action is also required) he will supply cash, goods and services (or any of them) on credit, or
> (b) that where, on the production of it to a third party (whether or not any other action is also required), the third party supplies cash, goods and services (or any of them), he will pay the third party for them (whether or not deducting any discount or commission), in return for payment to him by the individual.

Section 14(2) states that: 'A credit-token agreement is a regulated agreement for the provision of credit in connection with the use of a credit-token.'

ACTIVITY 8/9

Derek, a debtor, has various cards, under agreements with various creditors, as listed below. In each case indicate whether or not the agreement is a credit-token agreement. If the agreement is not a credit-token agreement write down why it is not. (First, you will need to decide whether or not the card in question is a credit-token. Second, you must decide whether or not the agreement is a regulated agreement for the provision of credit in connection with the credit-token.)

218 THE CONSUMER CREDIT ACT 1974: HISTORY, STRUCTURE AND DEFINITIONS

(a) An Access card, which enables Derek to buy goods from shops which have an agreement with the creditor.

(b) A cash card, which enables Derek to withdraw up to £100 cash per week from his bank account via the bank's cash dispensers.

(c) A cheque guarantee card. (The creditor agrees to honour cheques to the value of £50 if the supplier follows the correct procedures when taking the cheque.)

(d) An American Express card, with a limit of £1,000.

(e) A store charge card which allows goods to the value of £500 to be bought on credit.

(a) An Access card is a credit-token. In return for payment by Derek, the bank agrees to pay third parties for cash, goods or services supplied. The agreement under which the credit is provided in connection with the credit token is a regulated agreement, and is therefore a credit-token agreement.

(b) A bank cash card is not normally a credit-token, as it neither provides credit nor guarantees payment by the bank to a third party. However, if the card does permit the holder to go overdrawn, then it will be a credit token by virtue of s. 14(4).

(c) A cheque guarantee card is not a credit-token, as is made plain by example 21 in sch. 2 of the Act. The bank is not providing the holder with credit. Nor is the bank paying for goods or services supplied. It is merely guaranteeing that the holder's cheque will be honoured.

(d) An American Express card is a credit-token. In return for payment by the card holder, the bank agrees to pay third parties for cash, goods or services supplied. However, the agreement under which the card is supplied is an exempt agreement, and therefore not a regulated agreement, because the account must be settled by the making of a single payment at the end of each month. (See **8.4.1.3** above.) Therefore the agreement is not a credit-token agreement.

(e) A store card is a credit-token. On production of it, goods or services are provided on credit. The agreement under which the credit is provided in connection with it is a regulated agreement, and is therefore a credit-token agreement.

8.4.5 LINKED TRANSACTIONS

A linked transaction is defined by s. 19 of the 1974 Act. The definition is complex. Essentially a linked transaction is one entered into by the debtor or a relative of the debtor in relation to an actual or prospective regulated agreement (the principal agreement) if one of three conditions is fulfilled. The conditions are:

(a) the transaction is entered into in compliance with a term of the principal agreement, or

(b) the principal agreement is a three-party debtor-creditor-supplier agreement and the transaction is financed, or to be financed, by the principal agreement, or

(c) the creditor, owner or negotiator initiates the transaction by suggesting it to the debtor or hirer who enters into it for a purpose related to the principal agreement.

Section 19(3) provides that: 'A linked transaction entered into before the making of the principal agreement has no effect until such time (if any) as the agreement is made.'

Linked transactions are also important in calculating the total charge for credit and in respect of the cancellation and termination rights of the debtor.

CHAPTER NINE

CONSUMER CREDIT: ADVERTISING, CANVASSING AND ENTRY INTO AN AGREEMENT

9.1 Objectives

By the end of this chapter you should be able to:

- recognise the advertisements to which Part IV of the Consumer Credit Act 1974 applies;

- outline the offences relating to advertisements which are created by Part IV of the Act;

- explain what is meant by canvassing;

- outline the offences relating to canvassing, the sending of circulars to minors and the sending of unsolicited credit-tokens;

- recognise whether negotiations will be 'antecedent negotiations', as defined by s. 56 of the Act;

- explain the circumstances in which a party can withdraw from a prospective agreement, and the effect of such a withdrawal;

- explain the creditor's duty to send copies of the agreement to the debtor;

- explain the creditor's duty to give notice of cancellation rights;

- outline the effect of an agreement being improperly executed;

- explain the circumstances in which an agreement will be cancellable, and how such cancellation can be effected.

9.2 Introduction

Part IV of the Consumer Credit Act 1974 deals with advertising and canvassing. It is an offence to advertise credit other than in the prescribed form, to advertise to provide credit for goods which are not for sale for cash, and to make false or misleading advertisements.

ADVERTISING, CANVASSING AND ENTRY INTO AN AGREEMENT

It is an offence to canvass regulated debtor-creditor agreements off trade premises unless the canvassing is in response to a request made on a previous occasion. It is also an offence to send a circular offering credit to a minor, or to supply a credit-token to a person who has not asked for it in a signed document.

Part V of the Act deals with entry into credit or hire agreements. First we examine the complex definition of antecedent negotiations, the importance of which becomes apparent when we consider cancellable agreements. Then we examine the agreements to which Part V of the Act does not apply, and the right to withdraw from a prospective agreement.

The creditor or owner under a regulated agreement must supply copies of agreements and notice of cancellation rights. If these copies and notices are not served in the correct way the agreement will be improperly executed.

A regulated agreement is cancellable by the debtor or hirer if the antecedent negotiations included oral representations made in the presence of the debtor or hirer and if the agreement was not signed at the creditor or owner's place of business. Linked transactions are also cancelled. If an agreement is cancelled any sums paid or payable by the debtor are repayable or cease to be due. However, any credit actually received by the debtor must be repaid.

9.3 Advertising

Part IV of the 1974 Act, headed 'Seeking Business' deals with advertising and canvassing.

9.3.1 ADVERTISEMENTS TO WHICH PART IV APPLIES

Section 43(1) states that Part IV applies to any advertisement, published for the purposes of a business carried on by the advertiser, indicating that he is willing to provide credit or to enter into an agreement for the bailment or hiring of goods by him. 'Advertisement' is defined very widely by s. 189(1) as including every form of advertising.

Part IV only applies if the advertiser carries on a consumer credit business, or a consumer hire business, or a business in the course of which he provides credit to individuals secured on land (s. 43(2)). The definitions of 'consumer credit business' and 'consumer hire business' provided by s. 189(1) make it plain that making consumer credit agreements or consumer hire agreements does not need to be the main activity of the business. However, s. 189(2) states that 'a person is not to be treated as carrying on a particular type of business merely because occasionally he enters into transactions belonging to a business of that type'. This raises a difficult question as to when a person 'occasionally' makes regulated agreements. Part IV does not apply to advertisements which indicate that credit is available only to companies or to advertisements which indicate that the credit must exceed £25,000 and that either no security is required or the security is to consist of property other than land (s. 43(3)). An advertisement to hire goods is not covered if the advertisement indicates that the advertiser is not willing to enter into a consumer hire agreement (s. 43(4)).

The Consumer Credit (Exempt Advertisements) Order 1985 (SI 1985 No. 621) also excludes:

(a) fixed-sum debtor-creditor-supplier agreements where the number of payments does not exceed four;

(b) advertisements for debtor-creditor agreements where the rate of the total charge for credit does not exceed either 13 per cent or 1 per cent above the current base rate;

(c) advertisements for consumer hire agreements made by public bodies relating to metering equipment;

(d) advertisements to provide credit exceeding £25,000;

(e) certain consumer credit advertisements which have a connection with a country outside the UK.

SAQ 9/1

Does Part IV apply to the following advertisements?

(a) Fred, a retired teacher, advertises his car in the newspaper, stating that he will accept payment in 12 monthly instalments.

(b) Bert, a car dealer, has always sold cars only for cash. Last week he advertised six old cars in the newspaper, indicating that payments for these can be made in 12 monthly instalments. What if Bert places such an advertisement in a newspaper once a month?

(c) A garage regularly advertises that cars can be paid for in three-monthly instalments?

(a) This is not covered as Fred did not make the advertisement in the course of a business.

(b) This first advertisement would appear not to be covered. Bert must be regarded as only occasionally providing credit, and so s. 189(2) means that he is not to be regarded as carrying on a consumer credit business. If Bert placed such an advertisement once a month he would be carrying on a consumer credit business as far as his car dealing business relates to to the providing of credit under regulated consumer credit agreements. Applying the definition of 'consumer credit business' in s. 189(1)).

(c) These advertisements would not be covered as the advertisements indicate that the number of payments does not exceed four.

9.3.2 FORM AND CONTENT OF ADVERTISEMENTS

Section 44 allows the Secretary of State to make regulations about the form and content of advertisements. It is an offence to contravene these regulations. The regulations currently in force are the Consumer Credit (Advertisement) Regulations 1989 (SI 1989 No. 1125). These create three categories of advertisements: simple credit advertisements, intermediate credit advertisements and full credit advertisements. Different rules apply to each category. It is beyond the scope of this book to examine the regulations in any detail. The Regulations specify the exact words which must be used as regards the different categories. Consequently, most people are familiar with some of these. For example, where an advertisement in any of the three categories states that a charge on a debtor's home is or may be required, the advertisement must state: 'Your home is at risk if you do not keep up repayments on a mortgage or other loan secured on it.' As regards each of the three categories of advertisements the APR must be given special prominence. The APR is the Annual Percentage Rate of interest which is calculated according to statutory formulae. The APR can be most easily calculated by reference to consumer credit tables published by HMSO.

9.3.3 OFFENCES RELATING TO ADVERTISEMENTS

Section 45 of the 1974 Act makes it an offence for an advertiser to whom Part IV applies to indicate that he is willing to provide credit under a restricted-use credit agreement relating to goods or services to be supplied by any person, if at the time when the advertisement is published that person is not holding himself out as prepared to sell the goods or services for cash. (Some mail order firms are excluded from this provision.) This offence was deemed to be necessary because if there is no cash price then it is not possible to work out the whether the rate or amount of the credit charge stated is true.

Section 46 makes it an offence for an advertiser to whom Part IV applies to convey information which is false or misleading. Information stating or implying an intention on the advertiser's part is false if the advertiser does not have that intention.

If an advertiser commits an offence under ss. 44–46, then s. 47 makes publishers, devisers and procurers of the advertisement guilty of a like offence.

Section 168 provides advertisers with the defence of due diligence and having taken all reasonable precautions to prevent the commission of the offence. Section 47 provides an additional defence to publishers, devisers of advertisements and to those who procure advertisements if they published the advertisement in the course of a business and did not know and had no reason to suspect that it would be contrary to Part IV of the Act.

Breach of any of the advertising regulations does not affect the validity of any agreement entered into by a consumer (s. 170(1)). Neither of course does it preclude the possibility of an action by the debtor for misrepresentation or breach of contract.

SAQ 9/2

Acme Ltd advertises that it will provide restricted-use credit so that consumers can buy cars from Dodgy Motors Ltd. In what circumstances will Acme commit an offence under s. 45?

Acme would commit an offence if at the time of the advertisement Dodgy Motors Ltd were not holding themselves out as prepared to sell the cars to which the advertisement related for cash.

9.4 Canvassing

ACTIVITY 9/1

Section 48 defines canvassing off trade premises. *Cases and Materials* (9.1) and answer the following questions:

(a) Does s. 48 apply only to regulated agreements?

(b) What, essentially, does canvassing mean?

(c) **In what circumstances will oral representations made to a consumer not amount to canvassing?**

(a) Section 48 does apply only to regulated agreements.

(b) Canvassing means the soliciting of an individual (the consumer), off trade premises, to enter into a regulated agreement by making oral representations to the consumer or to someone else.

(c) Oral representations will not amount to canvassing if: (a) they are made in response to a request made on a previous occasion; or (b) the consumer is canvassed at a place where business is carried on by the creditor or owner, or the supplier, or the canvasser or the consumer.

Obviously the debtor's home would be 'off trade premises' but the debtor's place of business, like the place of business of the creditor, owner or canvasser would all be regarded as trade premises.

Section 49 creates two offences. First, it is an offence to canvass debtor-creditor agreements off trade premises. Second, it is an offence to solicit entry into a debtor-creditor agreement during a visit requested by the debtor on a previous occasion if the request by the debtor was not in writing and signed. It is not an offence to canvass a debtor-creditor-supplier agreement, or a consumer hire agreement. However, a canvasser of a debtor-creditor-supplier agreement will need a licence (s. 23(3)), and the debtor will be able to get out of the agreement under the 'cooling-off period', which is considered below at **9.5.7**.

Although s. 49 creates two offences, it does not affect the validity of an agreement which was canvassed or solicited. (s. 170(1)).

9.4.1 CIRCULARS TO MINORS

Section 50 of the 1974 Act creates an offence of sending circulars to minors. Section 50(1) defines a circular as any document, sent to a minor with a view to financial gain, inviting the minor to borrow money, hire goods, obtain goods or services on credit or apply for information or advice on borrowing money, obtaining credit or hiring goods. The offence can be committed even if the circular invites the minor to make an unregulated agreement. The offence relates only to the sending of documents, it will not be committed if the circular was delivered personally.

The offence is one of strict liability. However, it is a defence for the person charged to prove that he did not know, and had no reasonable grounds to suspect, that the person to whom the document was sent was a minor (s. 50(2)). However, this defence is not available if the document was received by a minor at a school or other educational establishment for minors and the person sending the document knew or suspected that it was such an establishment (s. 50(3)). This section applies to all forms of credit. Breach of the section does not automatically make an agreement which the minor subsequently enters into unenforceable (s. 170(1))).

9.4.2 PROHIBITION OF UNSOLICITED CREDIT-TOKENS

Section 51 of the 1974 Act makes it an offence to supply a credit-token to a person who has not asked for it in a signed document. If the credit token agreement is a small debtor-creditor-supplier agreement the request does not need to be in a signed document (s. 51(2)). The offence is not committed by the renewal or replacement of previously accepted credit tokens, nor if the credit-token is supplied under a credit-token agreement previously made (s. 51(3)).

ADVERTISING, CANVASSING AND ENTRY INTO AN AGREEMENT

If s. 51 is breached, the credit-token agreement will not be automatically unenforceable (s. 170(1)). However, the agreement will be improperly executed. The effect of this is considered below at **9.5.5**.

9.4.3 QUOTATIONS

Section 52 of the 1974 Act allows regulations about quotations to be made. The Consumer Credit (Quotations) Regulations 1989 (SI 1989 No. 1126) are the regulations currently in force. These set out the form and content of quotations, giving particular importance to the prominence to be afforded to the APR. Quotations relating to credit must display the warning, 'Be sure you can afford the repayments before entering into a credit agreement'. It is an offence to breach these regulations but the validity of any agreement entered into as a consequence will not be affected (s. 170(1)).

Section 53 allows regulations to be made requiring those who carry on a credit business to display information about the business. No such regulations have yet been made.

9.5 Entry into Credit or Hire Agreements

Part V of the 1974 Act deals with entry into credit or hire agreements. It begins with several preliminary matters, then deals with the making of the agreement, before going on to give the debtor or hirer the right to cancel certain agreements within the cooling-off period. Finally, there are exclusions of certain agreements from Part V.

9.5.1 PRELIMINARY MATTERS

The preliminary matters specified are disclosure of information, antecedent negotiations, withdrawal from prospective agreements, withdrawal from prospective land mortgages and agreements to enter future agreements. Section 55 of the 1974 Act gives the power to make regulations requiring specified information to be disclosed before a regulated agreement is made. As yet no such regulations have been made and so we begin by looking at the rules on antecedent negotiations.

9.5.1.1 Antecedent negotiations

Section 56 of the 1974 Act defines antecedent negotiations. These are important in two ways. First, they may be made by a negotiator as the agent of a creditor. This statutory agency is considered in the following chapter. Second, they are important in the context of cancellable agreements. (Which are considered below at **9.5.6**.)

Antecedent negotiations are defined by s. 56(1) as:

> ... any negotiations with the debtor or hirer—
> (a)   conducted by the creditor or owner in relation to the making of any regulated agreement, or
> (b)   conducted by a credit-broker in relation to goods sold or proposed to be sold by the credit-broker to the creditor before forming the subject-matter of a debtor-creditor-supplier agreement within section 12(a), or
> (c)   conducted by the supplier in relation to a transaction financed or proposed to be financed by a debtor-creditor-supplier agreement within section 12(b) or (c),
> and 'negotiator' means the person by whom negotiations are so conducted with the debtor or hirer.

Section 56(1)(a) is relatively straightforward. There are only two parties involved; the creditor (or owner) and the debtor, and the only requirement is that the agreement is a regulated agreement. (Section 56(1)(a) has significance only in relation to cancellable agreements. It does not play a part in the statutory agency created by s. 56(2).)

A credit broker introduces individuals desiring to obtain credit to those who carry on a consumer credit or a consumer hire business (ss. 189(1) and 145(2)). Section 56(1)(b) makes the negotiations of credit brokers antecedent negotiations where the credit broker sells or proposes to sell the goods to the creditor, so that the goods can become the subject of a creditor-debtor-supplier agreement within s. 12(a). An example of negotiations under s. 56(1)(b) would be the typical hire-purchase contract where the debtor, having conducted negotiations with the dealer (the credit broker), takes the goods from a finance company introduced by the dealer.

Section 56(1)(c) would apply where the supplier makes the negotiations and where the transaction is to be financed by a debtor-creditor-supplier agreement within s. 12(b) or (c). (You should remember from **Chapter 8** that s. 12(b) and (c) cover loans to the debtor (or payments to the supplier at the debtor's request) made under a pre-existing arrangement, or in contemplation of future arrangements, between the creditor and the supplier.

Antecedent negotiations begin when the negotiator and the debtor or hirer first enter into communication (including communication by advertisement) and include any representations made by the negotiator to the debtor or hirer and other dealings between them (s. 56(4)).

ACTIVITY 9/2

Consider whether the following examples constitute antecedent negotiations. If you decide that they are, indicate whether they are within s. 56(1)(a), (b) or (c).

(a) Representations are made about goods in a poster displayed by a shopkeeper near the goods, the goods being selected by a customer who has read the poster and then sold by the shopkeeper to a finance company introduced by him (with whom he has a business relationship). The goods are disposed of by the finance company to the customer under a regulated hire-purchase agreement.

(b) Discussions take place between a shopkeeper and a customer about goods the customer wishes to buy using a credit-card issued by the D Bank under a regulated agreement.

(c) Correspondence passes between an employee of a money-lending company (writing on behalf of the company) and an individual about the terms on which the company would grant him a loan under a regulated agreement.

(d) Discussions take place and correspondence passes between a secondhand car dealer and a customer about a car, which is then sold by the dealer to the customer under a regulated conditional sale agreement. Subsequently, on a revocation of that agreement by consent, the car is resold by the dealer to a finance company introduced by him (with whom he has a business relationship), who in turn dispose of it to the same customer under a regulated hire-purchase agreement.

ADVERTISING, CANVASSING AND ENTRY INTO AN AGREEMENT

(a) The representations in the poster constitute antecedent negotiations falling within s. 56(1)(b), the shopkeeper being the credit-broker and negotiator and the finance company being the creditor.

(b) The discussions constitute antecedent negotiations falling within s. 56(1)(c), the shopkeeper being the supplier and negotiator and the D Bank being the creditor.

(c) The correspondence constitutes antecedent negotiations falling within s. 56(1)(a), the moneylending company being both creditor and negotiator.

(d) The discussions and correspondence constitute antecedent negotiations in relation to both the conditional sale agreement and the hire-purchase agreement. They fall under s. 56(1)(a) in relation to the conditional sale agreement, the dealer being the creditor and the negotiator. In relation to the hire-purchase agreement they fall within s. 56(1)(b), the dealer continuing to be treated as the negotiator but the finance company now being the creditor.

These examples are in fact given in Part II of sch. 2 of the 1974 Act. Example (a) being Example 2 under the Act, Example (b) being Example 3, Example (c) being Example 1 and Example (d) being Example 4.

9.5.1.2 Agreements excluded from Part V

Section 74 excludes certain agreements from Part V of the 1974 Act, but these exclusions do not apply to statutory agency under s. 56. Excluded from all of Part V, except s. 56, are:

(a) Non-commercial agreements (s. 74(1)(a)). (In **Chapter 8** we saw that a non-commercial agreement is one made otherwise than in the course of a business.)

(b) Debtor-creditor agreements enabling the debtor to overdraw on a current account from specified organisations such as banks (s. 74(1)(b)).

(c) Small debtor-creditor-supplier agreements for restricted-use credit (s. 74(2)). (In **Chapter 8** we saw that a small agreement is one involving credit of less than £50, or involving hire payments of less than £50.) However, if any term of a small agreement is in writing then that term is not exempt from regulations on form and content under s. 60 (s. 74(4)).

9.5.1.3 Withdrawal from prospective agreements

In the case of a prospective regulated agreement, s. 57 extends the common law right to withdraw from an agreement before the offer and acceptance have been concluded. (Where the debtor signs first, the acceptance by the creditor will only be effective when notice of it is communicated to the debtor, subject to the postal rule.) If a party does withdraw from an agreement it is cancelled and so are any linked transactions or any other things done in anticipation of the making of the agreement (s. 57(1)). A written or oral withdrawal notice indicating an intention to withdraw, however expressed, may be given to the creditor or owner at any time before the agreement is concluded (s. 57(2)). The notice may be given to a credit-broker or supplier who acted as a negotiator, or to any other person who negotiated the agreement in the course of a business (s. 57(3)). Once the notice has been given the agreement and any linked transactions are cancelled. Section 57 applies to all agreements, whether cancellable agreements or not (s. 57(4)).

9.5.1.4 Opportunity for withdrawal from prospective land mortgages

Section 58 requires that at least seven days before a debtor is asked to sign an unexecuted regulated agreement secured on land, an advance copy of the agreement must be sent to him. This advance copy must include details in the prescribed form of the right to withdraw from the agreement. If the creditor does not do this then the agreement will be unexecuted and enforceable only by court order (s. 61(2)). This section does not apply to bridging loans or to restricted-use credit agreements to finance the purchase of the mortgaged land (s. 58(2)). It can therefore be seen that the section is aimed primarily at second mortgages. If the requirements of s. 58 are not met then the agreement is an unexecuted agreement and will only be enforceable by court order.

9.5.1.5 Agreements to enter future agreements

Section 59 makes such agreements, and any linked agreements, void.

9.5.2 MAKING THE AGREEMENT

Section 60 of the 1974 Act requires the Secretary of State to make regulations as to the form and content of regulated agreements. In particular the amount of credit and the total charge for credit, the APR, the number of payments and their timing, and the protection and remedies available under the Act must be included. The Consumer Credit (Agreements) Regulations 1983 (SI 1983 No. 1553) are the regulations currently in force. They set out in great detail, as regards each different type of agreement, the information which must be contained in relevant documents, the precise form of statements on debtor's rights which must be included and the precise forms of signature boxes which must be included in the various agreements. The language used in the statement of debtor's rights and in signature boxes is clear and simple. For example, the signature box on a conditional sale relating to goods must take the following form.

> This is a Conditional Sale Agreement regulated by the Consumer Credit Act 1974. Sign it only if you want to be legally bound by its terms.
>
> Signature(s)
> of Debtor(s)
>
> Date(s) of signature(s)
>
> The goods will not become your property until you have made payments. You must not sell them before then.

If s. 58(1) applies, the following statement of rights must be included:

> YOUR RIGHTS
>
> Under the Consumer Credit Act 1974, the creditor should have given you a copy of this agreement at least seven days ago to allow you time to consider whether to go ahead. If he did not, the agreement cannot be enforced without a court order.

A regulated agreement is not properly executed unless a document conforming to the regulations is signed by both the debtor or hirer and the creditor or owner. The debtor or hirer must sign personally but an agent can sign on behalf of the creditor or owner. The document must contain all the terms of the agreement other than the implied terms, and must be legible (s. 61(1)).

ADVERTISING, CANVASSING AND ENTRY INTO AN AGREEMENT

9.5.3 DUTY TO SUPPLY COPIES OF AGREEMENTS

ACTIVITY 9/3

The 1974 Act distinguishes here between executed and unexecuted agreements. What do you think the term 'executed agreement' means? Write down your thoughts and then check s. 189(1) in *Cases and Materials* (9.1) to see if you were correct.

You may have guessed that an executed agreement is defined as a document embodying the terms of a regulated agreement signed by or on behalf of the parties. Therefore, until both parties have signed the agreement it is unexecuted, once both have signed it is executed.

Section 62(1) deals with the situation where a document which has not been signed by the creditor is presented personally to the debtor or hirer for signature. When the debtor or hirer signs the document does not become executed, as the creditor has not yet signed. Section 62(1) requires that if such an unexecuted document is presented personally to the debtor or hirer for signature he must there and then be given a copy of the agreement and of any document referred to in it. Within seven days of the making of the agreement the creditor or owner must send a copy of the executed agreement, and of any other document referred to in it, to the debtor or hirer (s. 63(2)). The agreement will be made when the debtor or hirer has notice that the creditor or owner has signed it. If this notice is sent by post then the postal rule will apply.

If the unexecuted document is sent to the debtor, and it has not yet been signed by the creditor, then a copy of the agreement and of any document referred to in it, must also be sent (s. 62(2)). Within seven days of the making of the agreement the creditor or owner must send a copy of the executed agreement, and of any other document referred to in it, to the debtor or hirer (s. 63(2)).

If the creditor has already signed a document which is presented personally to the debtor for signature then the debtor must there and then be given a copy of the executed agreement and any documents referred to in it (s. 63(1)). There is no need to send another copy later (s. 63(2)(a)). If the document was sent to the debtor for signature, having already been signed by the creditor, then a copy of the executed agreement and of any document referred to in it must be sent to the debtor at the same time (s. 62(2)). Again, there is no need to send another copy later. If any of these requirements are not met then the agreement is not properly executed (ss. 62(3) and 63(5)). An improperly executed agreement is not enforceable without a court order, and may not be enforceable at all.

The purpose of ss. 62 and 63 is obvious enough. If the debtor were not provided with a copy then once he had returned the agreement he would not be able to give proper consideration to revoking the agreement, and would not know what the terms of the agreement, particularly the cancellation rights, were. (See also the diagram below.)

230 ADVERTISING, CANVASSING AND ENTRY INTO AN AGREEMENT

Copies of Agreements

Situation	Initial copy	Further copy
Unsigned agreement presented personally to debtor or hirer for signature	A copy of the agreement, and of any document referred to in it, must there and then be delivered to debtor or hirer (s. 62(1)).	Within seven days of the debtor receiving notice of the creditor having signed, a copy of the agreement, and of any document referred to in it, must be sent to the debtor or hirer (s. 63(2)).
Unsigned agreement sent to debtor or hirer for signature	A copy of the agreement, and of any documents referred to in it, must be sent at the same time (s. 62(2)).	Within seven days of the debtor receiving notice of the creditor having signed, a copy of the agreement, and of any document referred to in it, must be sent to the debtor or hirer (s. 63(2)).
An agreement signed by the creditor is presented personally for debtor's or hirer's signature	A copy of the executed agreement, and of any document referred to in it must there and then be delivered to the debtor or hirer (s. 63(1)).	No further copy need be sent (s. 63(2)(a)).
An agreement signed by the creditor is sent for debtor's or hirer's signature	A copy of the executed agreement, and of any document referred to in it, must be sent at the same time (s. 62(2)).	No further copy need be sent (s. 63(2)(b)).

If these rules are not complied with the agreement is improperly executed (ss. 62(3) and 63(5)).

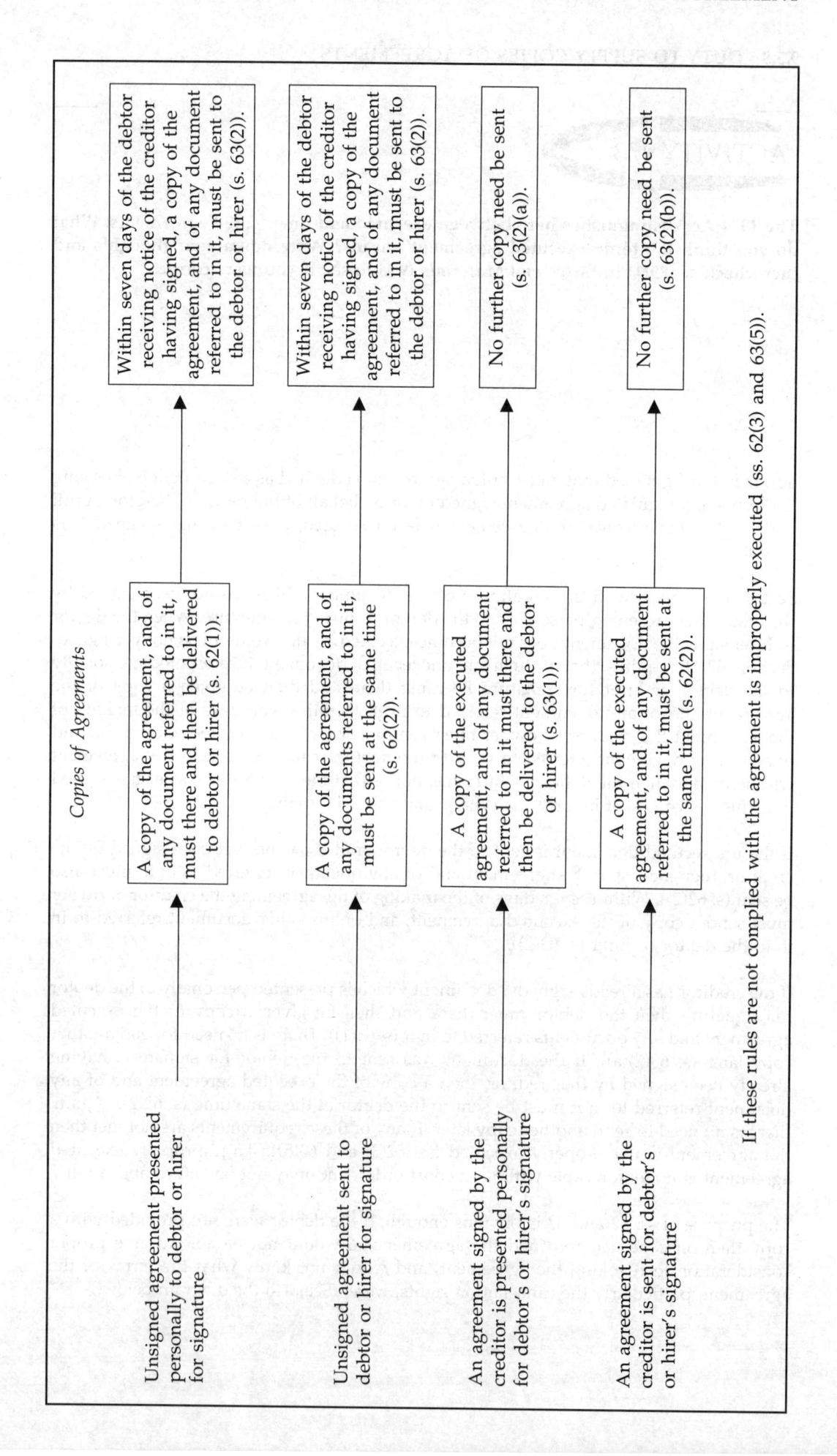

9.5.4 DUTY TO GIVE NOTICE OF CANCELLATION RIGHTS

In the case of a cancellable agreement, a notice in the prescribed form indicating the right of the debtor or hirer to cancel the agreement, how and when that right is exercisable, and the name and address of a person to whom notice of cancellation must be given must be included in every copy which is required to be given or sent to the debtor or hirer under ss. 62 or 63 (s. 64(1)(a)). Such a notice must also be sent by post to the debtor or hirer within seven days of making the agreement unless s. 62(3) applies (s. 64(1)(b)). If s. 64(1) is not complied with then the agreement is not enforceable even by court order (s. 127(4)(b)).

9.5.5 THE CONSEQUENCES OF IMPROPER EXECUTION

The 1974 Act distinguishes between those agreements which can only be enforced by court order and those which cannot be enforced at all.

If regulated agreement is improperly executed it can only be enforced by order of the court (s. 65(1)). In an application to enforce an improperly-executed agreement the court shall dismiss the application if, and only if, it considers it just to do so, having regard to the prejudice caused to any person by the contravention in question, and the degree of culpability for it, and the court's powers to discharge or reduce any sum payable by the debtor, and its power to impose conditions and vary agreements (s. 127(1)).

In the following circumstances an agreement cannot be enforced at all, not even by order of the court:

(a) if the agreement, or a document containing all of the prescribed terms, has not been signed by the debtor or hirer (s. 127(3));

(b) the document signed by the debtor did not contain all of the prescribed terms (s. 127(3));

(c) if, in the case of a cancellable agreement, the provisions of ss. 62 and 63 were not complied with and the debtor was not given a copy of the executed agreement before the commencement of proceedings. If the debtor is given a copy late, but before the commencement of proceedings, then the cooling-of period begins at the time when the copy was received (s. 127(4)(a));

(d) if s. 64(1) was not complied with. (That is to say where the debtor was not sent notice of cancellation rights in a copy, under ss. 62 and 63, or was not sent a separate notice of cancellation rights when such a notice was required. In such a case the relevant notice cannot be sent late and the agreement is totally unenforceable (s. 127(4)(b)).)

9.5.6 CANCELLABLE AGREEMENTS

Section 67 provides that a regulated agreement may be cancelled by the debtor or hirer if the antecedent negotiations included oral representations made in the presence of the debtor or hirer by an individual acting on behalf of the negotiator. We examined the meaning of antecedent negotiations earlier in this chapter. Here the negotiations must include oral representations, that is to say that there must have been face to face negotiations. An agreement cannot be cancelled under s. 67 if it is:

(a) secured on land, or a bridging loan to purchase land or a restricted-use credit agreement to finance the purchase of land; or

(b) if the creditor signed the unexecuted agreement at the business premises of the creditor or hirer, or a linked party or the negotiator. (Notice that it is where the debtor signed, rather than where the negotiations took place that is important here.)

ACTIVITY 9/4

Read s. 67 of the 1974 Act in *Cases and Materials* (9.1). Then look back to Activity 9/2, example (d). If the negotiations had taken place entirely by telephone, would the agreement be cancellable?

Example 4 in sch. 2 of the 1974 Act makes it plain that the agreement would not be cancellable as the oral representations would not have been made 'in the presence of the debtor or hirer'.

Any term which seeks to restrict the debtor's right to cancel is void (s. 173(1)).

9.5.7 THE COOLING-OFF PERIOD

Section 68 of the 1974 Act sets out the time limits within which a cancellable agreement can be cancelled. The debtor or hirer must serve notice of cancellation between his signing of the unexecuted agreement and the end of the fifth day following the day on which he received a copy under s. 63(2) or statutory notice of cancellation rights under s. 64(1)(b), or if s. 64(1)(b) does not apply (because of regulations made by the Director under s. 64(4)), the end of the fourteenth day following the day on which he signed the unexecuted agreement.

Earlier in this chapter we examined the circumstances in which s. 63(2) imposes a duty to send a copy of an unexecuted agreement to the debtor or hirer within seven days of making the agreement. (When the debtor or hirer's signature did not make the agreement an executed agreement because the creditor had yet to sign.) Section 64(1)(b) requires that where the agreement is a cancellable agreement, and where s. 63(2) does not apply, notice of cancellation rights must be sent to the debtor or hirer within seven days. What is important for the purposes of the cooling-off period is when the debtor or hirer *received* the copy or notice. If the copy or notice is sent late then the cooling-off period does not begin until they are received.

The notice can be served on the creditor or owner, the person specified in the notice under s. 64(1), the agent of the owner or creditor, or a person who carried on antecedent negotiations on behalf of the creditor or owner in the course of a business carried on by him (s. 69(1)). The notice must be in writing (s. 189(1)) and can be expressed in any way as long as it indicates an intention to withdraw from the agreement (s. 69(1)).

If a notice of cancellation is sent by post, it is deemed to be effective at the time of posting and this is the case even if the notice is lost in the post (s. 69(7)).

Cancellation has the effect of meaning that the agreement shall be treated as an agreement which was never entered into (s. 69(4)).

ADVERTISING, CANVASSING AND ENTRY INTO AN AGREEMENT

SAQ 9/3

(a) Alice visits Acme Superstore and enters into a regulated hire-purchase agreement after listening to a salesman. She signs an unexecuted agreement in the shop. What copies or notices must Alice be supplied with? Is there a cooling-off period?

(b) Alan visits Acme Superstore and listens to a salesman extolling the virtues of the goods on sale there. Alan says that he is interested in buying but has little money. Next week Alan phones to say he would buy if he was given credit. Alan is sent a copy of an unexecuted conditional sale agreement. Alan signs this and returns it to Acme. What copies or notices must Alan be supplied with? Is there a cooling-off period?

(c) Alan sends notice of cancellation within five days of receiving a copy of the executed agreement. This notice is lost in the post. What is the effect of this?

(a) Under s. 62(1), when Alice signs the agreement she must there and then be given a copy of it and of any other document referred to in it. Under s. 63(2) Alice must be sent a copy of the executed agreement, and of any other document referred to in it, within seven days of the making of the agreement, that is to say within seven days of having notice that the creditor has signed. There will be no cooling-off period as the agreement is not a cancellable agreement. (It was signed at Acme's place of business.)

(b) Along with the unexecuted agreement, a copy of it and of any document referred to in it must have been sent to Alan at the same time (s. 62(2)). Under s. 63(2) Alan must be sent a copy of the executed agreement, and of any other document referred to in it, within seven days of the making of the agreement. This is a cancellable agreement. The oral representations may have been made at Acme's place of business, but Alan signed the unexecuted agreement at home.

(c) The notice of cancellation would be deemed to have been served on Acme at the time of posting (s. 69(7)). Therefore the regulated agreement would be cancelled.

9.5.8 THE EFFECT OF CANCELLATION

If a regulated agreement, or any linked agreement is cancelled the effect is as follows:

(a) Any sum paid by the debtor or hirer under or in contemplation of the agreement becomes repayable. This includes any item in the total charge for credit (s. 70(1)(a)).

(b) Any sum payable by the creditor or hirer ceases to be due. This includes any item on the total charge for credit which would have been payable had the agreement not been cancelled (s. 70(1)(b)).

(c) In the case of a debtor-creditor-supplier agreement falling within s. 12(b), any sum paid on the debtor's behalf by the creditor to the supplier becomes repayable to the creditor (s. 70(1)(c)).

(d) The debtor has a lien on any goods which he has in his possession under the terms of the agreement for any sum repayable under s. 70(1) (s. 70(2)).

(e) A sum repayable under s. 70(1) is repayable by the person to whom it was originally paid. However, in the case of a debtor-creditor-supplier agreement within s. 12(b) the creditor and the supplier are jointly and severally liable to repay the sum (s. 70(3)).

(f) Linked agreements are also cancelled (s. 69(1)). However, if the agreement was a debtor-creditor-supplier agreement for restricted-use credit to supply the doing of work or supply of goods to meet an emergency, or the agreement was to supply goods which have at the time of cancellation become incorporated into land or into any thing not supplied under the agreement or under any linked transaction, the debtor will only have to pay the cash price for the goods and will not have any liability in relation to credit or other charges (s. 69(2)).

(g) If the total charge for credit included a fee or commission payable to a broker, the credit broker can retain £5, but must return any excess (s. 70(6)).

(h) When a regulated agreement is cancelled, other than a debtor-creditor-supplier agreement for restricted-use credit, the agreement shall continue in force so far as it relates to repayment of credit and payment of interest (s. 71(1)). (If the agreement had been for debtor-creditor-supplier agreement for restricted-use credit then the creditor would never have received any money and obviously therefore would not have to repay anything to the creditor.) However, if the debtor repays all or some of the credit either within one month of service of the notice of cancellation, or before the date on which the first instalment is due, no interest is payable on the amount repaid (s. 71(2)). If the whole of the credit repayable is not repaid before the first instalment, the debtor only has to repay the amount outstanding on receipt of a request in writing in the prescribed form, signed by the creditor or on his behalf, stating the amounts of the remaining instalments, but excluding any sum other than principal and interest (s. 71(3)).

(i) Any person possessing goods acquired under a cancelled agreement has a duty to restore the goods to the other party, and until this is done to retain possession of the goods and to take reasonable care of them (s. 72(4)). The possessor of goods has a duty to make them available at his own premises for collection rather than to return them. The duty to take reasonable care of the goods ends after 21 days if a written request for their return is not received within that period (s. 72(8)). Section 72 does not apply to perishable goods, goods which you would expect to be consumed and which have been consumed, goods supplied to meet an emergency, or goods which before cancellation have become incorporated into land or into some thing not comprised in the agreement. (Section 72(9).)

(j) If the debtor or hirer gave goods in part exchange then these must be returned to him in substantially the same condition as that in which they were taken within ten days of cancellation. If this is not done, the debtor or hirer can recover from the negotiator the amount of the part-exchange allowance given (s. 73(2)). In the case of a debtor-creditor-supplier agreement within s. 12(b) the creditor and the negotiator are jointly and severally liable to pay this sum (s. 73(3)). Until the debtor receives part-exchanged goods or the amount allowed in part-exchange, he will have a lien on the goods supplied under the cancelled agreement (s. 73(5)). The debtor will therefore be able to keep possession of the goods until he has received all that he is due.

(k) Any term which attempts to evade the provisions protecting the debtor or hirer is void (s. 173(1)).

ADVERTISING, CANVASSING AND ENTRY INTO AN AGREEMENT

9.6 Summary

This chapter covered the following topics:

- It is an offence to publish an advertisement offering credit other than in the form set out in regulations made by the Secretary of State. It is also an offence to publish a false or misleading advertisement offering credit, or to advertise that goods or services are available on credit where they are not held out as available for cash.

- It is an offence to canvass debtor-creditor agreements off trade premises. It is also an offence to solicit entry into a debtor-creditor agreement during a visit requested by the debtor if the request by the debtor was not in writing and signed. Canvassing means the soliciting of a consumer to enter into a regulated agreement, off trade premises, by making oral representations to the consumer or to someone else.

- It is an offence to send a circular offering credit to a minor. It is also an offence to give a person a credit-token if he has not asked for it in a signed document.

- A party can withdraw from a prospective agreement before it has been concluded.

- When a regulated agreement is made the creditor will have to send the debtor a copy of the executed agreement. If the agreement is a cancellable agreement the creditor must also send a copy of cancellation rights. Failure to do either of these things will mean that the agreement is not properly executed.

- A regulated agreement is cancellable by the debtor if the antecedent negotiations included oral representations made in the presence of the debtor by an individual acting on behalf of the negotiator, and if the agreement was not signed at the creditor's place of business.

- Cancellation must be done within five days of the debtor receiving the copy of the executed agreement or the notice of cancellation rights. If an agreement is cancelled, linked transactions are also cancelled and the debtor is entitled to repayment of any money already paid.

9.7 End of Chapter Assessment Question

A representative of Shady Finance Ltd knocks on the door of Derek's house and tries to persuade Derek to take out a loan. Derek replies that he is not interested. Later however Derek thinks that he might like to buy a new car. He therefore finds the salesman's card and telephones asking for another visit. During this second visit Derek is persuaded to take out a loan of £4,000, repayable over three years at 42 per cent APR. Derek now wishes to cancel this agreement.

Explain how the Consumer Credit Act 1974 might help Derek.

See *Cases and Materials* (9.3) for an outline answer.

CHAPTER TEN

MATTERS ARISING DURING CURRENCY OF CREDIT OR HIRE AGREEMENTS

10.1 Objectives

By the end of this chapter you should be able to:

- recognise the circumstances in which a negotiator of a credit agreement will be regarded as the agent of the creditor;

- explain the circumstances in which a creditor will be made liable for a supplier's breaches of contract and misrepresentations;

- describe the circumstances in which a creditor must give notice before taking action under a regulated agreement against a debtor who is not in breach of the agreement;

- outline the protection conferred on a debtor whose credit facility has been misused.

10.2 Introduction

In this chapter we examine matters arising under a regulated agreement. Some of these matters are considerably more important than others. The two most important are the statutory agency set out in s. 56(2) and the creditor's liability for breaches by a supplier under s. 75(1) of the Consumer Credit Act 1974.

Section 56(2) provides that where, in debtor-creditor-supplier agreements, antecedent negotiations are conducted by a credit-broker or a supplier these negotiations are conducted as agent of the creditor. Therefore if the antecedent negotiations made by the credit-broker or supplier amount to a misrepresentation or become a breached term of the contract the creditor is liable for them.

If the debtor under a debtor-creditor-supplier agreement has any claim for breach of contract or misrepresentation against the supplier, then s. 75(1) gives the debtor a like claim against the creditor. This is not the case in respect of any single item costing less than £100 or more than £30,000. A creditor made liable under s. 75(1) has an indemnity against the supplier.

A creditor has a duty to give the debtor seven days' notice before taking certain types of action under a regulated agreement. The creditor also has a duty to give a debtor copies of a regulated agreement or statements of account, on payment of a small fee.

If a credit token is misused by a third party the debtor is given protection against liability to the creditor, as long as the debtor takes certain precautions.

10.3 Liability of Creditor for Breaches by Supplier

10.3.1 ANTECEDENT NEGOTIATIONS MADE AS AGENT OF CREDITOR

At common law a creditor will not have any liability for the actions of a supplier unless the supplier was the agent of the creditor. Section 56(2) creates a statutory agency, making a credit-broker or supplier the agent of a creditor in certain circumstances.

In **Chapter 9** we examined s. 56(1), which defines antecedent negotiations. Section 56(2) states that: 'Negotiations with the debtor in a case falling within subsection (1)(b) or (c) shall be deemed to be conducted by the negotiator in the capacity of agent of the creditor as well as in his actual capacity.'

If you look again at s. 56(1), you will see that s. 56(1)(a) deals with the situation where there are only two parties, the creditor (or owner) and the debtor (or hirer). There is no need for s. 56(2) in these situations. The creditor or owner is obviously liable for antecedent negotiations made by himself or by his employees.

Section 56(1)(b) makes negotiations conducted by a credit broker with a debtor antecedent negotiations where they relate to goods sold or proposed to be sold by the credit-broker to the creditor before forming the subject matter a creditor-debtor-supplier agreement within s. 12(a). A typical case of this would be one where the dealer in goods sells the goods to a finance company which then arranges a contract of hire-purchase or conditional sale with a debtor, who was introduced to the finance company by the dealer.

Section 56(1)(c) makes negotiations antecedent negotiations if they were conducted with the debtor by the supplier in relation to a transaction financed or proposed to be financed by a debtor-creditor-supplier agreement within s. 12(b) or (c). Typical examples would be a supplier accepting payment for goods by a credit card issued by a third party, or a motor dealer selling a car to a debtor for cash which the debtor had taken on loan from a finance company introduced by the motor dealer.

Any liability of the creditor under s. 56(2) is in addition to any personal liability of the credit-broker or supplier.

Section 56(2) does not apply to contracts of hire. Nor does it apply to debtor-credit agreements, even if a credit-broker conducted negotiations for the creditor. (Such a credit-broker would be the agent of the creditor at common law.) Nor does s. 56(2) apply to cases where there is no existing or contemplated connection between negotiator and creditor. It does apply to debtor-creditor-supplier agreements where the legal supplier and the creditor are the same person, and to agreements where there is an existing or contemplated future arrangement between negotiator and creditor.

SAQ 10/1

Deidre wants to buy a car from Dodgy Motors Ltd because Dodgy's salesman has told her than the car is suitable for towing a caravan. Deidre cannot afford the car, so the salesman arranges credit with a finance company. As soon as Deidre takes possession of the car she discovers that it is quite unsuitable for towing a caravan. Dodgy Motors Ltd is in liquidation. How can s. 56 help Deidre?

Dodgy Motors Ltd conducted antecedent negotiations with Deidre (within s. 56(1)(c)). Therefore the statements made by Dodgy's salesman were made as agent of the finance company in addition to having been made as agent of Dodgy Motors. No effective remedy is likely to be gained against Dodgy Motors, as they are in liquidation. However, as Dodgy's statements will be regarded as having been made as agents of the finance company, the finance company will therefore assume liability for them. (The liability will arise in contract if the description was a term of the contract, or in fraudulent or negligent misrepresentation if the description did not amount to a term. The definition of 'representation' under the 1974 Act makes it plain that statements made by the negotiator which become terms of the contract can be included.)

It can be seen that s. 56 can be extremely useful to a debtor who might otherwise be left with no remedy in respect of representations made. Furthermore, any agreement which purports to avoid this statutory agency is void (s. 56(3)). It should be noticed however that antecedent negotiations must relate to the goods sold or proposed to be sold by the credit-broker or to the transaction financed or to be financed by a s. 12(b) or (c) debtor-creditor-supplier agreement. It should also be noticed that s. 56(2) only applies to regulated agreements (because the debtor-creditor-supplier agreements set out in s. 12(b) and (c) are defined as being regulated agreements.)

10.3.2 LIABILITY OF CREDITOR FOR BREACHES BY SUPPLIER

Section 75 provides additional protection to a debtor where the creditor and the legal supplier are not the same person. (It does not therefore apply to hire-purchase, where the creditor and the legal supplier are the same person.) In cases where s. 75 applies, a debtor who has a claim for breach of contract or misrepresentation against the supplier has a like claim against the creditor. Along with s. 56, this section can provide important protection where a supplier has gone into liquidation. Many dealers in cars and other goods are financially flimsy. Finance companies are much more likely to be financially sound, and any finance company to which the debtor is still making payments must necessarily still be in existence.

Section 75(1) of the 1974 Act states:

> If the debtor under a debtor-creditor-supplier agreement falling within section 12(b) or (c) has, in relation to a transaction financed by the agreement, any claim against the supplier in respect of a misrepresentation or breach of contract, he shall have a like claim against the creditor, who, with the supplier, shall accordingly be jointly and severally liable to the debtor.

(As we have just seen, when examining s. 56(2) above, s. 12(b) and (c) encompass debtor-creditor-supplier agreements where the supplier and the creditor are not the same person, but have an existing or contemplated connection.)

Section 75(3) of the 1974 Act states:

> Subsection (1) does not apply to a claim—
> (a) under a non-commercial agreement, or
> (b) so far as the claim relates to any single item to which the supplier has attached a price not exceeding [£100] or more than [£30,000].

The points to note about s. 75 are as follows:

(a) The section only applies where the creditor and the supplier are different persons. So it only applies where the credit is given as a loan to the debtor, so that the debtor can finance a transaction with a supplier. It does not therefore apply where a finance company supplies goods on hire-purchase. (However, as we have seen in this chapter, s. 56(2) will help the debtor if the dealer made antecedent negotiations and, as we saw in **Chapter 4**, the Supply of Goods (Implied Terms) Act 1973 will impose liability directly on the finance company if it breaches a term as to correspondence with description.)

(b) The section only applies to regulated agreements (because the debtor-creditor-supplier agreements set out in s. 12(b) and (c) are defined as being regulated agreements).

(c) Section 75 makes the creditor liable for the misrepresentations and breaches of contract of the supplier. If the supplier has no liability for breach of contract or misrepresentation, perhaps because of an effective exclusion clause, then the creditor will have no such liability under s. 75.

(d) The creditor is jointly and severally liable. The debtor can sue the supplier or the creditor or both. Gaining judgment against one does not prevent an action from being taken against the other (Civil Liability (Contribution) Act 1978, s. 3).

(e) Liability under s. 75 arises only where the transaction as regards which the debtor is claiming is the same transaction financed by the debtor-creditor-supplier agreement.

(f) Section 75 does not apply to non-commercial agreements.

(g) Section 75 only applies to claims in respect of a single item to which the supplier has attached a price of between £100 and £30,000. It does not apply if several items costing less than £100 are bought under the same debtor-creditor-supplier agreement, even if the total price of all the items is well over £100.

(h) Section 75 applies even if the debtor, in entering into the transaction, exceeded the credit limit or otherwise contravened any term of the agreement (s. 75(4)).

(i) The creditor's liability under s. 75 may far exceed the amount of credit given. For example, let us assume that goods costing £5,000 are bought from a supplier. The purchaser pays £4,500 cash and £500 with a credit card. Before delivery of the goods the supplier goes into liquidation. The creditor is liable to refund the full £5,000. Similarly, if the goods had been delivered, but had proved defective and had caused serious injury, then the creditor would be liable to pay contract damages to compensate for the injury.

(j) It is not possible to contract out of the provisions under s. 75 (s. 173(1)).

(k) Section 75 does not apply to contracts of hire.

10.3.3 CREDITOR'S RIGHT OF INDEMNITY

Section 75(2) of the 1974 Act states:

Subject to any agreement between them, the creditor shall be entitled to be indemnified by the supplier for loss suffered by the creditor in satisfying his liability under subsection (1), including costs reasonably incurred by him in defending proceedings instituted by the debtor.

MATTERS ARISING DURING CURRENCY OF CREDIT OR HIRE AGREEMENTS 241

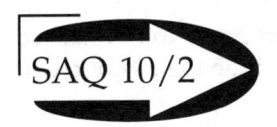

SAQ 10/2

Under a pre-existing arrangement between the supplier and a finance company, Denise borrows £5,000 from the finance company to buy a car from the supplier. The car is not as described by the supplier. In respect of this failure to match the contract description, Denise successfully sues the finance company, under s. 75(1), for £2,000 damages. What is the legal position between the finance company and the supplier?

If there is no agreement to the contrary, then under s. 75(2) the supplier will have to indemnify the finance company for the damages paid under s. 75(1). The supplier will also have to pay any legal costs reasonably incurred in defending the action.

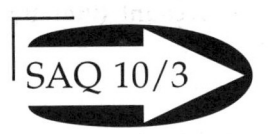

SAQ 10/3

Does s. 75 apply to the following transactions?

(a) A contract of hire-purchase where the dealer sells the goods to a finance company, which makes a hire-purchase agreement with the debtor.

(b) Anne borrows £1,000 from her bank, at 20 per cent interest, so that she can buy a car from a dealer. The price of the car is £2,000.

(a) Section 75 would not apply because the creditor and the (legal) supplier are the same person, the finance company. (The debtor would have a remedy against the finance company if the goods supplied broke any of the conditions contained in the Supply of Goods (Implied Terms) Act 1973. These conditions were explained in **Chapter 4**. If the dealer made false claims about the goods in antecedent negotiations, the creditor would assume liability for these claims under s. 56(2) of the Act.)

(b) Section 75 would not apply to this agreement. This is not a debtor-creditor-supplier agreement falling within s. 12(b) or (c) (because there is no existing or contemplated connection between the creditor and the supplier).

10.3.4 SECTIONS 56 AND 75, AS THEY RELATE TO CREDIT TOKENS

In **Chapter 9** we defined credit tokens and credit token agreements. It would probably pay you to have a quick look at these definitions before reading on.

Where a credit-token is used to acquire goods or services, this constitutes a three party debtor-creditor-supplier agreement. Consequently, the issuer of the credit-token can be jointly and severally liable with the supplier, under s. 75(1) of the Act.

Section 56(2) may also apply, so as to make a negotiator the agent of the creditor. It might be remembered that s. 56(1)(c) included negotiations with the debtor which were conducted by the supplier in relation to a transaction financed or proposed to be financed by a debtor-creditor-supplier agreement. This definition would include the use of credit cards at approved outlets.

SAQ 10/4

Does whether the card issuer have any liability under s. 56(2) or s. 75(1) as regards the following matters? Assume that all of the goods bought are faulty and that in each case the retailer conducted negotiations which made the debtor enter into the transaction.

(a) David uses his American Express card to buy a new television for £399.

(b) Diane uses her bank cash card to withdraw £150 from her account (thereby going overdrawn) so that she can buy a new tape recorder.

(c) Derek buys a radio costing £49. He pays the retailer with his Access card.

(a) American Express would not be liable under s. 56(2) or under s. 75(1), as the agreement under which the card was supplied would be an exempt agreement (see **8.4.1.3**).

(b) The bank would not be liable under s. 56(2) as there is no connection between the bank and the retailer. Nor would the bank be liable under s. 75(1), as this is not a debtor-creditor-supplier agreement within s. 12(b) or (c).

(c) Access could be liable under s. 56(2). There could be no liability under s. 75(1) as the item purchased cost under £100.

10.4 Duty to Give Notice Before Taking Certain Action

Section 76(1) of the 1974 Act deals with the situation where the debtor has not breached the agreement, but the creditor wants to take certain types of action under the terms of the agreement. The creditor cannot enforce a term of a regulated agreement to:

- demand earlier payment of any sum, or

- recover possession of any goods or land, or

- treat any right conferred on the debtor or hirer by the agreement as terminated, restricted or deferred,

without giving the debtor or hirer at least seven days' notice of his intention to do so.

The notice must take the form required by the Consumer Credit (Enforcement, Default and Termination Notices) Regulations 1983 (SI 1983 No. 1561). In order for s. 76(1) to apply, the agreement must be for a fixed time, although either party might be able to terminate it before that time has expired (s. 76(2)(a)). 'Acceleration clauses', under which the creditor can demand payment in full before the end of the agreement, are not uncommon. Generally they will only become operative where the debtor has breached the agreement. However, the agreement can also specify that they should take effect in circumstances which do not amount to breach, for example where the debtor has an unsatisfied court judgment against him. Section 76(1) does not prevent a creditor from refusing any fresh credit (s. 76(4)). A debtor who receives a s. 76 notice is entitled to apply for a time order (Section 129(1)(b)(ii)).

10.5 Duty to Give Notice of Termination in Non-default Cases

Where a regulated agreement is for a fixed-time which is specified in the agreement, the creditor or owner is not entitled to end the agreement early unless seven days' notice of the termination is given to the debtor or hirer (s. 98). This section does not prevent a creditor from treating the right to draw on any credit as restricted or deferred or from taking such steps as may be necessary to make the restriction or deferment effective (s. 98(1)).

10.6 The Duty to Give Information

Sections 77–79 require the creditor or owner to give information to the debtor or hirer. This information can be either copies of agreements or statements of account, and the debtor or hirer must pay 50p for each agreement requested. The copy of the agreement or the statement of account must then be provided within 12 working days. If a creditor fails to comply with these requirements he cannot enforce the agreement while the default continues, and if the default continues for more than one month he commits an offence.

Section 80(1) applies where, under a regulated agreement other than a non-commercial agreement, a debtor or hirer is required to keep goods under his possession or control. Upon receiving a written request from the creditor or owner, the debtor or hirer must tell the creditor or owner where the goods are within seven working days. If the debtor or hirer fails to comply with s. 80(1), and the default continues for 14 days, he commits an offence (s. 80(2)).

10.7 Appropriation of Payments

If a debtor or hirer is liable to make payments to the same person under two or more regulated agreements, and sends less than the total sums due, he can allocate the payments towards one or more of the agreements as he sees fit (s. 81(1)). If the debtor makes no such appropriation then the sum sent is allocated between the various agreements in proportion to the amount due under each (s. 81(2)).

10.8 Variation of Agreements

Section 82(1) of the 1974 Act states: 'Where, under a power contained in a regulated agreement, the creditor or owner varies the agreement, the variation shall not take effect before notice of it is given to the debtor or hirer in the prescribed manner.' The prescribed manner is set out in the Consumer Credit (Notice of Variation of Agreements) Regulations 1977 (SI 1977 No. 328). Where a 'modifying agreement' does vary the effect of an earlier agreement, the earlier agreement is regarded as revoked and the modifying agreement shall be treated as containing the combined effect of the two agreements

(s. 82(2)). If the original agreement is a regulated agreement but the modifying agreement is not, then the modifying agreement is treated as if it were a regulated agreement, unless the modifying agreement is for running-account credit (s. 82(3)).

10.9 Liability for Misuse of Credit Facilities

Section 83(1) of the 1974 Act provides that: 'The debtor under a regulated consumer credit agreement shall not be liable to the creditor for any loss arising from the use of the credit facility by another person not acting, or to be treated as acting, as the debtor's agent.' This does not apply to a non-commercial agreement, or to any loss in so far as it arises from misuse of an instrument to which s. 4 of the Cheques Act 1957 applies (s. 83(2)).

The protection conferred by s. 83(1) cannot be excluded by any term of the agreement (s. 173(1)).

ACTIVITY 10/1

Read ss. 83 and 84 of the 1974 Act in *Cases and Materials* (10.1). Then answer the following questions. In all of the examples assume that the credit card has been accepted by the debtor.

(a) Derek's Access card is stolen. The thief uses the card to obtain goods to the value of £1,000. To what extent, if any, is Derek liable for this loss if (i) the thief's action reduced Derek's credit from £1,200 to £200, and (ii) the thief's action increased Derek's debt from £300 to £1,300?

(b) Denise gives her Access card to Mary for safe-keeping while she goes swimming. Mary steals the card and uses it to order £1,000 of goods on credit. To what extent, if any, is Denise liable for this loss?

(c) Denise gives her Access card to Mary for safe-keeping while she goes swimming. Mary steals the card and uses it to order £1,000 of goods on credit. This increases Denise's deficit from £400 to £1,400. Denise phoned the creditor to say that the card had been stolen. The creditor asked for written confirmation of this, and Denise immediately posted a letter giving such confirmation. At the time of the phone call Mary had ordered £100 of goods on the card, at the time at which the letter was sent she had ordered £500, by the time the letter arrived she had ordered £1,000. To what extent, if any, is Denise liable for this loss?

    (a)(i) Section 83 has no application, as no question of liability for loss to the creditor has arisen. The section does not provide indemnity against loss.

    (ii) Section 83 tells us that Derek should not be liable to the creditor for this loss of the £1,000. However, s. 84(1) says that Derek can be liable, despite s. 83, to the extent of £50 or to the limit of his credit limit, whichever is lower. Assuming that Derek's credit limit is at least £50, Derek will therefore be liable to the extent of £50.

(b) Section 84(2) tells us that Denise cannot avail herself of the protection conferred by s. 83, as she consented to Mary's possession of the credit token. Denise is therefore liable 'to any extent for loss to the creditor', that is to say for the amount by which the account goes into deficit, or the amount to which any deficit is increased, up to the full £1,000.

(c) Denise is only liable to the creditor for £100. Section 84(3) tells us that further liability ceases when the creditor is given oral or written notice that the card has been stolen. However, assuming that the agreement requires this, the oral notice is treated as not taking effect unless it is confirmed in writing within seven days (s. 84(5)). Denise of course did satisfy this requirement.

Notice that when considering s. 84 we have again been considering 'loss to the creditor'. Thus the section will only protect the debtor to the extent that his account is taken into deficit or taken further into deficit. Section 84 does not require the creditor to indemnify the debtor for loss suffered by the misuse of a credit card.

10.10 Duty on Issue of New Credit-tokens

Section 85(1) provides that: 'Whenever, in connection with a credit token agreement, a credit-token (other than the first) is given by the creditor to the debtor, the creditor shall give the debtor a copy of the executed agreement (if any) and of any other document referred to in it.' If the creditor fails to comply with these requirements, he cannot enforce the agreement while the default continues, and he commits an offence if the default continues for more than one month (s. 85(2)). The section does not apply to small agreements (s. 85(3)).

SAQ 10/5

Why should s. 85 not apply to the first credit-token agreement?

There is no need for s. 85 to apply to the first agreement, as the rules contained in ss. 60–66 will apply.

10.11 Death of Debtor or Hirer

If the debtor or hirer under a regulated agreement should die, s. 86(1) prevents the creditor or owner from doing the following things if at the death the agreement is fully secured:

(a) terminating the agreement, or

(b) demanding earlier payment of any sum, or

(c) recovering possession of any goods or land, or

(d) treating any right conferred on the debtor or hirer by the agreement as terminated, restricted or deferred, or

(e) enforcing any security.

If at the time of the death the agreement was only partly secured then the creditor or hirer cannot do any of the five things without a court order.

10.12 Summary

Antecedent negotiations made by a credit-broker, in relation to goods sold or proposed to be sold to a creditor before forming the subject matter of a debtor-creditor-supplier agreement within s. 12(a), are made as agent of the creditor.

Antecedent negotiations made by a supplier in relation to a transaction financed or proposed to be financed by a debtor-creditor-supplier agreement within s. 12(b) or (c) are made as agent of the creditor.

If a debtor under a three party debtor-creditor-supplier agreement has any claim for breach of contract or misrepresentation against the supplier, s. 75 gives him a like claim against the creditor. The liability of the creditor and supplier is joint and several. Section 75 only applies as regards items which cost between £100 and £30,000.

The creditor must give the debtor 12 days' notice before taking certain actions to enforce the agreement. The creditor must supply the debtor with copies of the agreement and with statements of account, on payment of a small fee.

If the debtor or hirer is liable to make payment to the same creditor or owner under two or more agreements, and sends less than the total sum due, he can allocate the sum sent towards one or more of the agreements as he sees fit.

10.13 End of Chapter Assessment Question

Explain how the Consumer Credit Act 1974 might help Derek in respect of the following unrelated circumstances. Explain also whether any offences under the Act have been committed.

(a) Derek visits a shop with a view to buying a new television. The shopkeeper describes one particular type of television and persuades Derek that it is a good buy. Derek buys the television, paying the price of £375 with his bank credit card. The description applied to the television by the shopkeeper turns out not to be true. The shopkeeper refuses Derek any remedy.

(b) A thief steals Derek's bank credit card. At the time of the theft Derek's bank balance stood at £5,360. Three days later Derek phoned the bank to inform them of the theft. At the time of the phone call Derek's balance had been reduced by the thief to £132. Three months before the theft of his credit card Derek had made a hire-purchase agreement to buy a second-hand car. Under the agreement Derek paid a deposit of £1,000 and committed himself to paying £100 a month for 36 months. Derek now wants to end this agreement as he feels that he can no longer afford it.

See *Cases and Materials* (**10.3**) for an outline answer.

CHAPTER ELEVEN

CONSUMER CREDIT: TERMINATION AND REMEDIES

11.1 Objectives

By the end of this chapter you should be able to:

- explain the circumstances in which a creditor will need to serve a default notice on a debtor;

- outline the circumstances in which a debtor can repay a loan early and gain a rebate of charges for credit;

- calculate the financial position of a debtor who cancels a hire-purchase or conditional sale agreement early;

- outline the circumstances in which the hirer can terminate a consumer hire agreement early;

- explain the remedies available to a creditor in the event of a debtor breaching a regulated agreement;

- compare the damages payable to the creditor when a debtor repudiates a hire-purchase agreement with the damages payable where the creditor terminates the agreement;

- outline the debtor's protection against the creditor 'snatching back' goods which are the subject of a regulated hire-purchase or conditional sale agreement;

- explain the court's power to reopen an extortionate credit bargain.

11.2 Introduction

We begin this chapter by looking at default notices. Such notices must be served on a debtor who is in breach of a regulated agreement before the creditor can terminate the agreement, demand earlier payment of any sum, or recover possession of goods or land. The notice specifies the nature of the debtor's breach and gives him seven days to rectify it. If the debtor does rectify the breach then it is deemed never to have occurred.

We then examine the debtor's right to terminate regulated agreements early. First we see that a debtor can discharge a fixed-term agreement ahead of schedule and thereby claim a rebate of charges for credit. This right does not apply to hire-purchase and conditional sale agreements, nor to consumer hire agreements.

CONSUMER CREDIT: TERMINATION AND REMEDIES

Special provisions apply to debtors under hire-purchase or conditional sale agreements who terminate early. The debtor must return the goods to the creditor and must bring total payments made up to half of the total price. (If this figure has not already been reached.) Hirers under long-term consumer hire agreements are given the option of terminating the hire agreements early. This right cannot be exercised until the agreement has run for at least 18 months.

We move on to examine the remedies available to a creditor faced with a breach by the debtor. The four main remedies are to sue for arrears, to terminate the contract, to sue for damages or to repossess the goods.

An owner cannot enter premises to repossess goods without a court order. Nor can an owner repossess goods taken on hire-purchase or conditional sale without a court order once the debtor has paid at least one third of the total price.

11.3 Need for Default Notices

Where a debtor or hirer is in breach of a regulated agreement, s. 87 requires the creditor or owner to serve a default notice before doing any of the following:

(a) terminating the agreement, or

(b) demanding earlier payment of any sum, or

(c) recovering possession of any goods or land, or

(d) treating any right conferred on the debtor or hirer by the agreement as terminated, restricted or deferred, or

(e) enforcing any security.

The default notice must be in the form prescribed by the Consumer Credit (Enforcement, Default and Termination) Regulations 1983 (SI 1983 No. 1561), and s. 88(1) requires it to specify:

(a) the nature of the alleged breach;

(b) if the breach is capable of remedy, what action is required to remedy it and the date before which that action is to be taken; and

(c) if the breach is not capable of remedy, the sum (if any) required to be paid as compensation for the breach, and the date before which it is to be paid.

The date specified must be at least seven days after the date of service of the default notice and the creditor or owner cannot take any action before the seven days have expired (s. 88(2)).

If before the date specified the debtor or hirer takes the action specified, the breach shall be treated as not having occurred (s. 89).

A default notice is not needed if the agreement is a non-commercial agreement. Nor is a default notice needed to prevent the debtor from having any further credit (s. 87(2)). So, for example, a bank would not need to issue a default notice to stop a cheque or demand the return of a credit card. It should also be noticed that a default notice is not necessary where a creditor or owner is suing for arrears, as this is not demanding early payment of any sum. If the agreement stipulates that a specified default, typically non-payment of an instalment, is to activate an acceleration clause (whereby all of the instalments become payable immediately) a default notice is only required for the first breach of the agreement. A default notice is not required for breach of the acceleration clause (s. 88(3)).

A default notice is not necessary for an owner or creditor to recover goods supplied under a hire-purchase or conditional sale agreement and then wrongly disposed of to a third party. The owner will sue the third party in conversion to recover the goods. This is not affected by s. 87(1), which is restricted to rights which are exercisable 'by reason of any breach by the debtor or hirer of a regulated agreement'. The owner's right to sue arises in tort, not in contract.

11.3.1 INTEREST NOT TO BE INCREASED ON DEFAULT

Section 93 provides that if a debtor is in breach of a regulated consumer credit agreement, the rate of interest payable on arrears shall not be greater than the contractual rate of interest specified in the total charge for credit. If the contractual rate of interest is not specified, the interest payable on arrears must not exceed the rate of the total charge for credit, excluding any charges relating to linked transactions.

11.4 Early Payment by Debtor

The debtor under a regulated consumer credit agreement is entitled, at any time, to discharge the debt by giving the creditor notice and by repaying the whole debt (s. 94(1)). The debtor is then entitled to a rebate of charges for credit (s. 95(1)). Notice means notice in writing (s. 189(1)). There is no entitlement to a rebate unless the original agreement fixed a definite time for repayment. Details of the right to a rebate are contained in the Consumer Credit (Rebate and Early Settlement) Regulations 1983 (SI 1983 No. 1562). These regulations exclude a rebate on running-account credit because the interest is calculated on the amount outstanding from time to time and so there is no need for a rebate if the whole debt is paid off. There is no right to a rebate where the debtor terminates a hire-purchase or conditional sale agreement, as ss. 99 and 100 deal with the debtor's liability. (The effect of ss. 99 and 100 is considered below at **11.5**.) Nor is there any right to a rebate where the debtor terminates a hire agreement. (The effect of a consumer terminating a consumer hire agreement early is considered below at **11.6**.)

If a debt under a regulated consumer credit agreement is discharged early for any reason, the debtor is also discharged from any liability under a linked transaction, other than a debt which has already become payable (s. 96(1)).

The creditor under a regulated consumer credit agreement is obliged, upon receiving a written request from the debtor, to give the debtor a statement showing how much is needed to pay off the debt and how this amount was calculated. The Consumer Credit (Settlement Information) Regulations 1983 (SI 1983 No. 1564) require that the creditor provides the information within 12 working days of receiving the request to do so.

The provisions relating to early settlement cannot be contracted out of to the detriment of the debtor (s. 173(1)). However, the agreement can give the debtor additional rights.

11.5 Termination by the Debtor of Hire-purchase and Conditional Sale Agreements

Section 99(1) of the 1974 Act states:

> At any time before the final payment by the debtor under a regulated hire-purchase or regulated conditional sale agreement falls due, the debtor shall be entitled to

CONSUMER CREDIT: TERMINATION AND REMEDIES

terminate the agreement by giving notice to any person entitled or authorised to receive the sums payable under the agreement.

If the debtor does choose to terminate under s. 99(1) this does not affect any liability which has already accrued under the agreement (s. 99(2)). So arrears continue to be due.

Section 99(1) does not apply to a conditional sale agreement relating to land after the title to the land has passed to the debtor (s. 99(3)).

You should remember that the debtor's right to complete payments ahead of time, as set out in s. 94, does not apply to hire-purchase and conditional sale agreements. Nor will the right to terminate apply where the debtor is deemed to have repudiated the agreement. (See below at **11.7.3.1**.)

ACTIVITY 11/1

(a) Read s. 100 of the 1974 Act in *Cases and Materials* (11.1). Then calculate how much must be paid by the debtor to the creditor, or by the creditor to the debtor, when the debtor cancels the following regulated conditional sale agreements. Unless the contrary is stated, assume that the goods have been kept in good condition.

   (i) Denise made an agreement to buy a three piece suite on conditional sale. She paid a deposit of £100 and then committed herself to paying £20 a month for 24 months. At the time of cancellation, four months after making the agreement, she was two monthly payments in arrears.

   (ii) Dennis made an agreement to take a bicycle on a conditional sale agreement. Dennis paid a down payment of £50 and committed himself to paying £10 a month for three years. After making the first two monthly payments Dennis crashed the bicycle, bending the frame. Dennis cancelled the agreement under s. 99.

(b) Donald takes a television on hire-purchase over three years at £10 a month. Donald made a down payment of £40 and there was also an installation charge of £20. How is this installation charge to be treated when calculating the 'one-half of the total price' referred to in s. 100(1)?

(a)(i) To calculate the amount payable, we must apply the following provisions in the following order:

- First, arrears are payable (s. 99(2)).

- Second, assuming that the agreement did not provide for a lower sum to be payable, the debtor can be required to bring payments made up to half of the total price (s. 100(1)).

- Third, if the debtor has failed to take reasonable care of the goods, the amount payable should be increased to compensate the creditor for this (s. 100(4)).

These three measures can be shown by the following formula:

Amount payable = Arrears + $\dfrac{\text{Total price}}{2}$ − Sums paid (including arrears paid) + compensation

Denise is £40 in arrears, the total price payable is £580, and the amount already paid (including arrears) is £180. Therefore, applying this formula to Denise, the amount payable = £40 + £290 − £180 = £150. As the goods were kept in good condition no compensation will be added.

(ii) Applying the formula to Dennis. Dennis is not in arrears, the total price payable is £410, and the amount already paid is £70. Therefore:

Amount payable = £205 − £70 = £135 + compensation. The amount of compensation would be the amount needed to compensate the creditor for Dennis' not having taken reasonable care of the bicycle. The 1974 Act does not make it plain how this amount should be calculated.

Section 100(3) gives the court the power to reduce the amount payable under s. 100(1) to the actual loss suffered by the creditor as a result of the debtor's early termination. It is not certain whether or not this actual loss suffered by the creditor should include an amount for profit lost as a result of early settlement.

(b) Section 100(2) tells us that where there is an installation charge the 'one-half of the total price' in s. 100(1) shall be calculated as the aggregate of the installation charge and one-half of the remainder of the total price, i.e.:

$\tfrac{1}{2}$ of total price = installation charge + $\dfrac{(\text{total price} - \text{installation charge})}{2}$

In Donald's case $\tfrac{1}{2}$ of total price = £20 + $\dfrac{(£420 - £20)}{2}$ = £220

If the debtor gives goods in part-exchange, then the allowance given on the part-exchanged goods is counted as a payment made. This can mean that the debtor has paid half the total purchase price at the time of entering into the agreement.

Where the debtor terminates a hire-purchase or conditional sale agreement, the goods must of course be returned to the creditor. If the debtor wrongfully retains possession and the creditor brings an action to recover possession the court will not give the debtor the option of paying for the goods and keeping them. (Unless it would be just to make such an order.)

It is not possible to contract out of s. 100 (s. 173(1)). However, an accelerated payment clause is allowed. Such a clause would state that on default, or on the happening of a specified event, all of the payments become due immediately. If such a clause were invoked then the debtor's rights under s. 100 would be lost.

SAQ 11/1

Which provisions (already considered in this chapter or the previous one) give the debtor the chance to prevent an accelerated payments clause depriving him of his rights under s. 100?

CONSUMER CREDIT: TERMINATION AND REMEDIES

If the accelerated payment clause took effect because the debtor had defaulted, then s. 87 requires that the creditor serve a default notice giving the debtor seven days' notice before any action is taken. Therefore, before these seven days have expired the debtor must remedy the default so as to be able to terminate under s. 99. If the debtor had not defaulted, then s. 76 would require the creditor to give seven days' notice before invoking the accelerated payment clause. Again the debtor could terminate within these seven days.

11.6 Right to Terminate Regulated Consumer Hire Agreement

Section 101 gives a consumer who is locked into a long-term hire agreement the option of terminating the agreement early.

ACTIVITY 11/2

Read s. 101 of the 1974 Act in *Cases and Materials* (11.1) and then answer the following questions:

(a) Can a hirer under a regulated consumer hire agreement end the agreement at any time?

(b) When such an agreement is terminated by the hirer, what is the position as regards payments which have already accrued?

(c) How much notice must the hirer give?

(d) In what three circumstances does s. 101 not apply?

(e) Can s. 101 give a right to terminate where the hirer is a company?

(a) Section 101(1) does give the right to terminate by giving notice to any person entitled or authorised to receive the sums payable under the agreement. However, s. 101(3) says that the notice cannot expire earlier than 18 months after the making of the agreement.

(b) Section 101(2) tells us that termination does not affect any liability under the agreement which has already accrued before the termination.

(c) Unless the agreement provides for a shorter period of notice, the hirer must either give three months' notice, or the shortest interval between payments, whichever is the shorter period of time (s. 101(4)–(6)). This does not change the rule that the agreement cannot be ended within the first 18 months.

(d) Section 101 does not apply if the hirer has to make total payments exceeding £1,500 a year, or if the goods are bailed to the hirer for business purposes, or if the hirer chooses goods which the owner subsequently acquires from another person at the hirer's request (s. 101(7)).

(e) Section 101 cannot apply where the hirer is a company, because in such circumstances the agreement would not be a regulated agreement.

It is not possible to contract out of s. 101 (s. 173), therefore any additional payments or penalties will be void.

11.7 Remedies of the Creditor

ACTIVITY 11/3

If a debtor breaches a credit agreement the creditor might possibly have four rights. Write down what these rights are.

You should have written that the rights which a creditor might have are: to bring an action for arrears, to terminate the contract, to bring an action for damages or to bring an action to repossess the goods. We need to consider each of these matters in turn.

11.7.1 AN ACTION FOR ARREARS

Regardless of the 1974 Act, a creditor has a common law right to sue a debtor for arrears which have accrued. The Act makes four provisions in respect of this right. First, as we saw above, s. 93 provides that the rate of interest payable on arrears should not be higher than the interest rate specified in the total charge for credit. Second, the court may make a time order under s. 129 (explained immediately below). Third, as we saw above, the creditor must give the debtor notice (under either s. 76(1) or s. 87(1)) before demanding early payment of any sum under an acceleration clause. Fourth, the court may re-open an extortionate credit bargain, a matter considered at the end of this chapter.

11.7.1.1 Time orders

A court may make a time order under s. 129 in three situations. First, on application for an enforcement order. (An enforcement order is necessary for a creditor to enforce a regulated agreement which is unexecuted because it did not comply with all the provisions of the Act.) Second, where the debtor or hirer applies for a time order because he has received a default notice or a notice under s. 76(1) or s. 98(1). Third, where the creditor has brought an action to enforce a regulated agreement, or any security, or recover possession of any goods or land to which a regulated agreement relates s. 129(1)). Such an order would apply to a sum due under a regulated agreement and make it payable by instalments at intervals which the court would set. The court can make such changes as it considers reasonable, having regard to the means of the debtor or hirer and any surety given. The time order only relates to sums actually owed, except in the case of hire-purchase and conditional sale agreements where it can also apply to sums which would become payable if the agreement remained in force (s. 130(2)).

When a time order is in force, the creditor may not terminate the agreement, or demand earlier payment of any sum, or recover possession of any goods or land, or treat any

CONSUMER CREDIT: TERMINATION AND REMEDIES

right conferred on the debtor or hirer by the agreement as terminated, restricted or deferred, or enforce any security s. 130(5)).

11.7.2 TERMINATION OF THE AGREEMENT

SAQ 11/2

At common law, on what two grounds could the creditor terminate the agreement on account of breach by the debtor?

You should have written that the creditor could terminate if the terms of the agreement allowed him to do so, or if the breach by the creditor was such that it amounted to a repudiation of the contract. You should remember from the contract programme that a person repudiates a contract if he expressly or impliedly indicates that he does not intend to be bound by the contract. For example, in a hire-purchase contract a debtor who disposed of goods to which he did not have title, contrary to the terms of the agreement, would be taken to have repudiated the contract.

The 1974 Act does not prevent the creditor from terminating the agreement, but does insist that the provisions of ss. 87–89 (see **11.3**) and s. 98 (see **Chapter 10**) are observed. If there is an acceleration clause, then on payment of the sum demanded the creditor must allow for an early settlement rebate (see s. 95 at **11.4**).

11.7.3 DAMAGES

If a hire-purchase or conditional sale agreement is breached then the creditor can sue for damages. (Damages is not an appropriate remedy for breach of a loan or credit sale. Here the breach will consist of not repaying the instalments and the creditor can sue to recover payment of the unpaid instalments plus interest. This would be an action for an agreed sum rather than an action for damages.)

SAQ 11/3

How will the measure of damages be assessed under the common law? How much will the debtor need to pay if he terminates the agreement?

You should have written that under the common law the damages will be assessed, under the rule in *Hadley* v *Baxendale* (1854) 9 Exch 341, to put the creditor in the position which he would have been in if the contract had been performed as agreed. (See *Yoeman Credit Ltd* v *Waragowski* [1961] 1 WLR 1124 below.) If a debtor terminates a hire-purchase or conditional sale agreement early then the damages will be calculated according to s. 100(1), as explained above at **11.5**.

The measure of damages differs depending upon whether the debtor repudiated the agreement or whether the creditor terminated on account of a breach by the debtor which did not amount to a repudiation.

11.7.3.1 Damages where the debtor repudiated

The following case represented the law before the 1974 Act came into force.

Yoeman Credit Ltd v *Waragowski* [1961] 1 WLR 1124
The plaintiffs made a hire-purchase agreement with the defendant in respect of a second-hand van. The defendant paid £72 down and was to make 36 monthly instalments of £10-0s-9d. The defendant was paying £360 for the van, but the total price including interest and charges was £434-7s-0d. The defendant did not pay any of the monthly instalments and so six months into the agreement the plaintiffs terminated the agreement and repossessed the van. The plaintiffs sold the van for £205 and then sued for arrears of £60-4s-6d and damages.
Held: The Court of Appeal held that the plaintiffs were entitled to damages for breach of contract. These damages were assessed as the difference between the amount of money which they had received and the amount which they would have received if the defendant had continued with the agreement for the full three years. The damages were therefore £92-2s-6d. (£434-7s-0d − (£72 + £205 + £60-4s-6d).)

This case predates the Consumer Credit Act 1974 and Professor Goode has argued that the debtor's right to escape paying the whole of the agreed price (under ss. 99 and 100) would now have to be taken into account. Damages, he argues, should be based on the maximum amount which might be recovered under s. 100(1) less any payments actually made. Whether or not this view is correct is not yet certain.

Upon payment of the amount due, the debtor would be entitled to a rebate for early settlement under s. 95.

11.7.3.2 Termination by creditor where debtor does not repudiate

If the creditor terminates when the debtor has not repudiated, then the damages will be only amount to arrears and interest plus any amount to compensate for the defendant having failed to take reasonable care of the goods. There will be no damages for the loss of the bargain.

In *Financings Ltd* v *Baldock* [1963] 2 QB 104 a debtor took a truck on hire-purchase. He paid a deposit and agreed to pay monthly instalments for two years. The defendant missed making the first two payments. The creditor repossessed the truck and sold it. The Court of Appeal held that the debtor's behaviour did not amount to repudiation. A term in the agreement stating that if the debtor defaulted and the creditor repossessed the debtor would pay as damages an amount equal to two-thirds of total payments as compensation for depreciation of the goods was void as a penalty. Accordingly the debtor was ordered to pay the two instalments in arrears, plus ten per cent interest up to the date of judgment. (You should remember from the contract programme that where the damages are fixed in advance this will amount either to liquidated damages or to a penalty. If the amount fixed is a 'genuine pre-estimate of the loss' then it will amount to liquidated damages and this will be the amount of damages payable. If the amount fixed is not a genuine pre-estimate of the loss then it will be a penalty. The courts will ignore the penalty and calculate damages according to ordinary common law principles.)

CONSUMER CREDIT: TERMINATION AND REMEDIES

If you think it strange that the measure of damages should differ greatly depending upon whether or not the debtor repudiated, you are not alone. In *Financings Ltd v Baldock* Lord Denning MR said, at 113, that he thought that the measure of damages should be the same whichever party did the terminating.

In *Lombard North Central v Butterworth* [1987] 1 All ER 267 the Court of Appeal considered a hire contract in which a term stated that prompt payments of all instalments was of the essence of the contract. The defendant made several late payments. This would not ordinarily have amounted to a repudiation of the contract. However, as the term making prompt payments of the essence was a condition of the contract, the creditor could terminate the contract and recover damages for the loss of the whole bargain. Hire-purchase and conditional sale agreements now commonly include a term that prompt payment of all instalments is of the essence.

11.7.4 REPOSSESSION OF THE GOODS

If a debtor under a hire-purchase or conditional sale agreement does not make all of the payments then the creditor is entitled to terminate the agreement and repossess the goods. The hirer only ever acquired possession, never ownership, and the agreement will almost invariably have stipulated that the debtor's right to possess was conditional on sticking to the terms of the agreement. The Act protects a debtor in three ways, as without this protection a debtor who had made substantial payments before defaulting could suddenly lose all rights when the creditor 'snatched-back' the goods.

11.7.4.1 Notice required before action

You should remember that the creditor will not be able to repossess goods without observing the provisions of ss. 76, 87–89 and 98.

11.7.4.2 Protected goods

Section 90(1) of the 1974 Act states:

> At any time when—
> (a) the debtor is in breach of a regulated hire-purchase or a regulated conditional sale agreement relating to goods, and
> (b) the debtor has paid to the creditor one-third or more of the total price of the goods and
> (c) the property in the goods remains in the creditor,
> the creditor is not entitled to recover possession of the goods from the debtor except on an order of the court.

If an installation charge is included in the total price for the goods, the debtor must have paid the whole of the installation charge and a third of the remainder of the total price (s. 90(2)).

Section 90(5) states: 'Subsection (1) shall not apply, or shall cease to apply, to an agreement if the debtor has terminated, or terminates, the agreement.'

ACTIVITY 11/4

Harry takes a car on hire-purchase from Motors Ltd. Harry pays a deposit of £1,000 and commits himself to paying £100 a month for 36 months. After 10 monthly payments Harry defaults on his next payment. Motors Ltd immediately repossess the car.

(a) Applying s. 90 and s. 91 (which can be read in full in *Cases and Materials* (11.1)) what is the legal position?

(b) What would have been the legal position if after 10 monthly payments Harry had written to say that he no longer wanted the car, and was not making any more payments?

(a) If Motors Ltd repossessed the car without a court order then they would be in breach of s. 90. Section 91 would therefore terminate the agreement, and entitle Harry to recover all sums paid under the agreement. As the agreement would be terminated, Motors Ltd would be entitled to possession of the car. Harry, however, would be entitled to the return of the £1,000 deposit and the 10 instalments of £100 already paid.

(b) Harry would appear to have terminated the agreement under s. 99. Therefore, applying s. 90(5), s. 90(1) would not apply. As owners of the car, Motors Ltd would have the right to repossess it. Harry would not be able to recover money already paid. Harry would, under s. 100(1) have to make his payments up to half the total price. As Harry has paid £2,000 and the total price was £4,600, Harry would have to pay a further £300. However, if the court was satisfied that Motors Ltd's loss was less than £300 then Harry would not have to pay this extra £300 (s. 100(3)).

It is possible for the debtor to consent to the repossession of protected goods (s. 173(3)). However, if a term of the contract states that the debtor gives such consent then the term will be void under s. 173(1).

The creditor can repossess the goods where they have been abandoned, as this is not recovery of goods 'from the debtor'.

11.7.4.3 Entering premises to recover possession of goods or land

Section 92(1) gives further protection to a debtor or hirer who has taken goods under a regulated hire-purchase agreement, conditional sale agreement or consumer hire agreement. The creditor or owner is not entitled to enter premises to retake possession of the goods without a court order. This applies even if the goods are not protected goods under s. 90. Section 92(2) provides that when a debtor is in breach of a regulated conditional sale agreement relating to land, the creditor cannot recover possession of the land without a court order. Breach of either of these two subsections is actionable as breach of statutory duty (s. 92(3)).

The debtor or hirer can agree to repossession or entry into premises without a court order (s. 173(3)). There is of course no obligation to give such consent (s. 173).

11.8 Provisions Protecting Hirers of Goods

Section 90 only applies to regulated hire-purchase and conditional sale agreements. Section 132 gives financial relief to a hirer where the owner takes the goods back without taking court action. (Sections 127–140, which deal with judicial control, are set out in *Cases and Materials* (11.1).) The hirer can apply for a court order that

- the whole or part of any sum paid by the hirer to the owner in respect of the goods shall be repaid, and

CONSUMER CREDIT: TERMINATION AND REMEDIES

- the obligation to pay the whole or part of any sum owed by the hirer to the owner in respect of the goods shall cease.

The court will only grant the order if it appears just to do so, having regard to the extent of the enjoyment of the goods by the hirer.

11.9 The Court's Powers in Hire-purchase and Conditional Sale Agreements

Section 133 applies to regulated hire-purchase and conditional sale agreements. It enables the court to make a return order or a transfer order when the creditor sues to recover goods or when there is an application for an enforcement order or a time order. Under a return order the court orders that goods to which the agreement relates are returned to the creditor. Under a transfer order the creditor's title to some of the goods to which the agreement relates can be transferred to the debtor. Section 135 gives the court the power to impose conditions and s. 136 the power to vary the agreement. If the debtor contravenes a return order or a transfer order the court can revoke the order and order the debtor to pay the creditor the unpaid portion of the price which relates to those goods (s. 133(6)).

11.10 Protection Orders

If a creditor or owner under a regulated agreement applies to the court to do so, the court may make such order as it thinks fit for protecting any property belonging to the creditor or owner from damage or depreciation pending court proceedings. Such an order can restrict or prohibit the use of the property or give directions as to its custody (s. 131).

11.11 Extortionate Credit Bargains

Section 137(1) allows a court to reopen an extortionate credit bargain so as to do justice between the parties. This provision is not restricted to regulated credit agreements, but applies to any agreement where a creditor supplies credit of any amount to a debtor.

Section 138(1) defines an extortionate credit bargain as one under which the debtor has to make payments which are grossly exorbitant, or which otherwise grossly contravenes ordinary principles of fair dealing. Section 138(2)–(4) require regard to be had to the following matters:

(a) the prevailing interest rates at the time when the agreement was made;

(b) the debtor's age, experience, business capacity and state of health;

(c) the degree to which the debtor was under financial pressure when making the agreement, and the nature of that pressure;

(d) the degree of risk to the creditor, having regard to the value of any security provided;

(e) the creditor's relationship with the debtor;

(f) whether or not a colourable (plausible) cash price was quoted for any goods or services included in the bargain;

(g) any other relevant consideration.

If a credit bargain is extortionate, s. 139 gives the court the power to alter it, and in effect to rewrite it. The rate of interest can be changed, the court can set aside obligations imposed on the debtor and can order the creditor to repay sums already received.

Ketley, A., Ltd v *Scott and Another* [1981] ICR 241
The plaintiff company lent £20,000 to the defendant and his wife, to enable them to buy a house. On the same day that the money was lent the sum to be borrowed had gone up from £18,000 because the defendant (a businessman) could not borrow as much as he had expected from his bank. The defendant did not reveal that the bank had been given a legal charge over the property or that the property had been valued at less than the price he was paying for it. In the presence of solicitors acting for both sides, the defendant signed an agreement that the loan was to be for three months, at an interest rate of 48 per cent per annum. The loan was not repaid, and the plaintiff company gained repossession of the property. The question arose as to what sum the defendant ought to pay. In order to decide this the court had to decide whether or not the bargain was extortionate, within the meaning of the Consumer Credit Act 1974.

ACTIVITY 11/5

Read the extract from Foster J's judgment in *Ketley* v *Scott* in *Cases and Materials* (11.2) and write down what the court decided.

You should have written that Foster J did not think that the rate of interest was extortionate, and did not think that it would be just and equitable to reopen the bargain.

11.12 Summary

If a debtor is in breach of a regulated agreement, the creditor cannot terminate the agreement, or demand earlier payment of any sum, or recover possession of any goods or land without serving a default notice on the debtor. This notice gives the debtor seven days to remedy the default.

When a debtor is in breach of a regulated agreement the rate of interest payable on arrears must not be greater than the contractual rate of interest.

A debtor under a fixed-sum credit agreement has the right to repay the agreement early and thereby gain a rebate of charges for credit.

A debtor has the right to cancel a hire-purchase or conditional sale agreement before the expiry of the agreement. If the debtor has not paid half of the total price at the time of cancellation he must make an extra payment to bring the amount he has paid up to half the total price. The debtor must of course return the goods to the creditor. If the debtor has not taken reasonable care of the goods the amount payable to the creditor can be increased to compensate for this.

A hirer under a consumer hire agreement can terminate the agreement early. However, this will not be possible in the first 18 months of the agreement.

If a debtor breaches a credit agreement the creditor has four principal remedies: bringing an action for arrears; terminating the contract; suing for damages or repossessing the goods.

By making a time order a court can order that a debtor pay a sum owed under a regulated agreement by such instalments, payable at such times, as the court thinks reasonable.

If the debtor repudiates a hire-purchase or conditional sale agreement then the creditor can sue for the whole loss of the bargain. If the creditor terminates the agreement on account of a non-repudiatory breach by the debtor then the damages will only amount to arrears and interest plus any amount to compensate for the defendant having failed to take reasonable care of the goods. There will be no damages for the loss of the whole bargain.

Once a debtor under a hire-purchase or conditional sale agreement has paid one third of the total price of the goods they become protected goods and the creditor cannot repossess them without a court order. Nor can the owner enter premises to retake goods, whether protected goods or not, without a court order.

The court has the power to reopen an extortionate credit bargain and to change the terms of it.

CHAPTER TWELVE

THE TRADE DESCRIPTIONS ACT 1968: GOODS

12.1 Objectives

By the end of this chapter you should be able to:

- outline the history and the structure of the Trade Descriptions Act 1968;

- identify the circumstances in which a person will be acting in the course of a trade or business, for the purposes of the Act;

- explain what is meant by applying a false trade description to goods;

- explain what is meant by supplying or offering to supply goods to which a false trade description is applied;

- analyse the ways in which a person can apply a trade description to goods;

- analyse the definition of a trade description which is given by s. 2 of the Act;

- explain the extent to which a trade description can be made impliedly;

- explain the meaning of a false trade description, and the circumstances in which a description can be deemed to be false;

- analyse the extent to which a disclaimer can prevent a false trade description from being applied.

12.2 Introduction

The Trade Descriptions Act 1968 (in this chapter referred to as 'the Act') imposes criminal liability on those who misdescribe goods or services in the course of a trade or business. The Act replaces the Merchandising Marks Acts 1887 to 1953. Four major offences are created by the Act. Two of these concern the misdescription of goods, the other two concern the misdescription of services. In this chapter we examine the offences relating to goods, in the following chapter we examine the offences relating to services.

The Act only imposes liability only on those acting in the course of a trade or business. The two offences relating to goods are: applying a false trade description to goods (s. 1(1)(a)); and supplying or offering to supply any goods to which a false trade description is applied (s. 1(1)(b)). Both are offences of strict liability. The offence created by s. 1(1)(a) is more serious than the offence created by s. 1(1)(b). A person convicted under s. 1(1)(a) will generally have acted dishonestly, whereas a person convicted under s. 1(1)(b) may well have been only careless.

THE TRADE DESCRIPTIONS ACT 1968: GOODS

Even though the two s. 1 offences are offences of strict liability, defences are available. It is a defence for a defendant to show that the offence was committed due to a mistake; or to reliance on information supplied to him; or to the act or default of another person, an accident or other forces beyond the defendant's control. As regards all three of these matters the defendant must also show that he took all reasonable precautions and exercised all due diligence to prevent the commission of the offence. Another defence applies only to the s. 1(1)(b) offence of supplying or offering to supply goods to which a false trade description is applied. This defence requires the defendant to prove that he did not know, and could not with reasonable diligence have ascertained, either that the goods did not conform to the description or that the description had been applied to the goods. These defences are considered in **Chapter 13**.

12.3 False Trade Descriptions of Goods

Section 1 of the 1968 Act sets out the two offences which concern false trade descriptions of goods. Section 1 states:

ACTIVITY 12/1

Read s. 1 of the Act in *Cases and Materials* (12.1) and answer the following questions:

(a) **Can a person who has not described goods be guilty of either offence created by s. 1?**

(b) **Can a person who has not supplied or offered to supply goods be guilty of either offence?**

(a) You should have written that a person who has not described goods can be guilty of an offence under s. 1(1)(b). To commit that offence goods to which a false trade description is applied need to be supplied or offered for supply in the course of a trade or business. There is no requirement that the supplier is also the person who made the false trade description.

(b) A person who has not supplied or offered to supply goods can be guilty of an offence under s. 1(1)(a). That offence is committed by any person who in the course of a trade or business applies a false trade description to goods. There is no requirement that this person also supplies the goods to a customer. Of course, it is commonly the case that the person who applies the false description also does supply or offer to supply the goods.

12.3.1 ANY PERSON

SAQ 12/1

Could a company be guilty of an offence under s. 1 of the Act?

A company is a legal person and therefore could be guilty of an offence under the Act. In several of the cases considered in this chapter it is a company which is prosecuted.

When a company commits an offence under the Act with the consent or connivance of a company officer, or any person purporting to act as a company officer, then the officer can be prosecuted as well as the company (s. 20).

12.3.2 IN THE COURSE OF A TRADE OR BUSINESS

Only a person acting in the course of a trade or business can commit an offence under the Act. (However, a person acting privately may be caught by the 'by-pass' provision in s. 23. This provision is considered in **Chapter 13**.)

To commit an offence under s. 1(1)(b) a person must supply or offer to supply goods to which a false trade description is applied in the course of a trade or business. As we have seen, s. 1(1)(a) requires that a person applies a false trade description to goods. This false trade description must be applied to goods in the course of a trade or business. Generally the false description will be made in respect of goods which the defendant also supplies or offers to supply. But what if the false trade description, although made in the course of the defendant's trade or business, is not connected with any supply or offer to supply by the defendant? Can the defendant still be guilty of an offence under s. 1(1)(a)?

Wycombe Marsh Garages Ltd v *Fowler* [1972] 1 WLR 1152

The defendant company took in a car to see if it qualified for an MOT certificate. A foreman mechanic examined the car and failed it because he said that two tyres suffered from tread lift. The manufacturers of the tyres examined them. After eight days of tests an expert established that that the defect was mould drip (which would not cause the car to fail its MOT) rather than tread lift. The High Wycombe justices convicted the defendant company of applying a false trade description to the tyres, contrary to s. 1(1)(a) of the Act. The defendant appealed to the Divisional Court.

ACTIVITY 12/2

Read the extract from Lord Widgery CJ's judgment in *Wycombe Marsh Garages* v *Fowler* in *Cases and Materials* **(12.2.1)** and answer the following questions:

(a) Would a literal reading of s. 1 mean that the defendant was guilty?

(b) Which rule of statutory interpretation, and which minor internal aid to statutory interpretation, did Lord Widgery apply?

(c) Was the appeal allowed? On what grounds was this decision reached?

(a) You should have written that a literal reading of s. 1 would mean that the defendant was guilty.

(b) Lord Widgery applied the mischief rule, thinking that Parliament could not possibly have intended that the defendant could have been guilty of an offence under s. 1(1)(a). Lord Widgery gained encouragement for this view in the long title to the Act, which is a minor aid to statutory interpretation.

(c) The appeal was allowed. The first four sections of the Act were intended to penalise the provision of goods for sale or otherwise with a misleading

THE TRADE DESCRIPTIONS ACT 1968: GOODS

description attached to them. The Act did not intend to criminalise the honest making of a statement regarding goods which is given as an incidental part of providing a service of advising in regard to some matter affecting the goods.

SAQ 12/2

Would a garage be acting in the course of a trade or business if it falsely issued an MOT certificate to an unroadworthy car in order that the car could be sold?

Clearly the garage would have made the false description in the course of its trade or business. As Lord Widgery indicated, this was just the type of mischief which the Act did seek to penalise.

In *Davies v Sumner* [1984] 3 All ER 831 the House of Lords had to decide whether or not a self-employed courier acted in the course of a trade or business when he traded in his old Ford car for a new one. (The odometer on the car which was traded in showed a mileage of 18,100, but should have shown 118,100 because it had been right around the clock.) The car in question was the first one which the defendant had bought for use in his business, and therefore the first such car he had sold. Before buying the car in question the defendant had rented cars for use in his business.

ACTIVITY 12/3

Read the judgment of Lord Keith of Kinkel in *Davies v Sumner* in *Cases and Materials* (12.2.1) and answer the following questions:

(a) Was the defendant guilty of an offence under s. 1(1)?

(b) In the course of his speech Lord Keith considered *Havering London Borough v Stevenson* [1970] 3 All ER 609. In that case the defendant carried on a car-hire business and regularly sold cars off after about two years. The money generated was used to buy new cars. The cars were sold at the current trade price and no car was ever sold at a profit. On what grounds was *Havering London Borough v Stevenson* distinguished by Lord Keith?

(c) Could a one-off adventure in the nature of trade be within s. 1(1)?

You should have written that:

(a) The defendant was not guilty of an offence under s. 1(1) of the Act. The car was a business asset which was sold, and the sale was reasonably incidental to the carrying on of the business. However, the Act did not intend to catch all such sales, but only those which occurred with some degree of regularity. (As the long title of the Act indicated.) A normal practice of the defendant buying and selling cars had not been established at the time of the offence. It was also possible that in the future the defendant would revert to his old practice of hiring vans rather than buying them.

(b) *Havering London Borough* v *Stevenson* was distinguished because the regularity of the sales in question made the sales an integral part of the business of a car-hire firm. The cars were sold as part of the normal practice of the business.

(c) A one-off adventure in the nature of trade, carried through with a view to profit, would be within s. 1(1). Such a transaction would itself constitute a trade, and therefore there would be no need to prove regularity of such adventures.

ACTIVITY 12/4

In the following case the Divisional Court considered both *Davies* v *Sumner* and *Havering London Borough* v *Stevenson*. Read the facts of the case and write down what you think the court decided.

Devlin v *Hall* [1990] RTR 320

The defendant, a taxi driver, owned two cars for business purposes, a blue Peugeot and a similar green car. He offered both of these cars to a buyer. The buyer chose the blue Peugeot and the defendant sold this car to him with a false odometer reading, taking a Sierra in part exchange. The blue Peugeot was the first car used in the taxi business which the defendant had sold. However, the Sierra was then sold, in order to buy a white Granada. Later the defendant sold the Granada to a different taxi firm. A Nissan Bluebird used only for private purposes was also sold. In relation to the sale of the blue Peugeot, the defendant was charged with offences under s. 1(1)(a) and s. 1(1)(b). It was accepted that the sale of this car was not a one-off adventure in the nature of trade with a view to profit.

You should have written that the Divisional Court held that the blue Peugeot was not sold in the course of a trade or business, as it was the first car which the business had sold. Therefore when it was sold there was no regularity about such sales. The situation was closer to *Davies* v *Sumner* than to *Havering London Borough* v *Stevenson*. Therefore the defendant was not guilty of either offence.

SAQ 12/3

Consider the following:

(a) Arthur sets up in business, selling used cars. The first car Arthur sells has a false odometer reading. No cars subsequently sold by Arthur have a false odometer reading. Has Arthur committed an offence under the Act?

THE TRADE DESCRIPTIONS ACT 1968: GOODS

(b) Bill, a mechanic who works as an employee at a garage, decides to buy an old car and do it up so that he can sell it for a profit. While repairing the car Bill winds back the odometer and sells the car bearing this false odometer reading. Bill has never engaged in this type of scheme before and never does so again. Has Bill committed an offence under the Act?

Both Arthur and Bill will have committed an offence under s. 1 of the Act. The purpose of this question is to remind you that in *Davies* v *Sumner*, *Havering London Borough* v *Stevenson* and *Devlin* v *Hall* the defendants were not in the business of selling cars at a profit. If this was the business of Arthur, or if Bill was doing so as a one-off adventure in the nature of trade with a view to profit, then both would commit both of the offences set out in s. 1, even as regards the first car sold.

Roberts v *Leonard* (1995) 94 LGR 284
The defendants were a firm of vets who were employed by the Ministry of Agriculture, Fisheries and Food to issue health certificates in respect of calves which were to be exported. The certificates were issued after each calf had been examined and said that the calves were fit to travel. The defendants certified that a large number of calves were fit to travel when many of these calves had not been inspected. The defendants were charged with an offence under s. 1(1)(a) of the Act.
Held: 'Trade or business' in the Act included professions. The issuing of the certificates was an essential, integral and direct part of the export of the calves. Without the certificate there could have been no export, as the defendants knew. The defendants were therefore guilty even though they were not directly party to the export of the calves. The defendants would also have been guilty of an offence under s. 1(1)(b). (An extract from the judgment of Simon Brown LJ is set out in *Cases and Materials* (**12.2.1**).)

SAQ 12/4

When a false trade description is applied during a contract of sale, in almost every case it is the seller of goods who applies the false trade description. But can a buyer apply a false trade description?

The matter was considered by the Divisional Court in the following case.

Fletcher v *Budgen* [1974] 1 WLR 1056
The defendant, a motor dealer, was considering buying a Fiat 500. The defendant made three disparaging remarks about the car: that it was impossible to repair; that repairs could not make the car safe; and that the only thing to do was to scrap the car. Believing these remarks, the owner sold the car to the defendant for £2. The owner spent £56 repairing the car, and then advertised it for sale for £135. The defendant knew that his remarks about the car were false when he made them.

ACTIVITY 12/5

Read the extract from the judgment of Lord Widgery LJ *Fletcher* v *Budgen* in *Cases and Materials* (**12.2.1**). Write down whether or not the defendants were guilty of an offence under s. 1(1)(a).

You should have written that the defendants were guilty of the offence. There was no reason why the offence should not be committed by a buyer of goods, although the situation is unusual. It should be noted that this did not mean that every buyer of goods runs the risk of committing an offence by making deprecating or derogatory remarks about the goods. Only a buyer who made the remarks while conducting a trade or business could be liable in this way.

In *Fletcher v Budgen* Lord Widgery considered the decision in *Fletcher v Sledmore* [1973] RTR 371. The facts of that case were that the defendant, a panel beater who repaired and bought and sold cars, bought a car with a defective engine. The defendant agreed to sell the car to car dealers, but the car was to remain on the defendant's premises while he carried out repairs. The defendant knew that the car dealers intended to sell the car on. While the engine was dismantled the car dealers introduced a prospective customer for the car. The defendant told the customer that the car had a good engine and that he had driven it himself. The customer, influenced by the defendant's statement, bought the car from the dealer. The defendant was charged with an offence under s. 1(1)(a) of the Act. He had two defences. First, that his statement about the car was just an opinion. Second, that the statement had not been made in the course of a trade or business, because at the time of making it the car had already been sold (to the dealer.)

ACTIVITY 12/6

Read s. 1(1) of the Act in *Cases and Materials* (12.1). Write down whether or not you think either of the two defences in *Fletcher v Sledmore* were successful.

You should have written that neither defence was successful. The defendant's 'opinion' did amount to a false trade description, and the statement was made in the course of the defendant's trade or business because he was still interested in the fate of the car when he made the statement. (The statement was made as part of the defendant's business activities. He knew that his statement was capable of influencing the sale by the dealer, and he was still interested in doing the repairs so that the dealer could not allege he had committed a breach of contract.)

Car dealers who replace an odometer with another one which shows a lower mileage are very likely to commit an offence, especially if the car is subsequently sold. But this is not always the case. In *R v Shrewsbury Crown Court, ex parte Venables* [1994] Crim LR 61 a car dealer, having replaced the odometer with a different one which showed a lower mileage, sold the car to another dealer, T. (We shall see later in this chapter that turning back an odometer, or replacing one, will amount to the application of a false trade description if it was done in the course of a trade or business. The offence is committed at the time the odometer is turned back.) However, the Divisional Court held the seller of the car was not guilty of an offence under s. 1(1)(a) because when he replaced the odometer he had been using the car himself in the course of his trade or business and had later sold it to the other dealer purely fortuitously when the two met at a third party location. The false trade description was not therefore applied in the course of a trade or business because at the time of turning the odometer back the defendant had no intention of selling or offering to sell the car. (Nor was an offence committed under s. 1(1)(b) when the car was sold, because T knew that the odometer reading was false. See **12.6** below.)

12.3.3 SECTION 1(1)(a): APPLYING A FALSE TRADE DESCRIPTION TO ANY GOODS

The offence under s. 1(1)(a) requires that any person, in the course of a trade or business, applies a false trade description to any goods. The word 'applies' is also relevant to s. 1(1)(b). That offence concerns supplying or offering to supply goods to which a false trade description is applied. Thus it is still necessary to decide whether or not any such description is applied (either by the defendant or by some other person). Here then we first need to examine the meaning of 'goods' in this context and then examine the meaning of 'applies' in this context. The meaning of a 'false trade description' is considered below at **12.4**.

12.3.3.1 Goods

The word 'goods' is not defined by the Act, except that s. 39(1) says that 'goods' includes ships and aircraft, things attached to land and growing crops.

12.3.3.2 Applies

ACTIVITY 12/7

Arthur works with his brother Bill in a firm which deals in tea. In the firm's warehouse Arthur tells Bill that a certain batch of tea is Darjeeling. The tea is not Darjeeling but Assam, and Bill soon convinces Arthur of this. Read s. 1 of the Act in *Cases and Materials* (12.1) and state whether or not Arthur would have committed an offence if: (a) the literal rule of statutory interpretation; and (b) the mischief rule were applied. Which rule do you think the courts apply?

(a) You should have written that if the literal rule were applied then Arthur would have been guilty of an offence under s. 1(1)(a).

(b) If the mischief rule were applied then Arthur would not be guilty. The mischief which the Act sought to remedy was that goods or services might be provided by sale or otherwise with a misleading trade description attached to them. (See *Wycombe Marsh Garages Ltd* v *Fowler* in *Cases and Materials* (12.2.1).)

In *Cavendish Woodhouse Ltd* v *Wright* (1985) 149 JP 497 the defendants were charged with several offences under s. 1. The offences concerned several different customers. Miss Crawley visited the defendant's shop and looked at bedroom furniture. She was told that identical furniture was in stock and that this could be supplied to her. No such identical furniture was in stock and the furniture supplied was far from identical. At no time was Miss Crawley disabused of the notion that the furniture supplied would be identical. Mr and Mrs Mayo examined a suite in the defendant's shop. They were told that all the cushions were reversible and that the suite was perfect. They checked that this was the case and then Mr and Mrs Mayo ordered such a suite. The suite supplied to them had one cushion which was not reversible. Mr and Mrs Stewart bought a corner table. They saw one in the defendant's shop which was absent a glass top, but which was plainly meant to have one. They were told that the table supplied to them would have a glass top but in fact, due to an error made in the course of supply, it did not.

ACTIVITY 12/8

Read the extract from the judgment of Watkins LJ in *Cavendish Woodhouse* v *Wright* in *Cases and Materials* (12.2.1). Then write down whether or not the defendants had committed an offence under either s. 1(1)(a) or s. 1(1)(b), as regards:

(a) the bedroom furniture,

(b) the suite, and

(c) the table.

You should have written that:

(a) The defendants had committed an offence under both s. 1(1)(a) and s. 1(1)(b). They committed an offence under s. 1(1)(a) when they falsely stated that an identical suite was available in stock and could be supplied to Miss Crawley. This trade description, which they had applied at the time of the agreement to sell, was carried along to the time of supply, as no attempt had been made to correct it. Therefore the defendants were guilty of an offence under s. 1(1)(b), in that they supplied goods to which a false trade description is applied.

(b) On the same reasoning as applied above, the defendants had committed an offence under s. 1(1)(b). They were not charged with an offence under s. 1(1)(a) but would presumably have been guilty of the offence. The description of the particular suite in the shop was not false, but the same description would have been carried along and impliedly applied to the suite delivered. As regards the suite delivered, the description was false and this was therefore the application of a false trade description.

(c) The defendants had not committed an offence under either s. 1(1)(a) or s. 1(1)(b). Here there had been no attempt to misdescribe what the Stewarts ultimately received. It was just an accident in the supply of the table.

If the false description is applied after the goods have been supplied then no offence will have been committed.

Hall v *Wickens Motors Ltd* [1972] 1 WLR 1418
The defendants, who were car dealers, sold a car. About 40 days-later the customer returned with a complaint about the car's steering. The defendants said that there was nothing wrong with the car. A subsequent examination revealed that the car's chassis was distorted and that the steering was defective, and had been defective at the time of sale. The Gloucester City justices convicted the defendants of an offence under s. 1(1)(a). On appeal the deputy recorder of Gloucester quashed the conviction. The prosecutor appealed to the Divisional Court.
Held: The appeal was dismissed. Parliament had not intended to create an offence where the description was not associated with the actual sale or supply of the goods. As the description was made after the sale had been concluded, no offence was therefore committed.

Section 4 gives a statutory definition of the ways in which a person can apply a trade description to goods (see *Cases and Materials* (12.1)). This definition is exhaustive.

THE TRADE DESCRIPTIONS ACT 1968: GOODS

Donnelly v Rowlands [1971] 1 WLR 1600
A milk retailer, in the course of his trade or business, offered to supply 180 pint bottles of milk. The bottles were owned by other parties and were embossed with the names of those other parties (167 bottles were embossed with 'Northern' because they belonged to Northern Dairies Ltd, seven which belonged to the Co-operative Wholesale Society Ltd were embossed 'C.W.S.' etc.). The defendant filled the bottles with his own milk. That the milk was the defendant's could be ascertained from the foil caps, which legibly stated: 'Untreated milk produced from T.T. Cows, Rowlands, Plas Meiford, Henllan.' The defendant had used the bottles embossed with other names because he was waiting to get bottles embossed with his own name.

ACTIVITY 12/9

Read s. 4 of the Act and the judgment of Lord Parker CJ in *Donnelly* v *Rowlands* in *Cases and Materials* (12.1 and 12.2.1), and write your answers to the following questions.

(a) Under which part of s. 4 could the embossed words on a milk bottle amount to the application of a trade description of the milk in the bottle?

(b) Did the defendant apply a false trade description to the milk?

You should have written that:

(a) the embossed words on a milk bottle could have amounted to an application of a trade description of the milk inside the bottle under s. 4(1)(a) or s. 4(1)(b).

(b) The defendant did not apply a false trade description to the milk. The words on the caps accurately described the milk and the words on the bottles indicated to whom the bottles belonged.

You should notice that by virtue of s. 4(2) an oral statement may amount to the use of a trade description. (This was a significant change from the Merchandising Marks Acts.)

SAQ 12/5

Above, in Activity 12/8, we saw that in *Cavendish Woodhouse Ltd* v *Wright* the defendants applied a false trade description to the suite supplied to Mr and Mrs Mayo. Under which part of s. 4 would this description have been applied?

The description would have been applied under s. 4(1)(c). The description was used in a manner likely to be taken as referring to the goods.

SAQ 12/6

What does s. 4(3) mean?

Section 4(3) means that if the customer makes a trade description when ordering goods, then the supplier of the goods will be regarded as having made the trade description if he supplies goods filling the order, in circumstances which make it reasonable to infer that the goods supplied correspond to the description. For example, if a customer entered a delicatessen and asked for a quarter of Edam cheese, a shopkeeper who supplied Cheddar cheese in response to the customer's request would be deemed to have described it as Edam.

In *R v Ford Motor Co. Ltd* [1974] 1 WLR 1220 a car dealer completed an order form asking Ford Motor Co. Ltd to supply a Ford car. This order form indirectly indicated that the car to be supplied would be new. By supplying a car in response to this order form, Ford Motor Co. were deemed to have described it as a new car. Similarly, in *Routledge v Ansa Motors (Chester-Le-Steet) Ltd* [1980] RTR 1 the false trade description of a car was contained in a sales invoice which was also an order form.

SAQ 12/7

A person can apply a false trade description even without making any oral or written statement. In which case, already considered, did the defendant apply the false trade description in this way?

In the false odometer reading cases the defendants applied the false trade descriptions without making an oral or written statement. For example, in *Davies v Sumner* Lord Keith said, 'There can be no doubt that the respondent, when he traded in his car, applied a false trade description to it, in respect that he represented that it had travelled 18,100 miles when the true mileage was 118,100 miles.'

12.3.4 TRADE DESCRIPTIONS USED IN ADVERTISEMENTS.

ACTIVITY 12/10

Read s. 5 in *Cases and Materials* (12.1). Then write your answer to the following questions:

(a) Is a separate offence relating to advertisements created?

(b) What is meant by s. 5(2) 'The trade description shall be taken as referring to all goods of the class, whether or not in existence at the time the advertisement is published'?

THE TRADE DESCRIPTIONS ACT 1968: GOODS

(c) Why should s. 5(2) not ordinarily cause a defendant hardship?

(a) A separate offence relating to advertisers is not created. Section 5 explains how the use of an advertisement can create liability under s. 1(1)(a) or s. (1)(1)(b) of the Act.

(b) An example might make the meaning of s. 5(2) clearer. If a motor company advertised that 'our cars are fitted with airbags' this trade description would be taken as referring to all cars manufactured by the motor company (all goods of the class) including cars which had not yet been manufactured (goods not yet in existence at the time the advertisement is published).

(c) Section 5(2) should not ordinarily cause hardship because of s. 5(3) which provides that when deciding whether goods are in a class to which a trade description used in an advertisement relates, regard shall be had to the form and content of the advertisement and to time, place, manner and frequency of the publication and to all other matters which would make it likely or unlikely that the person to whom the goods are supplied would think that the goods belonged to the class in relation to which the trade description is used in the advertisement.

Section 39 of the Act, the interpretation section, says that 'advertisement' includes a catalogue, a circular and a price list.

Advertisers who publish material supplied by another have a defence under s. 25 if they did not know, and had no reason to suspect, that an offence was being committed under the Act. They may also avail themselves of the general defence in s. 24. Defences are considered in **Chapter 13**.

12.3.5 SECTION 1(1)(b): SUPPLYING OR OFFERING TO SUPPLY GOODS TO WHICH A FALSE TRADE DESCRIPTION IS APPLIED

The s. 1(1)(b) offence is committed by a person who, in the course of a trade or business, supplies or offers to supply goods to which a false trade description is applied. It is less serious than the s. 1(1)(a) offence of applying a false trade description. (In *R v Southwood* [1987] 3 All ER 556 Lord Lane CJ, at 562, approved a Crown Court judge's statement that those who offend against s. 1(1)(a) are unscrupulous, whereas those who offend against s. 1(1)(b) are irresponsible.) It is not necessary that the person committing an offence under s. 1(1)(b) should also have applied the false description, or have known that a trade description applied was false. However, it is necessary that the person who supplies or offers to supply should at least know that a trade description has been applied. (See *Cottee v D. Seaton Ltd* [1972] 1 WLR 1408 below.)

A person who supplies or offers to supply goods not knowing that a trade description applied to the goods is false may be able to rely on one of the defences set out in s. 24 of the Act.

12.3.5.1 Supplies

SAQ 12/8

The Act does not define the word 'supply'. How wide do you think supply is? Obviously a contract of sale is included. But what about a contract of hire, or hire-purchase? Is a promotional gift supplied? What if goods are sold by a non-profit making organisation, such as a Working Men's club? Write down your answers now. We shall find the answers shortly.

Cahalne v *Croydon LBC* (1985) 149 JP 561
The defendant was charged with offering to supply goods to which a false trade description was applied. The charges related to the defendant's hiring out of video cassettes which were falsely described as being produced by certain companies. In fact they were copies. Held: The defendant had offered to supply for the purposes of the Act. Stephen Brown LJ said, at 565:

> I am, further, clearly of the view that by offering to hire the goods to members of the public on payment of a fee, the person making that offer was offering to supply the goods. Supply is, in effect, distribution and the hiring of goods on payment of a fee is a method of distribution. It is not necessary, in my judgment, that a sale should be established in order for the supply of goods to be made out under s. 1(1).

In *Formula One Autocentres Ltd* v *Birmingham City Council*, *The Times*, 29 December 1998, the Divisional Court held that when a car taken in for a service was returned to the customer by the garage the car was supplied to the customer for the purposes of s. 1(1)(a) and (b). The garage in question offered a 'Master Service' and their documents described what this entailed. Trading standards officers submitted a car for this Master Service. When the officers collected the car they were given an invoice saying that the Master Service had been carried out. However, nine pre-existing faults which the Master Service should have detected were still present. The defendants argued that they should not have been charged under s. 1 of the Act, but under s. 14, which creates offences relating to the provision of services. (The s. 1 offences are offences of strict liability, the s. 14 offences are not.) Rose LJ held that the car had been supplied within the meaning of both s. 1(1)(a) and (b) because in returning the car the defendant was doing more than simply transferring physical control of it. The transfer of the vehicle enabled the recipient to apply the vehicle to purposes for which he desired to apply it. There was no requirement that the vehicle should have been supplied from the personal resources of the defendants.

As to the question of whether an unincorporated association can commit an offence under the Act, the Divisional Court considered the question in the case which follows.

John v *Mathews* [1970] 2 QB 443
The defendant was charged under s. 29(1)(a) of the Act with wilfully obstructing an officer who was acting in pursuance of the Act. The defendant was the secretary of the Gorse Hill Working Men's Club. The club had sold cigarettes marked '3d. off' at the full manufacturer's recommended price (i.e. without the 3d off) to a club member who had complained to an inspector of weights and measures. The inspector, who was employed by Swindon Borough Council, visited the club to investigate the matter. He was allowed into the hall of the club but not any further.
Held: The Act was only concerned with the supply of goods in the course of a trade or business. A private member's club did not supply goods to its members in this way. Therefore the officer was not acting in pursuance of the Act because the club could not have committed an offence under the Act. (The judgment of Lord Parker CJ is set out in *Cases and Materials* (**12.2.2**).)

In answer to **SAQ 12/8** it can therefore be seen that the word 'supply' is construed widely to incorporate any method of distribution. It would therefore include the distribution of a promotional gift. However, an unincorporated association cannot supply goods within the meaning of the Act.

12.3.5.2 Offers to supply

You should remember *Partridge* v *Crittenden* [1968] 1 WLR 1204 and *Fisher* v *Bell* [1961] 1 QB 394 from your study of the contract programme. In the former case a person who advertised bramblefinches for sale in a magazine was not guilty of offering for sale a wild bird contrary to s. 6(1) of the Protection of Birds Act 1954. In the latter case a shopkeeper who displayed a flicknife in his shop window, with a price tag attached, was not guilty of offering for sale an offensive weapon, contrary to s. 1(1) of the Restriction of Offensive

THE TRADE DESCRIPTIONS ACT 1968: GOODS

Weapons Act 1959. In both of these cases the defendants were not guilty because they made an invitation to treat rather than an offer.

ACTIVITY 12/11

Read s. 6 of the Act in *Cases and Materials* (12.1). Would the display of the knife in the shop window or the advertisement for the bramblefinches amount to an offer to supply for the purposes of the Act?

In both cases the defendants would have offered to supply. In *Partridge* v *Crittenden* the defendant did this by having the goods in his possession for supply. In *Fisher* v *Bell* the defendant offered to supply in the same way and also by exposing the goods for supply.

12.4 False Trade Descriptions

Section 2 of the Act contains an exhaustive list of what can amount to a trade description. (See *Cases and Materials* (12.1) for the full text.)

Section 2(1)(a)–(e) deals with physical characteristics; s. 2(1)(f)–(j) deals with past history. It can be seen that all of the matters which can amount to a false trade description are matters of fact. Therefore matters of opinion are not included, just as mere matters of opinion cannot be misrepresentations or terms of a contract. If a trade description is factual enough to amount to a misrepresentation, then it should also be factual enough to be a trade description for the purposes of the Act. However, it was never intended that the Act should make criminal a mere breach of warranty. Lord Widgery in *Becket* v *Cohen* [1972] 1 WLR 1593 stated, at 1596, 'In my judgment Parliament never intended or contemplated for a moment that the Act of 1968 should . . . make a criminal offence out of what is really a breach of warranty.'

In *Denard* v *Smith and Dixons Ltd* (1990) 155 JP 253 the defendants advertised a Spectrum computer for sale. The advertisement listed five items included in the deal. The box containing the computer contained items 1 and 2, but items 3, 4, and 5 were in a separate package. The defendants ran out of items 3, 4 and 5, but continued to display a placard in their shop, offering the whole package for sale. The defendants were charged with supplying and offering to supply goods to which a false trade description is applied contrary to s. 1(1)(b) of the Act. The defendants argued that they did intend to deliver items 3, 4 and 5, soon afterwards and that they had only committed a breach of warranty.

SAQ 12/9

(a) Which of the matters listed in s. 2(1)(a)–(j) had the defendant's description contravened?

(b) Were the defendants guilty of the offence?

(a) You should have written that the defendants had contravened s. 2(1)(c). The composition of the goods was not as described.

(b) The defendants were guilty of the offence. As they continued to display the placard at a time when they knew that items 3, 4, and 5 were out of stock this amounted to more than a mere breach of warranty.

Similarly, in *Queensway Discount Warehouses Ltd* v *Burke* (1985) JP 150 a wall unit was sold in a flat pack, but an advertisement showed the unit as ready assembled. The Divisional Court held that the word 'composition' under s. 2(1)(c) went wider than what would be regarded as the usual meaning of the word. It included not just the materials and the ingredients of an item but also the separate components of a package and the way in which those components were arranged and put together.

The matters listed in s. 2(1)(d) are all concerned with the quality of the goods. If the quality claimed cannot be scientifically disproved then it is obviously a difficult matter to say that it is absent in the goods. A claim by a garage that a car is a 'beautiful car' is likely to be regarded by the civil law as a mere sales puff. (If the car is not of satisfactory quality then s. 14(2) of the Sale of Goods Act 1979 will provide a remedy to the purchaser as long as the car was supplied in the course of a business.) But can such a sales puff give rise to criminal liability under the Act? In *Robertson* v *Dicicco* [1972] RTR 431 a secondhand car dealer described a car as a 'beautiful car' in an advertisement. One Mrs Walker examined the car and found that its appearance was very pleasing. Mrs Walker bought the car, which was subsequently shown to be in a very poor condition, and unroadworthy and unfit for use. The defendant claimed that as Mrs Walker found the car pleasing to the eye it was indeed a beautiful car. The Divisional Court held that an offence had been committed as the description was a false indication in respect of the car's performance, within s. 2(1)(d). In the following year, in *Kensington and Chelsea (Royal) London Borough Council* v *Riley* [1973] RTR 122 Melford Stevenson J explained that when words were alleged to constitute a false trade description for the purpose of the Act the primary question for consideration was what impression or impact was likely to be made on the mind of the ordinary man by the words used. Lord Widgery CJ agreed. At 124 he said that although in *Robertson* v *Dicicco* the Divisional Court had decided what the ordinary man would consider the word 'beautiful' to mean in the context of that case, the question ought ordinarily to be one of fact and therefore a matter for the magistrates to decide.

In *R* v *Anderson* (1987) 152 JP 373 the managing director of a garage which sold Nissan cars was convicted in the Crown Court of both applying a false trade description to goods and supplying goods to which a false trade description is applied, under s. 1(1)(a) and 1(1)(b) respectively. The British and Japanese governments had an agreement that Japanese cars should not amount to more than 11 per cent of total car sales in any one year. Nissan's own share of this amounted to 6 per cent of the market. If Nissan failed to reach this figure one year, the shortfall would be allocated to another Japanese supplier. For this reason, and to appear higher in the list of best-selling cars, Nissan required their managers to register a certain number of cars in their own names before selling them on to customers. The defendant later sold three previously registered cars as 'new'. The trial judge refused to rule as a matter of law that the word 'new' was incapable of being false when applied to each of the three cars at the time of sale. The jury decided that the word 'new' was a false description when applied to a previously registered car. Having been convicted, the defendant appealed to the Court of Appeal against the judge's ruling, arguing that the word 'new' did not carry any indication as to the registration position of the vehicles.

ACTIVITY 12/12

Read the judgment of Waterhouse J in *R* v *Anderson* in *Cases and Materials* (12.3) and answer the following questions.

(a) Were the cars sold in mint condition?

THE TRADE DESCRIPTIONS ACT 1968: GOODS

(b) Did the previous registration lower the value of the cars?

(c) In what way was *R v Ford Motor Co. Ltd* [1974] 1 WLR 1220 distinguished?

(d) Is the word 'new' capable of being exactly defined in this context?

(e) On appeal, was the conviction upheld?

(a) The cars sold were in mint condition.

(b) Both the purchasers and the vendors recognised that previous registration could reduce the value of the cars.

(c) *R v Ford Motor Co. Ltd* was distinguished because it concerned not previous registration, but minor repairs having been done to a car described as 'new'. The Court of Appeal ruled that as long as the car was perfectly repaired, so that it was as good as new, the description 'new' would not be false.

(d) The word 'new' is not capable of being exactly defined in this context. Rather it is 'susceptible of a variety of interpretations, depending upon the context in which it is used'.

(e) The conviction was upheld.

If goods are falsely described as being 'new' then obviously this might be within s. 2(1)(j). In *R v Anderson* Waterhouse J considered only s. 2(1)(j) to be relevant to the facts of the case. However, the description of a car as 'new' might also be within s. 2(1)(d), in that it might indicate expectations as to performance.

Section 2(1)(e) is a catch-all designed to cater for any physical characteristics not caught by s. 2(1)(a)–(d).

Section 2(1)(f) sets out that an indication of 'testing by any person and results thereof' will amount to a trade description.

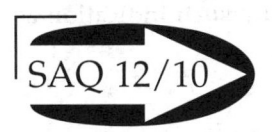

SAQ 12/10

A car is described by a garage as AA tested. The car has been tested by the AA and has failed the test on many counts. This failure is not revealed to a customer, who buys the car on account of the description 'AA' tested. Does the indication that the car was 'AA tested' amount to a false trade description?

A literal reading of s. 2(1)(f) would suggest that there has been no false trade description. However, it seems a better approach to regard statements about goods having been tested as implying that the goods have passed the test unless there is an indication that they have not.

SAQ 12/11

In *Beckett* v *Kingston Brothers (Butchers) Ltd* [1970] 1 QB 606 the Divisional Court accepted that the description 'Norfolk King Turkeys' was a false trade description when applied to Danish turkeys. Why then is it not an offence to sell soup described as 'Scotch Broth' or meals described as 'Irish stew' when the goods are manufactured in England?

It would seem that 'Scotch broth' and 'Irish stew' are recognised conventionally as referring to a style of cooking rather than to the meal having been produced in any particular country. But 'Norfolk King Turkeys' suggests that the birds were reared in Norfolk.

R v *Veys* (1992) 157 JP 567 concerned the appeal of a street trader to the Court of Appeal. The street trader had sold shirts outside Manchester United's football ground. The shirts bore an emblem which was very similar to the Manchester United registered trade mark. Above this were the words 'Manchester United' and underneath it the words 'Football Club'. On the reverse of the shirts was a picture of Brian McClair, the club's leading goal scorer, with the words 'He's here, he's there, he's every f***in where, Brian McClair'. The trader was convicted of offering to supply goods to which a false trade description had been applied. The grounds of the appeal were that the goods did not amount to a representation or indication that they had the approval of the football club or that they were manufactured by the football club.

ACTIVITY 12/13

Read the judgment of Staughton LJ in *R* v *Veys* in *Cases and Materials* (12.3) and answer the following questions.

(a) Under which two parts of s. 2 did the prosecution allege that there had been a false trade description?

(b) Did the words on the shirts and the trademark contain any such indication as is contained in s. 2 of the Act?

(c) Can it be said that the use of a trademark either will always or will never amount to a false trade description?

(d) On what grounds was *Durham Trading Standards* v *Kingsley Clothing* (1990) 154 JP 124 distinguished?

(e) Was the appeal allowed?

(a) The prosecution alleged that a trade description had been made under s. (2)(1)(g) or s. 2(1)(i).

THE TRADE DESCRIPTIONS ACT 1968: GOODS

(b) The word and the trademark did not contain any such indication as is contained in s. 2 of the Act. The words on the back gave a fairly clear indication that they were not authorised by Manchester United Football Club. Furthermore, the defendant had never suggested that the shirts were authorised by Manchester United Football Club, or that Manchester United Football Club had approved the sale of the shirts.

(c) It cannot be said that the use of trade mark either will or will not amount to a false trade description.

(d) *Durham Trading Standards* v *Kingsley* Clothing was distinguished on the grounds that the name 'Marc O Polo' is the name of somebody who deals only in clothing and there could be an indication from the name alone that the goods were produced by that company.

(e) The appeal was allowed and the convictions quashed.

When considering s. 2(1) it should also be borne in mind that no offence will be committed unless the description was false to a material degree (s. 3(1)).

Kent County Council v *Price* (1993) 157 JP 1161
The defendant was charged with six offences of offering to supply goods to which a false trade description had been applied, contrary to s. 1(1)(b) of the Act. The charges related to six T-shirts which were identical except that they sported different names, 'Fila', 'Levi's', 'Adidas', 'Puma' and 'Reebok'. None of the items were authentic. The defendant denied liability on two counts. First, a notice displayed on his stall stated 'Brand Copy'. Second, before each sale he indicated to members of the public that the garments were copies and were being sold for £1.99, whereas the genuine items would cost £12 or more. Held: In considering whether or not a description is false to a material degree the whole description has to be considered. The disclaimer notice and oral statements to the public were part of this description. No offence was committed because members of the public would have realised that they were not buying the genuine items. (An extract from Lord Stuart-Smith's judgment is reproduced in *Cases and Materials* (**12.3**).)

Section 2(1)(j) is again a catch-all section, covering matters which do not fall within s. 2(1)(f)–(i).

12.4.1 IMPLIED TRADE DESCRIPTIONS

Section 2(1) states that a trade description is an indication, direct or indirect, and by whatever means given, of any of the matters listed in s. 2(1)(a)–(j). We have already seen that the list is intended to be exhaustive. Although the indication given may be direct or indirect, it cannot be entirely passive.

Section 3(3) states: 'Anything which, though not a trade description, is likely to be taken for an indication of any of those matters [set out in s. 2(1)] and, as such an indication, would be false to a material degree, shall be deemed to be a false trade description.' Does this mean then that a trade description can be implied from the defendant's conduct?

In *Cottee* v *D. Seaton Ltd* [1972] 1 WLR 1408 the Divisional Court considered the effect of s. 3(3). A private motorist had effected an obvious and amateurish repair on the bodywork of his car surrounding the engine. The motorist had sold the car to the defendants, who were motor dealers. After failing to sell the car, the defendants had undertaken work to hide the repair. The defendants then sold the car to another dealer, Warry, who was entirely innocent of the repair. Warry sold the car to a private motorist. The defendants were charged with an offence under s. 23 of the Act. In order for this offence to be proved it was necessary to establish that Warry, who was not charged, had committed an offence under s. 1(1)(b) of the Act.

ACTIVITY 12/14

Read the extracts from *Cottee* v *D. Seaton* in *Cases and Materials* (12.3) and write down:

(a) Which of the indications under s. 2 did the prosecution allege was false to a material degree?

(b) Whether an antique restorer would commit an offence if he repaired goods and then sold them saying that they were undamaged.

(c) Whether an antique restorer who repaired goods but sold them without revealing that this was what he had done would commit an offence.

(d) Whether the defendants had applied a false trade description so as to make themselves guilty of an offence under s. 1(1)(a). (The defendants were not charged under s. 1(1)(a).)

(e) Whether Warry had committed an offence under s. 1(1)(b). (Thereby making the defendants guilty of an offence under s. 23.)

(f) There is no doubt that a person who supplies a car with a false odometer reading can be guilty of an offence under s. (1)(1)(b), even if he did not know that the reading was false. (See *R* v *Hammerton Cars Ltd* [1976] 1 WLR 1243 below, at 1246 in which Lawton LJ considering an offence under s. 1(1)(b) said, 'In our judgment a reading on a mileometer on a motor car is an indication of the use which it has had. It follows that it is a trade description and if the reading is false . . . it is capable of being a false trade description.' What is the difference between the odometer cases and the present case?

You should have written that:

(a) The prosecution alleged that s. 2(1)(d), an indication of the vehicle's strength, was false to a material degree.

(b) If the antique restorer sold repaired goods stating that they were undamaged then clearly an offence would be committed.

(c) If the antique dealer sold repaired goods but said nothing then no offence would be committed. Otherwise the doctrine of *caveat emptor* would be greatly reduced (Lord Widgery CJ). Milmo J thought that the Act did intend to make considerable inroads into the concept of *caveat emptor*, but did not disagree with Lord Widgery's example of the antique restorer.

(d) The defendants would have committed an offence under s. 1(1)(a) of the Act. The purpose of doing the repairs was to make it appear that the bodywork surrounding the engine was sound when it was not. This was an indication of one of the matters listed in s. 2(1)(d).

(e) Warry was not guilty of an offence under s. 1(1)(b). Warry did not even know that any trade description had been applied to the car. Without such knowledge

THE TRADE DESCRIPTIONS ACT 1968: GOODS

(which is a different matter from knowing that a trade description applied is false) he could not be guilty of an offence under s. 2(1)(b).

(f) The odometer cases are different because the trader who supplies the cars, not knowing that the readings are false, at least knows that there is a trade description. (The readings on the odometers.) Milmo J stated that, 'I think that knowledge that, at the time of supply or offer to supply, a trade description *is* applied to the goods is an essential prerequisite of an offence being committed by the supplier under s. 1(1)(b) of the Act.'

In *Cases and Materials* you should also read *Holloway* v *Cross* [1981] 1 All ER 1012 (**12.3**). In that case a motor dealer gave an expert opinion of the true mileage of a car. This opinion was a long way from the true figure, but it persuaded the member of the public to whom it was made to buy the car. Donaldson LJ thought that this might well have been an indirect trade description within s. 2(1) but that it was certainly within s. 3(3) because it was likely to be taken by the purchaser as an indication of the history of the vehicle. Hodgson J expressed the same view.

12.5 False Descriptions

Section 3(1) of the Act tells us that a false trade description is a trade description which is false to a material degree. Section 3(2) tells us that a trade description which is not literally false but which is misleading shall be deemed to be false, and that a misleading trade description is one which is likely to be taken for such an indication of any of the matters specified in s. 2 of the Act as would be false to a material degree. Section 3(3) states that anything which, although not a trade description, is likely to be taken as an indication of any of the matters listed in s. 2 and, as such an indication, would be false to a material degree, shall be deemed to be a false trade description.

We should consider the three subsections separately.

12.5.1 DESCRIPTIONS FALSE TO A MATERIAL DEGREE

Section 3(1) requires that a false trade description be false to a material degree.

Cadbury Ltd v *Halliday* [1975] 1 WLR 653
The defendants, who were manufacturers of chocolate bars, were charged under s. 23 of the Act. The alleged false trade description was the words 'extra value' on chocolate bar wrappers.

ACTIVITY 12/15

Read the judgment of Ashworth J in *Cadbury* v *Halliday* in *Cases and Materials* (12.4). Write down why the words 'extra value' did not amount to a false trade description.

You should have written that the words 'extra value' did not amount to a false trade description because they were neither dealing with physical characteristics nor the history of the goods (s. 2(1)(a)–(e) deal with physical characteristics; s. 2(1)(f)–(j) deal with past history). (Nor were the words likely to be taken as an indication of a trade description under s. 3(3).) Rather the words were a mere sales puff which would not induce people to buy the chocolate.

ACTIVITY 12/16

In *Cases and Materials* (12.2.1), look again at the judgment of Lord Parker CJ in *Donnelly* v *Rowlands*. Did Lord Parker think that the words embossed on the milk bottles were false to a material degree? Did Lord Parker consider the objective meaning of the words or the subjective meaning?

You should have written that Lord Parker did not consider the words false to a material degree or indeed to any degree. He based this view on an objective consideration of the words, considering what an ordinary member of the public would have made of them. Similarly, in *Kent County Council* v *Price* the descriptions on the T-shirts were not false to a material degree because no member of the public would have thought that they were authentic.

Can a description be materially false on the basis of what is not included in the description? In *Routledge* v *Ansa Motors* [1980] RTR 1 a car which was manufactured in 1972, but first registered in 1975, was sold as a new car. This description was false to a material degree because members of the public would have thought that it meant that the car was manufactured in 1975. (You should also remember that Waterhouse J in *R* v *Anderson* said that the word 'new' is 'susceptible of a variety of interpretations, depending upon the context in which it is used'. Whether or not such a description is false to a material degree would therefore depend upon all the circumstances of the case in question.)

Wolkind and Another v *Pura Foods Ltd* (1987) 85 LGR 782
A company sold vegetable fat labelled as 'Pura Vegetable Lard'. Lard generally means pig fat, but this product contained no pig or other animal fat. The label on the goods stated 'Pura Vegetable Lard is 100 per cent vegetable oils. It contains no animal fat'. The company which sold the lard was charged with supplying goods to which a false trade description had been applied, contrary to s. 1(1)(b) of the Act.
Held: The defendant was not guilty as no reasonably minded court could have concluded that lard was restricted to pig fat, particularly bearing in mind the words on the wrapping. The description was not therefore false to a material degree.

12.5.2 MISLEADING, BUT NOT LITERALLY FALSE, STATEMENTS

Section 3(2) tells us that a trade description which is not literally false but which is misleading shall be deemed to be false, and that a misleading trade description is one which is likely to be taken for such an indication of any of the matters specified in s. 2 of the Act as would be false to a material degree. An example of this is provided by *Robertson* v *Dicicco* above, where the unroadworthy car was described as a 'beautiful car'. As we saw earlier, the Divisional Court considered that this was a false indication in respect of the car's performance, within s. 2(1)(d).

In *R* v *Inner London Justices, ex parte Wandsworth London Borough Council* [1983] RTR 425 the defendants, who were motor dealers, sold a car saying that it had had only 'one

THE TRADE DESCRIPTIONS ACT 1968: GOODS

owner'. The purchaser of the car discovered that the car's registration document stated that the car had had five earlier keepers. The defendants were charged with an offence under s. 1(1)(b) of the Act. The one previous owner had been a leasing company, and over the five years of the car's life the company had hired the car to five hirers, each of whom was required to tax, insure, repair and maintain the car. The magistrates dismissed the charge on the grounds that there was no case to answer, because as a matter of strict legal meaning the car had had only one previous owner.

SAQ 12/12

Were the magistrates correct? Write down what you think.

The Divisional Court held that the justices had erred in law in deciding that there was no case to answer. The description 'one owner' was clearly capable of being a false trade description in the sense of a misleading trade description within s. 3(2) of the Act.

12.5.3 INDICATIONS OF THE MATTERS LISTED IN SECTION 2(1)

Section 3(3) states that anything which, although not a trade description, is likely to be taken for an indication of any of the matters listed in s. 2(1) and, as such an indication, would be false to a material degree, shall be deemed to be a false trade description.

ACTIVITY 12/17

In *Cases and Materials* (12.3), look again at the judgment of Donaldson LJ in *Holloway v Cross*. Did Donaldson LJ think that the expert estimation of the car's mileage fell within s. 2(1) or within s. 3(3)?

You should have written that Donaldson LJ did not rule that the estimation either was, or was not, within s. 2(1). He did, however, hold that it was within s. 3(3), and so when estimates of this kind are given this is the more appropriate section to use.

You should also look again at *Cottee v D. Seaton Ltd*, above, in which the Divisional Court considered the meaning of s. 3(3).

12.6 Disclaimers

Later we shall consider the defences allowed by s. 24 of the Act. Here we are considering disclaimers. Almost all of the disclaimer cases concern false odometer readings. The Act does not mention disclaimers, but the courts have allowed them. Lord Widgery CJ in *Waltham Forest London Borough Council v TG Wheatley (Central Garage) Ltd* [1978] RTR 157 said, at 162:

The disclaimer notice is a creation of the courts. It is not dealt with in the Act at all, and it has been developed in order to recognise the obvious justice of enabling a person to explain the falsity of a speedometer reading by saying, 'I am not suggesting that this is guaranteed. I disclaim any responsibility for it. You must not rely on it'.

Lord Widgery's full judgment is set out in *Cases and Materials* (12.4).

In *R v Hammerton Cars Ltd* [1976] 1 WLR 1243, at 1248, Lawton LJ made it plain that a disclaimer is not a defence, but rather that it prevents a false trade description from having been applied:

> He [the trial judge] went on to deal with disclaimer and did so in terms which may have led the jury to think that disclaimer was a defence in itself whereas, as we have already said, evidence of disclaimer may lead to the displacing of such inferences as arise from the presence on the motor car of a false mileometer reading.

In *Newman v Hackney London Borough Council* [1982] RTR 296 a motor dealer turned a car's clock back from 46,000 miles to 21,000. The dealer was charged with an offence under s. 1(1)(a) of applying a false trade description to goods and sought to rely on a disclaimer.

ACTIVITY 12/18

Read *R v Southwood* [1987] 3 All ER 556 in *Cases and Materials* (12.4). Could a disclaimer be used to prevent a defendant from being guilty of an offence under s. (1)(1)(a)? Could a disclaimer be used to prevent a defendant committing an offence under s. 1(1)(b) of supplying goods to which a false trade description is applied?

You should have written that the Court of Appeal decided that by turning the clock back himself, the motor dealer would be precluded from escaping liability by means of the disclaimer. However, the disclaimer could assist a defendant charged under s. 1(1)(b).

In *R v Southwood*, the defendant was appealing against a conviction under s. 1(1)(a). He had bought a number of used cars and deliberately turned the clock back on all of them. The invoices handed to purchasers stated, 'We do not guarantee the accuracy of the recorded mileage.' A sticker on the odometer of each car stated, 'We do not guarantee the accuracy of the recorded mileage. To the best of our knowledge and belief, however, the reading is incorrect.' A notice displayed in the sales office said, 'All mileage on cars offered are incorrect and sold and offered on this understanding.' The Court of Appeal held that the disclaimer did not alter the defendant's guilt under s. 1(1)(a) which is a strict liability offence. It was further held that a person who turned the mileometer back to zero was, in so doing, applying a false trade description contrary to s. 1(1)(a) and it was irrelevant that no-one was likely to be misled by a second-hand car which had zero miles on the clock.

In a more recent Court of Appeal decision, *R v Bull* (1996) 160 JP 240, a disclaimer did save the defendant, who had not himself turned the mileometer back, from committing an offence under s. 1(1)(a) of the Act.

R v Bull (1996) 160 JP 240

The defendant appealed against conviction under s. 1(1)(a) of the Act. He had displayed a car showing a mileage of over 47,526 miles, when the car had in fact travelled over 87,000 miles. The defendant had not himself turned the mileometer back. The defendant had placed a disclaimer on the odometer and on the sales invoice. He copied the mileage figure on the odometer onto the invoice, highlighting the following words with an asterisk, 'We have been unable to confirm the mileage recorded on this odometer and therefore it must be considered incorrect.'

Held: The offence of applying a false trade description could be committed by copying the mileage reading from the odometer onto an invoice. However, the disclaimer could prevent the trade description from being false at the time when it was applied in this way. It would have this effect if it prevented a reasonable person from regarding it as accurate. In cases such as this the court must have regard to the positioning of the disclaimer in relation to the quoted mileage reading and all the other relevant circumstances. In this case the highlighting with the asterisk was a relevant circumstance. The defendant's appeal was therefore allowed. (In *Cases and Materials* (**12.4**), you should read the judgment of Waterhouse J.)

As we have seen, disclaimers will generally assist only those defendants charged under s. 1(1)(b) of the Act. To be effective, the disclaimer must be 'as bold, precise and compelling as the trade description itself', per Widgery LJ in *Norman v Bennett* [1974] 1 WLR 1229 at 1232. Lord Widgery also said that 'the disclaimer must equal the trade description in the extent to which it is likely to get home to anyone interested in receiving the goods. To be effective as a defence to a charge under s. 1(1)(b) of the Act any such disclaimer must be made before the goods are supplied.' Lawton LJ reviewed *Norman v Bennett* in *R v Hammerton Cars Ltd* and said that supply could not be equated with delivery:

> The issue for the court of trial is whether when the purchaser takes possession of the goods he gets them with a false trade description applied to them. What he may have seen during the negotiations may have made such an impact upon him that an oral statement made when delivery was given might not be effective to displace the mileometer reading. Whether it had been would be a question of fact. If Lord Widgery CJ's judgment on the construction of the words 'is applied' amounts to the proposition that a dealer can never disclaim when making a delivery (which it probably does not) we do not agree. A dealer who delays disclaimer as late as this may have difficulty in persuading a court that a false trade description has not been applied; but he may be able to do so.

SAQ 12/13

Until *R v Bull* it was thought that a disclaimer could not save a defendant charged with applying a false trade description under s. 1(1)(a). To be effective the disclaimer must operate before any offence is committed. In cases such as *R v Southwood* and *R v Bull*, at what time is an offence committed under s. 1(1)(a)?

An offence is committed under s. 1(1)(a) as soon as the false trade description is applied. In cases such as *R v Southwood* a false trade description was applied when the defendant turned back the odometers. Therefore a subsequent disclaimer was too late to be effective. In *R v Bull* the description was not applied by the defendant until the mileage was copied on to the invoice. By this time the customer was aware of the disclaimer.

R v Hammerton Cars Ltd [1976] 1 WLR 1243
The defendants, motor dealers, were convicted of an offence under s. 1(1)(b). They had supplied two Jaguar cars. One had a mileometer reading of 25,600 miles when it should have been 53,714. The other mileometer showed 25,300 when it should have shown about 34,000. At or about the time of delivery the purchasers were given a printed document headed 'Specific guarantee of used motor vehicle'. In smaller print than the other paragraphs, one said, 'Any estimate or opinion of the mileage or date or model or past use of the vehicle which the suppliers may have given to the customer during negotiations for its purchase or hire-purchase was given according to their best information and belief.' Later in the same paragraph the document said, 'The suppliers are not answerable for the mileage shown on the vehicle's mileometer.' The jury rejected the defendant's evidence that he had specifically drawn the customer's attention to the fact that the mileage was not guaranteed.
Held: The defendants were guilty of the offence under s. 1(1)(b). Neither a casual oral remark nor a disclaimer in small print was likely to be an effective disclaimer.

In *R v Hammerton Cars Ltd* Lord Lawton said, at 1248, that it was unwise and likely to cause confusion to try and divide the evidence into that which established that a trade description had been applied and that which was said to be a disclaimer of that description:

> The evidence must be looked at as a whole. At the end of the case, when all the evidence has been heard, the right question for the court of trial is this: 'Have the prosecution proved that this defendant supplied goods to which a false trade description was applied?' If the evidence was positive that at the beginning of the negotiations a false trade description was applied but before they were concluded the defendant made it clear to the purchaser that the trade description should be disregarded, then the answer to the question will be 'no'; but if he did not make it clear then the answer will probably be 'yes'.

In *Waltham Forest London Borough Council v TG Wheatley (Central Garage) Ltd* [1978] RTR 157 the defendants displayed on their forecourt a car which displayed false odometer readings. They were charged under s. 1(1)(b) of the Act with supplying vehicles to which a false trade description was applied. On a wall in their office a disclaimer stated that they gave no guarantee of the mileage of cars which they supplied. Lord Widgery CJ said that:

> The cases show that, in order for such a disclaimer to be effective, it must be of equal power and penetration as the statement on the odometer which it seeks to counter ... in developing this doctrine of the disclaimer notice we never contemplated that a motor trader could put up a notice on the wall of his office and then forget all about his responsibility in this regard.

12.7 Summary

In this chapter we have covered the following:

- The Trade Descriptions Act 1968 imposes criminal liability on those who falsely describe goods and services in the course of a trade or business.

- Two offences relating to the misdescription of goods are created.

- It is an offence under s. 1(1)(a) of the Act to apply a false trade description to any goods.

- It is an offence under s. 1(1)(b) to supply or to offer to supply any goods to which a false trade description is applied.

- The s. 1(1)(a) offence is more serious than the s. 1(1)(b) offence.

- The two offences can only be committed by a person acting in the course of a trade or business.

- Section 2 of the Act sets out an exhaustive definition of the matters which can amount to a trade description.

- Section 4 of the Act gives an exhaustive definition of the ways in which a person can apply a description to goods.

- A trade description can be made impliedly.

- A trade description is false if it is false to a material degree.

- A disclaimer may prevent a false trade description from being applied.

12.8 End of Chapter Assessment Question

Dodgy Motors Ltd operate a car hire business. Mr D. Odgy is the managing director and the only shareholder in the company. When their hire cars are three years old Dodgy Motors then sell them off to members of the public. Dodgy Motors never sell a car for more than they paid for it. When selling the cars, Dodgy Motors do so from a garage forecourt which is two miles from their car hire premises. Last week Dodgy advertised two cars for sale in a local newspaper. The advertisement stated: '1995 Ford Fiesta. One owner. 23,000 miles. 1996 Ford Granada. One owner. 14,000 miles. Neither mileage can be guaranteed, but both cars in beautiful condition. First to see will buy.' Relying on the advertisement, Mr Smith went to view the Fiesta. A sticker was stuck across the Fiesta's odometer, saying that the mileage could not be guaranteed. In fact, Mr Odgy, the managing director of Dodgy Motors Ltd, had himself turned back the odometer from 76,000 miles. He had also effected repairs which disguised the fact that the car's bodywork was very rotten. Mr Smith bought the car for £5,000.

The Ford Granada was bought by Miss Jones. The car had not been used in Dodgy's car hire business. Mr Odgy had bought the car for his own personal use. One week later he inherited a new Rover and therefore decided to sell the Granada. Mr Odgy did not know this, but the Granada's odometer reading was false, having been turned back by the person from whom he had bought the car. Again, an identically worded disclaimer to that on the odometer of the Fiesta had been stuck across the Granada's odometer by Mr Odgy. Before he recorded the mileage on an invoice Mr Odgy said, 'As far as I know, that mileage is absolutely genuine. But in the car business you never know, so take a good look at that sign on the wall.' The sign to which Mr Odgy referred said, 'No guarantees on mileage. To the best of our knowledge and belief all recorded mileages are correct.'

Consider whether or not Dodgy Motors Ltd has committed any offences under the Trade Descriptions Act 1968.

See *Cases and Materials* (13.4) for an outline answer.

CHAPTER THIRTEEN

THE TRADE DESCRIPTIONS ACT 1968: SERVICES AND DEFENCES

13.1 Objectives

By the end of this chapter you should be able to:

- analyse whether a misdescription as to services, accommodation, or facilities is made in the course of a trade or business;

- explain the circumstances in which a false statement can be regarded as having been made for the purposes of s. 14 of the Trade Descriptions Act 1968;

- analyse the *mens rea* required by the s. 14(1)(a) offence of making a statement (about services etc.) which is known to be false;

- analyse the *mens rea* required by the s. 14(1)(b) offence of recklessly making a statement (about services etc.) which is false;

- evaluate the scope of 'services, accommodation and facilities';

- explain the extent to which a statement about the future can be regarded as a false statement;

- outline the defences available under the Act;

- explain how a defendant who has not committed one of the main offences can nevertheless by guilty of an offence under the 'by-pass' procedure.

13.2 Introduction

In **Chapter 12** we saw that the two offences relating to the misdescription of goods are offences of strict liability. Section 14 creates two offences relating to the false description of services, accommodation or facilities. These offences are committed either by making a statement which is known to be false, or by recklessly making a statement which is false. Both of these offences therefore require a *mens rea*, and we examine the different *mens rea* required by the two offences in some detail.

As with the two offences relating to goods, the offences relating to services, accommodation or facilities can only be committed by a person acting in the course of a trade or business. We begin the chapter by considering when a false statement as to services etc. is made in this way.

As the s. 14 offences only concern false or misleading statements as to 'services, accommodation or facilities', we need to examine each of these words in turn to ascertain their meaning. Section 14 prohibits the making of false statements as regards only five matters concerning services, accommodation and facilities. These matters are specifically set out and we therefore examine each of them individually.

We conclude the chapter by examining the defences available under the 1968 Act. These defences can apply to s. 1 offences as well as to s. 14 offences. When a defence is invoked it may be the case that another person is prosecuted for an offence under the 'by-pass' procedure.

13.3 Misdescription of Services, Accommodation or Facilities

13.3.1 ACTING IN THE COURSE OF A TRADE OR BUSINESS

In **Chapter 12** we examined the s. 1 offences and saw that these could only be committed by a person acting in the course of a trade or business. It can be seen from s. 14 that the two offences relating to services, accommodation or facilities can also be committed only by a person acting in the course of a trade or business.

ACTIVITY 13/1

In Chapter 3 read again the case of *Fletcher* v *Sledmore* [1973] RTR 371. Assume that the facts of the case were the same except that the dealer repairing the car had falsely told the prospective customer that he was going to fully service the car before it was sold on to the garage which would sell it to the customer. Would this false description as to a service to be provided have been applied in the course of the repairer's trade or business?

The same reasoning as was applied when considering the offence under s. 1(1)(a) can again be applied when considering s. 14. The statement would have been made as part of the dealer's business activities. He would have had an interest in the garage's sale to the customer, and therefore would have applied the false description as to services in the course of his trade or business. There is no requirement that the provider of the service etc. is to contract with, or be paid by, the person to whom the false statement was made.

R v *Breeze* [1973] 1 WLR 994
A potential customer engaged the defendant to draw up plans because the defendant falsely claimed to be a qualified architect. The Crown Court convicted the defendant of making a statement about the provision of a service which he knew to be false, in the course of any trade or business, contrary to s. 14(1)(a). The defendant appealed to the Court of Appeal, putting forward two arguments. First, that the services he provided were professional services and were not therefore provided in the course of a trade or business. Second, the false statement related to professional qualifications and not to the provision of any services.

THE TRADE DESCRIPTIONS ACT 1968: SERVICES AND DEFENCES

SAQ 13/1

Do you think either of these arguments were successful?

Neither argument was successful. First, the defendant could not claim that he was conducting an activity of a professional character when he did not have the qualifications to carry on that profession. Second, the statement that he was qualified as an architect would affect the likely quality of the service to be provided. It therefore amounted to a statement as to the provision of services. (An extract from Lord Widgery's judgment is set out in *Cases and Materials* (13.1.1).)

ACTIVITY 13/2

In Chapter 12, read again the facts of *Roberts* v *Leonard* (1995) 94 LGR 284. If the vets had falsely told the foreign purchasers of the cattle that they would all be inoculated before being handed over to the exporters would this false description have been applied in the course of a trade or business?

On the same line of reasoning as was applied when considering the s. 1 offences, the defendants would have applied the false description as to services to be provided while acting in the course of their trade or profession. It would not have mattered that they were not themselves selling or exporting the cattle. In *Roberts* v *Leonard* Simon Brown LJ said, 'I have not the least doubt that the term "trade or business" in the 1968 Act is apt to include professions too.'

In *R* v *Bow Street Magistrates Court, ex parte Joseph* (1986) 150 JP 650 the Divisional Court had to decide whether or not the Law Society carried on a trade or business for the purposes of the Act. (A solicitor wanted to bring a private prosecution against the Law Society, alleging that one of the Society's advertisements amounted to a breach of s. 14 of the Act.) The Divisional Court refused to accept that the Law Society was a body which carried on a trade or business. It offered services to solicitors, but did not offer services to the public and did not carry on any operation which had a commercial connotation.

13.3.2 MAKING A FALSE STATEMENT

Both parts of s. 14 require that a false statement be made. This inevitably raises the question of when a statement is made, and in the following case the Court of Appeal had to consider when a false statement contained in a holiday brochure was made. Was it made once, when the brochure was printed up, or was it made innumerable times when readers of the 2,000,000 brochures read the statement?

R v *Thomson Holidays Ltd* [1974] 2 WLR 371
In 1972 the defendants pleaded guilty to contravening s. 14(1)(b) of the 1968 Act. They had recklessly made false statements in their travel brochure that a particular hotel in Greece had a children's paddling pool, a private swimming pool and a nightclub on the

beach. The defendants were charged in 1973 with three new charges under s. 14(1)(b). These new charges arose because a second person had complained about having booked a holiday in the same hotel. This second person had relied on the same edition of the brochure in respect of the same amenities at the same hotel. The defendants entered a plea of autrefois convict (that they had already been convicted of the offence and could not therefore be convicted of it again). If a statement in the brochure is only made once, when the brochure is published, the defence would be successful. If a statement in a brochure is made every time a reader read the statement then the defence would not be successful.

Held: The true construction of s. 14(1)(b) was that the false statements in the brochure were made on each occasion when the brochure was read by the people for whom it was intended. It therefore followed that there were as many offences as there were readers. Lord Lawton: 'With the printed word the information would be given when the statements were read. In our judgment that was when the false statements were made, and they were made to each reader.' The defence of autrefois convict therefore failed. (Lord Lawton gave the judgment of the Court of Appeal, and an extract from this judgment is set out in *Cases and Materials* (13.1.2).)

Wings Ltd v *Ellis* [1985] 1 AC 272
Wings Ltd published a brochure in the course of their business. Unknown to anyone within the company, the brochure wrongly described a hotel in Sri Lanka as air-conditioned. The error was only discovered after the brochure had been issued to travel agents. On 1 June 1981 all staff of Wings Ltd were told to amend their brochures and sales staff were told to inform travel agents and customers of the error when holidays were booked. Customers who had already booked were informed by letter. On 13 January 1982 the complainant read an unamended brochure and booked a holiday through a travel agent. He could only be contacted through the travel agent and was not told of the error. On his return from Sri Lanka he complained to a trading standards officer that the hotel was not air-conditioned, as it had been described in the brochure. Wings Ltd were charged with making a statement which they knew to be false, on 13 January 1982, as to the nature of the accommodation at the hotel. The House of Lords therefore had to consider whether or not a defendant could be guilty of an offence under s. 14(1)(a) of the Act (making a statement which is known to be false) when he had no knowledge of the falsity of the statement at the time of publication, but did know of the falsity at the time when the statement was read by the complainant.

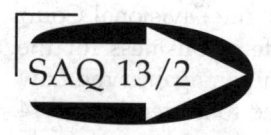

SAQ 13/2

What do you think the House of Lords decided?

The House of Lords held that the offence had been committed. A statement which was false was made by the company in the course of its business when it was read by the complainant, who was an interested member of the public doing business with the company on the basis of the statement. At the time when the statement was made the company knew that it was false. There was no requirement that the company should know that the statement was false at the time when it first made the statement. If the company became aware of the falsity of the statement then continuing to make the statement would constitute the offence. (Extracts from the judgments of Lord Hailsham of Marylebone and Lord Scarman can be read in *Cases and Materials* (13.1.2).) Although this approach seems somewhat harsh, all their Lordships thought that the defendants might have been better advised to try to prove that they had a defence, rather than to argue that no offence was committed.

THE TRADE DESCRIPTIONS ACT 1968: SERVICES AND DEFENCES

When we studied the s. 1 offences we saw that the false trade description must be connected to a supply of the goods. As regards the s. 14 offences, the false statement does not need to induce the making of a contract and may be made after the contract has been concluded. However, there is still a requirement that the statement is connected to the supply of a service, accommodation or facilities.

Breed v *Cluett* [1970] 2 QB 459
Contracts were exchanged, between the builder and the purchaser, on a partly built bungalow. Before completion, the builder of the bungalow made a false statement to the purchaser that the bungalow was covered by an NHBRC guarantee. The defendant was charged with recklessly making a statement which was false as to the provision of a service, contrary to s. 14(1)(b) of the Act. The justices decided that as there was already a binding contract between the builder and the purchaser, the statement could not be an inducement to make a contract and so the charge should be dismissed.
Held: The word 'statement' in s. 14 of the Act was not confined to statements which induced the making of a contract and could apply to a statement subsequently made. The builder was therefore guilty of an offence under s. 14(1)(b).

ACTIVITY 13/3

In Chapter 3, read again the facts of *Hall* v *Wickens Motors Ltd* [1972] 1 WLR 1418. Would the defendants have been guilty of an offence if, when the customer brought the car back with a complaint, they had stated that they had (40 days earlier) carried out a full service on the car, rather than stating that there was nothing wrong with the car?

The garage would have been guilty of an offence. It would not have been necessary to prove that the false statement as to services induced the contract of sale, and nor would there have been a requirement that the statement should have been made before the contract of sale was concluded. An offence would have been committed because a statement claiming that a service has been carried out on a car is one which carries with it a continuing obligation. (The garage might be called upon to rectify some matter which should have been covered by the service.) But a statement that the steering is in good working order imposes no such continuing obligation on the seller of the car.

R v *Bevelectric Ltd* (1992) 157 JP 323
The defendant company carried on a business repairing washing machines. The company's policy was to tell all customers whose washing machines were not working that a new motor would be required. This was the case even where the fault was very minor, and where the expense of having a new motor installed would not need to be incurred. The company was charged with offences under s. 14(1)(b).
Held: The company was guilty. The statements that new motors were needed was a false statement about a service provided in the past. (Examining the washing machines and ascertaining that a new motor would be needed.) False statements as to the nature of services provided in the past could be within s. 14(1)(b) as long as they are part of a transaction in the course of a trade or business. The statements that the motors needed to be replaced implied that a proper assessment had been made and they were clearly connected or associated with the supply of a service. (Staughton LJ gave the judgment of the Court of Appeal, an extract from which can be read in *Cases and Materials* (**13.1.2.**)

13.3.3 THE *MENS REA*

13.3.3.1 Making a statement which is known to be false

ACTIVITY 13/4

Read s. 14(1)(a) in *Cases and Materials* (12.1). Could the subsection be paraphrased to say that a defendant will be guilty of an offence if he knowingly makes a statement (about services etc.) which he knows to be false?

The subsection could not be paraphrased in this way. If it could, then clearly the offence would require *mens rea* and would not be an offence of strict liability. However, in *Wings Ltd* v *Ellis* the House of Lords held that the offence is one of 'semi-strict' liability. By this it is meant that the defendant must know that the statement he makes is false. But he does not need to know this when he first publishes the statement. In cases where the same statement is made many times, it will be sufficient if the defendant subsequently discovers that the statement is false. Once the defendant is aware that the statement is false, he will have the necessary *mens rea* every time the statement is subsequently made, even if the defendant did not know that the statement was being made. (In *Cases and Materials* (13.1.3.1) an extract from Lord Scarman's speech in *Wings Ltd* v *Ellis* is reproduced. In this extract Lord Scarman explains why the offence can be committed unknowingly, that is to say without knowledge of the act of making a statement. It will be seen that Lord Scarman thought that this approach advances the purpose of the Act. He also made the point that the approach should cause no injustice as a person who had acted innocently might be able to invoke one of the statutory defences.)

13.3.3.2 Recklessly

The word recklessly is in this context given a statutory definition. Section 14(2)(b) states that for the purposes of s. 14 'a statement made regardless of whether it is true or false shall be deemed to be made recklessly, whether or not the person making it had reasons for believing that it might be false'.

In **Chapter 1** we saw that a misrepresentation may be fraudulent, negligent or innocent. Put simply, a fraudulent misrepresentation is one made in any of three ways: either knowing that it was false, or not believing it was true or recklessly careless whether it was true or false. (As per *Derry* v *Peek* (1889) 14 App Cas 337.) A negligent misrepresentation is one made honestly believing that it was true, but without reasonable grounds for such a belief. An innocent misrepresentation is one made honestly believing it was true, with reasonable grounds for such a belief.

SAQ 13/3

Do you think either a fraudulent, negligent or innocent misrepresentation can be made 'recklessly', as defined by s. 14(2)(b)?

The following case will provide the answer.

THE TRADE DESCRIPTIONS ACT 1968: SERVICES AND DEFENCES

MFI Warehouses Ltd v *Nattrass* [1973] 1 WLR 307
The defendants advertised louvre doors for sale by mail order. A carriage charge of 25p was to be made for each door supplied. The advertisement also offered folding door gear for sale, 'carriage free'. The defendants intended that the folding door gear could only be bought with the louvre doors. The defendant's chairman studied the advertisement for five or ten minutes before it was published, but he did not appreciate that the folding door gear could be bought separately. A customer bought some folding door gear separately. The defendants charged the customer for carriage.
Held: The defendants were guilty of an offence under s. 14(1)(b). The statement about free carriage was made recklessly because it was made without regard to its truth or falsity. It was not necessary to prove that the chairman had any kind of dishonest mind or deliberately closed his eyes to the truth. What was necessary was to prove that he had not had regard to whether the advertisement was true or false, that is to say whether or not he had examined the advertisement with this end in view. As he had not, the advertisement was issued 'regardless of whether it is true or false.' (An extract from the judgment of Lord Widgery CJ is set out in *Cases and Materials* (**13.1.3.2**). You should read this extract and, if necessary, amend your original answer to **SAQ 13/3**.)

In the light of Lord Widgery's judgment we can now answer **SAQ 13/3**. It can be seen that a *'Derry* v *Peek'* fraudulent misrepresentation is within the meaning of 'reckless' here, but so is a negligent misrepresentation. The chairman who examined the advertisement was not fraudulent in the *Derry* v *Peek* sense. He was however negligent in that he should have appreciated what the advertisement actually said. It is unlikely that an innocent misrepresentation would be included. Widgery CJ stated, at 313, 'it is quite clear that this Act is designed for the protection of customers and it does not seem to me to be unreasonable to suppose that in creating such additional protection Parliament was minded to place upon the advertiser a positive obligation to have regard to whether his advertisement was true or false'. If the chairman had taken positive steps to see that the advertisement was true, and in the light of these steps had reasonably concluded that it was, then the company would not have made the statement recklessly.

In *Wings Ltd* v *Ellis* we saw that the defendant was guilty of knowingly making the false statement about the hotel's having air-conditioning because he knew that the statement was false when it was made to the complainant. (That is to say when the complainant read the statement.) The fact that Wings Ltd did not know that the statement was false when they published it, and that they had taken all reasonable steps to rectify the situation, did not prevent the commission of the offence. The same logic ought to apply to the offence of recklessly making a statement which is false. The statement must be made recklessly and, in the case of a brochure or advertisement, it will be made every time a customer reads it.

Cowburn v *Focus Television Rentals Ltd* [1983] Crim LR 563
The defendants advertised in their shops that anyone who hired a video recorder would be given free the hire of 20 films. On 9 November this offer was withdrawn and a new offer was made, this time giving the free hire of only six films. This amended offer was not communicated to one particular shop and a customer in that shop hired a video because of the original advertisement that 20 free films would be supplied. On being made aware of the customer's complaint to a trading standards inspector, the defendants sent the customer 20 free films and ensured that the advertisement was amended in the shop in question. The magistrates refused to convict on a charge under s. 14(1)(b) on the grounds that the defendant's subsequent conduct had rectified what was previously false. The prosecutor appealed.

SAQ 13/4

Did the Divisional Court allow the appeal?

You should have written that the Divisional Court did allow the appeal. The statement was made when the customer read it and hired the video. It was at this time false, and the defendants had made the statement recklessly. Their subsequent behaviour might mitigate the sentence, but it could not prevent the offence from having been committed.

13.3.4 SERVICES, ACCOMMODATION AND FACILITIES

Section 14 of the Act is concerned with false or misleading statements as to 'any services, accommodation or facilities'. We need therefore to consider the meaning of services, accommodation and facilities in turn.

13.3.4.1 Services

In **Chapter 12** we saw that s. 1 of the Act creates two offences relating to the false descriptions of goods. In this chapter we are considering s. 14 which creates offences relating to services. We now need to examine what is meant by 'services' in this context, and more particularly, whether a contract to supply goods can be classified as a contract to provide services.

Newell and Another v *Hicks* [1984] RTR 135
The defendants, motor dealers, advertised that if anyone bought a particular make of car they would be given a 'free' video cassette recorder. In fact the video recorders were not free, because anyone who tried to take advantage of the offer would have his discount on the cost price or trade in price of his old vehicle reduced by the price of the recorder. The justices convicted the defendants of an offence of recklessly making statements which were false as to the services or facilities provided in the course of a trade or business, contrary to s. 14(1)(b). The defendants appealed to the Divisional Court.

SAQ 13/5

What do you think the Divisional Court decided? Was this a case concerning the provision of a service? Write down your opinion.

The Divisional Court held that the conviction should be overturned. The supply of goods did not, save in exceptional circumstances, fall within 'services' or 'facilities' in s. 14(1). (The defendants might have been prosecuted for giving misleading indications on the price of goods available, a matter no longer dealt with by the Trade Descriptions Act, but by Part III of the Consumer Protection Act 1987. Part III of the 1987 Act is considered in **Chapter 14**.)

In the following case the Divisional Court considered this matter again.

Ashley v *Sutton London Borough Council* (1994) 156 JP 631
Ten people received unsolicited mailshots from the appellant. These offered for sale a book which gave a strategy to profit from betting on fixed odds football pools. The advertisement said that if the customers were not satisfied with the book which explained the strategy then they could have all of their money back. The ten people sent the defendant between £55 and £179 for the book. All ten returned the book, but none were sent their money back.
Held: The extravagant language of the mailshot, and the inflated price of the book, indicated that what was being sold was not the book itself but the information in the

THE TRADE DESCRIPTIONS ACT 1968: SERVICES AND DEFENCES 297

book. (The strategy to profit from the fixed odds football pools.) Therefore the defendants were properly convicted under s. 14(1)(b).

ACTIVITY 13/5

Read the judgment of Scott-Baker J in *Ashley* v *Sutton London Borough Council* and also Peter Cartwright's article 'A service fault in the Divisional Court' 1996 JBL 58 in *Cases and Materials* (13.1.4.1). Then answer the following questions. This activity may take between half an hour and an hour.

(a) Is the word 'services' defined by the Act?

(b) What question was asked of the Divisional Court? Was this the question answered by Scott-Baker J?

(c) On what basis can the following statement of Scott-Baker J. be criticised: 'The book itself was of no interest to him [the customer]. What he wanted was the information in it.'?

(d) In what circumstances does a sale of goods come within the provision of a service?

(e) Should the inflated price of the book and the extravagant language of the mailshot make the sale of that particular book the provision of a service?

(f) If Goff LJ's statement, in *Newell and Another* v *Hicks*, that '"services" in this context should be regarded as doing something for somebody' is correct, then why should a promise to refund money not be regarded as the provision of services?

(g) We examined *Breed* v *Cluett* earlier in this chapter and saw that the defendant was guilty of an offence under s. 14(1). There are two possible views as to what service was being supplied in that case. What are these views?

(h) In the light of s. 1 of the Act, why does it matter whether or not the supply of goods involves also the provision of a service?

(i) In the light of the House of Lords' decision in *BAB* v *Taylor* [1976] 1 All ER 65, at what time would the defendant have had to have had the intention not to refund the money, in order to be guilty of an offence under s. 14?

(a) The word 'services' is not defined by the Act.

(b) The Divisional Court was asked to decide whether or not the statement that the purchase price of the book would be refunded was a statement about the provision of a service. Scott-Baker J read the question as asking whether or not the provision of the book itself was the provision of a service.

(c) As Professor J.C. Smith pointed out, anybody who buys a book intended to teach them something, is likely to want only the information in the book. It seems extraordinary to therefore regard the sales of such books as the sales of a service.

(d) A sale of goods is within the provision of a service where it is ancillary to the provision of a service, such as changing the oil when a car is serviced.

(e) There seems no reason why these matters should have this effect.

(f) Goff LJ's statement must be read in the light of the facts of the case he was considering. Read out of context, it could be impossibly wide. Goff LJ did not intend it to cover the giving of a refund and the supply of goods.

(g) In *Breed* v *Cluett* the Divisional Court did not make it clear whether the service provided was the building of the bungalow with a guarantee, or the provision of the guarantee itself.

(h) As we have seen, the *mens rea* requirements for s. 1 and s. 14 are different. It can therefore be important to know whether or not the supply of goods also involves the provision of a service.

(i) The defendant would have had to have had the intention not to refund the money at the time when the statement about refunding it was made.

13.3.4.2 Accommodation

Several of the cases we have examined in this chapter have been concerned with the accommodation provided by holiday companies. It is therefore apparent that s. 14 covers short-term accommodation.

13.3.4.3 Facilities

The word 'facility' is, in every day use, a very wide one. *Collins* dictionary defines it as 'the means or equipment facilitating the performance of an action'. A shop would therefore come within this definition as it would provide the means of buying goods.

Westminster City Council v *Ray Allan Manshops Ltd* [1982] 1 WLR 383
The defendants displayed a sign saying 'Closing Down Sale' in their shop. In fact the sale was not a closing down sale, and the defendants later continued to trade at the shop. The defendants were prosecuted under s. 14. Their defence was that advertising a closing down sale did not amount to making a statement as to the provision of 'any services, accommodation or facilities'.

ACTIVITY 13/6

Read the judgment of Ormrod LJ in *Westminster City Council* v *Ray Allan Manshops* in *Cases and Materials* (13.1.4.2).

(a) What did Ormrod LJ mean when he said that the word 'facilities' should be construed *ejusdem generis* with the preceding words 'services' and 'accommodation'?

(b) Which presumption of statutory interpretation did Ormrod LJ apply?

(c) How did Ormrod LJ differentiate between services and facilities?

(d) In *Newell and Another* v *Hicks* Robert Goff LJ was prepared to broadly agree with counsel's submission that a facility is providing somebody with the wherewithal to do something for himself. Is this definition compatible with the examples given by Ormrod LJ?

(e) Were the defendants guilty of the offence?

(a) What was meant was that the word 'facilities' should be construed in relation to the preceding words 'services' and 'accommodation'.

(b) Ormrod LJ applied the presumption that penal words in a statute should be applied narrowly. Such an approach was necessary here because of the very wide meaning of the word 'facilities'.

(c) Ormrod LJ said that hotels provide services because they do something for customers. Others provide facilities in the sense that various things are made available to customers to use if they are so minded in a more passive sense than the activities implied in the word 'services'.

(d) The example given by Ormrod LJ is compatible with Robert Goff LJ's definition.

(e) The defendants were not guilty of the offence.

13.3.5 MAKING A FALSE STATEMENT

The *actus reus* of both of the s. 14 offences requires that a false statement is made as to one of the matters listed in s. 14(1), which are as follows:

(a) the provision in the course of any trade or business of any services, accommodation or facilities;

(b) the nature of any services, accommodation or facilities provided in the course of any trade or business;

(c) the time at which, manner in which or persons by whom any services, accommodation or facilities are so provided;

(d) the examination, approval or evaluation by any person of any services, accommodation or facilities so provided; or

(e) the location or amenities of any accommodation so provided.

SAQ 13/6

Would the prosecution need to establish exactly to which one of these five matters the defendant had applied a false description? Or would it be enough merely to prove that a false description had been applied to at least one of them, without specifying which one?

In *R v Piper* 1995 JP 116 Roch LJ held that it would not be enough for the prosecution to say that the statement was false as regards one or other of the five matters specified in s. 14(1)(b)(i) to (v). He said, at 122, 'Had that been Parliament's intention there would have been no need for Parliament to have enacted the sub-paras (ii) to (v); the provision in sub-para. (i) would have sufficed.'

13.3.5.1 The provision in the course of any trade or business of any services, accommodation or facilities

SAQ 13/7

The word 'provision' might mean the act of providing services, accommodation or facilities, or it might have a wider meaning, so as to include the terms on which services, accommodation or facilities are provided. Read the judgment of Robert Goff LJ in *Newell and Another v Hicks* [1984 RTR 135 in *Cases and Materials* (13.1.5.1) and answer the following questions:

(a) Which meaning did Goff LJ ascribe to the word?

(b) On what reasoning was this decision made?

(a) Robert Goff LJ said that it was impossible to read the word provision in s. 14(1)(b)(i) as referring to anything other than the act of providing.

(b) If the word provision were to be construed as including the terms on which services, accommodation or facilities were provided, then ss. 14(1)(b)(ii) to (v) would be rendered surplusage.

13.3.5.2 The nature of any services, accommodation or facilities provided in the course of any trade or business

R v Clarksons Holidays (1972) 57 Cr App R 38
The defendants, holiday tour operators, printed a brochure. On the strength of this a customer booked a hotel at the Calypso Hotel in Benidorm. Among other things, the brochure claimed that the hotel had been chosen for its cleanliness, good food and efficiency of service. These claims, being false, were matters within s. 14(1)(b)(ii). Claims that there were swimming pools, beach furniture, lifts, and showers or baths in the rooms were matters within s. 14(1)(b)(i).

13.3.5.3 The time at which, manner in which or persons by whom any services, accommodation or facilities are so provided

Generally, the meaning of this subsection is fairly self-evident. It would include matters such as that a hotel's bar is open all hours, that transport to the hotel from the airport will be by chauffeur-driven limousine and that a well-known singer would perform at the hotel.

13.3.5.4 The examination, approval or evaluation by any person of any services, accommodation or facilities so provided

Again, the meaning is fairly self-evident. For example, a hotel might state that it had been examined and approved by the AA or that it had been awarded a five star recommendation by the Michelin Guide.

THE TRADE DESCRIPTIONS ACT 1968: SERVICES AND DEFENCES

13.3.5.5 The location or amenities of any accommodation so provided

In *Airtours plc v Shipley* (1994) 158 JP 835 a tour operator claimed that a hotel had an indoor swimming pool. Shortly before going on holiday a customer was sent a letter saying that the pool would be closed during the winter months. In fact there was no indoor pool at all. This was a false statement as to the amenities of the accommodation. (It could equally have been a false statement as to the provision of any facilities under s. 14(1)(b)(i).)

In *R v Piper*, the defendant, a builder, did some work on a customer's house. The defendant sent a letter on headed notepaper. This notepaper had on it the logo of the Guild of Master Craftsmen and at the bottom of it were the words 'Corporate Member'. In fact the defendant was not a member of the Guild. The Court of Appeal held that the defendant was rightly convicted of an offence under s. 14(1)(b). The Court of Appeal recognised that the five sub-paragraphs of s. 14 overlap and that clearly there will be cases where the facts fall potentially within more than one of the sub-paragraphs. This was just such a case.

SAQ 13/8

(a) Within which two sub-paragraphs did the offence in *R v Piper* fall?

(b) Which was the most appropriate?

(c) Did the prosecution need to specify which sub-paragraph they were relying upon?

(a) The Court of Appeal recognised that the offence could have been committed under either s. 14(1)(b)(i) or s. 14(1)(b)(iii).

(b) The court regarded themselves bound by *R v Breeze*, which decided that a person providing a service, and adopting personal qualifications he did not in fact enjoy, committed an offence under s. 14(1)(b)(i). However, the court also expressed the opinion that s. 14(1)(b)(iii) would more directly cover the circumstances of *R v Piper*.

(c) As we saw earlier in this chapter, the court decided that the prosecution had to specify which of the sub-paragraphs they relied upon. It was not enough to say that it must fall within one or other of them.

We have seen then that in order for an offence to be committed under s. 14, a false statement must be made as regards one of the five sub-paragraphs. Section 14(4) deals with the meaning of 'false' and tells us that a statement is false if it is false to a material degree. (We considered the meaning of false to a material degree in **Chapter 12**, when examining the offences in relation to goods.)

Section 14(2)(a) says that for the purposes of s. 14 'anything (whether or not a statement as to any of the matters specified in the preceding subsection) likely to be taken for such a statement as to any of those matters as would be false shall be deemed to be a false statement as to that matter'. This subsection caters for drawings and visual representations which are not literally statements.

THE TRADE DESCRIPTIONS ACT 1968: SERVICES AND DEFENCES

Difficulties can arise when a statement made about the provision of a service which has yet to be provided subsequently turns out to be untrue. In **Chapter 12** we saw that Lord Widgery in *Becket v Cohen* [1972] 1 WLR 1593 stated, at 1595,

> In my judgment Parliament never intended or contemplated for a moment that the Act of 1968 should . . . make a criminal offence out of what is really a breach of warranty [and immediately before that Lord Widgery said] if at the end of the contract a person giving the service recklessly makes a false statement as to what he has done, the matter may well fall within section 14, but if before the contract has been worked out the person who provides the service makes a promise as to what he will do, and that promise does not relate to an existing fact, nobody can say at the date when the statement is made that it is either true or false.

R v Sunair Holidays Ltd [1973] 1 WLR 1105
The defendants advertised a hotel in their 1970 summer brochure. The description of the hotel read '. . . swimming pool. Modern restaurant: the food is good, with English dishes also available — as well as special meals for children . . . push chairs for hire'. The hotel was closed over the winter of 1969–70 so that the swimming pool could be built. A customer booked a holiday in the hotel, in reliance on the brochure, in January 1970. The customer was dissatisfied because during his family's stay at the hotel, at the end of May 1970, the swimming pool could not be used and his family were dissatisfied with the other services promised. The Crown Court convicted the defendants of an offence under s. 14(1)(b). The Court of Appeal quashed the conviction. Section 14(1) had no application to statements which amounted to promises with regard to the future and which, when they were made, could not have the character of being either true or false. However, a promise about the future could be within s. 14 if it could be construed as an implied statement of present intention, means or belief, which is false at the time of making and is made recklessly or knowingly. (Mackenna J gave the judgment of the Court of Appeal, and an extract can be read in *Cases and Materials* (13.1.5.2).)

R v Avro plc (1993) 157 JP 759
The complainant booked a return flight from Gatwick to Alicante. On the outward flight he was given a replacement ticket for the return flight. This ticket was for a flight leaving at 12 noon on April 17 and was to arrive at Southend. The original return ticket had been for a flight at 12.55 pm on April 17 and was for a return to Gatwick. The complainant felt obliged to take the 12 noon flight to Southend because he discovered that the original return flight did not exist.

ACTIVITY 13/7

Read the judgment of Lloyd LJ in *R v Avro plc* in *Cases and Materials* (13.1.5.2). Then answer the following questions.

(a) What would the outcome of the case have been if the original flight tickets setting out the time had been a forecast or promise or statement of future intent which subsequently proved to be inaccurate?

(b) What would be the outcome if the original flight tickets setting out the time constituted a statement of fact which the appellant knew to be false?

(c) Bearing in mind, s. 14(2)(a), the important question to ask was whether the statement was likely to be taken by a member of the public as a statement of fact. Is this a question of law or a question of fact?

(d) Bearing in mind your answer to part (c) in this Activity, what question should the judge ask himself?

THE TRADE DESCRIPTIONS ACT 1968: SERVICES AND DEFENCES 303

(e) The statement on the ticket referred to an event which was to take place in the future. How then could it be a statement of an existing fact?

(f) Why did the provision that the flight could be altered or cancelled not prevent there being a statement of fact?

(g) Why could *British Airways Board* v *Taylor* (1976) 140 JP 96 not be distinguished?

(h) The ticket was issued on 28 March and read by the customer on 3 April. On which of these dates was the statement made?

(a) If this had been the case then the Act would not have applied.

(b) If this were the case then clearly the appellant would have been guilty of an offence under s. 14(1) of the Act.

(c) As Lord Wilberforce pointed out in *British Airways Board* v *Taylor*, this is a question of fact for the jury.

(d) The judge should ask himself whether the ticket was capable of containing a statement of fact.

(e) A statement as to an existing fact was made by implication. There were in fact two statements as to existing facts. First that there was a flight which was timed to leave Alicante at 12.55. Second, that the customer was booked on that flight.

(f) Any provision as to alteration would be trying to alter an existing fact. Therefore a statement of existing fact must already have been made.

(g) In both cases the question was how the statement in the ticket would be likely to be read. The principle in *British Airways Board* v *Taylor* was not confined to bookings confirmed by letter.

(h) Following *Wings Ltd* v *Ellis*, the statement was made on both dates.

13.4 Defences

In **Chapter 12** we saw that the s. 1 offences are offences of strict liability. We also examined the way in which the courts have allowed disclaimers to prevent a false trade description from having been applied at all. Even though the s. 1 offences impose strict liability, the Act does allow certain defences which can apply to them. These defences do not prevent an offence from having been committed, rather they provide an excuse which exonerates the defendant from liability.

13.4.1 SECTION 24: DEFENCE OF MISTAKE, ACCIDENT ETC.

Section 24(1) states that:

In any proceedings for an offence under this Act it shall, subject to subsection (2) of this section, be a defence for the person charged to prove—
    (a) that the commission of the offence was due to a mistake or to reliance on information supplied to him or to the act or default of another person, an accident or some other cause beyond his control; and
    (b) that he took all reasonable precautions and exercised all due diligence to avoid the commission of such an offence by himself or any person under his control.

THE TRADE DESCRIPTIONS ACT 1968: SERVICES AND DEFENCES

This defence is available to a defendant charged under s. 14 or under s. 1(1)(b) (supplying or offering to supply goods to which a false trade description is applied). *R v Southwood* decided that this defence is not available to a defendant charged under s. 1(1)(a) (applying a false trade description to any goods) if the defendant himself applied the false description.

SAQ 13/9

(a) Upon whom does the burden of proof fall, as regards this defence?

(b) What standard of proof will be required?

(a) It is up to the defendant to prove both parts of the defence.

(b) The defendant will need to prove the defence on a balance of probabilities.

ACTIVITY 13/8

Section 24(1)(a) applies if the commission of the offence was due to one of four separate matters. Write down what these matters are.

You should have written that the matters are:

- a mistake;

- reliance on information supplied by another person;

- the act or default of another person;

- an accident or some other cause beyond his control.

The defendant must prove that the commission of the offence was specifically due to one of these matters. It is therefore necessary to examine each in turn.

13.4.1.1 Mistake

In *Birkenhead Co-operative Society v Roberts* [1970] 1 WLR 1497 the Divisional Court held that on the true construction of s. 24(1)(a) the word 'mistake' meant a mistake by the person charged and not a mistake by another person. The facts of the case were that the defendants, Birkenhead and District Co-op, had supplied to a customer a New Zealand leg of lamb, to which a label saying 'For roasting English' had been attached. The person in charge of the butchery department had been handing joints of English lamb to his assistant, but at some time had changed to handing her joints of New Zealand lamb. The assistant had been told this, but had inadvertently used the label on a joint of New Zealand lamb. The defendants were not allowed to rely on this mistake by one of their servants, as the mistake was that of another person rather than that of the person charged. They were therefore rightly convicted of an offence under s. 1(1).

The mistake must be one of fact.

13.4.1.2 Reliance on information supplied by another

It is a defence for a defendant to show that he relied upon information supplied by another. However, bearing in mind the defendant's need to prove that he also took all reasonable precautions and exercised all due diligence to avoid the commission of the offence, it is apparent that reliance on information supplied by another will not always be enough.

When this aspect of the defence is relied upon then s. 24(2) insists that the defendant give the prosecution seven clear days' notice of such information identifying the other person who supplied the information as the defendant then has in his possession. Failure to give this information will mean that the s. 24(1) defence cannot be relied upon. (The same is true when the defendant relies upon the defence of act or default of another person.) The prosecution may then choose to prosecute the other person who supplied the information, either under ss. 1 or 14, or under the by-pass provision in s. 23, which is considered below.

13.4.1.3 The act or default of another person

Here again, the defendant must give the prosecution seven days' clear notice of such information identifying the other person as the defendant then has in his possession. Again, the purpose of this is that the other person might be prosecuted.

When a company is charged with an offence difficulties can arise in deciding whether or not living persons who work for the company can be regarded as another person, or whether or not they might be regarded as the company's alter ego. The following landmark case examined the matter.

Tesco Supermarkets Ltd v *Nattrass* [1972] AC 153
The defendants, a large company owning supermarkets, were charged with an offence under s. 11(2) of the Act (now repealed). The offence had arisen because a shop assistant had put out ordinary packets of Radiant washing powder, which costs 11d. Posters in the shop advertised that 'flash packs' of Radiant were available at 2s 11d. The shop assistant did not tell the supermarket manager that she had put out the ordinary packet of Radiant. The supermarket manager was responsible for seeing that the proper packets were on sale, and had been trained to do this properly.
Held: Tesco Ltd were not guilty of the offence because the offence had been committed due to the act of another person, the supermarket manager. The very senior managers might be regarded as the controlling mind and will of the company, and therefore as the alter ego of the company, but a mere supermarket manager could not be so identified and was therefore another person.

In *Birkenhead Co-operative Society* v *Roberts* we saw that a person relying on a mistake can only do so if the mistake was his own. It would have been more appropriate for the defendant in that case to have relied upon the commission of the offence being due to the act or default of another person, but this would have meant giving the prosecution seven clear days' notice of such information identifying that other person as the defendant then had in his possession. Fisher J, giving the judgment of the Divisional Court said, at 393:

> As a matter of construction it seems clear to me that Parliament intended that where the matter sought to be raised by way of defence was the act or default of another person, it was to those words which the defendant must look, and on which he must rely, bringing in as they do the requirement to give seven days' notice under subsection (2). It would seem to me in the highest degree anomalous that, where an act by another person could be said to be a mistake, it should be open to a defendant to rely on it as a mistake thereby avoiding the necessity for giving the notice.

It can be seen from the above two cases that the Act does not impose criminal vicarious liability on employers.

13.4.1.4 An accident or some other cause beyond his control

There is little case law on the type of matters which would be included in this heading. Accidents caused by employees would not be included, as the more appropriate heading is that the offence was caused by the act or default of another person.

13.4.1.5 Reasonable precautions and the exercise of all due diligence to avoid the commission of an offence

In addition to proving that the commission of the offence was due to one of the four matters which we have just examined, it will also be necessary for the defendant to prove that he took all reasonable precautions and exercised all due diligence to prevent the commission of the offence.

What amounts to the taking of reasonable precautions and the exercise of all due diligence is an objective question of fact and will depend upon all the circumstances of the case, including the type of business carried on by the defendant. In false odometer cases it is unlikely that defendant who has neither issued a disclaimer nor made enquiries about the mileage can possibly have established a defence under s. 24(3) (*Lewis v Maloney* [1977] Crim LR 436).

ACTIVITY 13/9

In *Tesco Supermarkets Ltd* v *Nattrass* Lord Morris of Borth-y-Gest considered the circumstances in which a company could be said to have taken all reasonable precautions and exercised all due diligence. Read the extract from Lord Morris' judgment in *Cases and Materials* (13.2) and then answer the following questions.

(a) Does s. 24 contemplate the idea that the Act could be contravened by a person under the control of a company while at the same time the company could be said to have taken all reasonable precautions and exercised all due diligence?

(b) Why did the Divisional Court not think that the company had taken all reasonable precautions and exercised all due diligence?

(c) Were the Divisional Court correct in thinking as they did?

(a) Section 24 does contemplate such an idea. Indeed, such an idea is the very basis of s. 24. If both parts of the defence are not proved then there is no defence at all.

(b) The Divisional Court thought that the company had not taken all reasonable precautions and exercised all due diligence because the company had delegated its duty as regards these matters to the shop manager.

(c) The Court of Appeal held that the Divisional Court were not correct in thinking as they did. The company had created a system which could be rationally said to be so designed that the commission of offences would be avoided. It had not therefore delegated its duty to take all proper precautions and exercise all due diligence. The manager was the one being directed, he was not the controlling mind or will of the company. The duties imposed on the manager were the result of the company taking all reasonable precautions and exercising all due diligence. Lord Borth-y-Gest said of the manager, 'He was, so to speak, a cog in the machine which was devised; it was not left to him to devise it.'

It is of course before the offence has been committed that the reasonable precautions must be taken. In *Haringey London Borough Council* v *Piro Shoes Ltd* [1976] Crim LR 462, the defendant company, which owned a shoe shop, sold shoes which were not made entirely of leather as 'all leather'. The company issued a circular to the shop manager that the shoes were not to leave the shop with the words 'all' on them. At the cash desk, when the shoes were sold, the word 'all' was crossed out. The defendants were held to be guilty of an offence under s. 1(1)(b) in that they had offered to supply goods to which a false trade description is attached. The magistrates had believed that the company had a defence under s. 24(1) on the grounds that the offence was due to the default of the shop manager and the company had exercised all due diligence to prevent its commission. The Divisional Court disagreed. The company's instructions to delete the word 'all' related to the time when the shoes left the shop, not the time when they were offered for sale with a false trade description.

As mentioned earlier, the s. 24(1) defence is not open to a defendant charged under s. 1(1)(a) if the defendant has himself deliberately applied the false trade description. In *R* v *Southwood* Lord Lane CJ, at 564, said:

> It seems to us to be absurd to suggest that the actual falsifier could, by any stretch of the imagination, be said to have taken all reasonable precautions to attempt to avoid the commission of an offence merely by issuing a disclaimer, however expressed. By his initial actions in falsifying the instrument he has disqualified himself from asserting that he has taken any precautions, let alone all reasonable precautions.

The defence is available to a defendant charged with supplying or offering to supply a car with a false odometer reading.

Ealing London Borough Council v *Taylor* (1996) 159 JP 460
The defendant, a motor dealer, was charged with two offences under s. 1(1)(b). The first was that he offered to supply a car to which a false trade description had been applied. The second that he actually did supply a car with a false trade description applied to it. The car in question had a recorded mileage of 32,000, whereas the true mileage was over 55,000. The justices found that there had been a written disclaimer attached to the car and that although it had not been displayed prominently enough to be an effective disclaimer, the defendant had done enough to establish a defence under s. 24(1). The defendant had bought the car from another dealer who guaranteed the 32,000 mileage but provided no service record. The car was in good condition, so the defendant's belief that the mileage was correct was reasonable. The defendant did not try to contact any other previous owners to check the mileage. He had in the past made attempts to do this, but had never had any success.
Held: The magistrates' finding that the defendant had satisfied the requirements of the s. 24(1) defence should not be overturned.

In the above case the prosecution had argued that previous cases had established two things. First, that it was not possible for all reasonable precautions to be shown in a false odometer case if there was no effective disclaimer. Second, that it was a rule of law that in cases such as this there must always and in every case be a check with a previous owner before reasonable precautions have been shown. The Divisional Court rejected both of these arguments. Buckley J said, at 468:

> It cannot be a matter of law that in every case where a defendant seeks to make good a defence under s. 24 that a disclaimer has to be placed on the car, or that inquiries have to be made of the previous owner. What precautions it is reasonable to take in any particular case must depend upon all the circumstances of the case.

(It should be remembered that the the usual effect of an effective disclaimer will be to prevent the commission of an offence at all, rather than as a defence.)

13.4.2 THE SUPPLIER'S DEFENCE

Section 24(3) offers an additional defence to a person charged with an offence under s. 1(1)(b). Section 24 states:

> In any proceedings for an offence under this Act of supplying or offering to supply goods to which a false trade description is applied it shall be a defence for the person charged to prove that he did not know, and could not with reasonable diligence have ascertained, that the goods did not conform to the description or that the description had been applied to the goods.

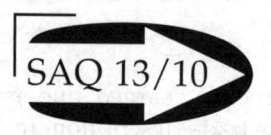

SAQ 13/10

(a) Upon whom does the burden of proof fall?

(b) In what two ways can the defence arise?

(a) It is up to the defendant to prove the defence.

(b) The defendant must prove that he did not know, and could not with reasonable diligence have ascertained:

   (i) that the goods did not conform to the description; or

   (ii) that the description had been applied to the goods.

'Reasonable diligence' in this subsection is the equivalent of 'due diligence' in s. 24(1). The fact of having taken reasonable precautions is not relevant to this defence. The defence is not concerned with what steps the defendant did take, but rather with what steps the defendant did not take.

13.4.3 THE BY-PASS PROVISION

Section 23, headed 'Offences due to fault of other person' reads as follows:

> Where the commission by any person of an offence under this Act is due to the act or default of some other person that other person shall be guilty of the offence, and a person may be charged with and convicted of the offence by virtue of this section whether or not proceedings are taken against the first-mentioned person.

SAQ 13/11

In *Tesco Supermarkets Ltd* v *Nattrass* Tesco had a successful defence under s. 24 because the commission of the offence was due to the act or default of another person — the supermarket manager.

(a) Who could have been prosecuted under s. 23?

THE TRADE DESCRIPTIONS ACT 1968: SERVICES AND DEFENCES

(b) How would the prosecution gain the necessary evidence to bring about this prosecution?

(c) Would it be possible for a person who is not in business to be prosecuted under s. 23?

(a) The supermarket manager could have been prosecuted under s. 23.

(b) As we saw earlier, a defendant cannot rely on the s. 24(1) defence that the offence was committed due to the act or default of another person without giving the prosecution seven clear days' notice of such information identifying that other person as the defendant then has in his possession.

(c) It would be possible for a person who is not in business to be prosecuted under s. 23, as the following case shows.

Olgiersson v Kitching [1986] 1 All ER 764
A private motorist sold a car to a garage. The motorist said that the car had done 38,000 miles although he knew that this was not true. The garage sold the car on to another garage, applying the false trade description of 38,000 miles. The owner of the purchasing garage discovered that the 38,000 mileage was far from true.
Held: The private motorist was guilty of an offence under s. 23, even though he could not have been guilty of an offence under s. 1 of the Act.

The wording of s. 23 can cause difficulty, in that it seems to require that the 'first person' has to be guilty of an offence in order for the 'other person' to be guilty under s. 23. However, when the offence is caused by the act or default of the 'other person', the 'first person' will have a defence under s. 24(1) and will not therefore be guilty of an offence. The Divisional Court resolved this difficulty in the following case.

Coupe v Guyett [1973] 1 WLR 669
S owned a car repair business but took no part in its management. S employed the defendant as the workshop manager. The defendant made a recklessly false statement as to the nature of repairs carried out by the business to a car. S was charged under s. 14(1)(b) and the defendant was charged under s. 23. S was acquitted as she had a defence under s. 24(1). The justices therefore decided that they could not convict the defendant of an offence under s. 23, because s. 23 starts by saying: 'Where the commission by any person [S] of an offence is due to the act or default of some other person [the defendant] . . .' As S had a defence she had not committed an offence and so s. 23, it seemed, would not apply. Lord Widgery CJ held that the defendant should be convicted. He agreed that there appeared to be something of a conflict between s. 23 and s. 24, but explained the solution in this way: 'The solution of the conflict is that, when the first mentioned person in section 23 has no defence to the charge except the statutory defence under section 24, he or she can properly still be regarded as as having committed "the offence" for the purpose of section 23.' It should be noted that if the 'first person' cannot be convicted for some reason other than having a defence under s. 24 then the other person cannot be convicted under s. 23.

If a person sells a car with a false odometer reading, and takes all proper precautions to see that the reading is not relied upon, so that no offence committed by him at the time of sale, he cannot be subsequently made guilty of an offence by s. 23.

K. Lill Holdings Ltd v White [1979] RTR 120
The defendants, who were motor dealers, bought a car with an odometer reading of 59,000 miles. They returned the odometer reading to zero and sold the car to S, with full disclaimers, in a transaction without fault. Later S sold the car to J, another dealer. J, having done 5,000 miles in the car, sold it with a false odometer reading of 5,000 miles

and thereby committed an offence of selling goods to which a false trade description is applied. The defendants were convicted by the justices of an offence under s. 23, on the grounds that the commission of the offence by J was due to the act or default of the defendants.

Held: The defendants were not guilty of an offence under s. 23. The commission of the offence by J was was not due to the act or default of the defendants, who ceased to be responsible before the sale by J took place. Wien J, at 125, said: 'It is only in the case of an act or default attributable to them [the defendants] that liability for the offence can be brought home . . . the act or default in section 23 must be a wrongful act or default.'

13.4.4 THE ADVERTISER'S DEFENCE

An advertiser who publishes an advertisement containing a false trade description can obviously be guilty of an offence of applying a false trade description to goods. Section 25 gives a defence to those whose business it is to publish advertisements if they received the advertisement in the ordinary course of business and did not know and had no reason to suspect that publication of the advertisement would amount to an offence under the Act.

13.5 Summary

Section 14 of the Trade Descriptions Act 1968 creates two offences relating to the false description of services, accommodation or facilities. Both offences can only be committed by a person acting in the course of a trade or business. Persons acting in the course of their profession come within this definition.

Both of the s. 14 offences require that a false statement be made. When a brochure is distributed by a business, the statements it contains are made not only when the brochure is first created but also on each occasion that a customer reads the brochure. There is no requirement that the statement induces the making of a contract, but it must be connected to the supply of a service, accommodation or facilities.

The s. 14(1)(a) offences of making a statement which is known to be false is one of 'semi-strict' liability. This is because, although the defendant does need to know that the statement he makes is false, he does not need to know this at the time when he first makes the statement.

The s. 14(1)(b) offence requires that the defendant recklessly makes a statement which is false. The word 'recklessly' is given a statutory definition and this is wider than the usual common law meaning of the word.

Section 14 is only concerned with false or misleading statements as to 'services, accommodation or facilities'. 'Services' in this context can be regarded as doing something for somebody, 'facilities' give someone the wherewithal to do something for themselves.

The *actus reus* of both of the s. 14 offences requires that a false statement is made as to one of the following matters: the provision in the course of any trade or business of any services, accommodation or facilities; the nature of any services, accommodation or facilities provided in the course of any trade or business; the time at which, manner in which or persons by whom any services, accommodation or facilities are so provided; the examination, approval or evaluation by any person of any services, accommodation or facilities so provided; or the location or amenities of any accommodation so provided.

A statement will be regarded as 'false' if it is false to a material degree. A statement about the future will not come within s. 14 unless it can be construed as an implied statement of a present intention, means or belief.

THE TRADE DESCRIPTIONS ACT 1968: SERVICES AND DEFENCES

Section 24(1) allows a defence that the commission of the offence was due to a mistake or to reliance on information supplied to the defendant or to the act or default of another person, an accident or some other cause beyond the defendant's control. However, the defence is not available unless the defendant can also prove that he took all reasonable precautions and exercised all due diligence to prevent the commission of the offence. The very senior managers of a company, who control the company, cannot be regarded as 'another person', separate from the company. Other company employees can be regarded as 'another person'.

Section 24(3) offers an additional defence to a person charged with the s. 1(1)(b) offence of supplying or offering to supply goods to which a false trade description is applied. The defendant will need to prove that he did not know, and could not with reasonable diligence have ascertained, that the goods did not conform to the description or that the description had been applied to the goods.

Where a person commits an offence due to the act or default of another person, the other person can be guilty of an offence under the by-pass provision contained in s. 23. This is the case even where this other person is not acting in the course of trade or business.

Section 25 gives a defence to advertisers who publish advertisements which they received in the ordinary course of business if the advertisers did not know and had no reason to suspect that the publication of the advertisement would amount to an offence.

13.6 End of Chapter Assessment Question

Mr D. Odgy is the only director of Dodgy Motors Ltd and owns all of the shares in the company. The company employs seven sales and office staff. Last year Mr Odgy introduced a 'special offer' whereby any customer who hired two separate cars in the same month would be given a free holiday weekend in Skegness. So many customers took advantage of this offer that Mr Odgy felt obliged to withdraw it. He ordered that all the leaflets which advertised the offer should be withdrawn and destroyed.

Last week Mr Odgy went on holiday, leaving two trainee managers in charge of his two branches. One of these managers did not know that the 'special offer' had been withdrawn and, finding some leaflets which advertised the offer distributed these to customers. The other trainee manager had been specifically told that the 'special offer' had been withdrawn. However, not wishing to be outdone, he printed up identical leaflets on the work computer and handed these out to customers. Several customers, in reliance on the leaflet, booked second hire cars within the same month. Mr Odgy flatly refused to give them the free holiday weekend. However, when he heard that one complainant was threatening legal action Mr Odgy immediately agreed to provide the free holiday weekends for all the customers who had relied on the leaflets.

Mr Odgy has become disillusioned with the car hire trade. He saw an advertisement in a newspaper for a book which guaranteed a foolproof way to win at roulette. The advertisement said that if any customer was not satisfied with the book, the purchase price of £350 would be refunded in full. Mr Odgy bought the book but found that following the book's system he lost more money at roulette than usual. He asked for a refund of the purchase price but this was refused. (You should assume that there cannot possibly be a foolproof way of winning at roulette. On each spin of the wheel the casino has a 3 per cent margin. The number on which the ball finishes is pure chance, unconnected with any previous spin of the wheel.)

Advise Dodgy Motors Ltd and the vendor of the book whether they are guilty of any offences under the Trade Descriptions Act 1968.

See *Cases and Materials* (13.4) for an outline answer.

CHAPTER FOURTEEN

MISLEADING PRICE INDICATIONS

14.1 Objectives

By the end of this chapter you should be able to:

- outline the nature of the two offences created by s. 20 of the Consumer Protection Act 1987;

- analyse the circumstances in which a person gives a misleading price indication 'in the course of any business';

- explain what is meant by a misleading indication as to price;

- outline the four defences specific to s. 20 of the 1987 Act;

- explain the status of the Consumer Protection (Code of Practice for Traders on Price Indications) Approval Order 1988;

- outline the content of the Code of Practice;

- apply the law on misleading price indications to problem situations.

14.2 Introduction

The Consumer Protection Act 1987, Part III (ss. 20–26) creates two offences relating to false price indications. These offences replace the offences created by s. 11 of the Trade Descriptions Act 1968 and the Price Marking (Bargain Offers) Orders 1979. Part III of the Act is backed up by a detailed Code of Practice.

We begin this chapter by distinguishing the two offences created by s. 20 of the 1987 Act. Then we examine the meaning of several key words or phrases used in s. 20. Four defences are specific to the misleading price offences and we conclude the chapter by examining these defences.

14.3 The Offence of Giving a Misleading Indication as to the Price

Section 20(1) of the Consumer Protection Act 1987 defines the main offence:

Subject to the following provisions of this Part, a person shall be guilty of an offence if, in the course of any business of his, he gives (by any means whatever) to any consumer an indication which is misleading as to the price at which any goods, services, accommodation or facilities are available (whether generally or from particular persons).

Section 20(2) defines a second offence:

Subject as aforesaid, a person shall be guilty of an offence if—
   (a) in the course of any business of his, he has given an indication to any consumers which, after it was given, has become misleading as mentioned in subsection (1) above; and
   (b) some or all of those consumers might reasonably be expected to rely on the indication at a time after it has become misleading; and
   (c) he fails to take all such steps as are reasonable to prevent those consumers from relying on the information.

SAQ 14/1

What, in essence, is the difference between the two offences?

You should have answered along the following lines. The main offence is committed by giving to a consumer a misleading indication as to price. The secondary offence is committed by failing to correct an indication as to price which has become misleading after it has been given to a consumer.

The difference between the two offences was considered in the following case.

Toys 'R' Us v Gloucestershire County Council (1994) 158 JP 338
Two brothers bought swimming goggles at the defendant's store. Attached to the goggles was a price sticker. The cashier on the till scanned the bar code on the first pair of goggles and this caused a higher price to be displayed on the till. This was pointed out to the cashier who voided the till and manually entered the lower price on the sticker. The cashier then manually entered the lower price on the sticker attached to the second pair of goggles. The defendants pleaded guilty to a s. 20(1) charge as regards the first pair of goggles, but pleaded not guilty as regards the second pair. Enforcement officers later seized 12 specimen items on which the price on the stickers was lower than the prices rung up on the till by the the bar codes. Enforcement officers subsequently visited the shop and found further discrepancies in the prices on the stickers and those on the bar codes. In total the defendants contested 34 offences with which they were charged. The defendants pleaded guilty to two charges where enforcement officers made test purchases and were charged the higher bar code prices.

ACTIVITY 14/1

(a) Write down your first impressions. As regards both the second pair of goggles and the items seized by the enforcement officers, do you think that the defendants were guilty of offences under either s. 20(1) or 20(2)?

MISLEADING PRICE INDICATIONS

(b) In *Cases and Materials* (14.1) read the judgment of Kennedy J. Then answer the following questions.

  (i) In cases where the prices differed, was the price which the defendants intended to charge the price on the bar codes or the price on the stickers?

  (ii) Was the court concerned with whether or not the goods were sold at the correct price?

  (iii) At what time was the relevant indication as to price given?

  (iv) In cases where the prices differed, at what price were the goods 'available'?

  (v) On what basis would the defendants have been guilty of a s. 20(1) offence if the evidence had showed that neither cashiers nor customers noticed the price changes and caused them to be corrected?

  (vi) Why was no offence committed under s. 20(2)?

(a) Your first impression might have been that the defendants were guilty of both s. 20 offences in respect of both the goggles and the items seized. The defendants might seem to be guilty of offences under s. 20(1) because the prices indicated on the items were lower than the prices which they might well have been charged at the till. They might seem to be guilty of s. 20(2) offences because the prices on the stickers had become misleading and consumers were likely to rely on these prices. As you answer part (b) of this Activity you will see that neither of these views is correct. If you thought that no offences had been committed then your first impressions would have been correct.

(b)(i) The price which the defendants intended to charge was the price on the stickers.

  (ii) The court was not concerned with whether or not the goods were sold at the correct price. The court was concerned to discover whether or not a misleading price indication had been given.

  (iii) The relevant indication as to price was given when the item was on the shelf with the sticker attached to it.

  (iv) The goods were available at the prices on the stickers as this was the price which the consumer would be required to pay.

  (v) If no-one noticed the price changes then the goods on the shelves would not have been available at the lower sticker price indicated and the court could have found that an offence under s. 20(1) had been committed.

  (vi) Section 20(2) was not applicable because it was intended to deal with a situation where a price indication *becomes* misleading because of an event which took place after it was displayed. Here the prices on the sticker did not become misleading.

14.3.1 IN THE COURSE OF ANY BUSINESS

In **Chapter 12** at **12.3.2** we considered the circumstances in which a person acts in the course of any trade or business. The word 'business' will have the same meaning here.

However, a defendant can only commit an offence under s. 20(1) and 20(2) if he acts 'in the course of any business of his'. The House of Lords considered the meaning of this phrase in the following case.

Warwickshire County Council v *Johnson* [1993] 1 All ER 299
The appellant was employed as the branch manager of a Dixons retail electrical shop. With the authority of the owners of the shop he put up a notice stating 'We will beat any TV HiFi and Video price by £20 on the spot'. While the notice was displayed a customer saw a television set offered elsewhere at £159.95. The customer took the appellant to see the set and then demanded an identical one at £139.95. The appellant had an identical television in stock but refused to sell it at £139.95. The appellant was charged with an offence under s. 20(1) of the Act. The employers were able to take advantage of the due diligence defence but the appellant was charged under the by-pass procedure (see below at **14.6.1**). The House of Lords had to decide two matters. First, could a notice which was not on the face of it misleading become misleading by a refusal to honour its terms? Second, for the purposes of s. 20(2)(a), could the words 'in the course of a business of his' include an employee?
Held: The notice constituted a continuing offer. The only way to discover whether or not such an offer was misleading was to try and take advantage of it. As the appellant had refused to allow a consumer to take advantage of it the notice was misleading. To hold otherwise would seriously restrict the efficacy of Part III of the Consumer Protection Act 1987. Second, the words 'in the course of any business of his' in s. 20(2)(a) meant any business of which the defendant was either the owner or in which he had a controlling interest. The shop manager, as a mere employee without a controlling interest, was not within the meaning of the phrase, even though it was his business to manage the shop in question.

As we saw in **Chapter 13** at **13.4.1.3** the very senior management of a company can be regarded as the controlling mind and will of the company. The actions of such a senior manager could therefore make the company guilty of an offence against s. 20 of the 1987 Act. In addition the senior manager in question could be personally guilty under s. 40(2) of the 1987 Act if the offence was committed with his consent or connivance or was attributable to his neglect.

Section 20(3), which applies to both s. 20 offences, states:

For the purposes of this section it shall be immaterial—
(a) whether the person who gives or gave the indication is or was acting on his own behalf or on behalf of another;
(b) whether or not that person is the person, or included among the persons, from whom the goods, services or accommodation or facilities are available; and
(c) whether the indication is or has become misleading in relation to all the consumers to whom it was given or only in relation to some of them.

SAQ 14/2

In *Warwickshire County Council* v *Johnson* the appellant was obviously acting on behalf of Dixons, his employer. So how does s. 20(3)(a) fit in with the House of Lords' decision?

Section 20(3)(a) allows an agent who sells on behalf of another to be guilty of either of the s. 20 offences. However, the agent must be carrying on a business of his own in order

MISLEADING PRICE INDICATIONS

to be guilty. In *Warwickshire County Council* v *Johnson* the House of Lords decided that the shop manager was not carrying on a business of his own. However some agents, such as those who sell others goods on a commission only basis, do of course carry on a business of their own. Section 20(3)(a) makes it plain that agents carrying on a business of their own can be guilty of s. 20 offences.

14.3.2 CONSUMER

Both of the offences require that a misleading price indication is given to a consumer. Section 20(6) gives a fairly lengthy definition of a consumer.

ACTIVITY 14/2

Read s. 20(6) of the 1987 Act in *Cases and Materials* (14.1). Then answer the following questions.

(a) Three different definitions of consumers are given, depending upon whether what is available is goods, services or accommodation. In essence, what is the definition of a consumer, as regards all three definitions?

(b) In Chapter 12 we considered *Fletcher* v *Budgen* [1974] 1 WLR 1056, in which a car dealer dishonestly told a customer that his car was fit only for scrap and worth only £2. These statements were far from true. Re-read the facts of that case (see SAQ 12/4) and then decide whether or not the car dealer would nowadays be guilty of an offence under s. 20(1) of the Consumer Protection Act 1987.

(a) As regards all three definitions a consumer is a person who wants to use the goods, services or accommodation for private purposes rather than for business purposes.

(b) The car dealer would not be guilty of an offence under s. 20(1). In relation to goods, s. 20(6)(a) defines a consumer as a person who might wish to be supplied with goods. In addition, s. 20(1) states that the misleading price indication must be as to the price at which goods are available.

In *Toys 'R' Us* v *Gloucestershire County Council* Kennedy J said that 'the definition of a consumer is probably formulated as it is to exclude retailers buying from wholesalers'. Whether or not this was the reason why s. 20(6)(a) defines a consumer as it does, it is plain that retailers buying from wholesalers would not be included as consumers. In *Toys 'R' Us* v *Gloucestershire County Council* Kennedy J also made it plain that a trading standards officer on duty is a consumer, because he is a 'person who might wish to be supplied with the goods for his own private use or consumption'. The fact that the trading standards officer on duty did not actually wish to be supplied with the goods was not material. The important word in s. 20(6) is 'might'.

14.3.3 PRICE

Section 20(6) defines price in the following way:

'price', in relation to any goods, services, accommodation or facilities, means—
(a) the aggregate of the sums required to be paid by a consumer for or otherwise in respect of the supply of the goods or the provision of the services, accommodation or facilities; or
(b) except in section 21 below, any method which will be or has been applied for the purpose of determining that aggregate.

SAQ 14/3

A trader advertises his goods at £100. A consumer decides to buy the goods but the trader says that the amount which must be paid is £117, as VAT was not included in the advertisement. The consumer refuses to pay this price. Has an offence been committed by the trader?

The trader has committed an offence under s. 20(1). The price is the aggregate amount which the consumer would be required to pay (£117) and the trader gave a misleading indication as to the price. There is of course no requirement that the consumer actually makes the purchase. Article 2.2.6 of the Code of Practice says that all price indications given to private consumers, by whatever means, should include VAT.

SAQ 14/4

(a) Write down your opinion as to the difference between an estimate and a quotation. Check your answer to this part of the SAQ before considering part (b).

(b) A builder replaces some windows and presents a consumer with a bill for £1,150. Would the builder have committed an offence under s. 20 if his estimate had been £1,000; or his quotation had been £1,000?

(a) You should have written that a quotation is a definite offer to supply at the price quoted. An estimate is merely a statement as to what the price is likely to be.

(b) If the builder only gave an estimate he would not have committed an offence under s. 20 as the estimate is not an indication as to the price (the sum which the consumer 'will be required to pay'). If the builder gave a quotation then he would have committed an offence as the quotation would have been an indication of the price.

14.3.4 THE PRICE AT WHICH GOODS, SERVICES, ACCOMMODATION OR FACILITIES ARE AVAILABLE

As s. 20 only applies to the price at which goods etc. are available. Where no goods are available, for example where a trader indicates the price of discontinued stock, then no offence is committed.

MISLEADING PRICE INDICATIONS

SAQ 14/5

A contract between a builder and a consumer is concluded under which the builder is to build a conservatory for a price of £3,455. Having completed the work, the builder sends an invoice for £4,000. This discrepancy is pointed out to the builder who agrees that the amount owing is £3,455. Has the builder committed a s. 20 offence?

The builder has not committed a s. 20 offence as the price indication in the invoice is not a price at which goods are available. (In *Miller* v *FA Sadd & Son Ltd* [1981] 3 All ER 285 the Divisional Court held that the concept of a false 'indication' in s. 11(2) of the Trade Descriptions Act 1968 (now repealed and replaced by s. 20 of the 1987 Act) was inapplicable in the context of a concluded contract.)

14.4 Goods, Services, Accommodation or Facilities

Section 45, the interpretation section, gives the following definition: '"goods" includes substances, growing crops and things comprised in land by virtue of being attached to it and any ship, aircraft or vehicle'.

Section 22(1) states that references to 'services or facilities' exclude services provided to an employer under a contract of employment, and also exclude services provided by investment businesses, but otherwise are to be taken to be any services or facilities whatever.

Accommodation is dealt with by the lengthy s. 23. Accommodation which is made available by the creation of or disposal of an interest in land is not included unless it was a business disposal of a new home by way of sale or by way of a lease of over 21 years' duration. Section 23 does not define what is meant by accommodation. However, the Code of Practice states that hotel and other holiday accommodation is included.

14.5 Misleading Indications

Both offences require that a consumer is given a misleading indication as to price. The indication can be given 'by any means whatever' (s. 20(1)). Section 21 defines 'misleading':

(1) For the purposes of section 20 above an indication given to any consumers is misleading as to a price if what is conveyed by the indication, or what those consumers might reasonably be expected to infer from the indication or any omission from it, includes any of the following, that is to say—
    (a) that the price is less than in fact it is;
    (b) that the applicability of the price does not depend on facts or circumstances on which its applicability does in fact depend;
    (c) that the price covers matters in respect of which an additional charge is in fact made;
    (d) that a person who in fact has no such expectation—
        (i) expects the price to be increased or reduced (whether or not at a particular time or by a particular amount); or
        (ii) expects the price, or the price as increased or reduced, to be maintained (whether or not for a particular period); or

(e) that the facts or circumstances by reference to which the consumers might reasonably be expected to judge the validity of any relevant comparison made or implied by the indication are not what in fact they are.

We need to consider the five matters specified in turn. First though we should note that s. 21(1) states that an indication is misleading if either what is conveyed by it includes any of the five matters, or if what consumers might reasonably be expected to infer from the indication or any omission from it includes any of the five matters. So if one of the five matters is not in fact included, but consumers might reasonably be expected to infer that it was included, an offence will have been committed.

14.5.1 INDICATIONS THAT THE PRICE IS LESS THAN IN FACT IT IS

The Code of Practice cites as examples showing one price in an advertisement, window display, shelf marking or on the item itself, and then charging a higher price at the point of sale or checkout (para. 2.1.1).

14.5.2 INDICATIONS THAT THE APPLICABILITY OF THE PRICE DOES NOT DEPEND ON FACTS OR CIRCUMSTANCES ON WHICH ITS APPLICABILITY DOES IN FACT DEPEND

If there are conditions attached to goods being available at an indicated price then this must be made clear. So, for example, if goods are available at a lower price only to the first few customers, or before a certain date, or to goods of a certain colour, or only to demonstration models, this must be made clear. The Code of Practice (para. 2.2.2) suggests that this can be achieved by using words such as: 'Available in other colours or sizes at additional cost.'

14.5.3 INDICATIONS THAT THE PRICE COVERS MATTERS IN RESPECT OF WHICH AN ADDITIONAL CHARGE IS TO BE MADE

An obvious example would be that VAT was not included or that there was an additional charge for postage and packing. The Code of Practice (para. 2.2.4) states that the trader must clearly show how the charges will be calculated, for example by stating 'Post Office rates apply'. The existence of delivery charges, and what those charges are, must be made clear before the consumer is committed to buying (para. 2.2.5).

14.5.4 INDICATIONS THAT A PERSON WHO HAS NO SUCH EXPECTATION EXPECTS THE PRICE TO BE INCREASED, REDUCED OR MAINTAINED.

Included could be notices such as: 'Buy now, these items won't be this price next week.' However, it will be necessary to prove that the person who gave the indication did not, at the time of giving the indication, intend that the price should be unaltered the following week. It is not necessary that details of the price increase or reduction should be spelt out.

14.5.5 INDICATIONS THAT THE FACTS OR CIRCUMSTANCES BY REFERENCE TO WHICH A CONSUMER CAN JUDGE THE VALIDITY OF A PRICE COMPARISON ARE NOT WHAT IN FACT THEY ARE

This provision is intended to be wide enough to catch anything not included in s. 21(1)(a)–(d).

Whereas s. 21(1) deals with misleading indications as to the price, s. 21(2), which can be read in *Cases and Materials* (14.1), deals with misleading indications as to the methods of determining the price. The five matters specified in s. 21(2)(a)–(e) are very similar to the five matters specified in s. 21(1)(a)–(e).

MISLEADING PRICE INDICATIONS

14.6 Defences

14.6.1 DUE DILIGENCE AND TAKING REASONABLE PRECAUTIONS

Section 39 makes it a defence for a person to show that he took all reasonable precautions and exercised all due diligence to avoid committing the offence. If the defence is that the offence was caused by the act or default of a third party then the defendant must serve a notice giving details of the third party to the prosecution who can prosecute the third party under the by-pass procedure. We have already examined the nature of the due diligence defence and the by-pass procedure in **Chapter 13** at **13.4.1.5**.

14.6.2 DEFENCES APPLICABLE ONLY TO THE SECTION 20 OFFENCES

Section 24 sets out four defences which relate to the s. 20 offences. The defences, which must be shown by the defendant, are as follows:

- that the acts or omissions which gave rise to the s. 20 offence were authorised by Regulations made by the Secretary of State under s. 26 of the Act (s. 24(1));

- as regards price indications published in books, newspapers, magazines, films, or radio or television broadcasts, that the indication was not part of an advertisement (s. 24(2));

- that an advertiser was given the material in the ordinary course of his business and at the time of publication did not know, and had no grounds to suspect, that the publication of the advertisement would amount to an offence (s. 24(3));

- that a person charged under s. 20(1) (with giving a misleading indication as to the price at which goods, services, accommodation or facilities are available) shows that the indication did not relate to availability from him, that there was a recommended price as regards all suppliers, that the price he had indicated was misleading because someone had failed to follow the recommendation and that it was reasonable for the person who gave the indication to assume that the recommendation was for the most part being followed (s. 24(4)).

SAQ 14/6

What defences, if any, would be available to the following defendants who have been charged under s. 20 of the Act?

(a) David, who publishes a free newspaper, is asked by a local trader to publish an advertisement. David publishes the advertisement in the format supplied to him. In fact the advertisement contains a misleading price indication.

(b) Doug, who publishes a consumer affairs magazine, publishes an article comparing the price of various vacuum cleaners. In this article Doug indicates that the price of one particular vacuum cleaner is much lower than it actually is.

(c) Off-Road-Cars Ltd, a manufacturer of cars, advertises the recommended retail price of all its vehicles in the national press. All retailers of the cars were expected to sell only at this price or lower. One retailer sold a vehicle at a price significantly higher than that recommended by Off-Road-Cars Ltd.

(a) As long as David did not know, and had no grounds for suspecting, that the publication would involve the commission of an offence David will have a defence under s. 24(3).

(b) Doug would be provided with a defence under s. 24(2).

(c) Off-Road-Cars Ltd would have a defence under s. 24(4), as long as it was reasonable for them to assume that the recommendation was for the most part being followed.

14.7 Time Limits

Section 20(5) provides that no prosecution can be brought (a) three years after the day on which the offence was committed, or (b) one year after the day on which the person bringing the prosecution discovered that the offence had been committed, whichever is the earlier.

14.8 The Code of Practice

The Consumer Protection (Code of Practice for Traders on Price Indications) Approval Order 1988 (SI 1988 No. 2078 is reproduced in *Cases and Materials* (**14.2**). Section 25(2) deals with the Code's legal status. A contravention of the Code does not of itself give rise to any criminal or civil liability (s. 25(2)). However, if a person contravenes the Code this may be relied upon either for the purpose of establishing that the person committed an offence or for the purpose of negativing any defence (s. 25(2)(a)). In addition, compliance with the Code may be relied upon to show that the commission of an offence has not been established or that a person has a defence (s. 25(2)(b)).

The Code is written in clear English and a reading of it is likely to enhance your understanding of Part III of the 1987 Act. Part 1 of the Code deals with price comparisons, Part 2 deals with the actual price to the consumer, Part 3 deals with price indications which become misleading after they have been given, and Part 4 with the sale of new homes.

14.8.1 THE CODE'S ADVICE ON PREVIOUS SELLING PRICES

If the trader is comparing the price with his own previous selling price then the previous price and the new lower price should both be stated (para. 1.2.1).

In any comparison with the trader's own previous selling price:

(a) the previous price should be the *last* price at which the product was available to consumers in the previous 6 months;

(b) the product should have been available to consumers at that price for at least 28 consecutive days in the previous six months; and

(c) the previous price should have applied for that period at the same shop where the reduced price is now being offered (para. 1.2.2).

If the previous price does not meet one or more of the conditions set out in para. 1.2.2:

(a) the comparison should be fair and meaningful; and

MISLEADING PRICE INDICATIONS

(b) the comparison should give a clear and positive explanation of the period for which and the circumstances in which the higher price applied. For example, 'these goods were on sale here at the higher price from 1 February to 26 February' or 'these goods were on sale at the higher price in 10 of our 95 stores only'. The explanation should be displayed as clearly and prominently as the price indication (para. 1.2.3).

In the case of food and drink or non-food perishables with a shelf life of less than six weeks there is no need to give a positive explanation if the previous price in a comparison has not applied for 28 consecutive days, provided it was the last price at which the goods were on sale in the previous six months and applied in the same shop where the reduced price is being offered (para. 1.2.4).

Paragraphs 1.2.2 and 1.2.3 were applied by the Divisional Court in the following case.

AG Stanley Ltd (T/A Fads) v *Surrey County Council* (1994) 159 JP 691
On 2 April 1992 the appellants priced a table at £7.99. From 14 October 1992 to March 1993 the price of the tables was reduced to £4.99 in a special promotion. In the meantime, on 10 November 1992, in what was described as a 13 day event which must end on 24 November, the tables were advertised as 'Occasional table was £7.99. Now only £4.99'. The tables remained at £4.99 until March 1993. The table was still at £4.99 on 21 December 1992 when a point of sale notice stated: 'Sale, round occasional table, now £4.99 was £7.99.' The justices convicted the appellants of two offences under s. 20 of the 1987 Act relating to the advertisement of 10 November and the point of sale notice on 21 December.
Held: The defendants were guilty of both offences because the facts or circumstances by reference to which the consumers might reasonably be expected to judge the validity of any relevant comparison made or implied by the indications were not in fact what they were. It was easily inferred that the price would revert to the higher price once the event or offer was over. In addition, the defendants had contravened paras 1.2.2 and 1.2.3 of the Code. The last price mentioned in para. 1.2.2 was the higher price immediately before the commencement of the special event or offers. It was not, as the appellants contended, the last numerically different price. (An extract from Scott Baker J's judgment is set out in *Cases and Materials* (**14.2**). It is worth reading this to see how he applied the Code of Practice.)

ACTIVITY 14/3

Find the relevant part in the Code (see *Cases and Materials* (**14.2**)) and then answer the following questions:

(a) If a series of price reductions is made, do all the reduced prices need to be shown and to have applied for 28 days?

(b) What are the four requirements for a trader to compare with another trader's prices?

(c) In what circumstances should a trader not claim that an offer is 'free'?

(a) If a series of reductions is made then, in the absence of a positive explanation, the highest price must have applied for 28 days in the previous six months at the same shop, and the highest price, the intervening price(s) and the current selling price must all be shown. The intervening prices need not have applied for 28 days in the previous six months (para. 1.2.6).

(b) A trader should only compare with another trader's prices if:

   (i) the trader knows that the other trader's price which he quotes is accurate and up-to-date:

   (ii) the trader can give the name of the other trader clearly and prominently, with the price comparison;

   (iii) the trader can identify the shop where the other trader's price applies, if that other trader is a retailer; and

   (iv) the other trader's price quoted applies to the same products or to substantially similar products and any differences are clearly stated (para. 1.5.1).

(c) A trader should not claim that an offer is free if:

   (i) the trader has imposed additional charges which he would not normally make;

   (ii) the trader has inflated the price of any product the consumer must buy or the incidental charges (for example, postage) the consumer must pay to get the 'free offer'; or

   (iii) the trader will reduce the price to consumers who do not take up the free offer (para. 1.10.4).

14.9 Summary

In this chapter we have covered the following:

- Section 20(1) of the 1987 Act makes it an offence to give a consumer a misleading indication as to the price at which goods, services, accommodation or facilities are available.

- Section 20(2) of the 1987 Act makes it an offence to fail to correct an indication as to price which has become misleading after it has been given to a consumer.

- Both offences can only be committed by a person acting 'in the course of any business of his'.

- The misleading indication must be as to the price, it must be given to a consumer and must relate to the price at which goods etc. are available.

- Four defences are specific to the s. 20 offences. In addition the defence of having taken all reasonable precautions and exercised all due diligence is available.

- The Code of Practice does not of itself give rise to civil or criminal liability. However, adherence to the Code is evidence that no offence has been committed or that a defence applies, and contravention of the Code is strong evidence that an offence has been committed or that a defence does not apply.

INDEX

Acceleration clauses 242–3
Acceptability test 70, 71–3
Acceptance of contracts 25–34
Accident defence 303–4, 306
Accommodation
  price *see* Price
  trade descriptions 298
    making false statement 299–303
Action
  action for arrears 254–5
  thing in action 51
Actual delivery 137
Advertisements 11–14
  consumer credit 221–3, 235
    application of Part IV of Consumer Credit act 1974 221–2
    form and content of advertisements 222
    offences related to advertisements 223
  trade descriptions in 272–3
    advertiser's defence 310
Affirmation of contracts 34–7
Agency 179
  in consumer credit agreements 237, 238–42
  misleading price indications 316–17
Appearance and finish of goods 74
Approval, sale of goods on 122–4
Arrears
  action for arrears 254–5
  interest on 250

Barter 57
Breach of contract 22
  damages 23, 38–43, 178, 182–5
  liability of creditor for breaches by supplier in consumer credit agreements 239–40
  remedies 23–4
By-pass provision 308–10

Canvassing
  consumer credit 223–5, 235

Canvassing – *continued*
  circulars to minors 224
  prohibition of unsolicited credit-tokens 224–5
  quotations 225
Care and skill, statutory implied terms in contracts for supply of services 82–6
Carrier, delivery to 138
Caveat emptor principle 2
Chattels
  personal 50–1
  real 51
Children/minors, canvassing consumer credit circulars to minors 224
Conditional sale agreements 55–6
  remedies 255–7
  termination by debtor 250–3
Consideration, statutory implied terms in contracts for supply of services 86
Constructive delivery 137–8
Consumer, definition 3, 317
Consumer credit
  advertising 221–3, 235
    application of Part IV of Consumer Credit act 1974 221–2
    form and content of advertisements 222
    offences related to advertisements 223
  canvassing 223–5, 235
    circulars to minors 224
    prohibition of unsolicited credit-tokens 224–5
    quotations 225
  Consumer Credit Act 1974 3, 55–6, 203–19, 220–35
    advertising 221–3, 235
    canvassing 223–5, 235
    definitions in Act 204–19
    entry into credit or hire agreements 225–34, 235
    history and structure 203–4

Consumer credit – *continued*
  entry into credit or hire agreements 225–34, 235
    agreements to enter future agreements 228
    agreements excluded from Consumer Credit Act Part V 227
    antecedent negotiations 225–7, 238–9
    cancellable agreements 231–2
    consequences of improper execution 231
    cooling-off period 232–3
    duty to give notice of cancellation rights 231
    duty to supply copies of agreements 229–30
    effect of cancellation 233–4
    making the agreement 228
    opportunity for withdrawal from prospective land mortgages 227–8
    preliminary matters 225–8
    withdrawal from prospective agreements 227
  extortionate credit bargains 259–60, 261
  linked transactions 218–19
  matters arising during currency of credit or hire agreements 237–46
    appropriation of payments 243
    death of debtor or hirer 245–6
    duty to give information 243
    duty to give notice before taking certain action 242–3, 246
    duty to give notice of termination in non-default cases 243
    duty on isuse of new credit-tokens 245
    liability of creditor for breaches by supplier 238–42
    liability for misuse of credit facilities 244–5
    variation of agreements 243–4
  regulated agreements 205–11
    consumer credit agreements 205–7
    consumer hire agreements 207–9
    exempt agreements 209–11
  remedies 249, 254–8, 259, 260–1
    action for arrears 254–5
    damages 255–7
    repossession of goods 257–8
    termination of agreement 255
  termination 248–50, 255, 260
    default notices 248, 249–50
    early payment by debtor 250

Consumer credit – *continued*
  types of agreements 211–16
    credit-tokens and credit-token agreements 217–18
    debtor-creditor-supplier and debtor-creditor agreements 213–15
    non-commercial and small agreements 205, 217
    restricted-use credit and unrestricted-use credit 213
    running-account and fixed-sum credit 211–13
Consumer law, development 1–3
Contra preferentum rule 157–8
Contract(s) 1–2
  acceptance 25–34
  affirmation 34–7
  breach of contract 22
    damages 23, 38–43, 178, 182–5
    liability of creditor for breaches by supplier in consumer credit agreements 239–40
    remedies 23–4
  discharge of contractual liability 22
  exclusion and limitation clauses 22, 152, 153–75
    common law approach 153–8, 174
    Unfair Contract Terms Act 1977 159–70, 174
    Unfair Terms in Consumer Contracts Regulations 1994 170–3, 174–5
  formation 7–14
  freedom of 152, 153
  frustration 22
  hire 58–9, 164
  hire-purchase 54–6, 77, 97–8
    exclusion and limitation clauses 161–3
  implied terms 2, 7, 14, 47
    statutory implied terms as to correspondence with description or title 89–107
    statutory implied terms as to quality and fitness 63–88
  misrepresentation 21–2
    damages 23, 38–43
    fraudulent 14, 38–40
    losing right to rescission 15, 24–5, 35–8
    negligent 14, 23, 40–2
    remedies 14–15, 23–4
    wholly innocent 14, 15, 42–3
  offers and invitations to treat 8–14
    advertisements 11–14
    goods displayed in shops 8–11
  pre-contractual statements 14–22
  privity of contract 14, 157, 177–86
    Law Commission Bill 186–8

INDEX

Contract(s) – *continued*
  product liability and   178–88
    contract damages   182–5
    Law Commission Bill on privity
      186–8
    liability under a contract   178–80
    manufacturers' guarantees   180–2
    specific performance   185–6
  remedies
    breach of contract   23–4
    misrepresentation   14–15, 23–4
    statutory implied terms as to
      correspondence with description
      or title   89–107
    statutory implied terms as to quality
      and fitness   63–88
  repudiation   22, 23
    losing right to   24–35
  rescission, losing right to   15, 24–5,
    35–8
  sale of goods   47, 48–54
    definition   49–52
    passing of property and risk   112–36
    statutory implied terms as to
      correspondence with description
      or title   89–107
    statutory implied terms as to quality
      and fitness   63–82, 87–8
    types of goods   52–4
  supply of services   51, 59–61
    statutory implied terms   82–6, 87–8,
    106
  terms and representations   15–22
    difficulties with pre–1967 cases
      19–21
    implied terms   2, 7, 14, 47, 63–88,
      89–107
    relative degrees of parties'
      knowledge   15–16
    reliance placed on statements   16–17
    statements of opinion   21
    statements which are both terms and
      actionable misrepresentations
      21–2
    strength of statements   17–18
    time at which statement is made   18
    written contracts   18–19
  transfer of property   56–8, 77, 164
Cooling-off period, consumer credit or
  hire agreements   232–3
Copyright   51
Credit *see* Consumer credit
Credit-tokens and credit-token
  agreements   217–18
  agency in   241–2
  duty on issue of new credit-tokens
    245
  prohibition of unsolicited credit-tokens
    224–5

Criminal law   3
Criminal liability
  for unsafe products   195–200
    Consumer Protection Act 1987 Part II
      195–7
    General Product Safety Regulations
      1994   197–200
Damages
  for breach of consumer hire or
    conditional sale agreements
    255–7
  breach of contract   23, 38–43, 178,
    182–5
  misrepresentation   23, 38–43
  product liability   182–5
De minimis rule   93, 141
Debtor-creditor-supplier and
  debtor-creditor agreements   213–15
Deceit   38–40
Default notices   248, 249–50
Defences
  accident   303–4, 306
  act or default of another person   304,
    305
  advertiser's defence   310
  by-pass provision   308–10
  due diligence   196, 306–7, 321
  misleading price indications   321–2
  mistake   303–4
  product liability   192–3, 196
  reliance on information from another
    303–4, 305
  supplier's defence   308
  trade descriptions   290, 303–10, 311
Delivery   112, 136–42
  actual delivery   137
  constructive delivery   137–8
  importance of   142
  by instalments   142
  place of delivery   138–9
  time of delivery   140–1
  ways of effecting delivery   137–8
  wrong quantity delivered   141–2
Description
  correspondence with   90–5
  see also Trade descriptions
Disclaimers, trade descriptions of goods
  283–6
Display of goods in shops   8–11
Due diligence   196, 306–7, 321
Durability   76–7

Emblements   51
Entering premises for repossession of
  goods   258
Estimates, price indications   318
European Union   2
  directive on product liability   189, 193,
    201

European Union – *continued*
  directive on unfair terms in consumer
    contracts 171
Exclusion and limitation clauses 22, 152,
  153–75
  common law approach 153–8, 174
    common law construction of
      exclusion clauses 157–8
    incorporation into contract 153–7
  Unfair Contract Terms Act 1977
    159–70, 174
    contracts of sale and hire-purchase
      161–3
    exclusion of liability for
      misrepresentation 168
    guarantee of consumer goods
      167–8
    liability arising in contract 164–6
    miscellaneous contracts under which
      goods pass 163–4
    negligence liability 159–61
    provisions against evasion of liability
      170
    requirement of reasonableness
      168–9
    Schedule 2 169–70
    scope of Act 159
    unreasonable indemnity clauses
      167
  Unfair Terms in Consumer Contracts
    Regulations 1994 170–3, 174–5
    consequences of inclusion of unfair
      terms in contracts 173
    construction of written contracts
      173
    prevention of continued use of unfair
      terms 173
    terms to which regulations apply
      171–2
    unfair terms 172–3
Extortionate credit bargains 259–60,
  261

Facilities
  price *see* Price
  trade descriptions 298–9
    making false statement 299–303
Finish and appearance of goods 74
Fitness for purpose 73–4, 77–82
Fixed-sum credit 211–13
Forfeiture, product liability 197
Formation of contracts 7–14
Fraudulent misrepresentation 14
  damages for 23, 38–40
Freedom of contract 152, 153
Frustration 22
  passing of property and risk on sale of
    goods 119, 133–6
Future goods 52–3, 54, 90, 113

Goods
  contracts for transfer of property in
    goods 56–8, 77, 164
  definition 50–2
  existing goods 52–3
  future goods 52–3, 54, 90, 113
  price *see* Price
  quality
    in business sales 64–6
    fitness for purpose 73–4, 77–82
    satisfactory quality 67–77, 81–2
  repossession of 257–8
    entering premises 258
    notice required 257
    protected goods 257–8
  specific goods 54, 90, 113
    passing of property and risk on sale
      of goods 114–24
  trade descriptions 262–87
    advertisements 272–3
    applying false trade description
      269–72
    in course of trade or business 264–8
    descriptions false to a material
      degree 281–2
    disclaimers 283–6
    false trade descriptions 275–81
    implied trade descriptions 279–81
    indications 283
    misleading but not literally false
      statements 282–3
    persons 263–4
    supplying or offering to supply
      goods to which false trade
      description is applied 273–5
  unascertained goods 54, 90, 113
    passing of property and risk on sale
      of goods 124–8, 133
  see also Product liability; Sale of goods
Guarantees *see* Warranties/guarantees

Hire
  consumer hire agreements 207–9
    entry into hire agreements 225–34,
      235
    matters arising during currency of
      hire agreements 237–46
    remedies 255–7, 258–9
    termination 253–4
  contracts 58–9, 77, 164
Hire-purchase
  contracts 54–6, 77, 97–8
    exclusion and limitation clauses
      161–3
  delivery of goods 137
  sale of motor vehicle obtained under
    hire-purchase 147–8
  termination by debtor of hire purchase
    agreements 250–3

INDEX

Hire-purchase and 148

Implied trade descriptions 279–81
Indemnity
   creditor's right of indemnity in consumer credit agreements 240–1
   indemnity clauses 167
Injunctions 24, 173
Innocent misrepresentation 14, 15
   damages for 42–3
Instalments, delivery by 142
Intellectual property rights 51
Interest
   on arrears in consumer credit agreements 250
   interest rates 222
Invitations to treat *see* Offers and invitations to treat

Land
   lease of 51
   opportunity for withdrawal from prospective land mortgages 227–8
   sale of interest in land 51
Late payment 143
Liability
   of creditor for breaches by supplier in consumer credit agreements 239–40
   criminal *see* Criminal liability
   discharge of contractual liability 22
   exclusion and limitation clauses 159–61, 164–6, 170
   product liability *see* Product liability
Lien, unpaid seller's lien 144–5
Limitation of actions
   misleading price indications 322
   product liability 194
Liquidated damages 23

Manufacturers' guarantees and product liability 180–2
Merchantable quality 69, 70–3
Minors, canvassing consumer credit circulars to minors 224
Misleading but not literally false statements 282–3
Misleading price indications 313–24
   Code of Practice 322–4
   defences 321–2
   goods, services, accommodation or facilities 319
   indications 319–20
   offence 313–19
   time limits 322
Misrepresentation 21–2
   damages 23, 38–43

Misrepresentation – *continued*
   exclusion of liability for misrepresentation 168
   fraudulent, damages 23, 38–40
   innocent 14, 15
     damages 42–3
   negligent 14
     damages 23, 40–2
   remedies 14–15, 23–4
     losing right to rescission 15, 24–5, 35–8
Misstatement, negligent 16
Mistake
   defence 303–4
   passing of property and risk on sale of goods 133–6
   sale by seller in possession after sale 112, 146–7
   wrong quantity delivered 141–2
Model, sale by 104
Mortgages, opportunity for withdrawal from prospective land mortgages 227–8

Negligence
   exclusion and limitation clauses 159–61
   product liability and 188
Negligent misrepresentation 14
   damages for 23, 40–2
Negligent misstatement 16
Non-commercial and small credit agreements 205, 217
Notice
   consumer credit agreements
     duty to give notice before taking certain action 242–3, 246
     duty to give notice of cancellation rights 231
     duty to give notice of termination in non-default cases 243
   repossession of goods 257

Offers and invitations to treat 8–14
   advertisements 11–14
   goods displayed in shops 8–11
Ownership
   contracts for transfer of property in goods 56–8, 77, 164
   passing of property and risk 112–36
   right to sell 95–101
   sale of motor vehicle obtained under hire-purchase 147–8
   sale by seller in possession after a sale 146–7
   warranties as to title 100–1

Parol evidence rule 18

Payment
   for goods 112, 142–6
   late payment 143
   right of resale 145–6
   for services 143
   unpaid seller's lien 144–5
   see also Arrears; Price
Penalties 23
Personal chattels 50–1
Place of delivery 138–9
Pre-contractual statements 14–22
   distinguishing terms and representations 15–22
Premises, entering premises for repossession of goods 258
Presumed intention rules 115–27
Price
   defined 317–18
   misleading price indications 313–24
      Code of Practice 322–4
      defences 321–2
      goods, services, accommodation or facilities 319
      indications 319–20
      offence 313–19
      time limits 322
Privity of contract 14, 157, 177–86
   Law Commission Bill 186–8
Product liability 177–201
   Consumer Protection Act 1987 189–97, 201
      damage giving rise to liability 193–4
      defences 192–3, 196
      forfeiture 197
      general safety requirement 195–6
      limitation of actions 194
      meaning of defect 191–2
      power to make regulations 196
      power to obtain information 197
      prohibition and warning notices 197
      suspension notices 197
      what is a product 191
      who is liable 189–90
   in contract and tort 178–88
      contract damages 182–5
      Law Commission Bill on privity 186–8
      law of tort 188–9
      liability under a contract 178–80
      manufacturers' guarantees 180–2
      specific performance 185–6
   criminal liability for unsafe products 195–200
      Consumer Protection Act 1987 Part II 195–7, 201
      General Product Safety Regulations 1994 197–200, 201

Prohibition notices 197

Quality
   appearance and finish 74
   in business sales 64–6
   durability 76–7
   fitness for purpose 73–4, 77–82
   freedom from minor defects 74–5
   merchantable quality 69, 70–3
   safety 75
   satisfactory quality 67–77, 81–2
Quotations
   canvassing consumer credit 225
   price indications 318

Real chattels 51
Remedies
   breach of contract 23–4
   in consumer credit agreements 249, 254–8, 259, 260–1
      action for arrears 254–5
      damages 255–7
      repossession of goods 257–8
      termination of agreement 255
   in consumer hire or conditional sale agreements 255–7, 258–9
   misrepresentation 14–15, 23–4
      losing right to rescission 15, 24–5, 35–8
   statutory implied terms as to correspondence with description or title 89–107
      correspondence with description 90–5
      no implied term in sale by model 104
      right to sell 95–101
      sale by sample 101–4
      status of implied terms 105–6
      supply of services 106
   statutory implied terms as to quality and fitness
      fitness for purpose 73–4, 77–82
      quality 63, 64–77, 81–2
      status of implied terms 81
      supply of services 82–6
   see also Damages
Repossession 257–8
   entering premises 258
   notice required 257
   protected goods 257–8
Repudiation 22, 23
   losing right to 24–35
      acceptance in a contract of sale of goods 25–30
      acceptance of goods forming a commercial unit 32–4
      acceptance of part of goods 30–2

INDEX

Repudiation – *continued*
    affirmation of contracts other than sale of goods   34–5
Resale, right of   145–6
Rescission
    losing right to   15, 24–5, 35–8
        affirmation and the right to rescind   35–7
        inability to restore pre-contract position   37
        third party acquired rights   37–8
Restricted-use credit   213
Risk
    goods in transit   133
    meaning   130–2
Running-account credit   211–13

Safety   75
    see also Product liability
Sale of goods
    agreements to sell   52, 95–6
        conditional   55–6, 250–3
    on approval   122–4
    contracts   47, 48–54
        definition   49–52
        passing of property and risk   112–36
        statutory implied terms as to correspondence with description or title   89–107
        statutory implied terms as to quality and fitness   63–82, 87–8
        types of goods   52–4
    delivery   112, 136–42
        actual delivery   137
        constructive delivery   137–8
        importance of   142
        by instalments   142
        place of delivery   138–9
        time of delivery   140–1
        ways of effecting delivery   137–8
        wrong quantity delivered   141–2
    passing of property and risk   112–36
        frustration   119, 133–6
        mistake   133–6
        risk   130–3
        rules in Sale of Goods Act 1979   113–36
        specific goods   114–24
        unascertained goods   124–8, 133
        undivided shares in goods forming part of bulk   128–30
    payment for   112, 142–6
        late payment   143
        right of resale   145–6
        unpaid seller's lien   144–5
    right to sell   95–101
    sale by model   104
    sale of motor vehicle obtained on hire-purchase   112, 147–8

Sale of goods – *continued*
    sale or return   122–4
    sale by sample   101–4
    sale by seller in possession after sale   112, 146–7
    unsolicited goods   112, 124, 148–9
Sample, sale by   101–4
Satisfactory quality   67–77, 81–2
Services
    care and skill   82–6
    consideration   86
    contracts for supply of services   51, 59–61
        statutory implied terms   82–6, 87–8, 106
    defective   184–5
    defined   296–8
    payment for   143
    price *see* Price
    time of performance   86
    trade descriptions   289–303
        in course of trade or business   290–1
        making false statement   291–3, 299–303
        mens rea   294–6
Shops, goods displayed in shops   8–11
Skill, statutory implied terms in contracts for supply of services   82–6
Small credit agreements   205, 217
Specific goods   54, 90, 113
    passing of property and risk on sale of goods   114–24
Specific performance   24
    product liability and   185–6
Supplier's defence   308
Suspension notices   197

Thing in action   51
Third parties, acquired rights and losing right to rescission   37–8
Time of delivery   140–1
Time limits *see* Limitation of actions
Time orders   254–5
Time of performance, statutory implied terms in contracts for supply of services   86
Title, warranties as to   100–1
Tort   2
    damages   23, 38–40
    deceit   38–40
    product liability and   188–9
Trade descriptions
    defences   290, 303–10, 311
        accident   303–4, 306
        act or default of another person   304, 305
        advertiser's defence   310
        by-pass provision   308–10
        due diligence   196, 306–7

Trade descriptions – *continued*
   mistake 303–4
   product liability 192–3, 196
   reliance on information from another 303–4, 305
   supplier's defence 308
  goods 262–87
   advertisements 272–3
   applying false trade description 269–72
   in course of trade or business 264–8
   descriptions false to a material degree 281–2
   disclaimers 283–6
   false trade descriptions 275–81
   implied trade descriptions 279–81
   indications 283
   misleading but not literally false statements 282–3
   persons 263–4
   supplying or offering to supply goods to which false trade description is applied 273–5

Trade descriptions – *continued*
  services 289–303
   in course of trade or business 290–1
   making false statement 291–3, 299–303
   mens rea 294–6
Trading stamps 61
Transfer of property in goods, contracts 56–8, 77, 164

Unascertained goods 54, 90, 113
  passing of property and risk on sale of goods 124–8, 133
Unpaid seller's lien 144–5
Unrestricted-use credit 213
Unsolicited goods 112, 124, 148–9
Usability test 70, 71–3

Warning notices 197
Warranties/guarantees
  guarantee of consumer goods 167–8
  manufacturers' guarantees and product liability 180–2
  as to title 100–1
Winding-up orders 120